AMINTAPHIL
The Philosophical Foundations of Law and Justice

More information about this series at http://www.springer.com/series/7372

Laurence D. Houlgate

Philosophy, Law and the Family

A New Introduction to the Philosophy of Law

Springer

Laurence D. Houlgate
Department of Philosophy
California Polytechnic State University
San Luis Obispo, CA, USA

ISSN 1873-877X ISSN 2351-9851 (electronic)
AMINTAPHIL: The Philosophical Foundations of Law and Justice
ISBN 978-3-319-51120-7 ISBN 978-3-319-51121-4 (eBook)
DOI 10.1007/978-3-319-51121-4

Library of Congress Control Number: 2016963753

Printed on acid-free paper

This Springer imprint is published by Springer Nature
The registered company is Springer International Publishing AG
The registered company address is: Gewerbestrasse 11, 6330 Cham, Switzerland

For my family

Acknowledgments

I would like to acknowledge the support and assistance of the California State University Emeritus and Retired Faculty Association whose generous grant made it possible to do the writing and editing necessary to complete the final draft of the manuscript. I am also thankful to the students in my philosophy of law classes at California Polytechnic State University who wrote helpful reviews of an earlier draft of the book: Kohl Kreutziger, Alex Delzell, Hunter Tasseff, Anthony Haddad, Shawn Farrington, Eden Moalem, Nicholas Brunner, Jorge Nozot, Scarlett Fivey, and Alexandra Ongman. And, although we have never met, I am indebted to Professor William P. Statsky for the many books he has written on United States family law since the mid-1970s. Although mainly intended for those studying to be paralegals, the clarity, organization, and precision of his writings about this important body of law have made it accessible to thousands of ordinary citizens, students, and professionals. My thanks also go out to Professor Andrew Altman whose book *Arguing About Law* influenced the structure of my book by convincing me to use a single theme (family law) throughout all chapters. Thanks also to the University of Pennsylvania Law School, Oxford University Press, Kluwer Academic Publishers, and Harcourt Brace for the permission to use selected parts of articles I have previously published in (respectively) the *University of Pennsylvania Journal of Constitutional Law*; *International Journal of Law, Policy and the Family*; *Law and Philosophy*; and the reader *Vice and Virtue in Everyday Life: Introductory Readings in Ethics.*

California
January 2017

Paso Robles

Contents

1 Introduction 1
1.1 A Plea for the Philosophical Study of Family Law 1
1.2 A Typology of Family Law 4
1.3 Jurisprudence vs Philosophy of Law 6
1.4 Plan of the Book 7
References 9

Part I Law, Morals and the Constitution

2 Natural Law Theory 13
2.1 Positive and Natural Law 13
2.2 The End of Miscegenation: *Loving vs. Virginia* 15
2.2.1 Historical Background 15
2.2.2 Factual Basis of the Case 16
2.2.3 Decision and Findings of the U.S. Supreme Court 17
2.3 Traditional Natural Law Theory 18
2.3.1 An Example of Traditional Natural Law Theory: John Locke 18
2.3.2 Assessing Traditional Natural Law Theory in the Context of Family Law 23
2.4 Modern Natural Law Theory: Lon Fuller 26
2.4.1 Principles of Legality 26
2.4.2 The Inner Morality of Law 27
2.4.3 The Social Purposes of Law 27
2.4.4 Objections to Fuller 28
2.5 Contemporary Natural Law Theory: Ronald Dworkin 28
2.5.1 Rules and Principles 29
2.5.2 Principles as Natural Law 30
2.5.3 Objections to Dworkin 31
References 33

3 Legal Positivism ... 35
3.1 The Separation of Law and Morals ... 36
3.2 Rape and Forced Marriage in Morocco ... 36
3.3 Traditional Legal Positivism: John Austin ... 37
3.3.1 Law as Sovereign Commands ... 37
3.3.2 Legal and Moral Validity ... 38
3.4 Assessment of Austin ... 41
3.4.1 Are Marriage Laws the Commands of a Sovereign? ... 41
3.4.2 Are Child Custody Laws the Commands of a Sovereign? ... 43
3.5 Modern Legal Positivism: H.L.A. Hart ... 45
3.5.1 Law and the Obligations Created by Law ... 45
3.5.2 The Key to Understanding the Nature of Law ... 46
3.5.3 The Application of Hart's Theory to Family Law ... 47
3.5.4 Objections to Hart's Theory ... 49
3.6 Hart's Compromise: The Minimum Content of Natural Law ... 51
3.7 Minimum Content of the Rules of Family Law ... 52
3.7.1 Rules of Marriage ... 53
3.7.2 Rules Protecting Infants and Young Children ... 54
3.7.3 Rules of Custody Assignments at Birth ... 54
References ... 57

4 Constitutional Interpretation ... 59
4.1 The Concept of "Person" in the Constitution ... 60
4.2 Three Supreme Court Family Law Cases ... 63
4.2.1 Parent's Right to Control Their Child's Education: *Meyer v. Nebraska* (1923) ... 63
4.2.2 Children's Rights of Free Speech: *Tinker v. Des Moines School District* (1969) ... 65
4.2.3 Marital Privacy: *Griswold v. Connecticut* (1965) ... 68
4.3 The Role of *Stare Decisis* in Supreme Court Decision-Making ... 69
4.4 Theories of Constitutional Interpretation ... 72
4.4.1 Originalism ... 73
4.4.2 Non-originalism ... 79
References ... 86

Part II State Intervention in the Family

5 The Moral Limits of Family Law ... 91
5.1 Legal Intervention in the Family ... 91
5.2 Is "Family" a Political Concept? ... 94
5.2.1 Relationship of Family Law to the Concept of Family ... 96
5.2.2 Resolving the Dispute Between Traditionalists and Radicals ... 99

5.3 Theories of Legal Intervention and Their Application to Family Law 100
5.3.1 Utilitarianism and the Harm Principle 100
5.3.2 Paternalism 105
5.3.3 Moralism 107
5.4 Testing the Limits of Intrafamily Sexual Behavior 111
References 113

6 Family Crime and Punishment 115
6.1 Public and Private Harms 115
6.2 Intrafamily Crimes: Justifications for Punishment 116
6.2.1 Punishment as Deterrence 117
6.2.2 Punishment as Retribution 120
6.3 Therapy, Not Punishment 123
References 126

7 Child Abuse and Neglect 127
7.1 Protecting the Child: The Family Court Option 127
7.2 Two Cases 128
7.3 The Standard of "Best Interests of the Child" 129
7.4 Using Family Models to Determine the Best Interests of a Child 132
7.4.1 Family Preservation vs Child Protection 134
7.4.2 Compassion vs Control 135
7.5 An Alternative Dispositional Standard 137
References 140

8 Family Torts and Remedies 143
8.1 Tort Liability and Remedies 144
8.2 Philosophical Questions About Torts and Tort Remedies 146
8.3 Theories of Justification for Tort Remedies 148
8.3.1 Corrective Justice 149
8.3.2 Retributive Justice 150
8.3.3 Distributive Justice 151
8.4 Intrafamily Torts and Immunities 152
8.4.1 Parental Tort Immunity 152
8.4.2 Interspousal Tort Immunity 155
8.5 Summary: Limits of Tort Intervention 158
8.6 Standards of Care in Intrafamily Negligence Torts 161
8.6.1 Objective and Subjective Standards of Care 162
8.6.2 H.L.A. Hart's Two-Question Proposal for Determinations of Negligence 164
8.6.3 Objections to Hart's Proposal: Standards of Care for Children 164
8.6.4 An Alternative Approach: Sub-categorization 165
References 168

Part III Marriage, Children and the State

9 Family Contracts: Marriage and Divorce 171
9.1 A Conversation About Marriage: Past and Present 172
9.2 Traditional Marriage: Rights, Duties and Benefits 173
9.3 Justice and the Distribution of Marital Benefits and Burdens 174
9.3.1 Egalitarian Principles 175
9.3.2 The Difference Principle 176
9.3.3 Utility-Based Principles 177
9.4 Legally Gendered Marriage 179
9.5 Access to Marriage 181
9.5.1 The Public Debate 181
9.5.2 The Constitutional Debate 184
9.6 Alternatives to Traditional Marriage 186
9.6.1 Contract Law and the Abolition of Legal Marriage 187
9.6.2 Marital Contracts as Private Contracts 187
9.6.3 Minimal Marriage 188
9.6.4 Assessing the Alternatives to Traditional Marriage 190
9.7 The Exit Rules 191
9.7.1 Divorce and the Vulnerability of Women 193
9.7.2 Divorce and the Vulnerability of Young Children 195
References 200

10 Children, Parents and the State 203
10.1 The Custodial Status of Children 204
10.2 Philosophical Theories on the Status and Rights of Children 204
10.2.1 A Typology of Rights 205
10.2.2 Parents as Owners of Children: Thomas Hobbes 206
10.2.3 The Perfect Freedom of Children: Herbert Spencer 207
10.2.4 Parents as Temporary Custodians: John Locke and J.S. Mill 209
10.2.5 Criticisms of Locke and Mill 211
10.3 Constitutional Theories About the Rights of Children 212
10.3.1 Socially Inappropriate Speech: *Bethel v Fraser* 214
10.3.2 "Reasonable" Censorship of Children's Speech: *Hazelwood v Kuhlmeier* 215
10.4 The Supreme Court's Dilemma of Classification 217
10.4.1 Limited Scope Rights 218
10.4.2 Rights-to-Be-Balanced 220
10.4.3 Rights-in-Trust 221
References 225

Part IV Contract and Property Disputes Arising from Alternative Birth Methods

11 Surrogacy 229
11.1 The Internal Oracle of Justice 230
11.2 Two Surrogacy Cases 231
11.2.1 *In re Baby M* (1987) 231
11.2.2 *Johnson v. Calvert* (1993) 232
11.3 The Biological Preference Principle and the Language of Surrogacy 232
11.4 Traditional Rules of Contract Law 234
11.5 Natural Law 235
11.6 Utilitarian Concerns 237
11.6.1 Best Interests of the Newborn Child 237
11.6.2 Interests of Parents and State 239
11.7 Exceptions to the Biological Preference Principle 240
11.8 Utilitarian Objections to Surrogate Mother Contracts 242
11.9 Kantian Objections: Selling Babies and Renting Bodies 244
11.9.1 Selling Babies 244
11.9.2 Renting Bodies 245
References 248

12 Frozen Embryos 249
12.1 Divorce and Cryopreserved Embryos 249
12.2 Four Cases 250
12.3 *A.Z. v. B.Z.*: A Closer Look 251
12.4 The Right to Procreate 252
12.5 The Right not to Procreate 254
12.5.1 Interpretations of the Right not to Procreate 254
12.5.2 Application to Legal Decisions 255
12.6 Appeals to Utility 258
12.7 Non-discretionary Standards 260
12.8 Pre-IVF Contracts 260
12.9 Limits on the Content of Pre-IVF Contracts 262
12.9.1 Forced Procreation 262
12.9.2 Interests of Future Persons 264
References 266

Part V Alternative Approaches to the Philosophy of Law

13 Critical Legal Studies and Feminist Jurisprudence 269
13.1 Formalism and Legal Realism 269
13.2 Critical Legal Studies 272
13.2.1 Legal Reasoning 273
13.2.2 *Stare Decisis* and the Rule of Law 276
13.2.3 Family Privacy 277
13.3 Feminist Legal Theory 277
References 282

Chapter 1
Introduction

> *"It is the case of trouble which makes, breaks, twists or flatly establishes a rule, an institution, an authority."*
>
> Adamson and Hoebel, *The Cheyenne Way* (1941)
>
> *"Perhaps more than in any other legal field, family law attempts to impose some measure of coherence and rationality upon an unruly, and often deeply irrational, domain of life."*
>
> Areen, et al., *Family Law*, 6th edition (2012)

Abstract Although family law is an area of the law most often used by the average citizen, and has seen the most modification as a response to changes in cultural mores, philosophers of law have largely ignored it as an area of inquiry. This book attempts to repair this omission by offering a unique introduction to the philosophy of law. It draws exclusively on family law cases as a way of introducing most of the traditional philosophical problems of legal philosophy: the nature of law and the relationship between law and morality, theories of constitutional interpretation, the moral limits of the law, theories of punishment, and tort liability. Other chapters are devoted to contemporary issues unique to family law, including justifiable limits of access to marriage, alternatives to marriage, child custody disputes involving surrogate mothers, quasi-property disputes involving custody of frozen embryos and the justifiable limits of the right not to procreate. This introductory chapter also draws a distinction between the philosophy of law and jurisprudence and gives a brief explanation of the typology of family law that will be used throughout the book.

1.1 A Plea for the Philosophical Study of Family Law

The family has long been an object of legal attention through statutory, judge-made and constitutional law. And almost everyone has had some kind of interaction with the legal system because of the pervasiveness of family law. If we lead a life filled with average human experiences, it is almost impossible to avoid some legal regulation or intervention at some point in our lives regarding a present or future family

L.D. Houlgate, *Philosophy, Law and the Family*, AMINTAPHIL: The Philosophical Foundations of Law and Justice 7,
DOI 10.1007/978-3-319-51121-4_1

relationship. We use the law to marry, divorce, achieve custody of a child through birth, adopt a child, and when we have children we are required by law to feed, clothe, shelter and educate them. When marriages break-up or families fail to live up to minimum standards governing child neglect, there is a heavy use of local courts for dispute resolution and responses to regulatory interventions. Some have estimated that up to fifty percent of time and legal effort in some civil courts is taken up resolving intrafamily legal disputes.

Most law schools require at least one course in family law and several case books are available devoted to descriptions of the complexity of its many rules, principles, statutes and precedent cases (sometimes published under the title "Domestic Relations Law"). But *philosophers* of law have generally ignored family law, focusing instead on the far more popular terrain of the criminal law, including theories of punishment and the limits to the kinds of conduct that ought to be criminalized. Although philosophy of law textbooks and compilations of readings include chapters on philosophical problems in criminal, tort, contract, property, and constitutional law, to my knowledge there has never been a textbook or a book of readings that has included a chapter or section devoted exclusively to the philosophical problems of family law. There has been some slight movement in that direction with the advent of interest in feminism and the law in recent years. This has spurred discussion of the validity of the public/private distinction, a topic which is also central to the question of justifiable interventions in the family. Textbooks will sometimes include material on the contemporary debates for and against gay marriage. There has also been some interest in recent years from philosophers who have published articles and books on the moral and legal rights of children, but very little of this debate appears in introductory philosophy of law texts. For the most part, textbooks and readers in the philosophy of law make little mention of most philosophical problems in family law.

Family law has undergone a radical transformation over the past 100 years that is unrivaled by any other body of American law. The evidence of this can be seen in the laws that define the formation and dissolution of marriage. In mid-twentieth century America there was a social consensus as to what marriage meant.

> Marriage was permanent and monogamous; children were automatic, essential, and central; husbands earned money and made decisions; wives stayed home taking care of house, children, and husband. The legal system reinforced the social norms for marriage. Now the clarity and unity of the domestic picture is gone. Only a small percentage of American families still have all the characteristics associated with the traditional nuclear family ideal. In place of a single socially approved ideal we have compelling demands for autonomy and privacy, and multiple models of intimacy: single parents, working wives, house husbands, living-together arrangements without marriage, serial marriage, and stepchildren (Schultz, 207).

Marjorie Schultz wrote those words in 1982. We can now add same-sex marriage to her list of "models of intimacy." This addition only serves to reinforce her concluding remark: "The changes are legion, and their message is clear: the destruction of traditional marriage as the sole model for adult intimacy is irreversible."

There are several other changes in family law that are worth noting, each of which are prime candidates for philosophical scrutiny (Statsky 2015:3). First, family law in the United States is no longer based on male dominance. The legal status of husbands and wives is now, to a large extent, equal. Second, Congress and federal courts have brought about several changes in family laws that were once entirely the province of the states (for example, federal laws on the legality of abortion and same-sex marriage). Third, there is much more opportunity now than there was 60 years ago for people who wish to marry to enter into contracts (premarital agreements) detailing the terms of their marriage, especially in the area of finances. Fourth, new technologies affecting reproduction (cryopreservation of embryos for future implantation) have brought new categories for legal dispute. Fifth, many of the restrictions on the privacy rights (liberty) of married persons to make their own decisions about sexual conduct and reproduction have been eliminated. Each of these changes in the law were contested on normative grounds when they were introduced and several are still in dispute. This is rich terrain for philosophers of law who should have much to contribute to these important debates.

Another (possible) reason for the lack of attention paid by scholars to the philosophical problems of family law is that laws concerning the family are a mix of rules having different functions. Unlike criminal, contract, tort or property law, there is no single set of rules having a common function that we can identify with the label "family law." The function of some family laws is mandatory, requiring or prohibiting behavior on pain of punishment (incest, bigamy) or requiring that a parent compensate a child she has injured through his neglect (intrafamily torts). Other family laws confer powers on persons to achieve a particular status (marriage rules, premarital agreements, and rules on adoption). As I shall discuss below, the only thing that ties these diversely functioning laws into a bundle is the fact that they are laws that concern a person either by virtue of his or her status as a family member (spouse, child, parent, and guardian) or by virtue of being in the process of family formation.

This book is an effort to correct this neglect by introducing readers to the main philosophical problems of law through an examination of family law cases contested in state, local and federal courts. Traditional problems in the philosophy of law such as the nature of law and legal systems, the relationship between law and morals, and interpreting the U.S. Constitution can just as well be illustrated using family law cases as it is now illustrated using cases from criminal law. And this book has the added benefit of introducing readers to special philosophical problems in family law rarely included in standard philosophy of law readers: access to marriage, the rights of children, custody disputes over children born to surrogate mothers, and disputes about whether cryopreserved embryos should be regarded as persons or property.

1.2 A Typology of Family Law

Family law is the body of law that concerns persons by virtue of their status as a family member or as an intending family member: a spouse, parent, child, legal guardian or fiancé. For example, a law that prohibits spousal abuse is a family law because it specifically prohibits persons from harming someone with whom he or she has a marital relationship. By way of contrast a law that prohibits assault is not classified as a family law because commission of the crime does not depend on the existence of a family status, identity as a family member, or a family relationship between perpetrator and victim.

There are other definitions of family law. Some have defined it as a set of laws "whose purpose is to regulate relationships among family members" (Hamilton 2006). Another definition says that family law "defines relationships, rights and duties in the formation, ongoing existence, and dissolution of marriage and other family units" (Statsky 2015). Thus, laws on marriage and divorce would be within the boundaries of these definitions, but not intrafamily conduct that could be classified as a crime or tort.

In this book I am going to take a more expansive view in constructing a typology of family law. My approach is based on the various *functions* of the law. For example, some laws have a *penal* or mandatory function. They impose or threaten to impose fines or imprisonment in order to ensure compliance. Some family laws also have this function. Spousal abuse, bigamy and incest are examples. Depending on the circumstances and the jurisdiction in which it is prosecuted, these have been treated as felonies subject to criminal punishment. Philosophical problems arising from the use of the penal function in family law are discussed in Chap. 6 ("Family Crime and Punishment").

A second function of the law is *remedial.* Laws in this category define particular grievances and specific remedies. Tort laws have this function, and some harms that occur in the family can be pursued by the individual harmed for damages in a civil lawsuit. Again, spousal abuse is an example of a family law that has a remedial function (in addition to the previously mentioned penal function). Philosophical problems arising from the use of the remedial function are explored in Chap. 8 ("Family Torts and Remedies").

Third, some laws have a *regulatory* function. These laws are designed to protect specific persons, usually children, from suffering harm, but they do not achieve this by penal or remedial methods. An example of laws having this function are found in statutory standards for child neglect and the power given to family court judges to measure parental behavior against such standards. Although criminal sanctions are rarely imposed for failing to meet the standards, children can be removed from the home, and in the more serious cases, parental rights to custody can be terminated. The regulatory function of family law is discussed in Chap. 7 ("Child Abuse and Neglect").

Fourth, a common function of the law is to confer power on individuals to alter or create rights and obligations involving others. These private *power-conferring* rules specify the procedures to be followed in order to invoke these powers, and they indicate the legal significance of the changes in rights and obligations, status and remedies that will result from their use. Marriage law, divorce law and adoption law are examples of family laws that have this power-conferring function. This function is front and center in debates about the employment of surrogate mothers for child birth, and in pre-divorce contracts for the disposition of frozen embryos. Philosophical problems arising from the use of this function are the subject of Chaps. 9 ("Family Contracts: Marriage and Divorce"), 11 ("Surrogacy"), and 12 ("Frozen Embryos").

Fifth, there is a large group of legal rules that function to *confer and distribute benefits* and, in some cases, to place *burdens* on individuals. The benefits are often conferred on families for child care, child welfare, family counseling, family planning, income maintenance, tax benefits and family housing. They are also extensively conferred on married couples: Social Security insurance, employment and retirement benefits, inheritance and estate benefits, and entitlements under federal immigration law (Hamilton, 44). The burdens are the constraints placed on some persons to do or to refrain from certain kinds of acts on pain of not receiving a benefit for which they would otherwise qualify (for example, under some cash assistance programs for indigent American families with dependent children, single parents are required to participate in work activities for at least 30 h per week. Failure to participate in work requirements can result in a reduction or termination of benefits to the family (Schott 2011). The philosophical issues involving the distributive functions of marriage law are part of the discussion in Chap. 9 (Sect. 9.3).

Finally, some legal rules have a *defining* function. In family law this function brings some measure of coherence to an otherwise ambiguous concept. The non-legal uses of the word "family" are examples of a "case of trouble" alluded to in the epigraph to this chapter. There are those who use "family" to refer only to a mother, father and children, while many of us apply it to their extended family, by including all their grandparents and cousins. Others will widen the scope of the word to include a married couple with no children, or an unmarried couple with children. Some genealogists use the word "family" to refer to all their ancestors, and college roommates are known to refer to one another as "my family." Statutes, codes and judicial decisions provide legal definitions that recognize some of these uses of "family" while ignoring others. The defining function of the law brings coherence to a disputed term, but not always to the satisfaction of those who feel that their type of intimate relationship should receive equal recognition. The defining function of family law is evident in the debates illustrated in most of the chapters of this book.

I realize that there are other possible typologies of family law. Instead of classifying family laws by their function, we could also classify them by the concepts they embody, for example conjugality, contract, privacy and *parens patriae* (Hamilton, 38). But this would limit my investigation to legal rules on marriage, divorce, parenting and child welfare, perhaps excluding criminal and tort rules that impact family relationships. Or one could simply point out that if certain harms occurring within the family are in fact treated by the legal system as crimes, torts or breach of contract, then this should disqualify the harm as a matter of family law concern. The problem with this suggestion is that one and the same harm occurring within the family is sometimes treated under the criminal law, but at other times is treated under family law (for example, some cases of sexual abuse of a child by a parent are transferred from criminal to juvenile or family court and treated as a ground for termination of parental rights).

Finally, the most important reason we should prefer the functional approach to the typology of family law provided above is that it allows us to discuss most of the issues and problems that arise in the philosophy of law, using family law cases as my illustrations. This would not be possible if we excluded intrafamily crimes and torts from the discussion, leaving us without an opportunity to examine the traditional debates about the limits of mandatory laws and the justification of punishment in the criminal law or the assignment of remedies in the law of torts.

1.3 Jurisprudence vs Philosophy of Law

The words "jurisprudence" and "philosophy of law" are often used interchangeably, as having the same meaning. In this book we will maintain a distinction between them.

The word "jurisprudence" derives from the Latin term *juris prudentia*, which means "the study, knowledge, or science of law." Black's Law Dictionary places the emphasis in its definition on the word *science*:

> In the proper sense of the word, "jurisprudence" is the science of law, namely, that science which has for its function to ascertain the principles on which legal rules are based, so as not only to classify those rules in their proper order, and show the relation in which they stand to one another, but also to settle the manner in which new or doubtful cases should be brought under the appropriate rules.

This definition does not apply to the philosophy of law. Philosophy is not science. Its aim is not to *explain* existing rules by searching for the principles on which the rules are based, but to determine whether the existing rules and principles are *justifiable*. The central concern of legal philosophy is the *moral evaluation of law and legal systems*. This is not to deny that philosophers will sometimes attempt to discover the principles from which existing rules *might* have been derived, but this is not done for any of the purposes mentioned in the definition of jurisprudence quoted above. Nor do we deny that legal philosophers should be concerned with basic factual questions about human nature. These facts might inform us of the conditions that will limit what can and cannot be proscribed by law. And, as illustrated in the previous section (Sect. 1.2), philosophical inquiry can be helped by a typology or classification scheme to aid us in sorting the areas of the law about which we wish to inquire.

But none of these tasks are within the province of philosophy. The central purpose of the philosophy of law is *normative*. It is a discipline that falls under the province of moral philosophy. If the existing rules cannot be derived from morally acceptable principles, then the philosopher of law will either reject the rules or recommend new rules derived from moral principles that are justifiable. And so it is with the philosophy of family law. Philosophers might look at a number of historical principles that are believed to be the basis for family law, and they can attempt to use these principles to justify the rules. But they may fail in this effort. For example, it has been persuasively argued that in the United States, rules on marriage enforcing conjugality have been influenced in part by the principle of "Biblical traditionalism" (Hamilton 2006). Notice that the key words here are "influenced by." Nothing is said or implied about whether these marriage rules are *justified by* Biblical traditionalism. If someone today were to attempt to use this principle to justify the restoration of the idea of marriage as a single unit headed by the husband, this would be immediately rejected on the ground that it conflicts with the contemporary liberal ideal of gender equality. In other words, contemporary scholars might accept Biblical traditionalism as an *explanation* of early American family law, but reject this principle as a *justification*. It is at this point – the search for a justification – where the philosopher joins the debate.

The other part of the philosophy of law is logical or conceptual. In order to present rationally grounded arguments for normative claims about the relationship between law and morals, for example, we need to present an analysis of the meaning of these concepts, in addition to many other concepts which figure importantly in family law such as "marriage," "family," "child," "parent," "privacy," "custody, "guardian," and "person." There is an important connection between this conceptual task of legal philosophy and its normative moral task, because a normative claim might stand or fall on how the concepts used in the claim are defined.

1.4 Plan of the Book

Each chapter begins with an abstract for quick review of its contents and ends with a set of discussion questions and references for further reading. In order to avoid redundancy, the following comments give only brief descriptions of each chapter and how the chapters have been organized into three major parts.

The first part (*Law, Morals and the Constitution*) has two chapters (2 and 3) discussing the traditional debate between natural law theory and legal positivism about the relationship between law and morals, and a chapter (4) about the conflict between several theories about the best way for Supreme Court judges (and the rest of us) to interpret the U.S. Constitution.

The second part of the book (*State Intervention in the Family*) has a chapter (5) on the moral limits of family law (to what extent ought the state, through the coercive power of law, intervene in family relationships?). The following chapter (6) looks at the problem of deciding on the type or manner of the state's response to intrafamily crime (through a system of punishment, therapy, or a mixture of both). Chapter 7 discusses the contentious issue of dealing, not with the perpetrator of harm, but the child victim. Should the emphasis be placed on preserving the family, on protecting the child from further harm, or again, on some combination of both approaches? Chapter 8 takes the first venture into private law by examining the philosophical problems that arise from special rules regarding intrafamily harms (torts). Should parents be immunized from tort liability for accidental harm caused to their children? Should married persons be immunized from liability for accidental harm they have caused to their spouse?

The third part of the book (*Marriage, Children and the State*) is about problems that are unique to family law: the justification of marriage (9), the moral and legal relationship between children and the state (10), and legal responses to the new science and technology of birth (11, 12). Chapter 9 raises several philosophical questions about marriage law, most of them about the justice of the state's regulation of this ancient institution. In Chap. 10 we will examine several philosophical theories about the moral and legal relationship between children and parents as a preliminary to a critical discussion of several confusing Supreme Court pronouncements about the status of children in public school settings. Chapters 11 and 12 are about the lag between new birthing methods and technologies of assisted reproduction, the practice of surrogacy, cryopreservation, and the resulting normative debate about whether and how to change the ancient rules governing motherhood and child custody.

The final part of the book is devoted to brief descriptions of two relatively recent theoretical movements in legal philosophy: Critical Legal Studies and Feminist Jurisprudence. We will show how these theories arose from early twentieth century Legal Realism and the effect these theories have had on debates about the rule of law, legal reasoning, and (of particular interest to a central theme of this book) disputes between advocates and opponents of the principle of family privacy.

In its strong form, the principle prohibits coercive state intervention in the family in all instances, including those situations in which one family member has caused or is threatening to cause harm to other family members. The principle was consistent with the early *doctrine of coverture* and the related understanding that upon marriage a woman lost her legal identity and became one with her husband, thereby making it difficult if not impossible for her to complain about his abusive treatment of her children. A weak (and more defensible) modern version of the privacy principle allows harm-preventing interventions, but prohibits the state from intervening in other behaviors that are regarded as private, for example parental decisions about the content of a child's education (sex education in the public schools), how a child should be disciplined for misbehavior, or a married couple's decision to use artificial contraceptives. The weak version is also seen in protests about rules that prohibit certain kinds of marriages (same-sex, polygamous), rules that prohibit non-harmful behavior within marriage (incest, bigamy, adultery), and rules that dictate whether and how a marriage can be terminated. The general question we shall explore in these final chapters is whether the state has any sound moral reasons for legally regulating behavior within the family that it does not have in regulating the same kind of behavior between persons who either are not in nor are attempting to be in some kind of family relationship. Should we treat individuals as individuals, or does family membership matter?

References

Areen, Judith, et al. 2012. *Family law: Cases and materials*, 6th ed. New York: Foundation Press.
Hamilton, Vivian. 2006. Principles of U.S. family law. *Fordham Law Review* 75: 1.
Schott, L. 2011. Policy basics: An introduction to TANF. *Center on budget and policy priorities*. http://www.cbpp.org/cms/index.cfm?fa=view&id=936 Accessed 02 Nov 2015.
Schultz, Marjorie Maguire. 1982. Contractual ordering of marriage: A new model for state policy. *California Law Review* 70: 204.
Statsky, William P. 2015. *Family law: The essentials*, 3rd ed. Stamford: Cengage Learning.

References

Part I
Law, Morals and the Constitution

Chapter 2
Natural Law Theory

"No human laws are of any validity, if contrary to the law of nature; and such of them as are valid, derive all their authority, mediately or immediately, from this."

Wm. Blackstone, *Commentaries on the Laws of England* (1765)

Abstract In this chapter we will critically examine natural law theory and the proposal that there is a necessary connection between *positive* (human-created) family law and natural family law (objectively valid, universal moral rules not created by humans). Natural law theory, as it applies to family law, proposes that the rules of positive family law are valid only if they conform to the rules of natural family law. Our question is whether this theory can be successfully defended. We begin with a description of a Supreme Court case invalidating a state statute prohibiting sexual activity and marriages between persons of different races, in which the prohibition was partly based on appeals to natural law. We will then test several versions of natural law theory, beginning with a classical version originally proposed in the seventeenth century by the English philosopher John Locke. We conclude with a discussion of two modern versions of the theory proposed and defended in the twentieth century by American philosophers Lon Fuller and Ronald Dworkin.

2.1 Positive and Natural Law

One of the standard problems in textbooks and readers in the philosophy of law is about the relationship of law and morals, usually discussed as the question "What is the relationship of positive law to natural law?" *Positive law* refers to laws or entire systems of laws that are created (legislated) by humans and enforced (executed) by them within a given state, country, or other jurisdictional locality. *Natural law* refers to the set of moral rules that both impose obligations and can be legislated and

L.D. Houlgate, *Philosophy, Law and the Family*, AMINTAPHIL: The Philosophical Foundations of Law and Justice 7,
DOI 10.1007/978-3-319-51121-4_2

executed as positive law for the human community.[1] These rules are called *natural* because they are not created by humans nor are they logically dependent on human enactment. They are believed to be objectively true, discoverable by the use of reason, and not restricted to any geographical or political territory. They are universal and apply to all persons, cultures and communities past, present and future. They *can* be legislated and executed as positive law in the sense that it is *physically* possible for those to whom the rules apply to do the acts that are proscribed or prohibited, but they cannot be legislated and executed in a way that will make these rules valid. People will sometimes obey an invalid law, not because they are under a moral obligation to obey, but only because they are coerced to obey by the threat of punishment.

The positive laws usually chosen by textbook authors for discussion are *criminal laws* and the natural laws selected are those that prohibit actions universally regarded as morally wrong. In asking the question whether there is a necessary connection between law and morals (that is, between positive and natural law), those who answer affirmatively will choose examples like murder and rape, proclaiming that laws prohibiting such acts are valid *only because* the acts themselves are universally believed to be morally wrong. Those who answer the question negatively will also choose their own examples, typically drawn from times past or from non-western cultures. For example, apostasy (the act of abandoning one's faith) and blasphemy (defined as speech or actions considered to be contemptuous of God or the divine) are regarded as crimes in many non-western countries, punishable by fines or even death (Pew Research 2014). Apostasy and blasphemy are not universally believed to be morally wrong, but laws prohibiting such acts are nonetheless valid in those countries that enforce them. Hence, the critic will argue that there is no necessary connection between law and morals: a law believed to be immoral can nonetheless be legally valid.

The examples of apostasy and blasphemy will not silence those who believe there is a necessary connection between law and morality. They will insist that rules prohibiting such acts are objectively true and can be known to be true by anyone using their natural powers of reasoning. They would argue that those who deny this are either ignorant of the laws of nature or they are so biased by self-interest that they refuse to recognize that these behaviors (apostasy, blasphemy) are condemned by the natural law. Acts that violate such acts are necessarily crimes, and any system of positive law that fails to criminalize them is defective.

These examples are taken from the existing criminal law of several sovereign states[2] and are here used only to outline the debate between various versions of

[1] The rules of natural law *can* be legislated and executed by human beings in the sense that it is *physically* possible for those to whom the rules apply to do the acts that are legally proscribed or prohibited by positive law.

[2] A Pew Research analysis finds that as of 2012, nearly a quarter of the world's countries and territories (22%) had anti-blasphemy laws or policies, and one-in-ten (11%) had laws or policies penalizing apostasy. The legal punishments for such transgressions vary from fines to death (Theodorou 2014).

Natural Law Theory and a second debate between all natural law theories and *Legal Positivism*. Legal positivists argue that the preceding internal debate between proponents of natural law theory about whether apostasy and blasphemy are prohibited by the natural law is *irrelevant* to deciding whether such laws are valid or invalid. Positivists contend that the validity of the laws of a community has nothing to do with their content "but with their *pedigree* or the manner in which they were adopted or developed" (Dworkin 1977, 38). If these laws have been enacted in accordance with the procedures for creating law that exist in the political community in which they are enforced, then this entirely decides the question of their validity.

It is the aim of this and the following chapter to recast the debate between these theories as a debate about the connection between positive *family law* and the moral rules governing *family relationships*. There are several versions of both theories, only one of which (to my knowledge) has ever cited rules of morality and law pertaining to family relationships as examples when attempting to support the theory. As I mentioned above, the examples have almost always been drawn from the criminal law, and little attention has been given to other branches of the law, especially the large body of law that deals with family relationships, or to those parts of the criminal law proscribing intrafamily harms.

Before we begin discussion of natural law theory let us examine a famous U.S. Supreme Court case that gives a clear description of how the theory was once used to influence positive laws on marriage and marital relations that had existed in America from the time of the British colonial period.

2.2 The End of Miscegenation: *Loving vs. Virginia*

2.2.1 Historical Background

Anti-miscegenation laws prohibit interracial sexual activity and marriages between persons of different races. The prohibition primarily bans the marriage of whites and blacks, but often also the marriages of whites and Native Americans and Asians. The first laws criminalizing marriage and sex between whites and blacks were enacted in the colonial era in Virginia and Maryland. The original intent of these laws was to prohibit sexual activity and marriages between slave owners and their indentured servants and slaves. But by 1691, Virginia also prohibited the marriages of free blacks and whites. Anti-miscegenation quickly spread to all of the colonies, and most of these laws were retained in the states after the independence of the United States had been secured from England. And they continued to be enforced in many states long after the abolition of slavery. However, by 1887 eleven states had repealed their anti-miscegenation laws, and an additional fourteen states had abolished such laws by 1967. This left Virginia and fifteen other states, most of them in the South, with anti-miscegenation laws still on the books at the start of the famous U.S. Supreme Court case of *Loving v. Virginia* on June 6, 1967.

2.2.2 Factual Basis of the Case

The incident that culminated in the *Loving* case began in June 1958 when two residents of Virginia, Mildred Jeter, a black woman, and Richard Loving, a white man, were married in the District of Columbia pursuant to its laws. Shortly after their marriage, the Lovings returned to Virginia and established their marital home in Caroline County. At the October Term, 1958, of the Circuit Court of Caroline County, a grand jury issued an indictment charging the Lovings with violating Virginia's ban on interracial marriages. The two statutes under which the appellants were convicted and sentenced are part of a comprehensive statutory scheme aimed at prohibiting and punishing interracial marriages. The Lovings were convicted of violating § 20–58 of the Virginia Code:

> *Leaving State to evade law.* —If any white person and colored person shall go out of this State, for the purpose of being married, and with the intention of returning, and be married out of it, and afterwards return to and reside in it, cohabiting as man and wife, they shall be punished as provided in § 20–59, and the marriage shall be governed by the same law as if it had been solemnized in this State. The fact of their cohabitation here as man and wife shall be evidence of their marriage.

Section 20–59, which defines the penalty for miscegenation, provides:

> *Punishment for marriage.* —If any white person intermarries with a colored person, or any colored person intermarry with a white person, he shall be guilty of a felony and shall be punished by confinement in the penitentiary for not less than one nor more than five years.

On January 6, 1959, the Lovings pleaded guilty to the charges and were sentenced to 1 year in jail; however, the trial judge suspended the sentence for a period of 25 years on the condition that the Lovings leave the State and not return to Virginia together for that period of time.

After their convictions, the Lovings took up residence in the District of Columbia. In late 1963 they filed a motion in the Virginia state trial court asking it to vacate the judgment and set aside their sentence on the ground that the relevant statutes violated the Fourteenth Amendment of the U.S. Constitution. After being ignored by the trial court, they brought a class action to the U.S. District Court for the Eastern District of Virginia. The state trial judge denied a motion to vacate the sentences and the Lovings appealed to the Supreme Court of Appeals. This court upheld the constitutionality of the anti-miscegenation statutes and, after modifying the sentence, they affirmed the convictions. The Lovings appealed this decision, and the U.S. Supreme Court noted probable jurisdiction on December 12, 1966.

2.2.3 Decision and Findings of the U.S. Supreme Court[3]

When the case reached the U.S. Supreme Court the justices heard arguments from both sides and unanimously ruled that the Virginia statutes were unconstitutional:

> This case presents a constitutional question never addressed by this Court: whether a statutory scheme adopted by the State of Virginia to prevent marriages between persons solely on the basis of racial classifications violates the Equal Protection and Due Process Clauses of the Fourteenth Amendment. For reasons which seem to us to reflect the central meaning of those constitutional commands, we conclude that these statutes cannot stand consistently with the Fourteenth Amendment.[4]

The justices noted that the state trial court judge had invoked natural law principles in his defense of the Virginia statutes. The Court quoted this passage:

> Almighty God created the races white, black, yellow, Malay and red, and he placed them on separate continents. And but for the interference with his arrangement there would be no cause for such marriages. The fact that he separated the races shows that he did not intend for the races to mix.

The trial court judge also referenced other natural law arguments used to justify miscegenation. In a previous case, the Virginia state court concluded that Virginia's legitimate purposes in enacting miscegenation laws were "to preserve the racial integrity of its citizens," and to prevent "the corruption of blood," "a mongrel breed of citizens," and "the obliteration of racial pride." All of this was obviously an endorsement of the doctrine of natural White Supremacy (*Naim v Naim*, 1955). These arguments assume that blacks are naturally inferior and that mixing the races is unnatural. The implied natural law is that there is a moral obligation to maintain the superiority of the white race.[5] "Natural law logic therefore underscored the following condition: If the laws of nature forbade miscegenation, and if the laws of man, to be valid, had to reflect the laws of nature, then legislators needed to promulgate statutes banning interracial sex" (Mendenhall 2013, 38).

---

[3] Twenty years prior to the U.S. Supreme Court's decision to consider the constitutionality of miscegenation laws, the California Supreme Court struck down all state and local laws prohibiting interracial marriage. (*Perez v Sharp*. 32 Cal. 2d 711, 198 P. 2d 17 Cal. 1948) Associate Justice Roger Traynor wrote for the majority: "Since the right to marry is the right to join in marriage with the person of one's choice, a statute that prohibits an individual from marrying a member of a race other than his own restricts the scope of his choice." He added: Equal protection laws could not be based on "arbitrary classifications of groups or races." Associate Justice Jesse Carter concurred with his colleague, but went further: Laws that barred interracial marriage were "the product of ignorance, prejudice and intolerance." (Cairns 2015).

[4] Section 1 of the Fourteenth Amendment to the United States Constitution: "All persons born or naturalized in the United States and subject to the jurisdiction thereof, are citizens of the United States and of the State wherein they reside. No State shall make or enforce any law which shall abridge the privileges or immunities of citizens of the United States; nor shall any State deprive any person of life, liberty, or property, without due process of law; nor deny to any person within its jurisdiction the equal protection of the laws."

[5] Justice Warren, writing for the majority, noted "the fact that Virginia prohibits only interracial marriages involving white persons demonstrates that the racial classifications must stand…as measures designed to maintain White Supremacy" (*Loving v Virginia*1967, 11).

All arguments of the Virginia state trial court justifying the prohibition of interracial marriage were rejected by the Supreme Court on the ground that the ultimate legal validity of a statute can only be secured by showing conformity to the provisions of the U.S. Constitution and its amendments, not by conformity to what some legislators or judges believe to be the laws of nature or laws that God or any other divine being had or had not ordained. Since the Virginia statutes "cannot stand consistently with the Fourteenth Amendment" the Court implied that it is irrelevant that they do or do not conform to what some believe to be the law of nature.

2.3 Traditional Natural Law Theory

Traditional natural law theory has two parts. The first part is the doctrine that "there are universally binding (objectively valid) moral rules, knowable by use of our natural faculties" (Simmons 1992, 103). The second part is the claim that positive laws are invalid and cannot have legal authority if they conflict with these moral rules. There have been many in the long history of philosophy who have argued for the traditional position, including the medieval philosopher Augustine who famously said "a law that is not just is not a law" (Augustine, 11) and Thomas Aquinas who wrote that a human law must be "derived" from the law of nature: " ... If in any point it deflects from the law of nature, it is no longer a law but a perversion of law" (Aquinas 1981, 58).

Although Augustine and Aquinas both saw the natural law as laid down by God, the claim that there are objectively valid moral rules need not be theologically based. Moral rules and principles can be called objectively valid even if these principles are not taken to be the commands of God, and even if the proposed rules are acknowledged to be created (not discovered) by human fiat. It is quite possible to use utilitarian or Kantian arguments to support a claim of objective truth for moral rules[6] and then proceed to the second part of natural law theory by taking the position that the positive law must conform to these rules in order to qualify as valid law.

2.3.1 An Example of Traditional Natural Law Theory: John Locke

I have chosen the seventeenth century English philosopher John Locke as representative of natural law theory for two reasons. First, Locke is one of the few natural law theorists who often defends natural law theory independent of any of his

[6]A utilitarian might argue that conventional moral rules are justifiable only if adherence to such rules promotes the greatest net utility (using the utilitarian or Greatest Happiness principle). Alternatively, one could take a Kantian position and argue for the justifiability of a conventional moral rule on the ground that it is a maxim through which one can will that it become a universal law (using the Categorical Imperative as a decision procedure for moral reasoning).

commitments to God's role as lawgiver and creator. His arguments can be judged on the basis of his promise that "reason alone" is sufficient to reveal the natural law. Second, Locke is one of the few philosophers to argue for the existence of natural laws governing family relationships. Although his ultimate motive was to show an important distinction between political and paternal power, his discussion of the paternal power reveals much about how he would have us construct a "just" system of family law.

The State of Nature

In his *Second Treatise of Government*, Locke writes that the original state (condition) that all men are naturally in is a state of perfect freedom and equality. Humans are free to do as they wish "without asking leave, or depending upon the will of any other man," so long as what they do does not violate "the law of nature." Second, all persons are equal in the sense that none has more power (rights) than any other person, "there being nothing more evident, than that creatures of the same species and rank, promiscuously born to all the same advantages of nature, and the use of the same faculties, should also be equal one amongst another without subordination or subjection …" (Locke, II, 4).

The pre-political condition of humankind is called the *state of nature*, and in that condition there is "a *law of nature* to govern it, which obliges everyone; and reason, which is that law, teaches all mankind, who will but consult it, that being all equal and independent, no one ought to harm another in his life, health, liberty, or possessions" (Locke, II, 6).[7] Before humans came together to form political society and develop systems of positive law, there was a natural law that conferred on them the moral obligations not to kill, injure, impede another's movements or damage another's possessions. These obligations reciprocally confer on all persons the rights to life, health, liberty and possessions. These rights ought to serve as the model for human creation of the laws governing civil society.

Our question in this chapter is about the relationship between natural and positive law. The relationship could take two forms in natural law theory. First, the theory might be construed as establishing requirements for *legal validity*. A positive law is valid only if it conforms to the law of nature. If it does not conform, then it is

[7] A. John Simmons says of this passage that Locke is suggesting "a kind of 'practical contradiction' involved in harmful conduct toward others. If I truly regard my fellow human beings as "all equal and independent," then it would be irrational or inconsistent to treat others as if they were different from me." We should note that Locke makes no reference to God's will or to his commands in the quoted passage (Simmons 1992, 40). In an earlier paragraph Locke quotes approvingly from Richard Hooker: "The like natural inducement, hath brought men to know that it is no less their duty, to love others than themselves, for seeing those things which are equal, must needs all have one measure; If I cannot but wish to receive good, even as much at every man's hands, as any man can wish unto his own soul, how should I look to have any part of my desire herein satisfied, unless myself be careful to satisfy the like desire, which is undoubtedly in other men, being of one and the same nature?" (Hooker, *Eccl. Pol. Lib.* 1).

invalid, and there is no moral obligation to obey an invalid law. For example, if a legal system contained rules giving a monarch arbitrary power over "the lives and fortunes of the people," then such rules would be invalid. They would not count as "law" because the fundamental law of nature is the preservation of mankind, and "no human sanction can be good, or valid against it" (Locke 1980, XI, 135). I will call this version of natural law theory the "strong" version. Second, natural law theory might also be interpreted as making recommendations for determining when positive laws are *good* or *bad.* In the event that a bad law is nonetheless enacted by a legislative body, it would remain valid and enforceable until it is repealed. For example, if natural law is interpreted to prohibit interracial marriage but the positive laws permit and regulate it, then these laws might be declared bad law but remain valid because they were duly enacted in accordance with the rules and procedures of the state legislature. I will call this the "weak" version of natural law theory.

Only the strong version of natural law theory claims that there is a necessary connection between positive law and morality. The rules of positive law must not conflict with the principles of natural law. Such rules are invalid, and they impose no obligations. This is what Locke means when he argues that the higher obligation of the law of nature to preserve mankind invalidates any obligation imposed by a positive law that would give a ruler the arbitrary power to decide whether a citizen should live or die, be enslaved or be free.

The strong version of natural law theory appears to deal only with existing positive laws, declaring them to be valid or invalid depending on whether or not they conform to or violate the fundamental law of nature (preservation of life, liberty and possessions). It does not tell us how we are to proceed when a legal system fails to enact any positive laws that enforce the laws of nature. Is the system itself to be declared invalid? Locke answers this question by declaring that there are a certain minimum number of positive laws that must be enacted if people are to escape the state of nature and "join in society with others, who are already united, or have a mind to unite, for the mutual preservation of their lives, liberties and estates" (IX, 123). These positive laws are those required to guarantee or insure that people *not* do whatever they individually think necessary for self-preservation of themselves and "the rest of mankind" (IX, 129). Locke does not mean that persons must give up the right to self-defense. He means that we must give up *to the community* the right to decide what laws are to be enacted, to be the final judge and executioner of the law of nature, and "by force to make good" any injustices we believe that has been done to us or others (IX, 124, 125, 126). If anyone insists on retaining any of these rights, then they cannot be a part of civil society.

We should notice that the natural rights we give up to the community are denoted by Locke as "powers" of which, Locke writes, there are two. "The first is to do whatsoever he thinks fit for the preservation of himself, and others within the permission of the law of nature … [and] the other power … is the power to punish the crimes committed against that law" (IX 128, 129). We give up both of these powers "to be regulated by laws made by society" (129). In the language of contemporary legal philosophers, the laws in question here are "power-conferring rules." These are rules which empower public officials to enact, repeal and change laws (legislative power), to apply and interpret them (judicial power), and to enforce them (executive power).

Power-conferring rules are different from the mandatory rules of the criminal law. They give both private persons and public officials the power or right to realize their wishes. If I want to see to it that my estate is given to my child after my death, then the private law on wills gives me the power to do this. If legislators want to see to it that murder is legally prohibited, then their status as legislators confers on them the public power to make this happen. But the law on murder itself is mandatory, not power-conferring. It commands people under threat of punishment to refrain from killing other persons, even if they may have a strong desire to do this. Power-conferring rules give us the legal ability to realize our wishes; mandatory rules prohibit or require us to do certain acts, despite our wishes.

If the unanimous agreement to give up our private power to create our own laws constitutes the social contract which creates civil society, then what mandatory rules should the first legislature create if they are to be guided in their decision-making by the laws of nature? The answer to this question has already been given by Locke. The first mandatory rules must be those that prohibit conduct that would harm persons in their "life, health, liberty and possessions." Hence, a minimum set of rules that comprise a criminal law would include prohibitions on murder, assault, kidnap, enslavement, theft, and damage to private property. These are the mandatory laws which are necessary to guarantee "the preservation of society," which is "the first and fundamental natural law, which is to govern even the legislative itself … and (as far as will consist with the public good) of every person in it" (XI, 134). Moreover, since the entire reason that persons left the state of nature to enter into society was to preserve their own lives, liberty and possessions, they cannot transfer to a legislative body more power than they had as individuals in the state of nature. Hence, there is a severe restriction on the positive laws that a legislature can enact. "Their power, in the utmost bounds of it, is limited to the public good of the society. It is a power that hath no other end but preservation and therefore can never have a right to destroy, enslave, or designedly to impoverish the subjects" (XI, 135).

Natural Law and Paternal Power

Prior to entering the social contract which creates political society, Locke wrote that "the first society" was *the family*, made up of man and wife, children and servants in which "the master or mistress of it had some sort of rule proper to a family" (VII, 77). Locke also uses the phrase *conjugal society* to describe the voluntary contract between a man and a woman which consists "chiefly in such a communion and right in one another's bodies as is necessary to its chief end, procreation" (VII, 78). The terms of the contract also commit the man and woman to give each other "mutual support and assistance" which is necessary not only for their own care and affection, "but also necessary to their common off-spring, who have a right to be nourished, and maintained by them, till they are able to provide for themselves" (id.) Finally, when the child attains the age of reason, his parents lose their power over him. But this freedom "exempts not a son from that honor which he ought, by the law of God and nature, to pay his parents." Children have a "perpetual obligation of honoring their parents," which includes not only outward expressions of "esteem and reverence," but also to never do anything that will "injure or affront, disturb or endanger, the happiness or life of those from whom he received his." This obligation extends to defending his parents from those who would harm them, and to providing them with relief, assistance and comfort" in their declining years (VI, 65, 66).

Locke does not clarify how we are to understand the nature of the relationship of positive family laws to the laws of nature that concern marriage, parent-child and filial relationships. Nor does he give any examples of family laws that would be null and void on the grounds that they violate the law of nature. However, we can create our own examples. First, imagine a society with a legal system that enforces the *paterfamilias* rule of ancient Rome, giving the oldest male in the family complete decision-making power over all things concerning the extended family. A male child of 65 years would still be under the control and direction of his 85-year-old father. This would violate Locke's natural law that says that the right of the parent to command the obedience of the child should end at the "at the age of reason."[8] Hence, we can safely assume that the *paterfamilias* rule would be void under the strong version of natural law theory. Here is a second example from early Roman law: It is allowable for a father to sell or even kill his child without suffering any legal consequences. This would certainly violate the natural law duty of parents to protect, educate, nourish and shelter their children. Third, although most would agree with Locke that adult children have a moral obligation to give aid to their parents when they are sick or infirm Locke does not recommend the enactment of positive laws requiring this behavior.

Another example mentioned by Locke is divorce. And here his position is markedly different from divorce law in eighteenth century England in which a divorce was possible only by private act of Parliament, a procedure that was "difficult, time consuming and expensive."[9] Moreover, fathers had an absolute legal right to custody of children after divorce, a law that was not changed until 1857. Locke has a much different view of these matters. After writing that the husband has the "last determination" in settling disputes about "things of their common interest and property," Locke quickly adds the remark that "he has no more power over her life than she has over his." Hence, "the wife has in many cases a liberty to separate from him, where natural right, or their contract allows for it; whether that contract be made in the state of nature, or by the customs or laws of the country they live in; and the children upon such separation fall to the father's or mother's lot, as such contract does determine" (VII, 81). These may be empty words. In eighteenth century England the marriage contract could not be altered by the marital partners and there was no state of nature to which those who wanted to marry could retreat in order to make their own marital contract.

---

[8] Locke writes that a man cannot be "under the law of England" until the age of twenty-one, which is the age at which we can presume that he has "a capacity of knowing that law" (58).

[9] Only 13 petitions were granted between 1700 and 1749, and in the remainder of the 18th century no more than 10 petitions were granted on average per year (Olsen 1999, 44).

2.3.2 *Assessing Traditional Natural Law Theory in the Context of Family Law*

Our question is whether traditional nature law theory, as represented by John Locke, gives us any guidance on the validity or legitimacy of positive family law. The first problem we confront in answering this question is whether we can accurately discern the relevant natural laws. As noted above, Locke's fundamental law of nature commands us not "to harm another in his life, health, liberty, or possessions." In creating positive law, including laws governing family relationships, the enlightened legislator must enact laws that serve this purpose, and *no other purposes.* The legislator's power, "in the utmost bounds of it, is limited to the public good of society," to which words Locke adds the clarification "it is a power that hath no other end but preservation" (XI, 135).

Let me refer to the miscegenation case of *Loving v Virginia* introduced earlier. Are the laws prohibiting interracial marriage justified by natural law? Certainly they were believed to be justified by their proponents. If the natural law is understood as God's law, then there were a large number of legislators prepared to provide quotes from religious writings showing that God prohibited both interracial marriage and sexual relationships. Although Locke quotes a great deal of Scripture in *Second Treatise*, he has nothing direct to say about its application to these practices, except in the opening paragraphs where the alleged natural *equality* of men might be used to invalidate laws prohibiting interracial marriage: "[There is] nothing more evident, than that creatures of the same species and rank, promiscuously born to all the same advantages of nature, and the use of the same faculties, should also be equal one amongst another without subordination or subjection … "(II, 4). This looks promising. If all human beings are equal, then any positive law that subjects or subordinates one class of persons to the rule of another class of persons would be an invalid law. It would seem that this voids all laws legalizing both slavery and miscegenation. However, among those who found a way to avoid this result was Thomas Jefferson, the author of the Declaration of Independence and a slave owner. Jefferson was an avid reader and follower of Locke's political theory, yet there is a loophole in the preceding quote from Locke about natural equality which was used by Jefferson and many others to justify the unequal treatment of black people. The loophole they exploited is found in the phrase "the use of the same faculties."

> According to fashionable philosophical principles of the day, if laws of nature and the universe applied equally to all humans, then blacks had to be conceptually remade as a lesser degree of human to validate any measure forbidding [slavery and] black–and–white sexual activity. Philosophy and law had to be rewritten to account for scientific revelations about racial distinctions. What is more, philosophy and law had to be rewritten so that equality was something (like the forces of nature or God's will) that each human *was subject to* but not that each human *possessed* (Mendenhall, 23).

In his *Notes*, Thomas Jefferson denied that black people have the same faculties as whites. Under the theory of "fixed nature," he described blacks as inherently inferior to whites in critical reasoning and beauty (Jefferson, 1955, 139–142, 162).

According to Mendenhall, quoted above, this theory was Jefferson's rationalized justification for the racial caste of slavery (Jefferson, 139–142). Because black people lack the same faculties as whites, they are not morally equal, and we can assume, whites and blacks ought not to be allowed to marry.

John Locke, like Thomas Aquinas before him, refers to promoting the public good of the community as a legitimate purpose of positive law, although Locke limits this to the goal of "preservation" (of life, liberty, health and possessions). Locke is also convinced that we can use our power of reasoning to discover the basic moral principles that comprise the law of nature (see fn. 6). And yet as shown above, there are fundamental disagreements about the content of the natural law between proponents of natural law theory. Legislators who adhere to natural law principles have put forward positive laws that many other legislators, using the same principles, would today regard as immoral or unjust. There are some who believe that divorce, gay marriage, interracial marriage, contraception and abortion violate the natural law, and consequently any legal rules enabling such activities are condemned as immoral. There are just as many others who deny this and would retain the same rules as promoting morality and justice.

Moreover, traditional natural law theory cannot support the general claim that an unjust rule of positive law fails to qualify as "law." The history of family law stands as testimony to several hundred years of laws on marriage, divorce and child custody (to name only a few laws) to disprove this. If the rules of natural law are those rules that are objectively valid for all persons at all times and universally apply to all cultures, then there is still plenty of room for disagreement about what constitutes the content of natural law. And, as mentioned earlier, utilitarians and Kantians, while agreeing with proponents of natural law that there are objectively valid moral rules, may also have profound disagreement about what these rules demand or prohibit for family members.

Finally, there are deep differences between seventeenth and twenty-first century Western cultures about the moral law governing decisions made within the family. The common law of England and its colonies prior to the nineteenth century "conceived of the family as an organism that had the husband/father at its head and his wife and children in its lower reaches" (Grossberg 1985). The law assumed that all members of the family had the same interests, and these were best represented by the male head of the family. This presents a dilemma for Locke. After arguing that man does not have a natural dominion over woman, he tries to align himself with the English patriarchal tradition by declaring that man does have a certain "priority" over her. The wife "owes" her husband a limited "subjection." Locke's argument is this:

> But the husband and wife, though they have but one common concern, yet having different understandings, will unavoidably sometimes have different wills too; it therefore being necessary that the last determination, i.e. the rule should be placed somewhere; it naturally falls to the man's share, as the abler and the stronger. (VII, 82–83).

The argument is clearly unconvincing. Greater ability and strength are not always a sufficient ground for granting greater authority in the family. Before authority is ceded it is important to know exactly what kind of ability is needed to carry out the relevant task. If a man is "abler and stronger" than his wife at tilling the fields behind a team of horses, these qualities have little relevance to success at other tasks requiring mental rather than physical ability, for example balancing the family budget or making decisions about a child's education.

Family planning is another area of contention between natural law proponents, especially when it involves abortion. Unlike reproductive rights in general, there is no universal consensus on abortion. The controversy is grounded in the belief held by the majority of legislators in some Roman Catholic countries that abortion involves two lives, that of the fetus as well as that of the mother, and the law of nature prohibits the intentional taking of any human life. This is contested by legislative majorities of other countries who may be of the opinion that the fetus, while human and innocent, does not have an absolute right to occupy a woman's body when her pregnancy is due to rape. Others may believe, also on grounds of natural law, that a woman has a right to make the final determination about what happens in and to her own body ("the right to choose").[10]

Among those states which recognize a public interest in the preservation of human life, moreover, there is a range of views as to when fetal life comes into being. The Inter-American Convention, for example, refers to "a right to life from the moment of conception." German law, in contrast, accepts as a matter of scientific fact that life begins 14 days after conception. Under the Hanafi School of Islamic law, "ensoulment" occurs at 4 months, before which abortion may be permitted (Stark 2005, 138–139).

The morality of divorce is another area in which one finds wide variation between the beliefs of different cultures and religions. Consider the way in which various cultures respond to adultery as a ground for divorce.

> In Nigeria, for example, a woman who has been raped may nevertheless be guilty of adultery. The practice of polygamy, similarly, which allows men in some Islamic states to take up to four wives, means that men may have multiple partners without committing adultery while women may not. In Egypt, following reforms in 1979, a woman had an automatic right to a divorce from a husband who took another wife. The 1985 law, in contrast, removed the presumption of injury and required the wife to prove that she had suffered harm by reason of her husband's subsequent marriage. This represented a return to the classical position. … In India, in addition to divorce by mutual consent, divorce is available for fault for adultery, cruelty, desertion, or if the spouse has 'ceased to be a Hindu by conversion to another religion'; or 'has been suffering continuously or intermittently from mental disorder of such a kind and to such an extent that the petitioner cannot reasonably be expected to live with the respondent.' In Uganda, fault is still required for divorce. While adultery is grounds for a divorce for either a wife or a husband, the wife must also prove that the husband was cruel or had deserted her (Stark 2005, 77).

[10] Although Locke never discussed abortion, at the beginning of his famous discussion *Of Property* he declares in *Second Treatise* that "every man has property in his own person: this nobody has any right to but himself" (V, 26). Using the word "man" in the generic sense, we can assume that a pregnant woman is the only one who has property in her own person – with all the rights of ownership, including the right to choose whether or not to abort the fetus she is carrying. It would be irrelevant how the fetus come into being, whether this was due to rape, failure of a birth control device, or to her intention to become pregnant.

Each of these cultures and religions would be quick to argue that the natural law is on their side when they enact laws opposing abortion and divorce, or when enacting the details of the exact time during a pregnancy when abortion is permissible, or the exact conditions when adultery ought or ought not to be allowed as a condition for divorce. In light of these extreme discrepancies it is difficult for proponents of natural law theory to launch a rational argument to convince us that there is a universal moral law to which we can appeal in constructing a valid body of family law.

2.4 Modern Natural Law Theory: Lon Fuller

One popular twentieth century attempt to make a necessary connection between positive law and morality is to have us look not at the conditions under which particular laws are deemed valid or invalid, but at the conditions under which systems of regulation and control qualify as *genuine systems of law*. The philosopher of law who best represents this approach is Lon Fuller.

2.4.1 Principles of Legality

According to Fuller there are eight ways in which a system of regulation and control could fail to qualify as a system of law. A person might be required to obey a legal rule that (1) does not exist or (2) is kept secret from him or (3) that came into existence only after he had acted or (4) was unintelligible or (5) was contradicted by another rule of the same system, or (6) commanded the impossible, or (7) changed every minute, or (8) is disregarded by those charged with its administration. (Fuller, 1969, 41).

Fuller refers to (1)–(8) as "abuses" of a legal system (Fuller, 43). Here is an example of (3), the "abuse of retroactive regulation": A policeman shows up at the home of Richard and Mildred Loving a few days after their return to Virginia as a married couple. The officer tells them that they are under arrest and will be prosecuted. They ask the prosecutor to explain. He says that a law was enacted *today* making it illegal for a black man to marry a white woman. He then tells them that legislators have made the law retroactive for the previous month.

Abuses (1)–(8) are violations of *principles of legality*. These principles impose on law makers and executors of the law the moral duties (a) to create rules and not make decisions on an ad hoc basis, (b) to publicize the rules that people are expected to obey, (c) not to create retroactive legislation, (d) to make rules understandable, (e) not to enact contradictory rules, (f) not to enact rules that require conduct beyond the powers of the affected party, (g) not to make frequent changes in the rules in such a way that persons cannot orient their actions by the rules, (h) to apply (execute) the rules that government expects all citizens to follow.

2.4.2 *The Inner Morality of Law*

The principles of legality represent an *inner morality* of positive law. It is this that imposes an *obligation* to obey the law. Inner morality is expressed in the moral principle that we have an obligation "to show respect for human agents capable of choosing their own conduct" (Altman 2001, 55). A system of regulation and control that violates even one of the procedural principles in (a)–(h) fails to address "humans as agents capable of deliberation and choice" (Altman, 55). Hence, there is no obligation to obey the laws of that system. Although it is possible that a law created in accordance with (a)–(h) may be an unjust law, Fuller's point is that a genuine legal system must contain the inner morality expressed by the eight principles of legality. And it is here that we see how Fuller makes the connection between law and morality. If we consider positive law from the standpoint of a system of law and not from the standpoint of individual laws, then the necessary connection between law and morality is between the inner morality of its procedural rules and the laws that are generated by that system.

2.4.3 *The Social Purposes of Law*

One of the debts owed to Fuller by natural law theorists is for his argument that there are social purposes behind the rules of positive law. For example, it is a reasonable assumption that the purpose of the First Amendment rule prohibiting Congress from creating a law abridging freedom of speech is to promote the free exchange of ideas – as much free exchange as is necessary for citizens and their representatives to make informed choices in a constitutional democracy. This purpose cannot be realized if persons are prevented by law from freely discussing their moral, political, and religious opinions. Suppose that Congress passes a federal law making it illegal for a person to falsely shout fire in a crowded theater, causing people to panic and make a rush for the exits, with the result that several are injured. Under a literal reading of the First Amendment, shouting the word "Fire!" would be regarded as constitutionally protected speech. But under an interpretation of the amendment that refers to the social purpose of the amendment it would become clear that falsely shouting "Fire!" with the intention of causing panic has nothing to do with promoting the free exchange of ideas.[11]

[11] This became known as the "clear and present danger test" for the permissibility of abridging speech. "The most stringent protection of free speech would not protect a man falsely shouting fire in a theater and causing a panic. … The question in every case is whether the words used are used in such circumstances and are of such a nature as to create a clear and present danger that they will bring about the substantive evils that Congress has a right to prevent" (O.W. Holmes in *Schenk v. United States* 1919).

2.4.4 Objections to Fuller

Let us consider a system of regulation and control of family relationships that generates unjust positive law even though it meets all of Fuller's criteria for possession of an inner morality. Is it logically possible that such a system could contain unjust laws? Andrew Altman cites examples of unjust laws enacted and enforced in Nazi Germany during the 1930s and 1940s. Among the most infamous cases of Nazi injustice were the Nuremberg laws prohibiting marriage and sexual intercourse between Jews and persons of "German blood." It would be difficult to argue that there was a *prima facie* obligation to be faithful to such laws on the ground that any system of positive law as such puts certain constraints on government evil-doing. In certain cases, those constraints are woefully short of what morality can tolerate, and the only reason for being faithful to such laws is fear of the awful consequences of disobedience (Altman, 57).

Even if it is objected that the system of laws that existed in Nazi Germany was not a genuine legal system because it violated so many of the principles of legality, it would still be possible to imagine a legal system enacting the same laws that did not violate these principles. In fact, Americans do not need to use their imagination. It has not been that long since we have had such laws in the United States. Both the rules granting white citizens the right to own slaves and the later anti-miscegenation laws that existed in many southern states until the mid-1970s were all duly passed in accordance with the principles of legality. They were clear in meaning, widely promulgated, and enacted according to established procedures. But this does not seem sufficient to confer even a *prima facie* moral obligation to obey them. Those who defied such laws believed them to be unjust and disputed any claim that they had a moral duty to conform.

2.5 Contemporary Natural Law Theory: Ronald Dworkin

As noted above, one problem with Fuller's purposive theory of interpretation is that it does not exclude laws whose social purposes are immoral or unjust. The Virginia miscegenation statute is a prime example. A law that prohibits interracial marriage and interracial sexual conduct had as its social purpose to promote a nineteenth century conception of equality that regards black people as inferior to whites. Most white people in Virginia still held this view in the mid-twentieth century and Virginia legislators and judiciary at the time apparently believed that it was no affront to equality to prohibit marriages between blacks and whites.[12] This view of what

[12] In *Naim v. Naim* (1955) the state court of Virginia concluded that the State's legitimate purposes were "to preserve the racial integrity of its citizens," and to prevent "the corruption of blood," "a mongrel breed of citizens," and "the obliteration of racial pride," obviously an endorsement of the doctrine of White Supremacy.

constitutes equality has now changed. We have long since rejected the idea that race is a relevant consideration when creating rules regarding eligibility for marriage.[13]

If Fuller's theory of law is to be rescued from the fate of promoting immorality by endorsing legal systems with laws that promote unjust social purposes, then he must introduce criteria for distinguishing between just and unjust purposes in order to correct this defect. But, as Andrew Altman observes, "nothing in the idea of law or the idea of a legal system guarantees that the law's purposes will be morally acceptable" (58). This is where Ronald Dworkin's "interpretive" version of natural law theory enters the conversation.

2.5.1 Rules and Principles

Dworkin begins by distinguishing between three types of standards that are used by lawyers when they reason or dispute about legal rights and obligations: rules, principles and policies. In family law, a *rule* would be equivalent to a statute or code, for example, "Except as otherwise provided by statute, all property, real or personal, wherever situated, acquired by a married person during the marriage while domiciled in this state is community property." (California Family Code 2016, 760). A *principle* is a standard to be observed because it is a requirement of justice or fairness or some other dimension of morality, for example, "Parents and guardians have the privacy right (liberty) to direct and control the upbringing of their children." A *policy* is a standard that sets out a goal to be reached, for example, "California will attempt to significantly decrease the rate of child abuse by 2020."

The differences between these standards are apparent. A rule is applied in an "all or nothing" fashion (Dworkin 1977, 45). It is either violated or it is not violated. If the husband claims most of the property acquired during the marriage, then he violates the statute (cited above). A rule does not function like an aspirational standard which one can "more or less" achieve. In the example provided above, if the facts are as stated (the husband claims most of the marital property), then it is logically impossible that he has the right to most of the real or personal property acquired during the marriage *and* for the relevant statute to be valid. This is not to deny that there are exceptions to legal rules,[14] but if these exist then "it is inaccurate and incomplete to state the rule so simply, without enumerating the exceptions." (Dworkin 1977, 46).

Principles function in a quite different way. Principles "do not set out legal consequences that follow automatically when the conditions provided are met" (Dworkin, 46) Most lawyers and judges involved in the process of reasoning about family law cases would agree with the principle (doctrine) of family privacy quoted

[13] It is plausible to predict that it will not be long before gender and sexual preference is also universally regarded as an equally irrelevant (and therefore unjust) consideration.

[14] There are several exceptions to California Family Code 760, for example "Nothing in this section affects the community character of property that is transferred before, on, or after July 1, 1987, in any manner or to a trust other than described in this section." (761e).

above. But they also know that the principle does not have the "absolute" feature of a rule. They do not say that the state can *never* justifiably intervene in the parent-child relationship. In fact, it often does this in cases of child neglect and abuse. And when such interventions occur they do not conclude that the family privacy principle is not a principle of family law, nor do they treat instances of state intervention as "exceptions" to the principle.

Second, unlike a rule, a principle like "Parents and guardians have the privacy right (liberty) to direct and control the upbringing of their children" does not set out the conditions that make its application necessary. It is not even clear how we would spell out these conditions. If the conditions are simply giving birth to a child or acquiring guardianship rights to a child through adoption, this does not imply that the state may not intervene. Instead, as Dworkin observes, the principle "states a reason that argues in one direction." In this case, it is a reason which the law will take into account when there is a cause for intervention. "All that is meant, when we say that a particular principle is a principle of our law, is that the principle is one which officials must take into account, if it is relevant, as a consideration inclining in one direction or another" (Dworkin, 47).

Finally, "principles have a dimension that rules do not – the dimension of weight or importance." When principles collide (the principle of family privacy in conflict with principles of child protection, for example), "one who must resolve the conflict has to take into account the relative weight of each" (47). It is an understatement to say that "the judgment that a particular principle or policy is more important than another will often be a controversial one," (Dworkin, 47) with no bright lines pointing the way to an obvious decision.

2.5.2 Principles as Natural Law

What does any of the above have to do with natural law theory? The answer is that Dworkin's "principles" are Lon Fuller's "social purposes," but with one important difference: Dworkin ties legal rules to those moral principles that express "the fundamental purposes of government and the proper relation between government and the individual" (Altman, 59). Fuller left his concept of "social purposes" an empty vessel, allowing that any regime that comes along could fill that vessel with purposes that most would reject as immoral. If the social purpose of the Virginia miscegenation law was to keep inferior people from marrying those who are judged to be superior, then Fuller appears to be committed to the unwelcome conclusion that a legal system will sometimes promote immorality. Dworkin's theory of "the best moral principles" underlying the rules of law appears to solve this problem.

The best way to understand this is to look at how Dworkin would deal with the *Loving* case. He would want us to consider a moral principle of the political community that is both logically consistent with the Virginia miscegenation statute and would justify it. Accordingly, a principle stating that (a) race is relevant to a determination of how people are to be treated under the law would make a good fit with the statute *when it was enacted in the nineteenth century*. By way of contrast, a principle stating that (b) race is *not* relevant to determining how people are treated under the law would *now* fail on both counts: it is neither consistent with the statute nor would it justify it. The former principle expresses the nineteenth century original understanding of equality that allowed the separation of the races.[15] The latter principle rejects that idea.[16] It expresses a conception of equality that was enunciated by Chief Justice Earl Warren in the concluding paragraph of the *Loving* decision.

> Marriage is one of the "basic civil rights of man," fundamental to our very existence and survival. To deny this fundamental freedom on so unsupportable a basis as the racial classifications embodied in these statutes, *classifications so directly subversive of the principle of equality* at the heart of the Fourteenth Amendment, is surely to deprive all the State's citizens of liberty without due process of law. The Fourteenth Amendment requires that the freedom of choice to marry not be restricted by invidious racial discriminations. Under our Constitution, the freedom to marry or not marry a person of another race resides with the individual and cannot be infringed by the State (*Loving v Virginia*, 388 U.S. 12).

Dworkin argues that the conception of equality expressed here by a unanimous Supreme Court is a *more advanced conception* of equality than the idea expressed 100 years earlier. Moreover, a principle that includes this advanced conception is *morally better* than the earlier principle justifying the use of race as a relevant consideration when creating laws governing marriage and the family. Finally, if the promise of natural law theory is that we cannot fully understand the nature of law and a legal system until we understand not only its rules but the fundamental moral principles that lie under and justify them, then the very idea of a legal system does appear to *guarantee* the moral acceptability of its principles.

2.5.3 *Objections to Dworkin*

One objection to Dworkin is that he does not give us a standard for determining when one principle is "morally better" than another. What are we to conclude when persons disagree over what is morally best?

---

[15] "The State argues that the meaning of the Equal Protection Clause, as illuminated by the statements of the Framers, is only that state penal laws containing an interracial element as part of the definition of the offense must apply equally to whites and Negroes in the sense that members of each race are punished to the same degree. Thus, the State contends that, because its miscegenation statutes punish equally both the white and the Negro participants in an interracial marriage, these statutes, despite their reliance on racial classifications do not constitute an invidious discrimination based upon race." *Loving v Virginia,* 388 U.S. 1 (1967).

[16] Over the years, this Court has consistently repudiated "distinctions between citizens solely because of their ancestry" as being "odious to a free people whose institutions are founded upon the doctrine of equality" (J. Earl Warren, *Loving v Virginia* quoting from *Hirabayashi v. United States* 1943, 100).

> Moral judgments are notoriously controversial. What is a judge, or anyone else, to do in the fact of such disagreement? Dworkin grabs the bull by the horns: each person must decide for him or herself about what is morally best. [For example, if a judge decides that the late 20th century conception of equality is best, then that is the one she should use in deciding the outcome of a case.] She may not arrive at the correct legal outcome; after all, she may be mistaken in her moral judgment. But a judge who follows Dworkin's method of legal interpretation will make a good-faith effort to determine what is morally best. And such a judge is, in Dworkin's view, fully authorized to make her legal decision on the basis of what she regards as the correct moral judgment (Altman, 62).

The fact that a judge is "fully authorized" to make a moral judgment when deciding a case does not imply that she should exercise her right to do so. She might understandably refrain on the ground that her choice of a moral principle to support her decision would be arbitrary. She might believe this because she once took a university course on ethical theory and came out of this experience with more questions about what mode of moral argument is best than she had before she took the course. She was confused when she went in and declared herself a skeptic when she came out. She tells us that she has no way to establish which mode of the many conflicting modes of moral argument she has studied is correct. We can understand why she also says "I was appointed to perform the role of judge, not the role of moral philosopher."

I suspect that Dworkin's response to her dilemma is to restate his theory: a judge often has no choice in the matter. She *must* employ a moral principle when making a judicial decision. An appeal to legal rules is not sufficient. Chief Justice Warren's interpretation of the Equality and Due Process clauses of the Fourteenth Amendment in the *Loving* decision is a prime example. He must answer the question: "What conception of equality should I choose when deciding whether the law treats people equally by prohibiting them from marrying one another if they are not of the same race or skin color? Should I use the conception employed by the Virginia state trial court (based on Jefferson's ideas of fixed nature and racial inferiority) or should I use a broader conception that rejects the relevance of racial distinctions?" This is a moral choice that the judge cannot avoid making.

A second objection to Dworkin is that he has only shown a connection between the laws and moral principles *such as we now have in the U.S.A. after 1970.* He has proved the hypothetical "If S is a legal system with positive laws resembling those that exist now, then the principles underlying the rules in S are morally acceptable." But he has not proved the much more ambitious hypothetical "If S is a legal system, then the principles underlying the positive laws in S are morally acceptable." That is, the *very idea* of a legal system does not guarantee the moral acceptability of its principles. There not only have been many legal systems in the past that did not have morally acceptable underlying principles (Nazi Germany and Fascist Italy in the 1930s come to mind), but there are many legal systems that exist at present that do not have such principles (North Korea, Saudi Arabia, Iran). A legal positivist would be quick to say that we can still refer to them as legal systems, albeit as bad, evil, or oppressive legal systems. That is, a legal system with some unjust or otherwise immoral laws is still a legal system. Hence, Dworkin faces the same dilemma faced by Lon Fuller. As there is no necessary connection between the concept of a legal system and laws serving morally good social purposes, so there is no necessary connection between the nature of a legal system and its laws being founded on universally acceptable moral principles.

Questions for Thought and Discussion

1. How would Dworkin's theory of law deal with the issues surrounding the arrest and conviction of Richard and Mildred Loving? Could the convictions be justified from the perspective of his theory? Does Dworkin's theory provide a convincing approach to the issues raised by the *Loving* case?
2. How would Fuller's theory of law deal with the issues surrounding the arrest and conviction of Richard and Mildred Loving? Could the convictions be justified from the perspective of his theory? Does Fuller's theory provide a convincing approach to the issues raised by the *Loving* case?
3. Before the 1946 *Perez* decision of the California Supreme Court, it had been argued by some scholars and progressive politicians that state laws prohibiting marriages between people of different races are invalid because they are unjust. Hence, judges and ordinary citizens alike had no obligation at all to enforce or obey them. Rather, they argued, everyone has an obligation to reject, subvert, and destroy the institutions that create anti-miscegenation laws. Do you agree with these recommendations? What if you agreed about the injustice of anti-miscegenation laws and (a) you are a judge who has sworn to uphold the state constitution and laws of the state? (b) You are a county clerk in charge of dispensing marriage licenses and you have taken an oath to obey all state laws regulating who will qualify for a marriage license? (c) You are a private citizen who has been asked to hide a young couple in your house, one white and the other black, who had been recently married but do not want their marriage discovered because they fear being arrested?

References

Altman, Andrew. 2001. *Arguing about law: An introduction to legal philosophy.* Belmont: Wadsworth.

Aquinas, Thomas. 1981. In *The political ideas of St. Thomas Aquinas: Representative selections*, ed. Dino Bigongiari. New York: Hafner Library of Classics.

Blackstone, William. 1765–1769. *Commentaries on the laws of England*, vol. 4. Oxford: Clarendon Press.

Cairns, Kathleen. 2015. California judge paved path for marriage ruling. *San Luis Obispo Tribune*, July 7. http://www.sanluisobispo.com/2015/07/073711189_california-judge-paved-path-for.html?rh=1.

California Family Code. 2016. http://www.leginfo.ca.gov/.html/fam_table_of_contents.html Accessed 25 Mar 2016.

Dworkin, Ronald. 1977. Is law a system of rules? In *Philosophy of law*, ed. Ronald Dworkin. New York: Oxford University Press.

Ferling, John. 2000. *Setting the world Ablaze: Washington, Adams, Jefferson, and the American Revolution.* New York: Oxford University Press.

Fuller, Lon. 1969. *The morality of law*. New Haven: Yale University Press.

Grossberg, Michael. 1985. *Governing the hearth: Law and the family in nineteenth century America*. Chapel Hill: University of North Carolina Press.
Hirabayashi v. United States, 320 U.S. 81 (1943).
Jefferson, Thomas. 1955. In *Notes on the state of Virginia*, ed. William Peden. Chapel Hill: University of North Carolina Press.
Locke, John. 1980. In *Second treatise of government*, ed. C.B. Macpherson. Indianapolis: Hackett.
Loving v Virginia. 388 U.S. 1 (1967).
Mendenhall, Alan. 2013. From natural law to natural inferiority: The construction of racist jurisprudence in early Virginia. http://www.academia.edu/2541976/From_Natural_Law_to_Natural_Inferiority_The_Construction_of_Racist_Jurisprudence_in_Early_Virginia Accessed 25 Mar 2016.
Naim v. Naim 197 Va. 80; 87 S.E.2d 749 (1955)
Olsen, Kirsten. 1999. *Daily life in the eighteenth century*. Connecticut: Greenwood Publishing.
Perez v Sharp. 32 Cal. 2d 711, 198 P. 2d 17 Cal. 1948.
Schenk v. United States, 249 U.S. 47 (1919).
Simmons, A. John. 1992. *The lockean theory of rights*. Princeton: Princeton University Press.
Stark, Barbara. 2005. *International family law*. Burlington: Ashgate.
Theodorou, Angelina. 2014. Which countries still outlaw apostasy and blasphemy? *Fact Tank: News in the Numbers*. Pew Research Center. http://www.pewresearch.org/fact-tank/2014/05/28/which-countries-still-outlaw-apostasy-and-blasphemy/ Accessed 7 Jan 2016.

Chapter 3
Legal Positivism

"The existence of law is one thing; its merit or demerit is another. Whether it be or be not is one enquiry; whether it be or be not conformable to an assumed standard, is a different enquiry."

John Austin, *The Province of Jurisprudence Determined* (1879)

Abstract This chapter provides descriptions and critical discussions of two versions of the philosophical theory known as Legal Positivism: the classical account of John Austin and the modern version of H.L.A. Hart. Legal Positivism makes what John Austin calls a "clean separation between law and morals," thereby refuting the central thesis of natural law theory. This is not a rejection of the idea that morality is a *source* of positive laws. Legal Positivists accept the notion that laws prohibiting murder, assault and theft reflect prohibitions of the same acts that we find in the rules of positive (human-made) morality. But this prompts the question "What is the *reason* why law and morals should include a specific content?" It is here that H.L.A. Hart enters the debate with a recommendation that ties together both the theory of natural law and legal positivism. Although he finds no logical relationship between law and morals, he believes that there are truths about human nature that "not only disclose the core of good sense in the doctrine of Natural Law but are of vital importance for the understanding of law and morals." (Hart 2012, 199) These truths or "simple truisms" provide us with the "minimum content of natural law." Using Hart's methodology, we here examine rules of family law in order to determine whether there are any facts about human nature and the environment in which we live that necessitate any specific rules concerning family formation or access to family relationships.

L.D. Houlgate, *Philosophy, Law and the Family*, AMINTAPHIL: The Philosophical Foundations of Law and Justice 7,
DOI 10.1007/978-3-319-51121-4_3

3.1 The Separation of Law and Morals

The theory known as Legal Positivism takes a position on the relationship of law and morality that is exactly the opposite of Natural Law theory. Legal Positivists argue that there is no necessary connection between positive law and morals. When laws prohibiting infanticide were enacted, the positivist would say that the validity of the laws bears no logical relationship to an alleged moral rule or a "law of God" that says infanticide is morally wrong. We may regard the anti-infanticide law as good or bad because it conforms or fails to conform to our moral sensibilities, but this moral evaluation "of approbation or disapprobation" has no relevance to the validity of the law.

As in natural law theory (Chap. 2) there are traditional and modern versions of legal positivism. We shall present authors who are representative of each version and discuss their theories in the context of family law. We begin with a test case for the legal positivist.

3.2 Rape and Forced Marriage in Morocco

Until 2014 the penal code of Morocco allowed the rapist of a minor to escape punishment if he marries his victim:

> *Whoever abducts or deceives a minor without using violence, threat or fraud, can escape prosecution and imprisonment if (1) the abductor marries the victim, or (2) those persons who have a right to request an annulment of the marriage do not file a complaint* (Article 475)

In one of many cases, a 15-year-old girl experienced constant harassment and threats from a 35-year-old man in her town. He waited for her each day outside of her school and on several occasions told her, "I will force you to marry me." One day, he abducted and raped her at knifepoint. The victim made a complaint to the police, who arrested the man. In his statement to the police, the rapist admitted his crime, declaring that he did it "because it was the only way I would be able to marry her." In order to avoid scandal, the victim dropped out of school and married him. "I am raped now every day," she told members of the local association that works with women survivors of domestic violence.

In a second case, Amina Filal was raped at the age of 15 by an older man. Instead of seeing her rapist punished for his crime, Amina was forced to marry him in order to preserve the honor and reputation of her family. A few months into an unconscionable marriage she told her mother that her rapist/husband was beating her. Her mother counseled her to try and bear it. Amina must have seen no way out, no future worth living. She was only 16-year-old when she took her own life by swallowing rat poison (Presthold 2014).

The public response to the Filal case, especially in Western countries, was universally condemnatory, forcing the Moroccan parliament to amend that part of the code that allowed rapists to avoid accountability by marrying his victim (Al Jazeera

2014). The strongest reason given for the Western condemnation was that the "marriage rape" provision violated the fundamental human rights of women and girls.

Although there is no evidence that either human rights activists or defenders of Article 475 joined the debate between natural law theorists and legal positivists about the validity of the code, it is clear what John Austin would have said. If Article 475 exists, then it is a valid law and it would remain valid until it is changed by the Moroccan parliament. The law's validity has nothing to do with whether its content is or is not "meritorious."

3.3 Traditional Legal Positivism: John Austin

John Austin was a nineteenth century legal theorist who was largely responsible for what is known as "analytical jurisprudence," an approach to legal theory requiring analysis of its key concepts (for example, "law," "legal validity" "command," "sovereign"). The theory of legal positivism developed out of this analytical approach. Austin saw the law as an object of "scientific" study (Austin 1879: 1107–1108), not as a body of rules to be morally evaluated and prescribed by those who undertake a study of legal systems. He argued that we cannot begin a scientific study of the law until we have a clear grasp of the meaning of legal concepts. In this respect, Austin's conceptual inquiry is well within the bounds of what we have previously referred to as "philosophy" (Sect. 1.3).

3.3.1 Law as Sovereign Commands

Austin defines *law* as "a rule laid down for the guidance of an intelligent being by an intelligent being having power over him" (Austin 1832, Lecture I). This definition includes under it both "the laws set by God to his human creatures, and laws set by men to men" (Lecture I). Austin equates the laws set by God with natural law or the law of nature. Laws set by men fall into two classes: those established by persons who are political superiors within an independent political society, and the rules of positive morality. The latter rules are not established by political superiors, nor by God. "The name *morality* severs them from *positive law*, while the epithet *positive* disjoins them from the law of God" (Lecture 1). If I say that the rule obligating us to keep our promises is a *moral* rule this tells us that the rule is not created by political superiors; and if I also call this rule *positive* I mean that it was created by humans, not by God.

To this general definition of law Austin uses the word "command" as signifying what he means by "laid down for guidance." Every law or rule is a species or type of command. Commands, in turn, are expressions of wishes or desires directed to rational beings to do or forbear from doing certain actions. And these expressions are backed by threats that some evil will be brought down upon those persons to whom the command is directed if they fail to comply. When you command me to close the door this is more than you expressing a desire that I close the door. It also implies that I will suffer certain unwanted consequences if I do not shut the door.

Austin further adds that laws are *general*, not *specific* commands. This means that laws command persons generally to acts of a determined class. They do not command specific acts to be done or avoided at specific times. When the Connecticut legislature prohibited the sale or dispensation of artificial contraceptives for a given period or indefinitely, and acts of this kind were generally forbidden, then their command is a law. But if a judge commands a specific person not to sell or give away artificial contraceptives, or orders her not to do this on specific days or at specific times of the day, this would be an order, not a law or rule. "... [A] law is a command which obliges a person or persons, and obliges generally to acts or forbearances of a class" (Austin 1832: Lecture 1).

The concept of a command also implies *superiority.* "For superiority is the power of enforcing compliance with a wish: and the expression or intimation of a wish, with the power and the purpose of enforcing, are the constituent elements of a command." It follows that the proposition "laws emanate from superiors" is analytically true. If laws are commands and commands emanate from superiors, then laws must emanate from superiors." (Lecture 1).

It is logically possible that a person or group of persons (superiors) command others (inferiors) to do or refrain from doing a certain class of acts under threat of punishment, even though they have no authority to do this. In that case, their commands do not yet constitute law. In order to repair this defect Austin introduces the concept of *sovereignty.* A sovereign is a person or body of persons in a given society who has most of that society "in a habit of obedience or submission" to him or them (Lecture 6). Moreover, "that certain individual, or that certain body of individuals, is not in a habit of obedience to a determinate superior." It is only when the commands emanate from a sovereign in a politically independent society that the commands constitute the laws of that society.

3.3.2 Legal and Moral Validity

Austin reiterates the central tenet of the theory of legal positivism in a blistering critique of the noted English jurist William Blackstone's claim that human laws have no validity if they are contrary to the laws of God (Blackstone, Vol. 1, Sect. 2). The implication of the words "have no validity" is "are not binding" and "are not laws."[1] (Lecture 5). Here is Austin's response:

[1] The exact quotation from Blackstone: "This is what is called the law of nature, which, being coeval with mankind, and dictated by God himself, is, of course superior in obligation to any other. It is binding over all the globe, in all countries at all times. No human laws are of any validity, if contrary to this; and such of them as are valid, derive all their authority, mediately or immediately, from this original" Volume 1, Introduction, section II ("Of the Nature of Laws in General").

> Now, to say that human laws which conflict with the Divine law are not binding, that is to say, are not laws, is to talk stark nonsense. The most pernicious laws, and therefore those which are most opposed to the will of God, have been and are continually enforced as laws by judicial tribunals. Suppose an act innocuous, or positively beneficial, be prohibited by the sovereign under the penalty of death; if I commit this act, I shall be tried and condemned, and if I object to the sentence, that [it] is contrary to the law of God, who has commanded that human lawgivers shall not prohibit acts which have no evil consequences, the Court of justice will demonstrate the inconclusiveness of my reasoning by hanging me up, in pursuance of the law of which I have impugned the validity. An exception, demurrer, or plea, founded on the law of God was never heard in a Court of Justice, from the creation of the world down to the present moment. (Lecture 5)

We began this chapter with what most would agree is a pernicious and immoral law from Morocco. A man rapes a woman in order to force her to marry because, under Article 75, the rapist will not be prosecuted if he marries his victim. Another man is threatened with jail if he refuses to marry the 15-year-old girl he has raped. He marries her and she later commits suicide. If someone tells the Moroccan court that Article 475 is an invalid law because it justifies rape and encourages forced marriages, this appeal will be rejected on the ground that the immoral content of the law is irrelevant to the question of its validity.

Some critics of Austin would argue that an appeal to examples like the Moroccan statute does not constitute a "reasoned argument" for the conclusion that a pernicious law is valid and genuine. A defender of natural law theory would agree that immoral laws have frequently been enacted and enforced, but this is not an argument for the conclusion that they are valid. She would simply respond that this law is invalid because it conflicts with natural law. We now have a standoff between two theories, each giving contradictory answers to the question "Is a rule enacted by the courts a valid law if it is contrary to natural law?"

This is clearly a dispute about the correct application of the word "valid" to positive laws. Legal dictionaries define it as "Binding; possessing legal force or strength; legally sufficient" (West, 2008). Using this definition, we can proclaim Article 475 as a valid law. It is "binding" and it possesses "legal force or strength." It was created in compliance with all the requisite formalities under Moroccan legislative procedure. But again, the natural law theorist would not dispute this. They would accept that this law is *legally* valid. However, they would insist that it is not *morally* valid. For a law to be morally valid it must possess moral force or strength. It must be morally sufficient. Since Article 475 has no moral force it fails the test of *moral* validity.

If this debate is about the correct answer to the question "How is the word *valid* used in positive law?" then the legal positivist give the correct answer to this empirical query: a law is valid if it possesses legal force or strength. The force or strength in a positive law is punishment or the threat of punishment. If the debate is about the correct answer to the question "How is the word *valid* used in natural law?" then the natural law theorist also gives a correct answer: a moral rule is valid if it possesses moral force or strength. The moral force or strength is either the *external* fear of Divine punishment, the hope of Divine reward, the fear of loss of reputation, the hope of approval from others in the community, or the *internal* promptings of one's own conscience.

However, legal positivists are not interested in the natural law answer to the latter question for they have already said that this answer has no relevance to the validity of positive law Suppose, however, that the debate is about the question "How *ought* the word *valid* be used in positive law?" This is where the debate between the two theories is finally joined. The logical positivist is committed to the answer already given, whereas the natural law theorist wants to change the criteria for legal validity and inject a moral component: the positive law ought to possess moral force or strength.

This puts the burden squarely on the shoulders of the natural law proponents. They must answer two questions: (1) Why do we need to add a moral component to the criteria for legal validity? (2) Where are we to find this moral component?

1. The natural law answer to the first question is that there must be a moral obligation to obey the law and this is not supplied by a mere enactment and enforcement of a rule. Austin's command theory is *obedience by threat* and threats do not constitute moral obligation. To use an oft-repeated example, if a gunman comes up to me and says "Your money or your life" and I hand over my money, my motive for doing this is not "I have a moral obligation to hand over my money," but "I do not want to be shot." Hence, Austin is wrong when he claims that "command, duty, and sanction are inseparably connected terms" (Lecture 1). The mere fact that the gunman has the power to enforce compliance with his wish for me to hand over my wallet does not impose on me any moral duty to do this.

Notice that this answer begs the question "Why do we need a moral obligation to obey the law?" If the answer is "Because this makes it more likely that people will obey the law," then this reply is relevant only to the *efficacy* of the law, not to its *validity*. If the law conforms to what we all understand to be what is demanded by common morality, then it is more probable that the law will command our obedience than when we cannot see a correspondence between law and morality. But probability of efficacy is an empirical prediction, presumably based on observation and experience. It does not prove a necessary connection between law and morals. Hence, it does not prove that legal validity *must* contain a moral component.

2. Austin says that positive morality includes both those moral rules "set and enforced by *mere opinion*" and those rules conforming to "the laws of God" (Lecture 1). Finding out the opinion of the people about what is and is not immoral can be easily discovered by empirical polling methods, although what might be found is that there is great disagreement about many moral issues, especially regarding the family.[2] Finding out what constitutes the laws of God makes this more difficult as soon as one is confronted with the questions "How

[2] For example, there are some who would deny that two gay men raising a child constitutes a family; others will just as vigorously reject this assessment.

do we know that God exists?", "If God exists, how do we know what laws God has communicated to humans?", and "How do we know that the laws God has communicated to humans are true or correct?"

A review of family law both during and after the colonial period of America, or a study of comparative contemporary non-European cultures shows an enormous disparity in the opinion of people about what is and is not morally approved behavior within the family. This disparity is only matched by the differences between world religions about what is and what is not approved. The natural law theorist must either prove that there is a universal morality that applies to all family relations, or she must argue that the positive law of each independent state must be based on the morality of the culture or religion of that country. Both options require some heavy lifting. The first implies that the natural law theorist show that the rules of other moral systems are false if they differ from what she regards to be "the laws of the one, true God." The second implies a relativism about family morality that most natural law theorists would reject.

Finally, Austin cautions that a requirement of conformity to morality or to the laws of God for legal validity would be "mischievous." It implies that people have no obligation to obey laws that they dislike, especially if their dislike is grounded in their beliefs about what God commands them to do. "To proclaim generally that all laws which are pernicious or contrary to the will of God are void and not to be tolerated, is to preach anarchy, hostile and perilous as much to wise and benign rule as to stupid and galling tyranny" (Lecture 5).

3.4 Assessment of Austin

Like most legal theorists before him, Austin gives few examples to illustrate the application of his theory, and among these examples none come from family law. This is partly because of the variety of types of laws that affect or concern the family. Only a few family laws are criminal (mandatory rules having a penal function). The function of most family laws are remedial, regulatory, or power-conferring (Sect. 1.2). It is with these types of laws that Austin's theory of law has the most difficulty.

3.4.1 Are Marriage Laws the Commands of a Sovereign?

The latter point can be seen in marriage law. These laws do not appear to command obedience on the threat of punishment. The rules created by marriage law are not mandatory. They are power-conferring. That is, they give private people the power to significantly alter their relationship with others. Imagine a man and a woman in Austin's England or in the United States in the mid-nineteenth century. Suppose that a young couple is engaged to be married. Before marriage the woman would have no legal obligation to be sexually available to her fiancé, and he would have no legal obligation to provide material/financial support for her, even if she were in dire need of such support. Their relationship changes immediately upon conclusion of the marriage ceremony that makes them husband and wife. The nineteenth century bride now has a legal obligation to be sexually available to her new husband and he has a legal obligation to provide his new wife with material and financial support. Their legal status has changed because, by exercising their power to marry, they have created legal rights and duties they did not have prior to their marriage. Of course prior to marriage they could have privately agreed with one another to do these things, but these agreements would not be legally binding.

Can power-conferring rules be seen as commands? The young couple in the previous example are not commanded by virtue of the law to get married. If they decide not to marry, they do not suffer any legal consequences as a result. Their legal status is unchanged. And if they are discovered to be under the legally proscribed age, they are not punished for this. Instead, the marriage is declared null and void.

Some have argued that private power-conferring rules that people use to marry "are like commands in an important way: the point of each is to alter the world in some way, rather than simply to describe the world as it is" (Altman, 71). But this seems to be a weak analogy, not unlike saying that commands and power-conferring rules are similar because both apply only to people, not to dogs and cats. The disanalogy between power-conferring and mandatory rules (commands) is that commands get people to do what they do *not* want to do, whereas power-conferring rules give them the ability to do what they *want* to do. Hence, marriage laws cannot be compared to commands without seriously distorting their actual function.

Other critics have argued that the power-conferring rules comprising marriage command behavior in the sense that they tell people they can *only* get married by following certain rule-based procedures, for example being of a certain age, giving an expression of consent at some point during the marriage ceremony, getting a blood-test, a marriage license, or appearing before a duly appointed officer of the court (a judge, minister, rabbi, priest) who conducts the ceremony. The threat behind the command is that the marriage will be null and void unless the procedures are followed. But this is like saying that the scoring rules in (American) football that inform players about how points can be scored in the game are actually threats backed by punishment: if a kicker fails to kick the ball between the goal posts, then his team is not awarded three points. But this is not a punishment that is imposed upon the team, as if the behavior (failing to get the ball between the posts) could be forgiven by the referee. It is a logical implication of the rule itself. If the referee should award three points after the ball goes wide of the posts, the content of the rule itself has been ignored. Similarly, if a marriage ceremony is conducted by someone not authorized by law to do this, resulting in a nullification, this is not punishment. The term "nullity" simply means that a marriage does not exist in the same way that a missed kick means that a goal does not exist. The young couple may be disappointed by the nullification, but it is not the object of the marriage law to cause disappointment (or happiness) in those who attempted to use the power of the law to get married.

3.4.2 Are Child Custody Laws the Commands of a Sovereign?

The complex laws on child custody are a combination of rules that define key concepts ("custody", "guardianship", "child"), and rules that regulate or determine the conditions under which a person shall be the legal custodian of a child. The question is whether such rules are a species of commands of the sovereign.

Let us begin with an example. Suppose that an unmarried woman gives birth. She is presumed to have the legal right to legal and physical custody of the newborn child. This means that she alone has "the right and the responsibility to make the decisions relating to the health, education, and welfare" of her child, and that the child "shall reside with and be under her supervision, subject to the power of the court to order visitation" (California Family Code, 3006, 3007). Her rights are superior to those of the biological father or any other person. Of course, these rights can be defeated if it can be shown that the mother is unfit or has abandoned the child.

Is the presumption of a right to custody a command, that is, is it an order backed by a threat of evil consequences unless there is compliance? In order to answer this question, we need to know (1) to whom the command is directed, (2) what would constitute disobedience, and (3) the kind and amount of punishment for the disobedience.

1. If the child custody rules in the California codes are commands (orders backed by a threat), then in our example the unmarried mother is the person at whom the order would be directed. But to inform her that she has a right to make the decisions noted in the codes is to inform her that she and she alone has these *powers*. She is not told what she *must* do under threat of punishment, but what she and no one else legally *can* do, pursuant to her wishes. The language of the code is not the language of coercion.
2. We do not think of a grant of legal rights (powers) as a burden, that is, as something that persons would ordinarily not want to assume. We are more acquainted with battles between divorcing parents who want to be granted custody than we are with the rare cases in which a parent refuses or attempts to escape custody. If it is objected that a birth mother's refusal to take custody of her newborn child constitutes *abandonment*, an act that is punishable under the penal code,[3] this does not constitute a counter-example to our contention that the rules of child custody are not commands of the sovereign. The example of abandonment proves only that a refusal to perform the legally proscribed duties of a parent would constitute disobedience. But there is no such thing as "disobedience" conceptually tied to a power-conferring rule. There is a distinction between having a legal power and exercising it. The birth-mother has the right to legal and physi-

[3] "If a parent of a minor child willfully omits, without lawful excuse, to furnish necessary clothing, food, shelter or medical attendance, or other remedial care for his or her child, he or she is guilty of a misdemeanor punishable by a fine not exceeding two thousand dollars ($2000), or by imprisonment in the county jail not exceeding 1 year, or by both such fine and imprisonment" (California Penal Code, 270).

cal custody of her child, and she has a duty to exercise these rights when the circumstances call for her to do this (for example, to make a decision about whether to get medical treatment for her ailing child). It is only the duty to exercise the right that can be construed as a command. But that it can be so construed is not relevant to answering the question whether the *right itself* can be disobeyed. It cannot.

3. If there is no such thing as disobedience to statutes granting the rights of custody of a child to a person or persons, then there is no punishment that would be tied to these codes. The concept of punishment implies not only the idea of a violation, but the imposition of a burden, some form of deprivation or the withholding of a benefit. It also implies that the person who suffers the burden or deprivation is believed to have acted wrongly and has been *found* guilty by persons authorized to make such a finding. Although there is a legal procedure by which the birth mother can voluntarily cede her parental rights to another person (for example, to the biological father), there is no implication that she is has behaved wrongly. Hence, custody rules cannot be conceived as commands of the sovereign without serious distortion of such rules.

Not all critics are convinced by the previous argument. Some have argued that even if we cannot easily conceive of power-conferring rules as commands, we can still see them as *declarations* of the sovereign, in the important sense that they would not exist unless persons with sovereign authority (for example, a state legislature) had enacted them. It is only because of the enactment of the sovereign that the people have the power to marry, divorce, and adopt children. Austin's central idea is that legal concepts are to be explained in terms of the power of a political sovereign. He can easily modify this central idea that takes account of the distinction between declarations and commands (Altman, 71).

I am not convinced by this defense. To say that a power-conferring rule can be "explained in terms of the power of a political sovereign" means that the sovereign has the right or authority to create such rules. This right, in turn, is the product of a *public* power-conferring rule, that is, a higher order rule that confers on a person or persons the right to make new law or change current laws. Suppose that the sovereign is a single person, a monarch. If her power is exhibited by her *declaration* that the people shall have certain *private* powers (such as the power to marry) this does not entail either the conclusion that her exercise of her public power to do this or that the private powers she declares to exist can be conceived as *commands* (orders backed by threats) to do something on pain of punishment. It is better conceived as a *gift* or *benefit* that allows them to do something they could not otherwise do (get married, adopt a child).

In summary, Austin is correct in his idea that we should maintain the distinction between what the law is and what it ought to be. The injection of a moral component into the criteria for legal validity is both unnecessary and would have bad consequences. The main problem with the classic version of legal positivism, as represented here by John Austin, is that by using the command model of the criminal law to determine the nature of all law, including the rules of family law, leads to the false conclusion that all law can be seen as a large set of mandatory rules backed by threats of punishment.

We turn now to another version of legal positivism that claims to correct these defects. It is a theory that supports the positivist attempt to separate laws and morals while at the same time providing us with a theory about the nature of law that will account for the types of rules we find in family law.

3.5 Modern Legal Positivism: H.L.A. Hart

H.L.A. Hart was a mid-twentieth century British philosopher who developed a theory about the nature of law and legal obligation that managed to repair the defects of traditional legal positivism while avoiding the pitfalls of natural law theory. Hart did this by replacing Austin's command theory of law with the theory that laws should be seen a type of *rule*. And he avoided the pitfalls of natural law theory by retaining Austin's distinction between the criteria for the validity of a law and the standards for judging whether a law is good or bad, reasonable or unreasonable. But he does not create the wide gap between law and morals argued for by most classical positivists. Hart contends that natural law theory is correct in thinking that there is a "minimum content" that all primary rules must have, even though we cannot use this content to invalidate particular laws. Let us examine both of these aspects of Hart's theory, beginning with the concept of a rule.

3.5.1 *Law and the Obligations Created by Law*

The advantage of conceiving laws as rules is that it allows us to explain why some laws cannot (without distortion) be understood as commands. Consider the rules of a game. For example, the rule in chess about the movement of the pawn is that the pawn can never move backwards. Suppose that Mary, who is just learning the game, moves her pawn backwards. If this rule is construed as a command, then there should be a perceived threat that Mary has ignored. The first thing that might come to mind is that her backwards move will not count as a *valid* move. Hence, she must return her piece to the square on which it sat prior to the move. But does the possibility that one's move might be declared invalid operate as a threat to players in the game of chess?

It is true that we use the words "must" and "not an option" when explaining the rules of a game, but this does not make all of them into commands. The consequence of making an incorrect move in chess is that the move is void, not that the person who made the move will now be subject to punishment. In order to see this, consider the fact that with *mandatory* rules we can logically separate or distinguish a violation of the rule from its proscribed punishment. For example, in some chess leagues there is an unsportsmanlike conduct rule that says players may not swear or "trash talk" their opponents before or during the games. The punishment for a violation is a 3-game suspension. Notice, however, that it is possible to distinguish the violation from the punishment. Suppose that John violates the swearing rule but is not punished for the violation. We can still say "John was playing the game of chess when swore at his opponent," even if he is not suspended for being unsportsmanlike. But we cannot imagine a player violating the "pawns do not move backwards" rule without nullifying the move. If Mary's illegal move is ignored by the referees during a chess match, then Mary *is no longer playing the game of chess*, but some other game in which pawns move backwards.

The same analysis applies to the power-conferring rules of family law. If the rules say that all couples must apply for and receive a *marriage* license from the County Clerk's office in order to get married, and the official conducting the marriage ceremony does not realize that the couple standing before her do not have a license, then the marriage she performs is null and void. The marriage does not exist, regardless of what the official and others might believe at the time. The invalidation of the marriage, like the invalidation of an incorrect chess move is not a punishment, but recognition of a failure to do what is logically necessary to get married.[4]

This explains why we cannot claim that all family laws are commands. Hart's theory that laws are rules allows us to understand and account for the great variety of rules in family law. Some of the rules are mandatory and can be conceived as commands of the sovereign, for example, criminal laws prohibiting child and spousal abuse. Other rules are power-conferring, for example the rules that make it possible for private persons to marry, divorce and adopt children. Some family law rules have both a mandatory and a power-conferring element. Domestic tort rules have this dual feature. For example, a husband with herpes might be restrained from sexual relations with his spouse by the knowledge that he might be sued for medical costs and emotional distress. If he succumbs and infects his wife, then she might exercise her right to bring a law suit to obtain compensation.

3.5.2 *The Key to Understanding the Nature of Law*

Hart realizes that the idea of a rule "is not a simple one." Using the examples cited earlier, he distinguishes two types of rule, both necessary to explain "the complexity of a legal system" (Hart, 80). The distinction between *primary* and *secondary* rules should by now be familiar to the reader as identical to the earlier distinction between *mandatory* and *power-conferring* rules:

> Under rules of the one type, which may well be considered the basic or primary type, human beings are required to do or abstain from certain actions, whether they wish to or not. Rules of the other type are in a sense parasitic upon or secondary to the first; for they provide that human beings may by doing or saying certain things introduce new rules of the

[4] The couple in this example might be punished for having a counterfeit license, but that would be a violation of another rule prohibiting this act.

> primary type, extinguish or modify old ones, or in various ways determine their incidence or control their operations. Rules of the first type impose duties; rules of the second type confer powers, public or private. (Hart, 81)

Examples of primary rules include the mandatory rules of criminal and tort law. Examples of secondary rules include the public power-conferring rules authorizing lawmakers to create, modify or remove a primary rule, or the private power-conferring rules giving individuals the ability to alter their legal relationship with others. As noted throughout this book, there are many examples of mandatory and private power-conferring rules to be found in family law (Sect. 1.2).

Hart writes that he has found what Austin wrongly claimed to have found in the notion of coercive orders, namely "the key to the science of jurisprudence." Hart's key to unlocking the door to understanding the nature of law is that *law and the obligations created by law are only to be found in the interplay of primary and secondary rules.*

What Hart means by this is that laws and the obligations created by law could not exist unless the primary rules have been created in a system that has given some persons the *authority* to create such rules. And this authority cannot exist unless there is another set of rules (secondary rules) that give persons or groups of person's legislative and executive power. Hence, primary rules prohibiting murder, rape and theft could not exist unless there was some authoritative person or persons who had the right to make such acts illegal. A command to cease and desist is ineffective unless it is given by a person who has the legal right or power to give this command.

This has important implications for both natural law theory and legal positivism. First, the natural law theory is wrong in arguing that the obligation to obey a positive law does not exist if the proscribed behavior is immoral according to the (objectively valid) natural law. If a legal system contains secondary rules giving authority to a group of persons (a legislative body) to create the primary rules, then this is sufficient to create an obligation to obey these rules even if the enacted rules do not correspond with the natural law. Second, classical legal positivism is wrong in arguing that the obligation to obey the law arises from orders backed by threats. If the orders are given by someone who has the physical capacity to make good on his threat, but has no authority to issue the order, then there can be no obligation to obey (Sect. 3.3.2).

3.5.3 The Application of Hart's Theory to Family Law

How does Hart's theory apply to family law? It appears that the only obligations created by family law are those that emanate from rules governing criminal and tortious behavior within the context of the family. For example, the laws prohibiting child abuse are both crimes and torts. But Hart would argue that they are made so only because there are public (secondary) rules giving legislatures the power to create such laws, executives the police power to enforce them, and the judiciary the power to punish offenders and order remediation for the victims.

Hart does not discuss the private laws enabling persons to marry, divorce or adopt children. But let us assume that he would count these among the primary rules, even though they create *private powers*, not *private obligations* (for example, marriage law creates a power, not an obligation, to marry). Assuming that this is an oversight, we can certainly agree that these private power-conferring laws are "made so" only because there are public (secondary) rules that give legislatures the power to create or change these rules and a judicial system to apply them in individual cases.

Second, we can agree with Hart that legal obligation "is not to be found in the gunman situation" (Sect. 3.3.2). The gunman forces or *obliges* me to hand over my wallet, but his order does not *obligate* me to do this. I am under no obligation to give him my wallet for the simple reason that he has no right to do what he is doing. The gunman is not the government. If a family court judge orders the non-custodial parent of a child to make child support payments owed to the custodial parent, then the judge has the *right* to do this by virtue of laws empowering the court to collect, and if necessary, to seize the funds owed. A gunman has no such authority.

Third, not all rules of family law are conceived in terms of obligation. We have already seen this in our discussion of the rules of marriage (Sect. 3.4.1) and child custody (Sect. 3.4.2). These are rules that function as definitions of key terms and as rules giving powers to individuals who are in or who desire to be in various kinds of family relationships. We distort the function of such rules by conceiving of them as mandatory rules imposing obligations to do or refrain from doing actions they do not want to do or refrain from doing.

Fourth, since so many of the rules of family law are power conferring, how do they fit in Hart's general theory of law? In order to answer this, let me quote again what Hart says about the key to understanding the nature of law: "The obligations created by law are only to be found in the interplay of primary and secondary rules" Sect. (3.5.2). The problem with Hart's theory is that it focuses too narrowly on the criminal law, as evidenced by his use of the term "obligations" in the previous sentence. It is this narrow focus that prompts him to ignore the *private powers* created by family law and other branches of the law (contract and property law). Here is a revision that applies Hart's "key" to the philosophy of family law: "The obligations *and private powers* created by family law are only to be found in the interplay of primary and secondary rules." These obligations are not to be found in morality, in natural law, or in the commands of the sovereign. They are to be found in those societies in which there are *public* secondary rules that empower "an individual or body of persons to introduce new primary rules for the conduct of the life of the group, or of some class within it, and to eliminate old rules" (Hart, 95). In a small jurisdiction, this may be a town council or a county board of supervisors. In a larger jurisdiction, it may be a state legislature. For example, if there is to be a law or a change in an existing law regulating the conditions under which a custodial parent can move out of the jurisdiction where custody was established without the consent of the noncustodial parent, then this can only be done by a body *empowered* to create or change the laws of the jurisdiction.[5]

3.5.4 Objections to Hart's Theory

Ronald Dworkin wrote the most significant objections to Hart's theory of law. His argument begins with the contention that rules tell only a part of the story about law and legal obligation. In the previous chapter we discussed Dworkin's distinction between rules, principles and policies (Sect. 2.5.1). To quote again from Dworkin:

> … when lawyers reason or dispute about legal rights and obligations, particularly in those hard cases when our problems with these concepts seem most acute, they make use of standards that do not function as rules, but operate differently as principles, policies and other sorts of standards. Positivism … is a model of and for a system of rules, and its central notion of a single fundamental test for law forces us to miss the important roles of these standards that are not rules (Dworkin 1977, 43).

Although the analogy is not exact, I would add to this the observation that to conceive of the law as only a system of rules is as inadequate as conceiving of *games* as only a system of rules. When people who know the game of chess reason or dispute about the game they no longer talk about the rules of chess, but are mainly concerned about differences in *strategy*. They know the rules that says the pawn cannot move backwards, the bishop only moves on the diagonal, and the king can only move one space but in any direction. What they want to know is what valid moves they can make with these pieces in order to gain an advantage over their

[5] *Rules of recognition* "specify some feature or features possession of which by a suggested rule is taken as a conclusive affirmative indication that it is a rule of the group to be supported by the social pressure it exerts" (Hart, 94). In the early law of a primitive society this feature might be that the suggested rule can be found carved on a public monument, or in a text of rules on an authoritative list. In a modern legal system, the rules of recognition are more complex. The primary rules may be identified "by the fact of their having been enacted by a specific body, or their long customary practice, or their relation to judicial decisions" (Hart, 95). For example, if a custodial parent wants to move out of the jurisdiction where custody was established without the consent of the noncustodial parent, then she will want to know what primary laws and practices governing relocation are authoritative in her state. She will identify such laws and practices by looking at existing statutes and judicial decisions of family courts, probably with the assistance of a family attorney.

Rules of change, in their simplest form, are rules which empower "an individual or body of persons to introduce new primary rules for the conduct of the life of the group, or of some class within it, and to eliminate old rules" (95). In a small jurisdiction, this may be a town council or a county board of supervisors. In a larger jurisdiction, it may be a state legislature. As Hart argues, there is a "close connection" between rules of change and rules of recognition: "for where the former exist the latter will necessarily incorporate a reference to legislation as an identifying feature of the rules" (96). If the legislature enacts a change in the law regulating the conditions under which a custodial parent can move out of the jurisdiction where custody was established without the consent of the noncustodial parent, then we know that the rule of recognition is that the change was enacted by the legislature.

opponent. Their question is not "What are the rules of chess?" but "What strategies can I employ in order to win the game?"

By (rough) analogy, once the court understands the relevant statutes and codes that apply to a case on which the court must rule, this knowledge may not be sufficient. They must also acquaint themselves with the relevant legal *principles*. Ronald Dworkin illustrates this with the court's reasoning in a famous case in which the judge had to decide whether a man who murdered his grandfather could inherit under his grandfather's will. The court chose not to base its decision on the statute governing wills, which would "give this property to the murderer" (*Riggs v Palmer* 1899, 188). Instead, the court chose to be guided by a fundamental principle of the common law that said "No one shall be permitted to profit by his own wrong." Similarly, when the U.S. Supreme Court struck down the Virginia miscegenation statute in *Loving v Virginia* (388 U.S. 1, 1967), they did so not on the strict application of the Fourteenth Amendment to the Constitution, but on the moral principles they said are contained therein: "Marriage is one of the basic civil rights of man, fundamental to our very existence and survival," and "the freedom to marry or not marry a person of another race resides with the individual and cannot be infringed by the State" *(Loving v Virginia*, 388 U.S. 12). These principles played an important part in the argument supporting the decision about the constitutional right to marry (Sect. 2.5.2). We should note that a rule giving persons of different races a constitutional right to marry did not exist before the *Loving* decision. In this respect it is not like a statute. Instead, the Court cited the principle of equality as its justification for creating and applying a *new* rule governing marriage law. Dworkin would say that these moral principles operate as "background standards" against which to read the Fourteenth Amendment, thereby justifying a new interpretation of that amendment (Dworkin 1977, 50).

Can Hart accommodate the use of principles in legal reasoning without abandoning one of the main tenets of legal positivism, namely that the law of a community is a set of special rules identified by tests having not to do with their content but with their pedigree? I think that he can. There is no reason why principles could not be placed with rules in the set of standards identified by their pedigree. Hart argues that rules get their pedigree from the legal system's "rule of recognition," defined as a secondary rule that allows us to discover whether a rule is indeed a rule of the system.[6] Principles get their pedigree in the same way. They are created by judges who formulate them to decide specific cases, thereby establishing them as precedents for the future. Consider, for example, the principle used by the Supreme Court majority in *Loving* proclaiming that "the freedom to marry or not to marry a person of another race resides with the individual." The proclamation establishes the pedigree. Although members of the Court certainly used their moral sensibilities in constructing the content of the principle, it has no validity until the principle is actually used in arriving at a judicial decision.

In rebuttal, Dworkin would point out that the use of principles implies that the current set of valid rules is *not* exhaustive of the law. New cases must be decided by a judge "exercising his discretion." This means "reaching beyond the law" for a

---

[6] See footnote 4 *supra*.

principle that will guide the judge in "manufacturing a fresh legal rule or supplementing an old one" (38). This is perhaps the strongest challenge that Dworkin makes against legal positivism and against Hart in particular. If the judge must reach beyond the law for a principle in order to make a judicial decision, then the wall that the positivist has set up between law and morals starts to crumble, especially if we add the proviso that judicial decisions *cannot* be made in a large number of cases without an appeal to moral principles.

I believe that Hart has a response to this final challenge, but it can only be made against the backdrop of his theory of minimum content of natural law. Let us now turn to Hart's discussion of this interesting idea and show its relevance both to Dworkin's challenge and to the understanding of family law.

3.6 Hart's Compromise: The Minimum Content of Natural Law

One possible criticism of Hart's brand of legal positivism is that the basic primary rules he says are needed for the survival of any society are identical to many of the laws of nature mentioned by John Locke and other natural law theorists. Locke writes that "the law of nature...teaches all mankind … that no one ought to harm another in his life, health, liberty, or possessions" (II, 6). Hart writes that the rules of any society, from the most primitive to the most modern, must contain, in some form, restrictions on acts harmful to others if we are to coexist in close proximity to each other (Hart, 91). Both agree that there must be a minimum set of laws prohibiting (for example) murder, assault, kidnap, and theft. The difference is that whereas Locke traces these rules to the natural law (or the laws of God), Hart derives them empirically from the conflict between the natural desire to survive and the propensity of some people in all societies to cause harm to others. The desire to survive cannot be satisfied unless we have primary rules to constrain those who refuse to exercise self-restraint.

None of this makes Hart a convert to natural law theory. Although he sees a close connection between law and morality, he does not believe this to be a necessary connection. It is logically possible, though highly unlikely, that there could be a legal system that lacks one or more of the aforementioned basic primary rules. Suppose, for example, that at some point in the future human beings are no longer vulnerable to bodily attack. This is not a logical impossibility,[7] but the lesson he draws from this thought-experiment is that "there would vanish one obvious reason for the most characteristic provision of law and morals: thou shalt not kill" (Hart, 194–5).

This is Hart's theory of "the minimum content of natural law." If survival is the aim, then this fact about human nature (our vulnerability) "affords a *reason* why... law and morals should include a specific content" (Hart, 193). There are five contin-

[7] I will leave it to the reader's imagination or to the writers of science fiction to imagine suitable scenarios of this change in the human exoskeleton.

gent facts or "simple truisms" on Hart's list: In addition to the fact of (1) *human vulnerability*, he mentions (2) the *approximate equality* of all persons ("no individual is so much more powerful than others, that he is able, without co-operation, to dominate or subdue them for more than a short period"); (3) our *limited amount of altruism* ("if humans are not devils, neither are they angels … human altruism is limited in range and is intermittent"); (4) *limited resources* (human beings need food, clothes and shelter, but "these do not exist in hand in limitless abundance"); (5) our *limited understanding and strength of will* ("All are tempted at times to prefer their own immediate interests and many would succumb to the temptation").

Each of the above provides a reason why the rules of law and morals should include a specific content. The first three (human vulnerability, approximate equality, and limited altruism) provide reasons why we need a system of rules requiring mutual forbearance and compromise. The fourth (limited resources) makes "indispensable some minimal form of the institution of property (though not necessarily individual property), and the distinctive kind of rule that requires respect for it" (for example, rules "excluding persons generally other than the 'owner' from entry on, or the use of land, or from taking or using material things"). The fifth natural fact (limited understanding and strength of will) is a reason we have rules creating a special organization for the detection and punishment of those who give in to selfish temptation and thereby "try to obtain the advantages of the system without submitting to its obligations. Sanctions are therefore required "not as the normal motive for obedience, but as a guarantee that those who would voluntarily obey shall not be sacrificed to those who would not" (Hart, 198).

Hart concludes with the remark that these simple truisms about human nature "not only disclose the core of good sense in the doctrine of Natural Law [but they] are of vital importance for the understanding of law and morals" (199). Although he does not support Aquinas's famous remark that an unjust law is not law, Hart does endorse the claim that the minimum forms of protection for persons, property and promises that are provided within a municipal system are a *natural necessity*.[8]

3.7 Minimum Content of the Rules of Family Law

Does the theory of minimum content apply to any of the rules of family law? Are there any "simple truisms" about human nature that make it contingently necessary to have minimal rules on marriage, divorce, parenting, child welfare, or rules encouraging (through provision of benefits) family formation? Let us begin with marriage.

[8]There is evidence that the germ of Hart's theory about minimum content can be found in the dialogue *Minos* (or *On Law*), attributed by ancient editors to Plato. Although there is a modern dispute about whether *Minos* should be included in the group of dialogues of Plato regarded as authentic, it is generally thought to have originated in Plato's Academy shortly after his death (348/7 B.C.). See R.F. Hathaway and L.D. Houlgate (Hathaway and Houlgate 1969) for a commentary and translation. We argue that *Minos* is not only an excellent introduction to Plato's *Laws*, but it deserves serious study, whether or not it is authentic (107).

3.7.1 Rules of Marriage

John Locke used the phrase "conjugal society" to refer to moral marriage, defined as a society of one man and one woman "made by a voluntary compact." The compact consists "chiefly in such a communion and right in one another's bodies as is necessary to its chief end, procreation." The other essential feature of the compact is that "it draws with it mutual support and assistance, and a communion of interests too, as necessary not only to unite their care and affection, but also necessary to their common off-spring, who have a right to be nourished, and maintained by them, till they are able to provide for themselves" (Locke 1980, VII, 78) These two features are essential because they are consistent with the ends of conjugal society," or else the compact cannot count as a *marriage* contract. But everything else can be altered by the man and wife, including the traditional presumption of eighteenth century marriage contracts that the man will make all important decisions for the family (Simmons, 170).

Our question is whether there are any natural facts that make necessary the "essential" provisions of the marital contract. Although Locke never answered this question he might fashion the follow reply. First, "the continuation of the species" requires the "conjunction between male and female" for the purpose of procreation. Second, this conjunction should last "as long as is necessary to the nourishment and support of the young ones, who are to be sustained by those that got them, till they are able to shift and provide for themselves." And because the female "is commonly with child again" while the first child is still dependent on his parents for help, the father is needed "to make provision and lay up goods for their common issue," (VII, 79, 80) at least until the mother is beyond her child-bearing years and the last child is "able to shift for himself." Third, Locke concludes with the radical remark that he can find no reason why "this compact … may not be made determinable" like any other compact "there being no necessity in the nature of the thing, nor to the ends of it, that it should always be for life" (VII, 81).[9]

Let us suppose that Locke's facts about the necessity for people to procreate and raise their children are true. What follows from this is not only that men and women could step forward and volunteer to procreate, but in the event of a lack of volunteers, women of child-bearing age *could be required* to have "conjunction" (sexual intercourse) with a man until she conceives. In other words, all that follows from the alleged necessity to continue the human species is sexual conjunction of male and female, not *voluntary* sexual conjunction. Second, although Locke would not know this, there is now no need for conjunction at all: conception and procreation can now be done artificially by *in vitro* fertilization and transfer of the embryo to the woman's womb.

[9] Locke is quick to remind the reader that this only applies to those who "are under no restraint of any positive law, which ordains all such contracts to be perpetual." This leaves us wondering why those who are under the restraint of a positive law forbidding divorce are *morally* compelled to continue their marriage after their last child leaves home.

Nor does it follow from the (alleged) need to continue the human species that men and women must enter into a marital contract that commits them to remain married and rear their children until the last one leaves home. This task could certainly be done without entering into a contract of marriage. Therefore, the "natural fact" that the human species requires procreative activity and the performance of subsequent lengthy child-rearing tasks in order to perpetuate the species does not require the creation of contracts for the purpose of sexual conjunction (marriage). In sum, laws creating the institution of marriage are not a natural necessity.

3.7.2 Rules Protecting Infants and Young Children

Another candidate for "simple truisms" about human nature that might require the minimum content of family law is the special vulnerability of newborns and young children. Locke refers to them as "weak and helpless, without knowledge or understanding" (VII, 56). Childhood is an "imperfect state … wherein [the child] has not understanding of his own to direct his *will*" (VII, 58). Young children are not only physically incapable of protecting themselves and providing the sustenance required for their survival, but they are mentally incapable of devising the means to achieve these ends. Hence, there is good reason for rules prohibiting child neglect and abuse. The content of these rules would require not only the assignment of specific caretakers and guardians, but the rules would charge them with the duty to protect the child from external threats to life and limb, and providing for food, shelter and clothing sufficient to keep the child alive and in good health.

3.7.3 Rules of Custody Assignments at Birth

Locke assigns the duties of custody and guardianship to the child's biological parents. And from this duty "which is incumbent on them, to take care of their offspring, during the imperfect state of childhood," Locke also gives parents the reciprocal *right* "to govern the actions of their yet ignorant nonage." Since the young child lacks the understanding to direct his own desire to obtain what is necessary to survive, the parent "must understand for him, must will for him too; he must prescribe to his will, and regulate his actions" (VII, 58).

It might be objected that this duty and its reciprocal rights could be assigned to any adult or group of adults, whether biologically related to the child or not. But if it is agreed that there is a minimum-content rule assigning presumptive custody of a newborn to the biological parents, and the concept of "custody" implies "care, control and maintenance", then the duty of protecting the child and providing for her basic needs would naturally go to her parents. Locke states this in the language of classical natural law:

> From [Adam] the world is peopled with his descendants, who are all born infants, weak and helpless, without knowledge or understanding, but to supply the defects of this imperfect state, till the improvements of growth and age hath removed them, *Adam* and *Eve*, and after them all parents were, by the law of nature, *under an obligation to preserve, nourish, and educate* the children they had begotten … (VII, 56).

Here is a restatement, in the language of a "minimum content of family law," in which the content of both rules respond not to religious mythology, but to facts about human nature which justify these rules:

> F1 There is a fundamental duty to provide for the basic survival needs of those children who are physically and mentally incapable of providing for themselves.
>
> F2 Initial (presumptive) custody of a newborn child should go to the biological parents who shall have both the duty to provide for the basic survival needs adumbrated in F1 and the rights (powers) required to carry out this duty.

F1 is justified by the special vulnerability of infants and young children due to their inability to protect or provide for themselves. F2 is justified by facts about human nature which afford a reason why family law and morals should have this particular content. However, whereas F1 is linked to the natural aim of survival, F2 does not have this link. Newborn and young children will not die if their custody at birth is given to adults who have no biological relationship to them.[10] Instead, the link is to the fact that "during pregnancy many – perhaps most –expectant parents form a poignantly embodied, but also emotional, intimate relationship with their fetus":

> Because children come into existence through gestation, pregnant women and their supporting partners have to invest a significant amount of resources into having birth children; this is an often conscious, intentional process, akin to other projects in which people engage: it contains much anticipation and planning, thinking and hoping, imagination and projection. Through their bodily connection with the baby and their various psychological investments, expecting parents normally build a relationship with their future baby, relationship which is sometimes highly emotional and already quite developed at birth. Bearing parents and their newborns already share a common history including numerous embodied common experiences ("you kicked me on the 1st of March," "you made me worry," "you made me so happy"). The fact that the body plays such a central part in pregnancy, makes pregnancy a uniquely privileged context for developing a bond that is at the same time physical and imaginative with the future child. (Gheaus 2012)

In this passage, Anca Ghaeus gives us an empirical basis for the universal practice of granting presumptive custody rights of a newborn child to its birth parents. The rules giving parents the moral and legal right to keep their birth baby "obviously depends on the way in which we come into the world." If human procreation were to change radically, such that babies would be born in artificial wombs, then a case for allocating babies to future parents in other ways (for example, *via* lotteries) would become significantly stronger. "Not only would the meaning of 'biological

---

[10] Although there is evidence that some newborn adoptees may have bonded *in utero* during pregnancy. If they are immediately handed over to adopting parents at birth, this may result in future psychological problems for the adopted child (U.S. Dept. of Health and Human Services. 2007, 2–7; Atwell, Barbara. Atwell 2012, 201).

parent' become less substantial, and signify a genetic connection only, but such change would pose a radical challenge to parents' right to keep their biological babies" (Gheaus 2012).

This is not unlike Hart's imagined scenario of a world in which all persons are encased in an impenetrable armor such that none are vulnerable to external efforts to cause them to suffer harm. In such a world the meaning of "murder" would eventually be forgotten and "Thou shalt not kill" would only be a curiosity for historians. By analogy, consider Plato's recommendation in *Republic* that all infants born to the ruling class of the ideal state should be permanently taken from them and given to professional child rearers at birth, so that no child would ever know its own biological parents, and no parents would know their own biological child (Book V).[11] As a result, when parents use the phrase "my child" they would be referring to any child born in the same month as the month in which "their" biological child was born. *All* children born in that month to any of the rulers would be "their children," the children would consider all the rulers to whom these children were born as "my parents," and the children would consider each other as "brother and sister." In Plato's imaginary world, the phrase "my child," would neither say nor imply anything about the parent's emotional and intimate relationship with the particular child they have borne. If we assume that there is sufficient evidence for such a relationship, we can safely conclude that rules giving presumptive custody to birth parents are a natural necessity.[12]

Questions for Thought and Discussion

1. What does a legal positivist mean by *separation* in the phrase "the separation of law and morals"? Use the Moroccan statute 475 on forced marriage as your example of law and use the Western conception of human rights as your example of morals.
2. Hart says that understanding the nature of law lies in our acknowledgement that *law and the obligations created by law are only to be found in the interplay of primary and secondary rules.* What does he mean by this? Explain how this compares to John Austin's earlier attempt to define the nature of law.
3. Why is Hart's discussion of "minimum content" seen as a compromise between the theories of natural law and legal positivism?
4. Are there any "simple truisms" about human nature that make it contingently necessary to have minimal rules on marriage, divorce, parenting, child welfare, or rules encouraging (through provision of benefits) family formation? What are these truisms? What kind of rules pertaining to the family do they justify?

[11] Plato's motive for this recommendation was to reduce the temptation of the rulers to give special favors to their biological children, thereby taking their attention away from their primary task of ruling the city-state. This motive was also behind his recommendation that the rulers not be allowed to have private possessions, nor claim exclusive sexual access to any person of the opposite sex by referring to them as "*my* husband," or "*my* wife."

[12] We will return to this discussion in Chap. 11 when we look at the role of the common legal practice of giving preference to the gestational mother in custody disputes between a surrogate gestational mother and the genetic parent(s) of a newborn child Sect. (11.7).

References

Al Jazeera. 2014. Morocco repeals 'rape marriage' law. http://www.aljazeera.com/news/africa/2014/01/morocco-repeals-rape-marriage-law-2014123254643455.html. Accessed 15 Jan 2016.

Atwell, Barbara. 2012. Nature and nurture: Revisiting the infant adoption process. *William & Mary Journal of Women and the Law* 18: 2.

Austin, John. 1832. *The province of jurisprudence determined*. London: John Murray.

———. 1879. *Lectures on Jurisprudence*, or *The philosophy of positive law*, 2 volumes, ed. R. Campbell, 4th edition, rev., London: John Murray; reprint, Bristol: Thames Press, 2002.

Blackstone, William. 1765–1769. *Commentaries on the laws of England*, vol. 4. Oxford: Clarendon Press.

Dworkin, Ronald, eds. 1977. *The philosophy of law*. New York: Oxford University Press.

Gheaus, Anca. 2012. The right to parent one's biological baby. *The Journal of Political Philosophy* 20(4): 432–455.

Hart, H.L.A. 2012. *The concept of law*. 3rd ed. Oxford: Oxford University Press.

Hathaway, Ronald, and Laurence Houlgate. 1969. The platonic *Minos* and the classical theory of natural law, with *Minos*, a Translation by R.F. Hathaway. *The American Journal of Jurisprudence* 14: 105–124.

Locke, John. 1980. ed. McPherson, C.B. *Second treatise of government*. Indianapolis: Hackett. (First published in 1690).

Loving v Virginia 1967. 388 U.S. 1.

Presthold, Jennifer. 2014. Morocco: Human rights violations under Article 475. *The Advocates for Human Rights*. http://theadvocatespost.org/2014/01/13/morocco_humanrightsviolationsunder-article475/ Accessed 15 Jan 2016.

Riggs v Palmer 1899. 115 N.Y. 506, 22 N.E. 188

U.S. Department of Health and Human Services. 2007. Helping your foster child transition to your adopted child. *Child Welfare Info Gateway*, 2–7. https://www.childwelfare.gov/ Accessed 3 Apr 2016.

West's Encyclopedia of American Law, 2nd edition. 2008.

Chapter 4
Constitutional Interpretation

> *"We deal with a right of privacy older than the Bill of Rights – older than our political parties, older than our school system."*
>
> – J. Wm. O. Douglas, *Griswold v Connecticut* (1965)
>
> *"With all deference, I can find no such general right of privacy in the Bill of Rights, in any other part of the Constitution, or in any case ever before decided by this Court."*
>
> – J. Potter Stewart, *Griswold v Connecticut* (1965)

Abstract In this chapter we examine the ongoing debate about how the U.S. Constitution should be interpreted. Although family law is traditionally the responsibility of the states, there are a few U.S. Supreme court cases that brought about a change in areas once controlled mainly by state laws: the right of parents to control their child's education; the right of children to freely express their political or moral views in school; and the right of married couples to use artificial contraception. We briefly look at these cases in order to get an understanding of the debate between proponents of two broad categories of theories of constitutional interpretation: Originalism and Non-originalism. Originalist theories insist that the only considerations to use when interpreting the Constitution and its provisions are those that are temporally "fixed" to the time when they were written or ratified. Non-originalism denies this and considers such non-temporal factors as the purpose of the Constitution or the underlying moral philosophy that might have inspired its authors. All of the interpretations are normative. They attempt to answer the question as "Why *ought* the justices on the Supreme Court to defer only to the intentions of those who wrote the Constitution and its amendments or to the intentions of those who had a hand in the ratification of these documents? "What moral standing do the framers, ratifiers and the general public in the 18th century have that gives them the final word on interpretation?" We begin the chapter by looking at how the word "person" was originally used in the Constitution in order to get some perspective on "originalist" theories of interpretation. We then examine three U.S. Supreme Court cases involving family law in order to illustrate the persistent arguments that occur

L.D. Houlgate, *Philosophy, Law and the Family*, AMINTAPHIL: The Philosophical Foundations of Law and Justice 7,
DOI 10.1007/978-3-319-51121-4_4

over how the doctrine of *stare decisis* is employed, and in the final sections of the chapter, to show how the various theories of constitutional interpretation have been employed by justices and legal scholars when deciding these and other cases that have come before the U.S. Supreme Court.

4.1 The Concept of "Person" in the Constitution

Debates about how the U.S. Constitution should be interpreted began almost as soon as the ink dried on this revered document. In what is generally regarded as the most important of the early cases before the Supreme Court (*Chisholm v. Georgia*, 1793), three of the four justices quarreled with the lone dissenting justice about the best way to interpret the meaning of key terms like "state," "suable" and "controversy" in Article III of the Constitution.[1] Ten years later, in a seminal case that changed the balance of power between all three branches of government (*Marbury v Madison*, 1803) the Supreme Court interpreted "judicial power" in the same article to mean that it and it alone was the only branch having the right of *judicial review* – the power to invalidate laws created by Congress and to nullify any actions of the executive that it deemed unconstitutional.[2]

[1] Chisholm, a citizen of South Carolina and executor of the estate of a South Carolina merchant, sued the State of Georgia in the U.S. Supreme Court to recover the value of clothing supplied to Georgia during the Revolutionary War. Georgia refused to appear, on the ground of sovereign immunity. A majority of the Court rejected this claim and rendered default judgment against the State.

The relevant sections of Article III of the Constitution referenced by the Court are these:

Section 1

The judicial power of the United States, shall be vested in one Supreme Court, and in such inferior courts as the Congress may from time to time ordain and establish. The judges, both of the supreme and inferior courts, shall hold their offices during good behavior, and shall, at stated times, receive for their services, a compensation, which shall not be diminished during their continuance in office.

Section 2

The judicial power shall extend to all cases, in law and equity, arising under this Constitution, the laws of the United States, and treaties made, or which shall be made, under their authority;–to all cases affecting ambassadors, other public ministers and consuls;–to all cases of admiralty and maritime jurisdiction;–to controversies to which the United States shall be a party;–to controversies between two or more states;–between a state and citizens of another state;–between citizens of different states;–between citizens of the same state claiming lands under grants of different states, and between a state, or the citizens thereof, and foreign states, citizens or subjects.

In all cases affecting ambassadors, other public ministers and consuls, and those in which a state shall be party, the Supreme Court shall have original jurisdiction. In all the other cases before mentioned, the Supreme Court shall have appellate jurisdiction, both as to law and fact, with such exceptions, and under such regulations as the Congress shall make.

[2] Congress had passed the *Judiciary Act of 1789*, giving the Supreme Court original jurisdiction over writs of mandamus. (These are judicial orders to any government subordinate court, corporation or public authority to do (or forbear from doing) some specific act which that body is obliged

The vagueness of ordinary and legal language has always been a problem for those jurists who attempt to interpret the Constitution and its amendments. The inclusion of some words and the omission of others is also of paramount importance. For example, the Constitution contains many instances of the words "person," "people," "male" and "citizen," but not a single instance of "female," "women," or "children." It was generally understood in the late eighteenth century that women and children were not persons for purposes of constitutional protections and rights. Women were not allowed to vote in state or federal elections and children did not have any of the rights guaranteed to adults under the first ten amendments. Women did not achieve the right to vote until passage of the Nineteenth Amendment in 1920 and it was assumed until the late 1960s that children had no free speech rights under the First Amendment, nor the right to counsel under the Sixth Amendment. It took a *new* constitutional amendment to get women the right to vote and it took an "interpretation" of *existing* amendments to determine that children should have free speech rights in school and the right to an attorney if charged with a crime.

A *theory* of constitutional interpretation provides an answer to the question "How *ought* the provisions of the Constitution and its amendments be interpreted?" This is a normative question, calling on us to state and defend a standard or principle that would give us the most plausible interpretation of a troublesome phrase, paragraph, section or amendment of the Constitution. There have been several attempts by philosophers of law to provide a theory of constitutional interpretation. However, some scholars have implicitly rejected making any such attempt by saying that a judge needs only to look at the text and plain meaning of the words in the Constitution.[3] No interpretation is needed. This is analogous to most of our non-legal day-to-day conversations. If my wife tells me she is going grocery shopping this afternoon, I do not need to "interpret" what she has told me. She is not speaking a foreign language, nor is she using technical terms that I cannot comprehend. I do not need to deduce what she means from her statement, as if she has given me the premises of an argument from which I am to arrive at a conclusion. By analogy, if the words used in the Constitution or in its amendments are in plain English, understandable by anyone who is conversant with the language, then there is no need for an interpretation or a deduction. Consider, for example, the "plain English" used by the framers in writing the First Amendment:

under law to do (or refrain from doing)—and which is in the nature of public duty, and in certain cases one of a statutory duty.) Justice Marshall held that Congress does not have the power to modify the Supreme Court's original jurisdiction. Consequently, Marshall found that the Constitution and the Judiciary Act conflict. This decision settled the important question of what happens when an Act of Congress conflicts with the Constitution. Marshall ruled that Acts of Congress that conflict with the Constitution *are not law* and the Courts are bound instead to follow the Constitution.

[3] In *Chisholm v Georgia*, Justice Wilson argued that the doctrine used to decide the case "rests not upon the legitimate result of fair and conclusive deduction from the Constitution: It is confirmed, beyond all doubt, *by the direct and explicit declaration of the Constitution itself.*"

> Congress shall make no law respecting an establishment of religion, or prohibiting the free exercise thereof; or abridging the freedom of speech, or of the press; or the right of the people peaceably to assemble, and to petition the Government for a redress of grievances.

There may be some otherwise intelligent people in the twenty-first century who are not familiar with the words "redress," or "abridging," but to many persons these words have a clear meaning. They certainly understand the phrase "*make no law*...abridging the freedom of speech or of the press." There is no need to launch into an interpretation of its meaning. As Justice Hugo Black famously put it in a free speech case:

> The First Amendment's language leaves no room for inference that abridgments of speech and press can be made just because they are slight. That Amendment provides, in simple words, that "Congress shall make no law ... abridging the freedom of speech, or of the press." *I read "no law ... abridging" to mean no law abridging* (Concurring opinion, *Smith v. California*1959)

It has been pointed out that those who use Justice Black's *textualist* or *literal* approach to reading the First Amendment makes it impossible for Congress to create a law prohibiting the disclosure of military secrets. They would argue that although the language of the amendment mentions no exceptions to the prohibition, "the framers never intended that it be applied in a perfectly literal way" (Altman, 98). I suspect that if Justice Black was alive today he would greet this conjecture about the framers' intentions by repeating the following statement he made in the first James Madison lecture:

> It is my belief that there are "absolutes" in our Bill of Rights, and that they were put there on purpose by men who knew what the words meant and meant their prohibitions to be "absolutes." (Black 1960).

If the framers knew what their words meant, then why shouldn't we also conclude that the words "person" and "people" includes women and children? If I say to you, in plain English, "Look at all the people in that crowd," I do not mean "Look at all the adult males." I mean all the human beings in the crowd, including women and children. Can we say, with the certainty of Justice Black, that the framers who put the words "person" and "people" in the Constitution did so "on purpose," knowing that these words included all human beings? Unfortunately, this is not what the framers intended by these words:

> The word "persons" was used [in the Constitution], which sounds gender neutral. However, common law, inherited from British precedents, informed the interpretation of the law. And many state laws were not gender-neutral. ...New Jersey accepted voting rights for women, [but] even those had been lost by a bill in 1807 that rescinded the right of both women and black men to vote in that state. The principle of coverture prevailed at the time the Constitution was written and adopted: a married woman was simply not a person under the law; her legal existence was bound up with that of her husband's (Lewis, 2014).

Although the framers might use the word "person" in everyday life outside of the law to refer to all members of the human species (young and old, male and female), they would use the prevailing legal meaning of the word when writing and enacting legislation. Notice that this does not refute the literalist position on how to read the Constitution and its amendments. The fact that the word "person" is ambiguous, having both an ordinary and a legal meaning, only implies that there are *two* textual or literal meanings of the word, and that when reading the Constitution, we should defer to the legal meaning that was in use in the nineteenth century.

4.2 Three Supreme Court Family Law Cases

The preceding remarks are not enough to satisfy the critics. They will continue to insist that we need a theory of interpretation if we are going to properly understand how we should read and apply the Constitution in the twenty-first century.[4] In what follows we will look at the factual basis and the finding of three U.S. Supreme Court case dealing with parent's rights, the rights of children, and marital privacy. We will then (Sect. 4.3) consider brief accounts of three theories of constitutional interpretation, showing how each would be used to arrive at a decision in the marital privacy case (*Griswold v Connecticut*) and how each theory compares with the actual ruling. This is by no means an exhaustive account of the existing theories of constitutional interpretation, but the cases and theories discussed below are representative of the current debate.

4.2.1 Parent's Right to Control Their Child's Education: **Meyer v. Nebraska** *(1923)*

In 1920 an instructor at a parochial school in Nebraska was arrested for teaching the German language to a 10-year-old child. He had violated a Nebraska state law which said: "No person, individually or as a teacher, shall, in any private, denominational, parochial or public school, teach any subject to any person in any language other than the English language." He appealed the decision to the Nebraska Supreme Court, but the court affirmed the decision, explaining their reasoning with the remark that the "salutary purpose" of the statute is clear:

> The [Nebraska] legislature had seen the baneful effects of permitting foreigners, who had taken residence in this country, to rear and educate their children in the language of their native land. The result of that condition was found to be inimical to our own safety. To allow the children of foreigners, who had emigrated here, to be taught from early childhood the language of the country of their parents was to rear them with that language as their mother tongue. It was to educate them so that they must always think in that language, and, as a consequence, naturally inculcate in them the ideas and sentiments foreign to the best interests of this country. The statute, therefore, was intended not only to require that the education of all children be conducted in the English language, but that, until they had grown into that language and until it had become a part of them, they should not in the schools be taught any other language. The obvious purpose of this statute was that the English lan-

[4] "The 'plain meaning' or 'textualist' theory of interpretation is not a theory at all; it is instead a description of what happens when constitutional meaning is not problematic" (Post 1990).

guage should be and become the mother tongue of all children reared in this state. The enactment of such a statute comes reasonably within the police power of the state.

The case was further appealed to the United States Supreme Court. Justice McReynolds, writing for the majority, began by noting that the constitutional problem is "whether the statute, as construed and applied, unreasonably infringes the liberty guaranteed to the plaintiff in error by the Fourteenth Amendment." The relevant part of the amendment is contained in the words "No State shall … deprive any person of life, liberty, or property, without due process of law." The phrase "due process" generally means operating within the law and providing fair procedures. If a person is in danger of losing her liberty because she has been arrested and charged with a crime, for example, then she has a right to not incriminate herself, to cross examine anyone who testifies against her, to be given notice of the proceedings and an opportunity to be heard. However, Justice McReynolds makes it clear that he is more interested in the word "liberty" in the amendment than he is in what constitutes fair procedure.

While this Court has not attempted to define with exactness the liberty thus guaranteed, the term has received much consideration and some of the included things have been definitely stated. Without doubt, it denotes not merely freedom from bodily restraint, but also the right of the individual to contract, to engage in any of the common occupations of life, to acquire useful knowledge, to marry, establish a home and bring up children, to worship God according to the dictates of his own conscience, and generally to enjoy those privileges long recognized at common law as essential to the orderly pursuit of happiness by free men.

Reading these words, we might plausibly respond by saying that as long as the state of Nebraska gave the appellant a fair trial, consistent with established procedures noted above, then the statute does not violate the Fourteenth Amendment. But Justice McReynolds has another interpretation of the amendment:

The established doctrine is that this liberty may not be interfered with, under the guise of protecting the public interest, by legislative action which is arbitrary or without reasonable relation to some purpose within the competency of the State to effect. Determination by the legislature of what constitutes proper exercise of police power is not final or conclusive, but is subject to supervision by the courts.

As the justice understands the Fourteenth Amendment, it is not sufficient that the German language teacher got a fair trial. The state of Nebraska must also show that the statute it uses to charge him with an offense does not "arbitrarily" interfere with his liberty. There must be "a rational relation to some purpose within the competency of the State to effect." Justice McReynolds is here making use of *substantive due process* – a doctrine which looks at the *content* or *substance* of the statute, as something distinct from *procedural due process* – used by the court to determine whether the *procedures* used to determine guilt or innocence are *fair*. For example, if the legislature exercised its police power to make it illegal to wear a tuxedo in public before 6 p.m., this would be an *arbitrary* or *unreasonable* interference with individual liberty under substantive due process standards. The statute would violate the Fourteenth Amendment, even if someone prosecuted for wearing a tuxedo before 6 p.m. was given a fair trial.

Writing for the Court, Justice McReynolds declared that the right of the Nebraska school teacher to teach the German language and the right of parents to engage him to instruct their children "are within the liberty of the Amendment." The justice then noted that the statute's restriction on this right is *arbitrary*. It does not prohibit the teaching of Latin, Greek, or Hebrew, but instead puts German, French, Spanish, Italian and every other alien speech within its ban. "Evidently the legislature has attempted materially to interfere with the calling of modern language teachers, with the opportunities of pupils to acquire knowledge, and with the power of parents to control the education of their own."

Finally, Justice McReynolds notes that there is no emergency which has arisen in Nebraska which makes it harmful for children to gain knowledge of some language other than English. "We are constrained to conclude that the statute as applied is arbitrary and without reasonable relation to any end within the competency of the State." The statute was found to be in violation of the Fourteenth Amendment to the U.S. Constitution. Accordingly, the judgement of the Nebraska Supreme Court was reversed.[5]

4.2.2 *Children's Rights of Free Speech:* Tinker v. Des Moines School District *(1969)*

On December 16, 1965 Mary Beth Tinker, 13 years old, her brother John, 15, and Christopher Eckhardt, 16, wore black armbands to their schools in order to publicize their objections to the hostilities in Vietnam. A few days earlier, the principals of the Des Moines (Iowa) schools became aware of the student's plan. The principals met and quickly adopted a policy that any student wearing an armband to school would be asked to remove it, and if he refused he would be suspended until he returned without the armband. The children were made aware of the regulation that the school authorities adopted, but kept to their plan. Shortly after arriving at their school they were sent home and suspended until they agreed to return without their armbands. Mary Beth, John and Christopher did not return to school until after their previously planned period for wearing armbands had expired on January 1 (New Year's Day).

The children, through their fathers, subsequently filed a complaint in the United States District Court asking for an injunction restraining the school officials from

[5]*Meyer* is usually discussed with another case in which the Court reached a similar decision: *Pierce v Society of Sisters 268 U.S. 510 (*1924*)*. In *Pierce* the Court held unconstitutional the Oregon Compulsory Education Act of 1922 that required all normal children between the ages of 8 and 16 years to attend public school. This was held a violation of the Fourteenth Amendment in that the Act "unreasonably interferes with the liberty of parents and guardians to direct the upbringing and education of children under their control" (573). No mention is made of the right of a child to choose to attend a public or private school. Instead, the only concern of the Court with children is to stress the judgment that in a conflict between their parents and the state over the general question of who should "nurture and direct [their] destiny," the parents should prevail.

disciplining them. The District Court dismissed the complaint on the ground that their suspension was a reasonable action needed to prevent disturbance of school discipline. On appeal, the U.S. Court of Appeals for the Eighth Circuit was equally divided, and the District Court's decision was accordingly affirmed, without opinion.

The U.S. Supreme Court agreed to take the case. When the Court reached a decision, Justice Fortas wrote for the majority. His first finding was that the wearing of an armband for the purpose of expressing certain views is the type of symbolic act that is within the Free Speech Clause of the First Amendment. Wearing or displaying a symbol to silently express a moral or political opinion should be treated under the law in the same way we now treat verbal or written opinions. Second, the wearing of armbands in the circumstances of this case was entirely divorced from any alleged actual or potentially disruptive conduct by those wearing the armbands. It was closely akin to "pure speech" (that is, speech without accompanying action), which is entitled to comprehensive protection under the First Amendment. Third, First Amendment rights, applied in light of the special characteristics of the school environment, are available to teachers and students.

> It can hardly be argued that either students or teachers shed their constitutional rights to freedom of speech or expression at the schoolhouse gate.... In our system, state-operated schools may not be enclaves of totalitarianism. School officials do not possess absolute authority over their students. Students in school as well as out of school are "persons" under our Constitution. They are possessed of fundamental rights which the State must respect, just as they themselves must respect their obligations to the State. (393 U.S. 503)

Fourth, Justice Fortas noted that the problem for the Court "lies in the area where students in the exercise of First Amendment rights collide with the rules of the school authorities." Although students have the right to freedom of speech, "the Court has repeatedly emphasized the need for affirming the comprehensive authority of the States and of school officials, consistent with fundamental constitutional safeguards, to prescribe and control conduct in the schools."

However, Justice Fortas observed, the record does not demonstrate any facts which might reasonably have led school authorities to forecast substantial disruption of or material interference with school activities, and no disturbances or disorders on the school premises in fact occurred.

> Their deviation consisted only in wearing on their sleeve a band of black cloth, not more than two inches wide. They wore it to exhibit their disapproval of the Vietnam hostilities and their advocacy of a truce, to make their views known, and, by their example, to influence others to adopt them. They neither interrupted school activities nor sought to intrude in the school affairs or the lives of others. They caused discussion outside of the classrooms, but no interference with work and no disorder. In the circumstances, our Constitution does not permit officials of the State to deny their form of expression.

The Supreme Court reversed the ruling of the Appeals Court in a 7-2 vote with justices Black and Harlan dissenting. Justice Black's dissent was long and vigorous. Although he had argued in many previous cases that the Court should accept the literal meaning of the First Amendment (Sect. 4.1) that "Congress shall make no law abridging freedom of speech," he argued that this does not mean that anyone can say anything he or she wants to say *in any place or at any time*. I cannot stand up in a church and loudly proclaim for atheism, not because the content of my speech is atheism, but because of the place and time I chose to speak.

> Assuming that the Court is correct in holding that the conduct of wearing armbands for the purpose of conveying political ideas is protected by the First Amendment, the crucial remaining questions are whether students and teachers may use the schools at their whim as a platform for the exercise of free speech–"symbolic" or "pure"–and whether the courts will allocate to themselves the function of deciding how the pupils' school day will be spent. While I have always believed that under the First and Fourteenth Amendments neither the State nor the Federal Government has any authority to regulate or censor the content of speech, I have never believed that any person has a right to give speeches or engage in demonstrations where he pleases and when he pleases.

Second, Justice Black attacks the Court majority's use of the "reasonableness" test that was used in the substantive interpretation of the Fourteenth Amendment in *Meyer* v. *Nebraska* (Sect. 4.2.1). He complains, first, that in cases that came after *Meyer*, the "reasonableness" constitutional test was left "dead on the battlefield," so much so that the Court was able to conclude in 1963:

> There was a time when the Due Process Clause was used by this Court to strike down laws which were thought unreasonable, that is, unwise or incompatible with some particular economic or social philosophy... The doctrine that prevailed ...that due process authorizes courts to hold laws unconstitutional when they believe the legislature has acted unwisely—has long since been discarded. (*Ferguson v. Skrupa*1963)

We have earlier referred to this doctrine as substantive due process (Sect. 4.2.1). Not only is there precedent for repudiating this doctrine, but Justice Black argues that the judges who discarded it were right to do so. Judges do not "have the power to hold laws unconstitutional upon the belief that the laws they are adjudicating 'shock the conscience' or that they are 'unreasonable,' 'arbitrary,' 'irrational,' 'contrary to fundamental decency,' or some other such flexible term without precise boundaries." If they had this kind of power, then judges "could strike down any law they do not like."

Further, even if it is true that the decision of the Des Moines school district to prohibit the wearing of armbands to school is unreasonable, this is a decision that only they have the power to make. This is because the "single purpose" of the public schools is to give students "an opportunity to learn." It is not to give students a platform for them to air their moral, religious or political opinions:

> Iowa's public schools... are operated to give students an opportunity to learn, not to talk politics by actual speech, or by "symbolic" speech. And, as I have pointed out before, the record amply shows that public protest in the school classes against the Vietnam War "distracted from that singleness of purpose which the State [here Iowa] desired to exist in its public educational institutions." Here the Court should accord Iowa educational institutions the right to determine for themselves to what extent free expression should be allowed in its schools...

4.2.3 Marital Privacy: **Griswold v. Connecticut** *(1965)*

On November 10, 1961, Estelle Griswold, Executive Director of the Planned Parenthood League of Connecticut and Dr. C. Lee Buxton, Medical Director for the League at its center in New Haven were arrested for violating statutes 53-32 and 54-196 of the General Statutes of Connecticut (1958, revised). Section 53–32 provides: "Any person who *uses* any drug, medicinal article or instrument for the purpose of preventing conception shall be fined not less than fifty dollars or imprisoned not less than sixty days nor more than one year or be both fined and imprisoned." Section 54–196 provides: "Any person who *assists, abets, counsels, causes, hires or commands another to commit any offense* may be prosecuted and punished as if he were the principal offender." Ms. Griswold and Dr. Buxton admitted to having given information, instruction, and medical advice to married persons as to the means of preventing conception. They examined the wife and prescribed the best contraceptive device or material for her use. They usually charged fees for this service, although some couples were serviced free. They were found guilty as accessories and fined $100 each.

After a lengthy process in which the conviction was upheld by both the Appellate Division of the Circuit Court, and by the Connecticut Supreme Court, the case was finally argued before the U.S. Supreme Court in March of 1965. Three months later, in a 7-2 vote the Court held that the Connecticut statutes were unconstitutional. Mr. Justice Douglas delivered the opinion of the majority. The following two passages are representative:

> Specific guarantees in the Bill of Rights have penumbras, formed by emanations from those guarantees that help give them life and substance. Various guarantees create zones of privacy. The right of association contained in the penumbra of the First Amendment is one… The Third Amendment, in its prohibition against the quartering of soldiers "in any house" in time of peace without the consent of the owner, is another facet of that privacy. The Fourth Amendment explicitly affirms the "right of the people to be secure in their persons, houses, papers, and effects, against unreasonable searches and seizures." The Fifth Amendment, in its Self-Incrimination Clause, enables the citizen to create a zone of privacy which government may not force him to surrender to his detriment. The Ninth Amendment provides: "The enumeration in the Constitution, of certain rights, shall not be construed to deny or disparage others retained by the people." Would we allow the police to search the sacred precincts of marital bedrooms for telltale signs of the use of contraceptives? The very idea is repulsive to the notions of privacy surrounding the marriage relationship.

> We deal with a right of privacy older than the Bill of Rights—older than our political parties, older than our school system. Marriage is a coming together for better or for worse, hopefully enduring, and intimate to the degree of being sacred. It is an association that promotes a way of life, not causes; a harmony in living, not political faiths; a bilateral loyalty, not commercial or social projects. Yet it is an association for as noble a purpose as any involved in our prior decisions.

In a biting dissent to the majority decision, Justice Potter Stewart argued that there is nothing either in the literal words of the amendments to the Constitution or in their intended meanings to support the conclusion that the Connecticut statutes cited above are unconstitutional.

> As to the First, Third, Fourth, and Fifth Amendments, I can find nothing in any of them to invalidate this Connecticut law… It has not even been argued that this is a law "respecting an establishment of religion, or prohibiting the free exercise thereof." And surely, unless the solemn process of constitutional adjudication is to descend to the level of a play on words, there is not involved here any abridgment of the freedom of speech, or of the press; or the right of the people peaceably to assemble, and to petition the Government for a redress of grievances. No soldier has been quartered in any house. There has been no search, and no seizure. Nobody has been compelled to be a witness against himself.
>
> What provision of the Constitution, then, does make this state law invalid? The Court says it is the right of privacy "created by several fundamental constitutional guarantees." With all deference, I can find no such general right of privacy in the Bill of Rights, in any other part of the Constitution, or in any case ever before decided by this Court (529).

Justice Black was equally dismissive of Justice Douglas's suggestion that there is a constitutional right to privacy:

> One of the most effective ways of diluting or expanding a constitutionally guaranteed right is to substitute for the crucial word or words of a constitutional guarantee another word or words, more or less flexible and more or less restricted in meaning. This fact is well illustrated by the use of the term "right of privacy" as a comprehensive substitute for the Fourth Amendment's guarantee against "unreasonable searches and seizures." "Privacy" is a broad, abstract and ambiguous concept which can easily be shrunken in meaning but which can also, on the other hand, easily be interpreted as a constitutional ban against many things other than searches and seizures. I have expressed the view many times that First Amendment freedoms, for example, have suffered from a failure of the courts to stick to the simple language of the First Amendment in construing it, instead of invoking multitudes of words substituted for those the Framers used. For these reasons, I get nowhere in this case by talk about a constitutional "right of privacy" as an emanation from one or more constitutional provisions. I like my privacy as well as the next one, but I am nevertheless compelled to admit that government has a right to invade it unless prohibited by some specific constitutional provision. For these reasons, I cannot agree with the Court's judgment and the reasons it gives for holding this Connecticut law unconstitutional (510).

4.3 The Role of *Stare Decisis* in Supreme Court Decision-Making

The Latin phrase *stare decisis* translates as "following precedent." The source of authority most frequently relied on by the Supreme Court in deciding cases that come before is *precedent*, that is, the Court's (or particular justices') own prior opinions. Robert Post provides a reason for this reliance.

> In American law, the principle [of stare decisis] constitutes a fundamental aspect of "the rule of law," for it requires courts to decide cases based on public and predictable rules, applied in an even-handed manner, upon which persons can rely in the conduct of their lives. In constitutional adjudication "adherence to precedent can contribute to the important notion that the law is impersonal in character, that the Court believes itself to be following a 'law which binds [it] as well as the litigants.'" The principle of stare decisis helps to ensure that our constitutional order retains the kind of stability and continuity that are prerequisite for institutional legitimacy (Post, 16).

Post here describes not only the doctrine of *stare decisis* but he justifies its role in constitutional decision-making. His argument is based on adherence to the rule of law and its role in ensuring stability and continuity in the "constitutional order." In order to retain this ideal, the people need public and predictable rules. Rules are both public and predictable when the court decides cases by an appeal to precedent.

The rule of *stare decisis* is not an "inexorable command." There are circumstances in which a prior decision is overturned. Here are the words of justices O'Connor, Kennedy and Souter in *Planned Parenthood v Casey* (1992), suggesting what circumstances might be relevant:

> When this Court reexamines a prior holding, its judgment is customarily informed by a series of prudential and pragmatic considerations designed to test the consistency of overruling a prior decision with the ideal of the rule of law, and to gauge the respective costs of reaffirming and overruling a prior case. Thus, for example, we may ask whether the rule has proved to be intolerable simply in defying practical workability…; whether the rule is subject to a kind of reliance that would lend a special hardship to the consequences of overruling and add inequity to the cost of repudiation…; whether related principles of law have so far developed as to have left the old rule no more than a remnant of abandoned doctrine…; or whether facts have so changed or come to be seen so differently, as to have robbed the old rule of significant application or justification (854).

Let us see how *stare decisis* is used in *Griswold* before we assess these and other remarks. As we might expect, the first thing that Justice Douglas does is to cite several previous cases decided by the Court in which there is no explicit mention of the specific action that the Court ruled to be constitutional, for example, the right to educate a child in a school of the parent's choice (*Peirce*), or the right to study any particular subject or any foreign language (*Meyer*). And yet, Douglas argues, the First Amendment has been interpreted by the Court to include some of these rights.

> By *Pierce v. Society of Sisters,* the right to educate one's children as one chooses is made applicable to the States by the force of the First and Fourteenth Amendments. By *Meyer v. Nebraska* the same dignity is given the right to study the German language in a private school. In other words, the State may not, consistently with the spirit of the First Amendment, contract the spectrum of available knowledge. The right of freedom of speech and press includes not only the right to utter or to print, but the right to distribute, the right to receive, the right to read…and freedom of inquiry, freedom of thought, and freedom to teach – indeed, the freedom of the entire university community…Without those peripheral rights, the specific rights would be less secure. And so we reaffirm the principle of the *Pierce* and the *Meyer* cases.[6]

Justice Douglas's argument is that since there is a general precedent for the Court's practice of locating "peripheral rights" *within* the ambit of the specific rights mentioned in the First Amendment, then there is no reason why this precedent should not be followed in the attempt to locate a (peripheral) right to privacy.

Douglas argues that the precedent cases provide the Court with a principle that can be used as the guide. For lack of a better term, I will call it the Principle of Non-Contraction. In the same way that "the State may not, consistently within the spirit of the First Amendment, contract the spectrum of available knowledge," so the State

---

[6] See fn 5 for a description of *Pierce v Society of Sisters.*

may not, consistent with the First, Third, Fourth, Fifth, Ninth and Fourteenth Amendments, contract the right to privacy of the people. To allow the state of Connecticut to prohibit married couples from using artificial methods of contraception contracts or diminishes their freedom to make their own choices about when and how to avoid pregnancy. The Principle of Non-Contraction prohibits the state from limiting personal privacy in a way that significantly impacts an important part of marital life.

What Justice Douglas has done is to use preceding Court decisions to tease out a principle that can be used to determine the constitutionality of the Connecticut statutes. Justice Black's response to this reading is that the amendments cited by Douglas should not be construed as precedent cases. For example, Black argues that the First and Fourth Amendments cannot be stretched "so as to afford protection to the conduct of these defendants in violating the Connecticut law":

> …The Court talks about a constitutional "right of privacy" as though there is some constitutional provision or provisions forbidding any law ever to be passed which might abridge the "privacy" of individuals. But there is not. There are, of course, guarantees in certain specific constitutional provisions which are designed in part to protect privacy at certain times and places with respect to certain activities. Such, for example, is the Fourth Amendment's guarantee against "unreasonable searches and seizures." But I think it belittles that Amendment to talk about it as though it protects nothing but "privacy." …The average man would very likely not have his feelings soothed any more by having his property seized openly than by having it seized privately and by stealth. He simply wants his property left alone. And a person can be just as much, if not more, irritated, annoyed and injured by an unceremonious public arrest by a policeman as he is by a seizure in the privacy of his office or home.

The most serious criticism made by Justice Black in his dissent is that Justice Douglas is using as precedents a range of earlier decisions that used a doctrine that had long since been discarded by the Court. The doctrine to which he refers is *substantive due process*, as described earlier in this chapter (Sect. 4.2.1). Justice Black says that the Court had long since discarded this interpretation of the Fourteenth Amendment. "We [the Court] have returned to the original constitutional proposition that courts do not substitute their social and economic beliefs for the judgment of legislative bodies, who are elected to pass laws." And yet, he argues, this is exactly what Justice Douglas has done in *Griswold*. By using *Meyer* as a precedent case he has ignored other precedents and returned to the practice of substituting his social beliefs (in this case, about the desirability of privacy for married couples) for those of the Connecticut state legislature.

We should notice that the debate between the two justices is not about whether precedent should be followed. I suspect that both Black and Douglas would agree with Robert Post's suggestion (quoted above) that the use of precedent in judicial decision-making is important for maintaining the rule of law as well as judicial stability and continuity. Instead, their disagreement is about *what precedent cases are authoritative* and how they should be interpreted. Justice Douglas uses *Meyer* to generate the Non-Contraction Principle and thereby to support his claim that the First and Fourteenth amendments imply several "peripheral rights" not explicitly mentioned in these amendments. Justice Black rejects *Meyer* and *Pierce* as authoritative and also rejects the idea of peripheral rights, as does Justice Stewart who writes the following dissenting words:

> What provision of the Constitution, then, does make this state law invalid? The Court says it is the right of privacy "created by several fundamental constitutional guarantees." With all deference, I can find no such general right of privacy in the Bill of Rights, in any other part of the Constitution, or in any case ever before decided by this Court.

This debate exposes one serious flaw in the doctrine of *stare decisis*. Judges have a great deal of discretion in deciding what prior cases will serve as precedents. Justice Douglas uses cases that Justice Black says are irrelevant, and *vice versa*. Second, even when there is agreement about what precedents are authoritative, there is often substantial disagreement about exactly what the precedent cases imply. One side might read the cases narrowly while the other side reads them broadly. Douglas interprets some of his precedents as supporting the idea that there is a right of marital privacy protected by the Constitution. Justice Hugo Black (joined by Justice Potter Stewart) interprets the same precedents in the opposite manner. Finally, as mentioned earlier, no precedent is an "inexorable command." Prior decisions can be and have been overturned by a later Court. We will return to a further discussion of judicial discretion and its impact on the doctrine of *stare decisis* in Chap. 13 where it will appear as part of the Critical Legal Studies (CLS) attack on the rule of law (Sect. 13.2.2).

Although *precedent* is often used to interpret the Constitution, the doctrine of *Stare Decisis* is not a theory of constitutional interpretation. It does not provide a guiding principle that tells the Court when a past case *ought* to serve as a precedent for the case at hand. The choice of one case rather than another as a precedent begs the question "Why ought we to defer to this case and ignore other possible candidates?" The answer to this question is to be found in a *theory* of constitutional interpretation – a theory that will tell us (for example) why Justice Douglas is convinced that the Bill of Rights contains a right to privacy and Justice Black writes that he can find "no such general right." We turn now to a discussion of some of the theoretical bases that have been suggested by legal scholars almost since the first cases were decided by the Supreme Court (1791–1794).

4.4 Theories of Constitutional Interpretation

The Constitution and its Amendments are documents that beg for interpretation. Many of its concepts are vague or ambiguous, and therefore susceptible of being given multiple meanings and appear to have been understood by citizens in multiple ways. The purpose of providing a detailed summary of the previous three Supreme Court cases (Sect. 4.2) is to illustrate how different theories of constitutional interpretation are at work in both the majority decisions and in the dissents to these decisions. Following a recommendation of the late Justice Antonin Scalia, we will categorize and discuss all theories as residing either under the banner of *originalism* or *non-originalism* (Scalia 1988). The terms "originalism" or "originalist" refer to theories that view the meaning of words and phrases in the Constitution and its amendments as fixed at the time of their origin. The terms "non-originalism" or "non-originalist" allows that the meaning of these words or phrases are not temporally fixed.

4.4.1 Originalism

Originalist theories come in several forms. Here are four variations: (1) The words of the Constitution should be taken literally (*Textualism*); (2) We should defer only to the *intent* of those men who created, ratified or framed the Constitution and its amendments (*Framers' Intent*); (3) We should rely on the *understanding* of those people who read the Constitution and its amendments and to whom it applied at the time it was enacted and ratified. (*Original Understanding*); (4) We should interpret the Constitution in terms of the political and intellectual atmospheres of the time leading up to ratification, the influence of British law on the framers and ratifiers, and the records of the ratifying debates in all the states (*Informed Understanding*).

Because Textualism has been previously discarded as a theory of interpretation (on the grounds that it calls for the Court *not* to interpret the words of the Constitution), and because it is usually confused with Framer's Intent theory, we will here discuss only variations (2)–(4).

Framers' Intent

Although Justice Black in both *Griswold* and *Tinker* shows himself to be an unrelenting textualist in his interpretation of the Constitution, no one who believes we should defer to the intended meanings of the framers would disagree with his textual analyses. For example, not only does the word "privacy" not occur in the Amendments, there is no evidence that it would be among the "multitudes of words" that the framers would have used to express their *intended* meaning when they wrote the Amendments. Nor would the framers agree with the words of Justice Fortas in *Tinker* that "Students in school as well as out of school are 'persons' under our Constitution." It was never the intention of the framers to include children as among those whose conduct is protected under the provisions of the amendments. And, harking back to Justice Black's dissent in *Tinker*, with reference to the use of substantive due process in *Meyer*, there is no evidence that the authors of the due process clause of the Fifth and Fourteenth Amendments intended any more than that accused persons should have all the protections of a fair trial when their case is being tried in a court of law. None of the framers intended that the due process clause implied standards of "reasonableness" to guide state legislatures when they create laws affecting individual liberty, especially including the liberty of children.

The theory of *Framers' Intent* says that the courts should always apply the intended, not the literal meaning of the framers when interpreting the provisions of the Constitution and its amendments. The fact that women were not regarded as legal persons in common law at the time when the Constitution was written is proof that the framers did not intend to include women in the category of persons who had the right to vote. And the fact that laws prohibiting the disclosure of military secrets were never affected by passage of the First Amendment shows that the framers never intended nor expected them to be rescinded. Hence, it could not have been their intention that the First Amendment's protection of freedom of speech would apply to these prohibitions. The intentions of the framers, not their literal words, should guide the courts in how they interpret the Constitution.

There are some intentions that the framers could not have had because they lacked knowledge of technologies that had yet been invented or even imagined. We can use the Fourth Amendment to illustrate this point. The amendment declares that there is a "right of the people to be secure in their persons, houses, papers, and effects, against unreasonable searches and seizures." It seems safe to conjecture that those who wrote and approved this language were thinking only about searches and seizures involving *physical* intrusions and confiscations. They did not intend it to apply to wiretapping of a suspected criminal's telephone by the government without a warrant (*Olmstead v United States*, 1928). They could not have intended this because they had no knowledge of telephones and wiretapping. On the basis of these facts, the *Olmstead* court had to make a choice between declaring that the Fourth Amendment does not apply (because there was no physical intrusion and confiscation) or declaring that the Fourth Amendment does apply. The theory of Framers' Intent requires the former choice, and this is exactly what the Court affirmed: "the use of evidence of private telephone conversations between the defendants and others, intercepted by means of wiretapping [is not] a violation of the Fourth Amendment" (277 U.S. 455). Critics of the theory would consider this result to be a counter-example and would urge that we discard Framers' Intent in favor of a theory of interpretation that allow considerations other than the intent of the framers (see section "Original understanding: Robert Bork" below).

Whether or not we take Olmstead as a destructive counter-example (see section "The democracy argument for originalism"), there are serious epistemological problems with the Framers' Intent theory, among them the implication that we can somehow *discover* the intentions of each of the men who signed and ratified the original document in 1787. "Different framers undoubtedly had very different and even conflicting intentions with respect to many of the provisions that require interpretation" (Altman, 98). Some of the framers may even have intended to protect individual privacy when they voted on the ratification of the Fourth Amendment. Second, it is not obvious that we can identify all of the authors of the Constitution. Who should we include and who should we exclude? For example, the Constitution was ratified by the men attending the conventions held in each of the early colonies. Even if these men carefully read the entire document, we cannot say with any certainty that they attached the same meanings to its provisions as those who wrote the document in Philadelphia.

Finally, there is an important normative question to add to the previous epistemological concerns. Why should the intent of the framers, an elite group of wealthy property owners, not elected by anyone, be given the privilege of determining the final meaning of the Constitution? It is the assumption that they have this privilege that drives the attempts of scholars to determine their intentions. If we deny that there exists a plausible basis for giving them this privilege, then perhaps we can find a better standard to use for constitutional interpretation.

The originalist response to this criticism is to remind the critic that the only option to interpreting the Constitution with reference to the origins of this document is for the Court to use non-originalist criteria, for example the moral ideas or substantive values held by the justices. This is response made by Stewart and Black in *Griswold* (Sect. 4.2.3), and each declares that the judicial use of moral ideas that happen to appeal to them is illegitimate.

Original Understanding: Robert Bork

Constitutional law scholar Robert Bork posited that the only relevant interpretive question the courts should ask is "How was the Constitution and its amendments *understood by the people* at the time of adoption?" He argued that there is no need to make guesses about what the framers were thinking or intending at the time of adoption. It is far easier to examine social history with its many reports about how common people understood the written words of the relevant documents. In *The Tempting of America*, Bork emphasized that originalists should not "search…for a subjective intention," but rather for "what the public of that time would have understood the words to mean" (1990, 7).

Based on this approach Bork contends that the Equal Protection Clause of the Fourteenth Amendment ensured newly freed blacks the same legal rights and privileges that were accorded to whites "because the Amendment was enacted after the Civil War and was understood as ensuring that newly freed blacks would not be discriminated against by state laws" (Altman, 99).

Bork gives the same interpretive analysis of the Cruel and Unusual Punishment clause of the Eighth Amendment. At the time the amendment was ratified (1791), few citizens thought that the death penalty was either cruel or unusual. But most persons did believe that ancient practices of torture such as tar and feathering, whippings, and the rack and screw constituted cruel and unusual punishment. Hence, on the basis of original understanding, although capital punishment is constitutional, torture is not.

We should add that no one in the late eighteenth century understood that women were to be accorded the same rights as men under the new Constitution (Sect. 4.1). They did not have the right to vote, and discrimination on the basis of gender was not affected by the adoption of any of the first ten amendments. We can add the observation that there was no general understanding during that time that parents had a right to teach their children a non-English language, nor that children had a right to either explicit or symbolic freedom of expression while attending public schools.

Bork's main target was the right to privacy. He argued passionately and at length that there is no historical evidence for the claim that ordinary people in the late eighteenth and early nineteenth centuries understood the amendments to the Constitution to include a right that would void all state laws prohibiting contraception or abortion. And since this was not a common understanding of the people during the time of the adoption of the constitutional amendments, Bork concludes that there is no constitutional right to contraception or abortion: "The original understanding of the Constitution's provisions did not include any right to privacy more general than the specific rights enumerated in the document" (Altman, 100).

Does Bork's switch from "intent of the framers" to "understanding of the people" allow him to avoid the central criticism made of the theory of Framers' Intent? That criticism was that no good reason has been provided to tell us why we should defer to the intent of the framers when interpreting the Constitution (section "Framers' intent"). We can ask the same question here. What good reason is there for deferring to the understanding of Americans alive in the early days of the Republic? Why should their understanding of the constitutional provisions put them in a privileged position? Why not defer to the understanding of contemporary U.S. citizens?

Bork's response to this line of criticism is to remind the critic that the only option to interpreting the Constitution with reference to the origins of this document is for the Court to use *non-originalist* criteria, for example the moral ideas or substantive values held by the justices and (perhaps) shared by the majority of the populace at the time they are considering the case. This is also the response made by Stewart and Black in *Griswold* (Sect. 4.2.3). They both declare that the judicial use of moral ideas in reaching a conclusion about constitutionality is illegitimate. Bork goes even further and contends that when this happens the Court becomes a "naked power organ," exercising might without right and illegitimately imposing its own moral views on society. The only views that the Court can legitimately impose on society through constitutional interpretation are those to be found during the time of its origins.

Informed Understanding: Antonin Scalia

The late Supreme Court justice Antonin Scalia gave a succinct description of originalism and "its warts" in a lecture delivered in 1988.

> [Originalism's] greatest defect, in my view, is the difficulty of applying it correctly…But what *is* true is that it is often exceedingly difficult to plumb the original understanding of an ancient text. Properly done, the task requires the consideration of an enormous mass of material–in the case of the Constitution and its Amendments, for example, to mention only one element, the records of the ratifying debates in all the states. Even beyond that, it requires an evaluation of the reliability of that material–many of the reports of the ratifying debates, for example, are thought to be quite unreliable. And further still, it requires immersing oneself in the political and intellectual atmosphere of the time–somehow placing out of mind knowledge that we have which an earlier age did not, and putting on beliefs, attitudes, philosophies, prejudices and loyalties that are not those of our day. It is, in short, a task sometimes better suited to the historian than the lawyer…. (Scalia 1988).

We should first note that this description is not identical to Robert Bork's variety of originalism. Scalia calls on the originalist to do much more than discover the understanding of the people living at the time the Constitution and its amendments were ratified. It is just as important (for a Supreme Court justice and a constitutional scholar) "to immerse oneself in the political and intellectual atmosphere of the time." We can assume that this atmosphere was not available to most citizens. Many were either illiterate or did not have the intelligence, education, time or energy to engage in the political debates of the time. Their understanding of the Constitution and its amendments, unaffected by this heady atmosphere, might not have been the same as the understandings of the educated who participated in the public discussions of the time.

There is ample evidence of Justice Scalia's diligent inquiry into both the understanding of common folk and the political and intellectual culture of the eighteenth century in the decision he wrote for the majority in *District of Columbia* v *Heller* (2008) – the case that held that the Second Amendment protects an individual right to possess firearms.[7] This approach to constitutional interpretation is also evident in cases involving or touching upon family law. Here is part of Scalia's dissent in the recent decision to extend the right of marriage to same-sex persons:

> When the Fourteenth Amendment was ratified in 1868, every State limited marriage to one man and one woman, and no one doubted the constitutionality of doing so. That resolves these cases. When it comes to determining the meaning of a vague constitutional provision—such as "due process of law" or "equal protection of the laws"—it is unquestionable that the People who ratified that provision did not understand it to prohibit a practice that remained both universal and uncontroversial in the years after ratification. We have no basis for striking down a practice that is not expressly prohibited by the Fourteenth Amendment's text, and that bears the endorsement of a long tradition of open, widespread, and unchallenged use dating back to the Amendment's ratification *(Obergefell v Hodges*, 2015).

And in an earlier dissent to a majority decision that struck down a Texas law criminalizing sodomy, Scalia wrote:

> Our opinions applying the doctrine known as "substantive due process" hold that the Due Process Clause prohibits States from infringing fundamental liberty interests, unless the infringement is narrowly tailored to serve a compelling state interest. We have held repeatedly, in cases the Court today does not overrule, that only fundamental rights qualify for this so-called "heightened scrutiny" protection—that is, rights which are "deeply rooted in this Nation's history and tradition." [W] e have insisted not merely that the interest denominated as a 'liberty' be 'fundamental'...but also that it be an interest traditionally protected by our society. (*Lawrence v Kansas* 2003)

In *Obergefell* v *Hodges* (2015) Justice Scalia writes of the "understanding" of those who ratified the Fourteenth Amendment, and refers to a "long tradition" of the unchallenged use of the text of the Fourteenth Amendment. He repeats these words in the last sentence of the preceding quote from *Lawrence* v *Texas*. "The Fourteenth Amendment protects "those privileges long recognized at common law as essential

---

[7] For example, Justice Scalia quotes from a 1794 thesaurus, and two other eighteenth century dictionaries in order to assure readers that the word "arms" in the Second Amendment meant "firearms" or "weapons of offense or armaments of defense." He also traced the individual right to bear arms to 1689 England as the result of the abuses of the Stuart kings Charles II and James II when they used select militias loyal only to them "to suppress political dissidents, in part by disarming their opponents" (Scalia in *Heller*, 59).

to the orderly pursuit of happiness by free men." The original understanding to which he refers is the understanding that the founders have of the common law of England and its American colonies and which served as the basis of much of the early law of the states.

The Democracy Argument for Originalism

Several arguments have been produced in favor of originalism.[8] One of the most popular is "the democracy argument."[9] This argument begins with a statement of *the democracy principle*: only the people or their elected representatives shall legislate, that is, create new law or change existing law. It is assumed that it is always wrong to violate this basic principle. But the democracy principle is necessarily violated when one uses non-originalist considerations. This is because any use by the Supreme Court of non-originalist considerations when interpreting the Constitution would be an act of legislation. This cannot be said of originalist considerations. Strict adherence to the text of a constitutional provision, the intention of those who created it, or the understanding of the law by those to whom the law applied or by those who were part of the "political and intellectual culture" at the time of enactment is perfectly consistent with the democracy principle.

In assessing this argument, we must first determine what constitutes strict adherence to originalist criteria and what does not. In our previous mention of the *Olmstead* decision that wiretapping did not violate the Fourth Amendment's prohibition of unreasonable searches, the stated reason was that the intention of the Framers could only have been to prohibit *physical* intrusions (section "Framers' intent"). The Framers had no knowledge of wiretapping or any other electronic intrusions. Moreover, the original understanding by the people of the Fourth Amendment at the time it was ratified would have been identical to the original intent of the Framers. Suppose, however, that we add a new category of "people" to

---

[8] Douglas Lindner (2011) has organized the following list of pro-originalist arguments: (1) Originalism reduces the likelihood that unelected judges will seize the reins of power from elected representatives. (2) Originalism in the long run better preserves the authority of the Court. (3) Non-originalism allows too much room for judges to impose their own subjective and elitist values. Judges need neutral, objective criteria to make legitimate decisions. The understanding of the framers and ratifiers of a constitutional clause provide those neutral criteria. (4) *Lochner v New York* (widely considered to be a bad non-originalist decision). (5) Leaving it to the people to amend their Constitution when needed promotes serious public debate about government and its limitations. (6) Originalism better respects the notion of the Constitution as a binding contract. (7) If a constitutional amendment passed today, we would expect a court five years from now to ask what we intended to adopt. [Can the same be said for a court 100 or 200 years from now?] (8) Originalism more often forces legislatures to reconsider and possibly repeal or amend their own bad laws, rather than to leave it to the courts to get rid of them.

[9] This is the author's name for the argument.

the larger group whose understanding we wish to consult. The new category is "contemporary people." These are the competent adults who were living at the time that *Olmstead* was being considered by the Supreme Court. Let us suppose that a majority of these people, when consulted, would know about the existence of wiretapping. Let us also assume that a majority of these (contemporary) people would say that *their* understanding of an unreasonable search *does include* wiretapping. On the basis of this information the Court reverses and decides that wiretapping without a warrant is an unreasonable search.[10]

This prompts the question: why does consideration of the people's *contemporary* understanding of what constitutes an unreasonable search constitute an act of judicial legislation (a change in existing law), but consideration of *original* understanding does not? The originalist has no reply to this question. If an appeal to original understanding is consistent with the democratic principle, then so is an appeal to contemporary understanding. In both cases, the Court can argue that it is affirming the right of *the people*, original or contemporary, to make or change the law.

4.4.2 Non-originalism

As stated at Sect. 4.4, the word "non-originalism" refers to any theory of constitutional interpretation that does *not* view the meaning of words and phrases in the Constitution and its amendments as fixed at the time of their origin. This broad definition of non-originalism can be applied to several theories of interpretation that have been offered by both judges and scholars of constitutional law.[11] In this section we will discuss two non-originalist theories, beginning with a theory recently presented by Supreme Court Associate Justice Stephen Breyer.

[10] Olmstead was reversed in 1967 by *Katz v. U.S.*

[11] Lindner (2011) provides a helpful list of some of the arguments in favor of non-originalism: (1) The framers at the Convention in Philadelphia indicated that they did not want their specific intentions to control interpretation. (2) No written Constitution can anticipate all the means that government might in the future use to oppress people, so it is sometimes necessary for judges to fill in the gaps. (3) Intentions of framers are various, sometimes transient, and often impossible to determine. Text is often ambiguous and judicial precedents can be found to support either side. In such cases, why not produce the result that will best promote the public good? It's better than flipping a coin. (4) Non-originalism allows judges to head off the crises that could result from the inflexible interpretation of a provision in the Constitution that no longer serves its original purpose. (The amendment process is too difficult and cannot be relied upon to save us.) (5) Non-originalism allows the Constitution to evolve to match more enlightened understandings on matters such as the equal treatment of blacks, women, and other minorities. (6) *Brown vs Board of Education* (on originalist grounds, it was decided incorrectly). (7) Originalists lose sight of the forest because they pay too much attention to trees. The larger purpose–the animating spirit–of the Constitution was the protection of liberty, and we ought to focus on that. (8) Nazi Germany: Originalist German judges did not exercise the power they might have to prevent or slow down inhumane programs.

Active Liberty: Stephen Breyer

Stephen Breyer defines democracy as "a form of government in which all citizens share the government's authority, participating in the creation of public policy." This democratic participation is what Breyer means by "active liberty." This fits well with the previously mentioned "democracy principle" used to justify originalist theories (section "The democracy argument for originalism"). Both Breyer and his originalist friend and colleague Antonin Scalia take seriously the admonition of the seventeeth century English philosopher John Locke not to put anyone under the political power of another "without his own consent" (Locke, VIII), and Thomas Jefferson's reminder in the Declaration of Independence 100 years later that governments must derive "their just powers from the consent of the governed." Why then does Breyer get classified as a non-originalist?

Breyer veers away from Scalia when he introduces a familiar distinction between ancient and modern liberty. Modern liberty is *negative.* It is the liberty of the individual to be *free from* tyranny, including the tyranny of a majority of citizens in a democracy who would impose their will on a minority unless restrained by law. In the United States it is the freedom guaranteed by the Bill of Rights. Ancient liberty is *positive*. It is the *freedom to* actively participate in the democratic process.

> It consisted of a sharing of a nation's sovereign authority among that nation's citizens. From the citizen's perspective it meant "an active and constant participation in collective power"; it included the citizen's right to "deliberate in the public place," to "vote for war or peace," to "make treaties," to "enact laws," to examine the actions and accounts of those who administer government, and to hold them responsible for their misdeeds (Breyer 2004:3).

Breyer writes that while taking account of the importance of modern liberty, his aim is to call increased attention to active liberty, the principle of participatory self-government that is found in ancient discussions of liberty (13). His thesis is that courts should take greater account of the constitution's democratic nature when they interpret constitutional and statutory texts. Breyer's thesis

> …finds in the constitution's democratic objective not simply restraint on judicial power or an ancient counterpart of more modern protection but also a source of judicial power and an interpretive aid to more effective protection of ancient and modern liberty alike. It finds a basic perspective that helps make sense of our constitution's structure, illuminating aspects that otherwise seem less coherent (5).

Breyer offers several examples of Supreme Court cases to illustrate his thesis. The examples are drawn from the areas of free speech, federalism, privacy, equal protection, statutory interpretation, and review of administrative action.

> Each example considers modern government-related problems that call for a democratically based response. and each raises difficult questions of constitutional or statutory interpretation. In each instance I shall explain why I believe that increased recognition of the constitution's democratic objectives (along with an appreciation of the role courts have to play in securing those objectives) can help judges deal more effectively with the interpretive issues, thereby helping communities deal better with the problems that have called those issues into being (21).

In order to see how this applies to family law cases, we will restrict discussion to the area of free speech, and in particular, children's speech in public schools, as illustrated earlier by *Tinker v Des Moines School District* (Sect. 4.2). How does Breyer's "increased recognition of the constitution's democratic objectives" help us interpret and apply the First Amendment in this case?

Breyer's first instruction is to read the First amendment, not in isolation, but as seeking to maintain a system of free expression itself designed to further a basic constitutional purpose: creating and maintaining democratic decision-making institutions. Second, Breyer would attempt to classify children's speech. Is it political speech or is it more like some other type of speech, for example commercial speech or economic regulation. This is important because political speech, unlike other types calls for a strong pro-speech presumption. Third, these presumptions are needed so we do not put "active liberty" at risk. Fourth, "That special risk … also justifies careful review where the speech in question seeks to shape public opinion, particularly where that opinion in turn will affect the political process and the kind of society in which we live" (23).

> To understand the First amendment as seeking in significant part to protect active liberty, "participatory self-government," is to understand it as protecting more than the individual's "negative" freedom. It is to understand the amendment as seeking to facilitate a conversation among ordinary citizens that will encourage their informed participation in the electoral process. It is to suggest a constitutional purpose that goes beyond protecting the individual from government restriction of information about matters that the constitution commits to individual, not collective, decision-making. It is to understand the First amendment as seeking primarily to encourage the exchange of information and ideas necessary for citizens themselves to shape that public opinion which is the final source of government in a democratic state. In these ways the amendment helps to maintain a form of government open to participation (in Constant's words) "by all citizens without exception" (26–27).

The obvious question to ask is whether the purpose of protecting active liberty applies to the speech of school children? Does a guarantee of free speech while at school, represented symbolically by the Tinker children's black arm bands, "facilitate a conversation among ordinary citizens that will encourage their informed participation in the electoral process"? Will it "encourage the exchange of information and ideas" necessary to shape public opinion? Children in the school who saw the armbands and asked the Tinker children about their symbolic meaning were not old enough to qualify as *participants in the electoral process*, although the armbands might have encouraged an exchange of information and ideas among the children and their parents about the Vietnam war and the justification for a U.S. military presence in that country.

"Basic democratic objectives, including some of a kind that the First amendment seeks to further, lie on both sides of the constitutional equation" (27). Seen in terms of "modern liberty," Breyer points out, these objectives would include protection of the citizen's speech from government interference. But seen in terms of "active liberty," they include promotion of a democratic conversation. The *Tinker* court appears to be interested only modern liberty – protecting children's speech from the interference of their school and the school district. This led the Court majority to almost *automatically* find that the decision to suspend the children from school to be an unconstitutional violation of the children's free speech rights. ("All persons have the constitutional right to freedom of speech. School children are persons. Therefore, school children have the constitutional right to freedom of speech."). But a "Breyer court," I believe, would not reach an easy conclusion. Seen in terms of active liberty, this hypothetical court would ask whether a "democratic conversation" would be promoted by giving school children the same speech rights enjoyed by university students or by the general adult population. The answer would probably be "no" because until they come of age, there is no electoral process in which children can participate (other than school elections). Hence, a Breyer court would be much less inclined than is the majority in *Tinker* to extend full free speech rights to school children.

If the purpose of the First Amendment is "first and foremost" to facilitate democratic self-government, then the speech of school children while in school fails to advance this purpose. It might even be said that this speech is not political at all, even while pretending to be such. The Tinker children were *practicing* political speech, no doubt imitating the speech of their parents. This is not to deny that imitation has value, especially if we want our children to actively engage in the political process as adults. It is the kind of *speech-related* activity that calls for a "totally relaxed presumption of unconstitutionality," rather than the strict presumption of unconstitutionality that we give to political speech (22).

If the Tinker children's speech is not political, their speech did convey to some of the other children in their school that they had strong negative feelings about the U.S. military presence in Vietnam. But in conveying this they were not contributing to the *public debate* outside of the school about the relative merits of the war. Symbolic displays of their beliefs, while important, are not so important that they justify striking down school district rules that regulate children's speech for sound reasons related to the traditional community regulation of public schools. Breyer might even join the *Tinker* dissenters and argue that a contrary view of the First amendment standard fails to further, indeed it impedes, the workings of a democratically determined school regulatory system. It restricts the Des Moines school district's regulatory powers, preventing the local schools from achieving related objectives that the community democratically determines to be important.

This does not mean that the First amendment leaves the public schools free to enact any rule it wishes to regulate children's speech. "Traditional, 'modern liberty'—the individual's freedom from government restriction—remains important" even though ancient liberty—the freedom to participate in democratic government—is not. Children need information in order to make decisions about their own lives, and, irrespective of context, "a particular rule affecting their speech might, in a particular instance, require them to act against conscience" (for example, a rule that prohibits them from saying a prayer important to their religion). Other rules might threaten a child's artistic expression, censor views in ways unrelated to the school's basic objectives, or create other risks of abuse. In each of these cases, those who wish to restrict children's speech must override the soft presumption in favor of freedom of speech. The burden is on those who would write and apply the rules.

Natural Law: Ronald Dworkin

In his dissent in *Griswold* Justice Black accuses justices who wrote the majority opinions of injecting "formulas based on natural justice" into their concurring decisions. This is a serious charge. It implies that these justices used moral principles that are not found in the Constitution. Black forcefully reminds the court that there is no provision in the Constitution that gives the Supreme Court the power to measure the constitutionality of a state law based on the "belief that legislation is arbitrary, capricious or unreasonable, or accomplishes no justifiable purpose, or is offensive to our own notions of 'civilized standards of conduct." The use of these standards to appraise legislation "is an attribute of the power to *make* laws, not of the power to *interpret* them." The Supreme Court has *only* the power to interpret laws.

Justice Black quotes passages from the opposing opinions of several of his colleagues on the Court: Douglas, Goldberg, Harlan and White. I have italicized the suspect phrases:

> Specific guarantees in the Bill of Rights have penumbras, formed by emanations from those guarantees that help give them life and substance... Various guarantees create *zones of privacy*... The present case, then, concerns a relationship lying within the zone of privacy created by several fundamental constitutional guarantees. (Douglas, opinion of Court, 381)

> In determining which rights are fundamental, judges are not left at large to decide cases in light of their personal and private notions. Rather, they must look to the "traditions and [collective] conscience of our people" to determine whether a principle is "so rooted [there] ... as to be ranked as fundamental." *Snyder v. Massachusetts*. The inquiry is whether a right involved is of such a character that it cannot be denied without violating those "*fundamental principles of liberty and justice* which lie at the base of all our civil and political institutions." ... (Goldberg, concurring, 493)

> In my view, the proper constitutional inquiry in this case is whether this Connecticut statute infringes the Due Process Clause of the Fourteenth Amendment because the enactment violates *basic values "implicit in the concept of ordered liberty,"*... While the relevant inquiry may be aided by resort to one or more of the provisions of the Bill of Rights, it is not dependent on them or any of their radiations. The Due Process Clause of the Fourteenth Amendment stands, in my opinion, on its own bottom. (Harlan, concurring, 500)

> It would be unduly repetitious, and belaboring the obvious, to expound on the impact of this statute on the liberty guaranteed by the Fourteenth Amendment against arbitrary or capricious denials or on the nature of this liberty. Suffice it to say that this is not the first time this Court has had occasion to articulate that the liberty entitled to protection under the Fourteenth Amendment includes *the right "to marry, establish a home and bring up children," ...and that these are among "the basic civil rights of man."* ...These decisions affirm that there is a "realm of family life which the state cannot enter" without substantial justification... Surely the right invoked in this case, to be free of regulation of the intimacies of the marriage relationship come [s] to this Court with a momentum for respect lacking when appeal is made to liberties which derive merely from shifting economic arrangements. (White, concurring, 503).

Justice Black does not dispute either the objectivity or the truth of the moral principles, values and rights enunciated above by justices Douglas, Goldberg,

Harlan and White. Instead, his claims are: (1) that these "natural justice" principles are not explicit in the Constitution, and therefore (2) although it is certainly justifiable for a state legislature to use them when creating or changing a law regulating "the intimacies of the marriage relationship," (3) it is not justifiable for members of the Court to refer to such principles, rights and values when constructing a decision about the constitutionality of a state law.

There is one legal philosopher in the twentieth century who mounted a vigorous defense of his own unique version of the natural law approach to interpreting the provisions of the Constitution and its amendments. I have discussed some of his ideas about the relationship between law and morals in earlier chapters (Sects. 2.5 and 3.5.4). Ronald Dworkin there maintained that it is impossible to construct an adequate theory about the nature of law and legal systems without mentioning the *moral principles* that were used by their authors to construct them. This also applies to the Constitution. We need to know the content of the moral principles that were not only explicitly used by the framers to justify its provisions, but the implicit principles that could justify the provisions if we were called upon to do this. And since the justices of the Supreme Court are the only persons authorized to interpret and apply the Constitution in deciding cases, it is not only appropriate but necessary to discover and apply these underlying principles.

Dworkin's "interpretive" version of natural law theory can serve as a philosophical defense of the approach taken by the Court majority in *Griswold.* In deciding a difficult constitutional case Dworkin would counsel the justices to think about the Constitution as the expression of an underlying "philosophy of government." The task is to identify the "strongest" philosophy of government that could justify the provisions of the Constitution and its amendments. The standard to determine whether one philosophy of government P is stronger than another Q is "true morality." P is stronger than Q if P reflects more of the true morality than Q. Of course this prompts the question "How are the justices to identify true morality?"

Dworkin's answer to this question begins with his distinction between *moral concepts* and *moral conceptions*. The Fourteenth Amendment is a good example of this distinction. It contains the concept of equality. As a formal concept the idea of equal treatment simply means treating like cases alike and different cases differently. However, the formal concept does not help resolve disputes about equal treatment because it does not tell us when two or more cases are relevantly alike or different. If it is decided that blue-eyed people will no longer be allowed to vote in federal elections, the formal definition of equality is of no help to those who think this is a violation of equality. It could be argued that blue-eyed people are in fact treated as equals because they are receiving different treatment as a response to their difference in eye color. What is needed is a standard of *relevant* differences that will exclude eye-color. Dworkin refers to this supplementary standard as a *conception.*

In the mid-nineteenth century the concept of equality was not understood by most people to include race, gender or sexual preference. Differences between persons in these respects were not part of their conception of equality. Everyone assumed that segregation of the races, prohibiting women from voting, and restricting marriage to one man and one woman did not constitute unequal treatment under the Fourteenth Amendment. In the late twentieth and early twentieth century, however, the conception of equality has radically changed. Race and gender are now largely seen as irrelevant differences between persons when legal burdens or benefits are distributed. And many U.S. states have made the same moral judgement about the way they legally treat same-sex persons under their marriage laws.

We can incorporate this into Dworkin's idea of "true morality." A morality is true when it contains the *best conception of a concept*. Hence, the true morality that makes one philosophy of government stronger than another is the one that has developed the best conception of the moral concepts explicitly espoused by those who wrote and ratified the Constitution. We have a "better understanding" of the conception of equality than people generally had in the mid-nineteenth century because our conception treats race, gender and sexual preference as irrelevant when making decisions about equal treatment.

Dworkin's theory of constitutional interpretation can be used to support Justice Douglas' finding in *Griswold* that the Constitution can be interpreted as containing a general right to privacy that goes beyond those rights explicitly mentioned in the text. Dworkin does not use the colorful language of "penumbras," "halos," or "emanations." Instead he uses the word "underlying" to characterize the relationship of the best philosophy of government to the enumerated provisions of the Bill of Rights. The particular philosophy of government Dworkin employs is the liberal conception of treating persons with equal concern and respect (Dworkin 1977, 262–3).

> Respect is of particular significance here. To treat persons with equal respect is to treat them as equally capable of forming and acting on intelligent conceptions of how their lives should be lived. An individual's right to equal respect is violated when his liberty is limited on the grounds that his conception of the good is less worthy than that of others, or when he is not treated as an equal, that is, when his concerns and wishes are not accorded equal weight with those of others in political decisions (Schopp, 98).

In *Griswold* the Connecticut statute that was struck down by the Court does not treat persons "as equally capable of forming and acting on intelligent conceptions of how their lives should be lived." By limiting the liberty of married couples to make their own decisions about contraception the state has done so in a way that fails to respect their conception of what constitutes a good marital relationship and family, substituting for it a religious conception disguised as a state prohibition.

The criticisms of Dworkin's interpretive theory are similar to those made earlier about his general theory of law (Sect. 2.5.3). The argument that the strongest philosophy of government is the one that best represents true morality looks suspiciously circular when we analyze true morality in terms of the best conceptions of the Constitution's moral concepts. In order to escape the circle Dworkin needs an independent argument proving that the conceptions used in cases like *Griswold* are better than the conceptions used in the mid-nineteenth century. Second, there may be some other philosophy of government represented by the Constitution than the one enunciated by Dworkin. It may prove to have the same kind of fit and perform the same task of justification. This possibility should alert us that there is not one and only one legitimate philosophy of government. Third, "we still need to know why the best conception of the Constitution's moral concepts should dictate the meaning of the document" (Altman, 105). Why not the conceptions of liberty and equality generally accepted in society at the current time, whether or not some philosophers have better ones? Fourth, there is the criticism of Justices Black and Stewart that philosophical questions about the true morality and the strongest philosophy of government are questions to be answered by the legislature, not by the judiciary. It is not the business of the Supreme Court to answer these or other moral and political questions as part of a judicial decision.

Questions for Thought and Discussion

1. Describe how Breyer's approach to constitutional interpretation might be used to decide the constitutionality of the *Meyer v Nebraska* case.
2. Describe how an originalist theory might be used to decide the constitutionality of the *Griswold v Connecticut* case.
3. Describe how Dworkin's Interpretive theory might be used to decide the constitutionality of the *Tinker v Des Moines School District* case.
4. Can you think of any good reason why we should prefer one of the several theories of constitutional interpretation to any of the others? Is there a good reason to prefer Original Understanding (for example) to Dworkin's Interpretative theory? Explain.
5. How would an originalist like Justice Scalia respond to the criticism that his theory of interpretation makes it impossible for the Constitution "to evolve to match more enlightened understandings on matters such as the equal treatment of blacks, women, and other minorities"? (Lindner 2011)
6. How would a non-originalist like Justice Breyer respond to the criticism that his theory of constitutional interpretation "allows too much room for judges to impose their own subjective and elitist values"? (Lindner 2011).

References

Altman, Andrew. 2001. *Arguing About Law: An Introduction to Legal Philosophy*. Belmont: Wadsworth.

Black, Hugo. 1960, April. The Bill of Rights. *New York University Law Review*, Vol. 35.

Bork, Robert. 1990. *The Tempting of America*. New York: Free Press.

Breyer, Stephen. 2004. Active Liberty: Interpreting Our Democratic Constitution. *The Tanner Lectures on Human Values*.http://tannerlectures.utah.edu/_documents/a-to-z/b/Breyer_2006.pdf. Accessed 21 Sept 2016.

———. 2005. *Active Liberty: Interpreting Our Democratic Constitution*. New York: Random House.

Chisholm v Georgia 2 US 419 (1793).

Dworkin, R. 1988. *Law's Empire*. Harvard University Press.

———., eds. 1997. *The Philosophy of Law*. New York: Oxford University Press.

Fallon, Richard H. 1999. How to Choose a Constitutional Theory. 87 *California Law Review* 535.

Ferguson v. Skrupa, 372 U.S. 726 (1963).

Griswold v Connecticut, 381 U. S. 479 (1965).

Lewis, Jone Johnson. 2014. Women in U.S. Constitutional History: Sex Discrimination. http://womenshistory.about.com/od/laws/a/Constitution-Sex-Discrimination.htm. Accessed 8 Apr 2016.

Lindner, Douglas. 2011. Theories of Constitutional Interpretation. http://law2.umkc.edu/faculty/projects/ftrials/conlaw/interp.html

Marbury v. Madison, 5 U.S. 137 (1803).

Meyer v Nebraska, 262 U.S. 390 (1923).

Pierce v Society of Sisters, 268 U.S. 510 (1924).

Planned Parenthood of Southeastern Pennsylvania v Casey, 505 U.S. 833 (1992).

Post, Robert C. 1990. Theories of Constitutional Interpretation. *Faculty Scholarship Series*. Paper 209. http://digitalcommons.law.yale.edu/fss_papers/209/. Accessed 8 Apr 2016.

Scalia, Antonin. 1988. Originalism: The Lesser Evil. 57 *University of Cincinnati L. Rev.* 849.

———. 1997. *A Matter of Interpretation: Federal Courts and the Law*. Princeton: Princeton University Press.

Schopp, R.F. 2016. Education and Contraception Make Strange Bedfellows: *Brown, Griswold, Lochner* and the Putative Dilemma of Liberalism. *College of Law, Faculty Publications Paper 98*. http://digitalcommons.unl.edu/lawfacpub/98/. Accessed 8 Apr 2016.

Smith v. California, 361 U.S. 147 (1959).

Tinker v. Des Moines Independent Community School District, 393 U.S. 503 (1969)

West's Encyclopedia of American Law, 2nd edn. 2008. New York: The Gale Group, Inc.

Part II
State Intervention in the Family

Chapter 5
The Moral Limits of Family Law

> *"The only part of conduct of any one, for which he is amenable to society, is that which concerns others. In the part which merely concerns himself, his independence is, of right, absolute. Over himself, over his own body and mind, the individual is sovereign."*
>
> John Stuart Mill, *On Liberty* (1860)

Abstract Questions about the moral limits of state intervention have usually been asked about intervention in the actions of individuals, and only rarely asked about intervention in the behavior of families. In this chapter we will discuss these questions as they pertain to families by using the same normative principles employed in familiar discussions about the limits of state intervention in the conduct of individuals: harm-to-others, legal paternalism, and moralism. In this discussion we will introduce and critically examine the doctrine of family privacy which says that the state has no business intervening in internal family conduct which does not harm the interests of anyone outside the family. Using the language of J.S. Mill (quoted in the epigraph), we will ask whether it is true to say "Over itself, over its own members, *the family* is sovereign." Before we attempt to answer this question we need to respond to the objection that questions about the limits of state intervention wrongly assume that there is a concept of the family that is pre-political or pre-legal. It has been argued that this assumption is false because the family, like the personal, is essentially political. Is the assumption false? Or is there a concept of family that allows us to refer meaningfully to unjust or wrongful legal interventions in family life?

5.1 Legal Intervention in the Family

In Chap. 4 we examined three normative theories of interpretation, each informing us of the best way to determine the *constitutional* limits of family law: the limits set by the U.S. Constitution regarding the amount and kind of control that parents should have over their children's education, that married couples should have over

L.D. Houlgate, *Philosophy, Law and the Family*, AMINTAPHIL: The Philosophical Foundations of Law and Justice 7,
DOI 10.1007/978-3-319-51121-4_5

their family planning choices, and that children should have over the amount and kind of freedom of expression they can exercise as students. In this chapter we will look generally at the *moral* limits of family law. To what extent is the state *justified* in creating legal rules allowing the state to intervene in the family? Although this question is yet to be clarified, it is a question that thoughtful legislators attempt to answer when they consider whether a proposed statute requiring intervention in marriage or family is or is not justifiable. Typical questions include rules on access to marriage ("Should same-sex persons be allowed to marry?"), family planning ("Should a married couple be allowed to abort a pregnancy?"), child-rearing decisions ("Should child abuse standards be modified to prohibit parents from using corporal punishment as a means of disciplining their children?"), and access to legal remedies for injuries caused by a spouse or parent ("Should a person be immunized from liability when their negligent conduct has caused injury to their spouse?" "Should parents be similarly immunized when the person they have injured is their child?").

Questions about the moral limits of family law are similar, but not identical to questions about the nature of the relationship between law and morals asked in Chaps. 2 and 3. We were there concerned with the debate between natural law theory and legal positivism about the possible existence of a necessary connection between law and morality. If natural law theory "wins" that debate, then this would provide a natural law answer to the question about limits: the positive law can demand no more of us than what is demanded under the natural law.[1] Any positive law that fails to prohibit immoral conduct, as determined by the law of nature, is to be declared invalid. However, if the legal positivists are correct about their claim that there is no necessary relationship between legal validity and the moral content of a law, then questions about the justifiable limits of positive law still remain. To quote John Austin again, "The existence of law is one thing; its merit or demerit is another. Whether it be or be not is one enquiry; whether it be or be not conformable to an assumed standard, is a different enquiry" (Austin, Lecture V). Having settled the question of existence (validity), a legal positivist can now raise a question about the standard we should apply to determine whether a valid law exceeds the justifiable limits of state intervention.

Questions in philosophy of law textbooks about the limits of the law are almost always asked in the context of the criminal law. This is undoubtedly because the criminal law imposes mandatory rules prohibiting what most would regard as "serious" or "important" kinds of wrongdoing: for example, murder, manslaughter, assault, rape, arson, kidnapping, robbery, burglary. Violations of these rules are responded to with various kind of punishment: loss of liberty (imprisonment), loss of property (fines and confiscation), and in some cases death by execution. It is largely because of the kinds of punishment imposed on those found guilty of a

[1] "[The legislative] power, in the utmost bounds of it, is *limited to the public good of* the society. It is a power, that hath no other end but preservation, and therefore can never have a right to destroy, enslave, or designedly to impoverish the subjects.... Thus, the law of nature stands as an eternal rule to all men, legislators as well as others" (Locke, XI, 135).

crime that the question about the limits of the criminal law arises: What is the dividing line between those behaviors that we regard as suitable for criminal prohibition and punishment and those behaviors that we believe cannot justifiably be prohibited by the criminal law?

Family law is not as amenable as is the criminal law to questions about its "limits." As explained in Chap. 1, this is partly because most of the laws affecting the family, unlike criminal and tort laws, have functions that are not mandatory (Sect. 1.2). For example, the rules governing marriage have the function of empowering people to change their status from "unmarried" to "married," thereby voluntarily imposing upon themselves new obligations and rights. It is not clear that a question about the "limits" of marriage law would have any meaning. And yet legislators and voters historically have had contentious debates about limiting the *qualifications* of those who will be granted the legal right to enter into the marital relationship, as seen in the debates over miscegenation (Sect. 2.2) and as will later be illustrated in contemporary debates about same-sex marriage (Sect. 9.4). There is also a long history of legal intervention in the marital relationship itself, for example, laws prohibiting the use of artificial methods of contraception,[2] restrictions on abortion,[3] and punishment for adultery.[4] Perhaps this is where we can find some commonality between the limits of criminal and family law. The limits of criminal law are about the kinds of behavior that are justifiably prohibited by mandatory law. The limits of marriage law are about the restrictions justifiably imposed by the state to prevent some persons from marrying, and about the kinds of behavior that can justifiably be practiced within the confines of the marital relationship.

There is a preliminary question that needs to be answered before we can begin a search about the limits of family law. There are some who argue that there is no line between the area in which society may legitimately use family law to regulate and control conduct and the area in which family law may not legitimately be used. They contend that this is because "family" is essentially a political concept. It is defined by the law. Hence, by definition, the law always and necessarily intervenes in the family. But if this is true, then it is impossible to ask about the extent to which the state ought to intervene in the family. To ask whether the state ought to intervene in the family would be as empty a question as one that asks whether bachelors ought to be unmarried. We need to respond to this conceptual challenge before we can begin to inquire (in Sect. 5.3) about the justifiable limits of family law.

---

[2] "Beginning in the 1800s, laws in the United States prohibited birth control, when temperance and anti-vice groups advocated outlawing birth control devices and information about birth control devices. These groups considered birth control information to be obscene, a belief that was popular enough that in 1873 Congress passed the Comstock Act outlawing the dissemination of birth control devices or information through the mail. Most states followed suit by passing their own laws outlawing the advertising, sale, and distribution, of contraception." (Anon., *Find Law,*2016b).

[3] Until 1967 abortion was classified as a felony in 49 states (Anon., *Chicago Tribune*, 2016a).

[4] "Under the law of many states, a single act of adultery constitutes a crime, whereas in others, there must be an ongoing and notorious relationship. The punishment set by statute may be greater for an individual who engages in repeated acts of adultery than for one who commits an isolated act" (*West's Encyclopedia of American Law, 2nd edition*. 2008).

5.2 Is "Family" a Political Concept?

There is a position within the philosophy of family law which holds that the family and the moral obligations of family life are one thing and the legal obligations created by family law are quite another. Let us call this the *traditional* position.[5] For example, in his description of the pre-political state of nature (Sect. 2.3.2), John Locke writes that a family is created when a man and a woman make a "voluntary compact" between them, which "consist chiefly in such a communication and right in one another's bodies as is necessary to its chief end, procreation (Locke, 1980, Ch. VII). When children are born, the parents are, "by the law of nature, *under an obligation to preserve, nourish, and educate the children* they had begotten" (Ch. VI). Although Locke believes that legal obligations created by political or civil society should generally imitate the obligations of "conjugal society" (marriage) and parenthood, he makes it clear that these family obligations are moral, existing entirely in the state of nature prior to the existence of civil society. Neither the family nor the moral obligations of family membership logically depend on the existence of positive law.

The traditional position separating moral and legal family obligations is not to be confused with Locke's natural law theory of the relationship between positive and natural family law. It is one thing to say that a positive family law is not valid unless it conforms to the natural law. It is quite another to say that the family and the moral obligations in family relationships can exist independently (in the state of nature) of a civil society with a legal system that creates positive family laws.

Second, the distinction made by the traditionalist between moral and legal familial obligation is not to be confused with some of the versions of the distinction often made between the *public* and *private* spheres of family life and behavior. One of the several uses of the *public/private distinction*[6] is to mark off those areas of family life into which the law ought to intervene from those into which it ought not to intervene. But for the traditionalist there is no necessary correlation between this use of the private/public distinction, on the one hand, and the moral and legal obligations of family life, on the other. Some traditionalists argue that there are important moral obligations of family life that ought to be public, that is, enforced by positive family law (for example, the obligations of parents not to injure, torture, sell, or kill their children). But there are other less important obligations, which some traditionalists believe ought to be private, that is, they are not the law's business (for example, the obligation of parents to teach their children about sexual behavior and its consequences).

---

[5] Some of those whose writings imply some version of the traditionalist position include Jean-Jacques Rousseau *On the Social Contract*, 1769; John Locke, *Second Treatise of Government*, 1690, Ch. VI and VII; and William James, A Review of Women's Suffrage, 1869, 362. More recently, traditionalist views have been espoused by Blustein, *Parents and Children*, 1982; Schoeman, *Rights of Children*, 1980; and Mohr, *The Case for Gay Marriage*, 1995.

[6] The public/private distinction has been variously used to distinguish (1) the unknown and unobserved from that which is known or observed; (2) the sphere of the "free" in which others do not or ought not interfere from the sphere in which others do or ought to interfere; and (3) individuals and perhaps small, voluntary groups from larger, more anonymous and non-voluntary groups. (See Gavison 1992).

When characterizing the public/private distinction the traditionalist typically uses the terms "intervention" and "non-intervention". That is, when an area of family life is believed to be public, this is expressed by saying that the law ought to intervene and/or enforce the corresponding moral obligation. If an area of life is believed to be private, this is expressed by saying that the law ought not to intervene and/or enforce the corresponding moral obligation.[7]

In recent years, the meaningfulness of the distinction between legal intervention and non-intervention in the family has been questioned, as has the corresponding distinction between public and private spheres of family life. We will call this the *radical position*.[8] The radical argues there is no such thing as the family as a separate and distinct entity into which the state sometimes legally intervenes. This view is sometimes expressed in a maxim that sums up the radical's position on the relationships between the family and family law. The maxim, now famous, is: "*The personal is political.*" In the present context this is taken to mean that the family itself is political, that is, law and social policy together determine which groups of persons count as a family and which do not, and what rights and duties people have within family groups. It follows that the notion of a private sphere of family life that is immune from state intervention is "incoherent" (Olsen 1985, 383). The terms "intervention" and "nonintervention" are meaningless. There is "no logical basis for considering any particular set of policies nonintervention" (*id.*). A legislative decision not to legally enforce parental duties is a political choice as much as is the decision to enforce them. Both choices can be characterized as examples of intervention in the family. "As long as the state exists and enforces any laws at all, it makes political choices" (*id.*). Since the state constantly defines and redefines the family and adjusts and readjusts roles within the family, there can be no such thing as non-intervention. The legal system *must* intervene in the family.

What would satisfy the claim of the traditionalist that the moral obligations of family life are one thing but the obligations of family law are quite another? What would count as a case of legal intervention in the family? Why does the radical reject these cases? Is legal intervention in the family only a myth? The object of this chapter is to clarify the relationship between family morality and family law in a variety of legal situations so that we have a better grasp of the kind of case to be included in the traditionalist claim that the idea of legal intervention in the family is a coherent notion. This analysis will provide the groundwork for a critical examina-

[7] A contemporary example of the traditionalist position is in Ferdinand Schoeman's influential essay. He defines the family as "an intense continuing and intimate organization of at least one adult and child, wherein the child is extensively and profoundly dependent on the adult, in which the adult supplies the child with its emotional and material needs, and in which the parent is dependent on the child for a certain kind of intimacy." (1980, pp. 9–10). Schoeman concludes this passage with the remark that "this relationship is to be understood as moral, not biological." He then argues that because the family is an intimate organization, it must be accorded privacy and autonomy, that is, legislators have an obligation to enact legislation that guarantees that others (including the state itself) will be excluded "from scrutinizing obtrusions into family occurrences." (p. 10).

[8] Some of those who hold some version of the radical position include Dworkin 1987, pp. 97, 122, 155–159; MacKinnon 1987, p. 100; Minow 1985; Olsen 1984, 1985.

tion of the radical claim that the very ideas of family and family law are somehow essentially related. Unless we clarify the idea of legal intervention itself we will not be in a position to assess this important second part of the radical thesis that the personal is political.

5.2.1 Relationship of Family Law to the Concept of Family

Is the radical correct in her claim that there is an *essential* relationship between family law and the concept of family? There are several possible interpretations of this claim.

First, the radical may have in mind no more than the empirical point that legal systems provide definitions of marriage and family and establish rules that set roles within the family. When confronted with a case in which there is something that we would call a family or a marriage the definition of which is not provided by the rules of a legal system she may simply limit her generalization and admit that there are exceptions to her claim.

Second, the radical may wish to put forward a moral demand. The claim might be construed as "it is morally undesirable for the state to refrain from intervention; it ought to define the family and roles within the family." The person who holds this view reacts to instances where the state does not intervene by regulating or defining the family in this way: (1) she doesn't withdraw her statement or claim, even when we provide examples of societies that refuse to intervene in the family; and (2) she is not necessarily inclined to say such things as "these are not really families."

Third, the claim that the state *must* intervene in the family may be understood as a conceptual remark. Something is being said about the *concept* of the family. This, I think, is the most favored interpretation of "the family is political." But exactly what is it that is being said? Let us look at three quite different analyses of the conceptual relationship between law and the concept of family.

(a) Some philosophers believe that all concepts of right and wrong, duty and obligation, justice and injustice are essentially linked to the law.[9] For them a necessary condition for the existence of rights or obligations is that there is a legal rule conferring such rights and obligations. Such philosophers may also believe that the family is defined in terms of rights and obligations. They might, then, conclude that there could not be families that exist independently of legal systems. They would reach this conclusion because they believe there exists some necessary connection between rights and obligations and the law. This is one possible line of argument, but it has all the limitations associated with the view that there are no obligations and rights independently of legal systems, that is, it has all the limitations associated with a failure to retain the distinction between what *is* and what *ought* to be law (Sect. 3.3.2).

[9] See, for example Hobbes Chap. 13.

(b) The connection between a group of persons being a family in a particular society *S* and *S* having laws defining the family and regulating conduct within the family might be like the connection between being a bachelor and being unmarried. That is, if *S* had no laws defining the family and regulating conduct within the family, then there would be no families in *S*. If there were any groups in *S* of two persons of the opposite sex who mated, procreated and resided permanently with their children, this philosopher would say, "Such groups are not really families." The radical might further object that since zones of privacy are defined and created by the legal system, this must be regarded as a kind of legal intervention. If so, this would make it conceptually impossible for there to be a "private" sphere of family life from which government should be barred. The state intervenes by virtue of the fact that it has created by law the very area that it makes private.

In reply, we should notice that the radical assumes that a state decision *not* to legally intervene in the family is to be construed as a kind of intervention. Although this assumption *guarantees* the conclusion that a sphere of family privacy does not exist, it gets to this conclusion at too dear a price. For the radical has now made her hypothesis that the state always intervenes in the family completely *untestable,* and therefore immune from refutation. On her view, the state *could never fail* to intervene in the family. For not only does the state intervene when it prohibits or requires conduct of family members, but it also intervenes when it does *not* prohibit or require conduct of family members! In other words, she has so defined the concept of legal non-intervention that no example of non-intervention that we choose to submit could possibly count as evidence against her hypothesis. It follows that her conclusion that there is no such thing as non-intervention is *logically empty.*

I think that what might have led the radical to this unfortunate result is that she correctly notices that the family is something more than a group of genetically related persons. Although a biologist might use the word "family" to indicate a group of genetically related individuals, the primary use of "family" is normative. That is, it is used to refer to a group of persons (not all of whom may be genetically related) who have rights and obligations with respect to each other (for example, the obligation of parents to satisfy the needs of their young children, and the correlative right of young children to have their needs satisfied by their parents [Macklin 1988]). Since legal systems define and enforce rights and obligations, the radical wrongly concludes that the concept of family must be connected in meaning with the concept of a legal system. But it seems clear that the concepts of family and law are not connected in this way. Not all rights and obligations are legal. Some are moral; others are derived from the (quasi-legal) proscriptions of religion and cultural mores.

(c) There is a third way in which the concepts of family and family law might be conceptually connected. It might be argued that these concepts stand to each other in the way that the legs of a chair stand to the idea of a chair. "Neither the absence nor the presence of such a feature is determinative of a thing being of a certain kind though it is *relevant* to a thing's being of a certain kind" (Morris,

1976). One can imagine a chair without legs, and the presence of legs is not sufficient to make something a chair. However, the absence or presence of legs is certainly relevant to (evidence for) a thing being (or not being) a chair.

In order to decide whether the concepts of family and family law stand to each other in this way let us imagine two different types of legal system both of which lack family law (that is, neither system contains laws that affect or concern persons by virtue of their status as a family member): (1) A system in which all laws are the result of either formal legislative enactment or precedent-setting decisions of the courts. (2) A legal system that in all relevant respects is like the preceding system with the single exception that in this system customary (moral) rules are regarded as an important source of law.

With respect to system (1), the question before us is not whether the presence of family law is a necessary condition for the existence of a normative concept of family, but whether its absence in a legal system is *relevant* to a determination that persons in that society lacked a normative concept of family. To put it another way, if family laws were entirely absent, would this weigh against our saying that persons in that society possessed a normative concept of family?

I have said that a normative concept is one the definition of which employs such ethical terms as "obligation," and "rights." Accordingly, a normative concept of "family" would be one in which the family is defined as a social group made up of persons who are related to each other by particular obligations and rights. One way to discover whether members of a social group possess this concept is to ask whether they have a critical reflective attitude about the rules governing family relationships.[10] For example, do they generally regard violations of the rules as lapses or faults open to criticism? Do they meet threatened lapses with pressure for conformity? Is the fact that a rule has been violated regarded as a good reason for making the criticism?

Since the only source of law in (1) is legislative enactment and judicial precedent, we need much more information about the beliefs and attitudes of those who are subject to the law if we are to answer these questions. Suppose, for example, that there is only one person (a monarch) who decides what law in the society is and that person has no interest in legislating rules pertaining to the family. It is doubtful that we would take the absence of family law in this society as at all relevant to the question whether its members had a normative concept of family. That the monarch does not enact any family law might show that he or she does not regard family relationships as important, but we can draw no conclusions from this either about what his or her subjects might think about the importance of family relationships or (consequently) whether they have a normative concept of family.

If we turn now to a consideration of legal system (2) described above, there is a much stronger pull toward the conclusion that persons in this system lack a norma-

[10] Hart refers to this feature as the "internal aspect" of rules. If a social rule is to exist, then some persons must look upon the behavior in question as a general standard to be followed by the group as a whole. (Hart 1961, p. 55).

tive concept of family. Since customary rules are a regarded as a source of family law, the complete absence of family law can certainly be regarded as a relevant sign that this society lacks a normative concept of family. Without customary rules to guide their behavior, it is likely that members of this society would not have a critical reflective attitude toward their own behavior or that of others within families. However, because a system of religious laws governing family relationships might take the place of custom in some societies, we cannot claim with certainty that the absence of customary rules is determinative of the absence of a normative concept of family.[11]

5.2.2 Resolving the Dispute Between Traditionalists and Radicals

The dispute between traditionalists and radicals is about the relationship of the concepts of family and law. Traditionalists emphasize an *essential* difference between the two, whereas some radical answers emphasize an essential likeness. According to the traditionalist, the family and the rights and obligations of family membership can and do exist independently of the legal system. They accept that the law establishes its own definition of the family and legal systems structure family relationships, but the family is not logically dependent on legal definitions. Moreover, when some traditionalists speak of an essential difference between the family and family law, they often imply a moral ideal of marriage, family and particular rights and obligations within the family that (they believe) the state should enforce through one or more of the various functions of law. These are the natural law traditionalists. However, as stated earlier, the traditionalism which we are discussing here confines its theory to the simple proposition that the family and relationships within the family exist independently of the rules of a legal system.

The analysis in the preceding section shows that the traditionalist position is consistent with only one of the various versions of the radical claim that there is an essential likeness between the family and family law ("the personal is political"). Although this version is plausible, it is the relatively weak position that when a society fails to use its legal system to enforce customary moral rules pertaining to the family, this is relevant (though not determinative) to establishing that it lacks a normative concept of the family. Although this may be a far cry from the strong version of the radical position that says we can have *no* concept of the family independent of a legal system containing family laws, the weak version is consistent with traditionalism. Indeed, I believe that the two positions are complementary. For if one agrees with the thesis that legal intervention in the family is a sign of the commitment of a society to morally ideal types of family relationships, then it is a short

[11] Of course the system of religious laws might be identical with the customary rules of the society, for example Islamic law on the family appears to be identical with custom in many mid-Eastern countries.

step to the thesis that where a normative concept of family exists, there you are *likely* to find a legal system that supports it through one or more of the techniques of family law.[12]

5.3 Theories of Legal Intervention and Their Application to Family Law

In the previous section we examined and rejected the radical claim that the very ideas of family and family law are essentially related. Hence, legal intervention in the family is a logical possibility. The family is not (or not entirely) a political/legal invention. There is such a thing as "the family" and relationships within the family that (logically) can exist apart from legal definition. This puts us in a position to re-examine the public-private distinction. How are we to draw the line between the *private* realm of the family where the law may not legitimately (legally) interfere with the choices of family members, and the *public* realm where it may so interfere? To put the question another way: Is there a limit to what is or ought to be private conduct within the family?

In the philosophy of criminal law several theories or principles have been recommended as candidates for setting a limit to the liberty of the individual. We shall discuss three of these principles below, while keeping in mind the diverse functions of the laws that concern the family. Principles that were developed within the context of criminal law may not easily apply to those family laws that do not have a mandatory function. Second, we should be aware that these principles pertain to the liberty of the *individual*, not to the *family*, conceived as a distinct type of *social group of individuals*. It is one thing to ask for conditions under which the state is justified in legally restricting the behavior of a person; it may be quite another to ask this about the behavior of a family.

5.3.1 Utilitarianism and the Harm Principle

In his 1860 essay *On Liberty*, the philosopher John Stuart Mill set out to answer a general question which is relevant to our question about the limits of family law. Mill's primary interest was in the extent of individual liberty, or (as Mill put it) "the nature and limits of the power which can legitimately be exercised by society over the individual" (*On Liberty*, Ch. I). If it is the case that at least some of the rules of family law can interfere with the liberty of the individual, then Mill provides a principle that tells us when this is legitimate and when it is not.

[12] Okin advocates the "just" family in which social roles are distributed between husband and wife without regard to gender as the ideal that should be promoted by a legal system (Okin 1989).

> That principle is, that the sole end for which mankind are warranted individually or collectively, in interfering with the liberty of action of any of their number, is self-protection. That the only purpose for which power can be rightfully exercised over any member of a civilized community, against his will, is to prevent harm to others.

This is called the "harm principle" or (more accurately) the "harm-to-others principle." Mill next explains the purposes for which power *cannot* be rightfully exercised:

> His own good, either physical or moral, is not a sufficient warrant. He cannot rightfully be compelled to do or forbear because it will be better for him to do so, because it will make him happier, because, in the opinions of others, to do so would be wise, or even right. These are good reasons for remonstrating with him, or reasoning with him, or persuading him, but not for compelling him, or visiting him with any evil in case he does otherwise. To justify that, the conduct from which it is desired to deter him, must be calculated to produce evil to someone else.

Mill concludes by re-stating the harm-to-others principle:

> The only part of conduct of any one, for which he is amenable to society, is that which concerns others. In the part which merely concerns himself, his independence is, of right, absolute. Over himself, over his own body and mind, the individual is sovereign.

The harm-to-others principle is derived from the moral principle of utility which says that our fundamental obligation is to promote the greatest happiness for the greatest number. Mill believed that the greatest happiness can only be achieved by providing opportunities for intellectual and emotional development. This development is in turn dependent on maximizing individual liberty. Liberty should only be restricted in those situations where there is harm or the threat of harm to the interests of others. In all other cases, the liberty of the individual to do as he or she wishes must not be restricted either by the law or by social opinion.

Other-Regarding and Self-Regarding Harms

Mill refers to conduct that causes or threatens to cause harm to others as "other-regarding." He places this conduct in the public realm as suitable for legal intervention. Conduct that harms only oneself, but does no harm to others is called "self-regarding." This conduct is placed in the private realm, and society ought not to intervene to prevent such behavior, even if what the person is voluntarily doing risks his own injury or death.

Although Mill does not define "harm," we can make a few remarks about this concept. First, not all harms hurt. If my house burns down when I am out of town for two weeks and I do not learn about this until I return, then although I was not hurt (in pain) during the two-week period, I was certainly harmed. If the house had a market value of $250,000 and I had no insurance, then I suffered an immediate financial setback during the period *before* I learned that my house burned down. The point is that we have interests other than avoiding physical or emotional pain ("hurting"). We also have economic interests, interests in our reputation, interests in our attachments and relationships to others, and many other interests, all of which can be harmed by others.

Second, harm can be caused by an omission, that is, by failing to do what one has a "distinct and assignable obligation"[13] to do. If a child is malnourished because her drug-addicted parents neglect to feed her (they have the resources to do this), then this would constitute harm as much as if they had intentionally injured her.

Intrafamily Harm and the Family Privacy Principle

I have alluded to a question about the identification of those who are responsible for causing harm. As individuals who are members of families as husbands, wives, parents, children, siblings, etc. there are many ways in which family members can be harmed by the behavior of others in the family. The obvious cases are those involving physical pain: child abuse, child neglect, spousal abuse, and marital rape. The limits of legitimate liberty are exceeded when a parent abuses or neglects her child, or a husband hits or rapes his wife. All of these types of acts and omissions are prohibited by law (usually under the heading of "domestic violence") and the justification of this can easily be found in the harm-to-others principle.

Let us use the phrase "internal family harm" to refer to those harms caused by one family member to another member of the same family. Consider a proposal that the legal system should treat internal family harm in the same way that Mill suggests the system treat harm that an individual does to oneself. The proposal is that we adopt Mill's sovereignty principle (quoted earlier) but make a slight change of wording in order to apply it to intrafamily harm. Instead of "Over himself, over his own body and mind, the individual is sovereign," we substitute "Over itself, over its own members, *the family* is sovereign." We can make similar changes to the rest of Mill's famous words: "The only part of a family's conduct, for which it is amenable to society, is that which concerns those individuals who are not part of the family. In the part which merely concerns itself, the independence of the family is, of right, absolute." Harms that are strictly internal, harms that occur within the family and affect only members of the same family are to be treated as self-regarding harms in which the "self" is the family.

We will refer to this as the *Family Privacy Principle* (FPP). In its *strong* version it recommends absolute prohibitions of state or legal intervention whenever there is *internal* family harm. By extension FPP also prohibits attempts of non-family members (including those acting in an official capacity) to detect or discover instances of

[13] This is extracted from the following quote in Ch. IV: "When, by conduct of this sort [for example, drug addiction], a person is led to violate a *distinct and assignable obligation to any other person or persons*, the case is taken out of the self-regarding class, and becomes amenable to moral disapprobation in the proper sense of the term. If, for example, a man, through intemperance or extravagance, becomes unable to pay his debts, or, having undertaken the moral responsibility of a family, becomes from the same cause incapable of supporting or educating them, he is deservedly reprobated, and might be justly punished; but it is for the breach of duty to his family or creditors, not for the extravagance [nor for the intemperance]." The words in brackets are by this author.

such harm without the invitation or express permission of the family. Hence, when a child is seriously harmed by a parent, or a woman is raped by her husband, the harm may never be discovered by a non-family person or by state authorities. If it should be accidentally discovered (for example, during an emergency room visit), FPP says that such harms should provide no justifiable ground for state or legal intervention.

There is a *weak* version of FPP which has historically been invoked to prevent the state from intervening in parental decisions about the content of a child's education (for example, sex education in the public schools), or the use of some types of corporal punishment in the home. By way of contrast, the strong version extends the scope of family privacy to include injurious behavior that might otherwise be prosecuted as a felony (for example, child sexual abuse and spousal rape) or would be treated in family court as a case suitable for termination of parental rights (for example, chronic child neglect).

There is one exception to both the weak and the strong versions of FPP. It is similar to the exception Mill makes to accommodate temporary forcible interventions in the behavior of a person who we believe may not know that what she is about to do will cause her to suffer harm. Mill's example is of someone forcibly, but temporarily preventing a person from crossing a decrepit foot bridge in order to determine whether they are aware that the bridge might collapse. The intervenor does so on the reasonable belief that this person would not walk across the bridge if she knew about its poor condition. But once she has received and understands the warning, further intervention is no longer justifiable. By analogy, if the internal harm-causing behavior in a family is reasonably believed to be such that it would not occur if the family member who caused the harm was aware of the detrimental consequences of his behavior, or if his behavior was not voluntary (for example, he was under the influence of drugs or alcohol or he was mentally ill) then a temporary intervention is permissible. And, to continue the analogy, once we are assured that internal conditions have been corrected, then further intervention in the family is not justifiable.

Why should we adopt FPP? Why should society treat intrafamily harm in the same way Mill recommends it treat cases of an individual's self-regarding harm? An appeal to the principle of utility would surely result in a complete rejection of the strong version of FPP. The probable bad consequences of adopting strong FPP (an increased rate of domestic violence, including the rates of child and spousal abuse and deaths due to abuse) would certainly outweigh any good consequences of non-intervention. There may be some relief felt by those family members that comes from knowing that they will not be prosecuted for the battery or sexual abuse of their children, but the pleasure of this relief hardly outweighs the enormous pain they cause.

The problem is that FPP is based on a flawed analogy in which the family is said to be relevantly similar to an individual. If the analogy is true, then (it is argued) the principle of non-interference in the self-regarding conduct of individual persons should be extended to the family. This places the burden on the proponent of FPP to prove that there are sufficient similarities between an individual person and an individual family to support the analogy.

One attempt to draw an analogy can be found in political philosophy. There is a type of utilitarianism that is *organic* or, *corporatist*. It views the individual as constituted by, rather than as constituting, society in that the individual is basically incomplete apart from society. It is the idea expressed by Aristotle in his famous assertion that "man is by nature a political animal, and that "the state is by nature prior to the individual." Now if we replace the word "family" for the word "society," then we get an organic notion of the relationship between the family and its individual members. This notion says that the individual is constituted by the family to which he or she belongs. The human being is by nature a member of a family. It follows that the goods enjoyed by individuals are "inherently social ones, that is, goods whose every enjoyment... directly involves a communal relationship," for example the goods of family love, caring relationships, and of participation in family life.

I doubt that this way of conceiving the relationship between a person and the family to which he or she is a member will give much utilitarian support to FPP. Even if utilitarians accept the idea that social goods should be counted when making our utility calculations about the consequences of FPP, these goods are heavily mitigated or non-existent in families suffering from domestic violence. Second, utilitarians like Bentham and Mill would hardly be counted among the ranks of organicists. If pressed they would probably classify their type of utilitarianism as *individualistic*. This means that they would view the family as composed of individual persons, of whom the adult members are basically complete apart from the family to which they belong. Adults use the family to fulfill their needs and desires, but most of these needs and desires can be specified independently of family membership, and that membership is at most a useful instrument for their satisfaction. Hence, most of the goods stressed by the individualistic utilitarian are those that can conceivably be enjoyed independently of the family, for example the goods of food, drink, satisfaction of sexual desire, clothing, health, safety and security. Children also have these basic needs, but they must depend on the family to provide them. I suspect that Mill would modify individualistic utilitarianism to accommodate the social goods that can only be fulfilled through family membership, as noted above: the goods of loving and being loved and cared for by a parent or spouse.

If we use either the individualistic or modified individualistic conception of the relationship between the family and its individual members, then we can derive a complete rejection of the strong version of FPP. Both of these conceptions stress health, safety and security as among the goods that are satisfied by family membership. FPP fails to guarantee the satisfaction of these goods. In fact, it worsens the family environment by making family members much more vulnerable to domestic violence (internal family harm) than they would be under contemporary legal prohibitions.[14] Utilitarian defenders of the organic conception of family relation-

[14] The statistics for child abuse are staggering. During the year 2013, a nationally estimated 3.2 million children received either an investigation or alternative response at a national disposition

ships point might counter by claiming that FPP promotes the social goods of "family unity and harmony among its members." They might support this claim by submitting evidence that family unity is best achieved when members are left to their own devices are allowed to work through internal family problems without outside interference. Even if this is true (and there is little evidence for this claim), it seems clear that the bad consequences of FPP would far outweigh the good. It is highly improbable that family harmony would improve to such an extent that the amount of instances of internal family harm would drop if there was no social intervention to help victims of child abuse, spousal abuse or intimate partner sexual violence. Our conclusion is that utilitarians would not endorse the Family Privacy Principle, preferring instead to treat each family member as a distinct individual for purposes of applying the harm-to-others principle to specify the conditions under which it is legitimate for the state to intervene in family affairs.

5.3.2 Paternalism

The principle of paternalism says that an additional reason for restricting individual liberty is the individual's own good, either physical or moral. This principle can also be derived from the general utilitarian principle. If we restrict individual liberty to those actions that promote an individual's own good while at the same time ensuring that they do not act in ways that are harmful to themselves, then this is perfectly consistent with the higher aim of promoting the greatest happiness for the greatest number, despite Mill's protestation that such interventions inhibit intellectual and moral development.

People often do not know what is for their own good, or they may sometimes know this but do not know how to achieve it, or how to avoid consequences that are not in their own best interests. Legislators believe they are well justified in making certain behaviors illegal on paternalistic grounds. We require automobile drivers and passengers to wear seat belts, motorcyclists to wear helmets, and everyone to have a valid prescription from a physician in order to purchase certain drugs at the pharmacy. But the justification for these paternalistic laws has more to do with preventing them from causing themselves physical harm than it does with promoting their intellectual and emotional development. It might be true that my development is best achieved if I carefully think through the risks of taking one medication rather than another for my arthritis instead of leaving this to my physician and the pharmacist, but the risk of not getting it right would probably far exceed the benefit of my having achieved a relatively small development of my intellectual capabilities.

---

rate of 42.9 children per 1000 in the population (U.S. Department of Health and Human Services 2015). The statistics on spousal or intimate partner violence in the U.S. is just as alarming. In 2013 there were 10,512,000 victims of physical violence by a spouse or intimate partner in the United States. That works out to 20 people each minute. (Centers for Disease Control and Prevention 2014).

How does the principle of paternalism apply to family law? The family is fertile territory for the paternalist. Paternalistic intervention in internal family affairs receives its most obvious iteration in the public policy called *parens patriae*. In law this Latin phrase refers to the power of the state to act as the parent of any child or individual who is in need of protection. The state is the ultimate parent of the child, and in theory, the state can use its police power to intervene whenever it determines that a child is in danger of causing harm to herself.

In addition to the *parens patriae* policy, most of the laws restricting the liberty of children are justified by an argument based on the child's own best interests. For example, the specific purpose of child labor laws is to safeguard children against harms such as exposure to hazardous, unsanitary, or immoral conditions, and overwork. Children are not consulted about whether they want to work under such conditions. The assumption is that children do not know their own interests, and thus are incapable of making a rational choice about where and when to work. Hence, under paternalism it is perfectly justifiable that the state enacts child labor laws in order to promote the child's own good, despite what the child or her parents want.[15]

But paternalism has also been used to justify treating married women as children. Under the doctrine of coverture that was not abandoned in England until the 19th century, "the husband and wife are one person in law: that is, the very being or legal existence of the woman is suspended during the marriage, or at least incorporated and consolidated into that of the husband" (Blackstone, *Commentaries*, Bk. 1, Ch. 15, sec.3). The doctrine was justified on the same paternalistic principle used to justify the legal treatment of children: a woman does not have the mental and emotional capacities sufficient to make rational decisions about many matters that concern her own best interests. Caroline Norton wrote about the extent to which paternalism affected the lives of married women in England:

> [She] has no legal existence: her being is absorbed in that of her husband. Years of separation or desertion cannot alter this position... She has no possessions, unless by special settlement: her property is his property... An English wife has no legal right even to her clothes or ornaments...An English wife cannot make a will...cannot legally claim her own earnings...may not leave her husband's house. Not only can he sue her for "restitution of conjugal rights," but he has a right to enter the house of any friend or relation with whom she may take refuge...and carry her away by force, with or without the aid of police...She cannot prosecute for a libel....cannot sign a lease, or transact responsible business...cannot claim support, as a matter of personal right, from her husband...She cannot bind her husband by any agreement...as her husband, he has a right to all that is hers; as his wife, she has no right to anything that is his (Norton, E. 8-13, as edited by Brake, 112).

The problem with paternalism is that it does not draw a line between those who do not possess knowledge of their own best interests sufficient to avoid causing harm to themselves, and those who have this capacity. Mill exempts children from

[15] Mill implicitly accepts paternalism for children when he writes that his "doctrine is meant to apply only to human beings in the maturity of their faculties. We are not speaking of children, or of young persons below the age which the law may fix as that of manhood or womanhood. Those who are still in a state to require being taken care of by others, must be protected against their own actions as well as against external injury" (Ch. 1).

the recommendation that everyone should have as much liberty as they want up to the point where they attempt to use it to cause harm to others. Because they are not "in the maturity of their faculties," they "must be protected against their own actions, as well as against external injury." Hence, paternalism is a justifiable reason for interfering with the liberty of children.

But the same cannot be said for women. There is no factual basis for the claim that women are not in the maturity of their faculties, or possess faculties which make them naturally inferior to men in any of the ways relevant to their intellectual capacities. Hence, there is no basis for one person to use *his* freedom to do as he likes in acting for another, "under the pretext" that *her* affairs are his own affairs. Mill uses this observation to maintain that "the State" should "maintain a vigilant control over his exercise of any power which it allows him to possess over others." He applies this to "the almost despotic power of husbands over wives":

> [N]nothing more is needed for the complete removal of the evil, than that wives should have the same rights, and should receive the protection of the law in the same manner, as all other persons; and because, on this subject, the defenders of established injustice do not avail themselves of the plea of liberty, but stand forth openly as the champions of power (Ch. V)

Since the central argument for liberty (constrained only by acts causing harm to others) and against paternalism applies to women as well as to men, there is no moral basis for application of the doctrine of coverture.[16] There is no justification for denying married women the same legal rights as those of their husbands.

5.3.3 *Moralism*

Moralism, as defined by Mill, is the practice of society exercising its power over the individual for the purpose of preventing immoral conduct, "regardless of whether the conduct harms or victimizes any other specific person" (Altman, 159). All acts that cause harm to others are regarded as immoral by the moralist, and therefore can justifiably be prohibited by law. But the moralist also argues that there are other actions which do not cause harm to others which are justifiably punished. This category of actions would include consensual conduct between adults in which there is no victim, for example, sexual activities such as homosexuality and prostitution.

Examples of the use of moralism in the formation of family law would include not only laws prohibiting violence (child abuse, marital rape), but any kind of conduct in the family that violates an established moral code. Procreative activities are often the target of advocates of moralism. The use of artificial forms of contraception and early term abortion as methods of family planning have been prohibited through the application of moralism, as are restrictions on the number of persons who can marry (two persons only) and restrictions on gender (one man and one woman). A reason often (but not always) given for these prohibitions and restric-

[16] Mill would later expand on this argument in his book *The Subjection of Women* (1869).

tions is that the dominant moral code of the society or culture should be enforced by law even if it could be shown that contraception, abortion, polygamy and gay marriage would cause no internal harm to the family or external harm to others.

But the moral rules to which the moralist appeals are often relative to the culture in which the rules have majority support. For example, in Middle East countries in which Islam is the dominant religion, male and female circumcision is morally obligatory. In boys and men circumcision is done "by cutting off the piece of skin on the glans of the penis." Circumcision of the female is accomplished by cutting out the clitoris."[17] In non-Muslim countries, especially in the Americas and in Western Europe, female circumcision is referred to as female genital *mutilation*. The morally charged word "mutilation" is used because the procedure is believed to be a serious moral wrong. Many girls bleed to death or die of infection and those who survive can suffer adverse health effects during marriage and pregnancy (von der Stocken and Uwer 2007). Perhaps the most serious objection of Western human rights advocates is based on the fact that the procedure, even when done under safe conditions, will result in a significant reduction in sexual desire when the young girl becomes an adult. Hence, she is permanently deprived of the future opportunity to make her own informed decision as an adult about whether she wants to be circumcised.[18,19]

There are two versions of moralism, each version agreeing that immorality includes not only acts that cause harm to individuals, but also acts in which there are no victims. The difference between these versions is in the way in which each justifies legal intervention. (1) Legal intervention is justified by the immorality of the act itself, not by its consequences; and (2) The justification for prohibiting immoral acts is to be found in the harm that is done *to society* by a failure to legally enforce its moral code. Let us examine whether either of these versions might be used to justify the genital circumcision of young girls.

1. The argument for the first version is that "immoral conduct is the sort of conduct that calls for punishment, just as morally upstanding conduct calls for reward of some sort" (Altman, 159). If it is obligatory for the Muslim parents of a young girl to have her circumcised, and they refuse to do this, then they are liable to

[17] Keller, *Reliance of the Traveler*http://wikiislam.net/wiki/%27an,_Hadith_and_Scholars:Female_Genital_Mutilation

[18] Performing female genital circumcision on anyone under the age of 18 became illegal in the U.S. in 1997 with the *Federal Prohibition of Female Genital Mutilation Act*. As of 2015, 23 US states have specific laws against FGM. States that do not have such laws may use other general statutes, such as assault, battery or child abuse. The *Transport for Female Genital Mutilation Act* was passed in January 2013, and prohibits knowingly transporting a girl out of the U.S. for the purpose of undergoing FGM. https://en.wikipedia.org/wiki/Female_Genital_Mutilation_in_the_United_States.

[19] Another example of this type of deprivation was the ancient Chinese custom of foot binding in which the feet of young girls was tightly and painfully bound to prevent further growth. Although believed to be a mark of beauty, it resulted in lifelong disabilities for most of its subjects.

various types of punishment (beatings, fines, punitive forced labor[20]). If they conform, then the honor of the family is preserved.

But the question asked by Western human rights advocates is not whether the concept of immorality implies punishment but whether parental refusal to have their girls circumcised is morally wrong. According to the first version of the theory, this question is not relevant. The principle makes no recommendations about what actions are moral obligatory and what actions are morally wrong. If the practice of female genital circumcision conforms to an existing moral code, then this satisfies the demands of the principle. But this also identifies the flaw in the theory. Since the theory provides no objective criteria for determining when an act is morally obligatory, leaving the determination up to the pronouncements of a culture or religion, then the limits placed on individual liberty are arbitrary. It is theoretically possible that the theory could also be used to justify the sacrifice of virgins and the slavery of people believed to be inferior.

2. The argument for the second version of moralism is a harm-based argument developed by Patrick Devlin.[21] The argument has three steps. First, society has the right to pass judgment on matters of morals, that is, morals are not always a matter of private judgment. "What makes a society of any sort is a community of ideas, not only political ideas but also ideas about the way its members behave and govern their lives; these latter ideas are its morals. ... The structure of every society is made up both of politics and morals" (131). Devlin uses the Christian idea of marriage as an example, noting that Christians "adopt monogamy as a moral principle."[22]

> Consequently, the Christian institution of marriage has become the basis of family life and so part of the structure of our society. It is there not because it is Christian. It has got there because it is Christian, but it remains there because it is built into the house in which we live and could not be removed without bringing it down.

Christianity is also "the basis of a moral code which condemns behaviors like fornication and adultery." This moral code would be "gravely threatened" if individual judgments were permitted about the morality of these behaviors. If it is accepted that (a) there is a public morality, and (b) society could not exist without shared ideas on what types of acts are immoral, then the public morality must be protected if society is to be kept from disintegration.

This leads to the second step of Devlin's argument. He argues that society has the right to protect its moral code because it has the right to do whatever is necessary to guarantee its own survival. One way to exercise this right is to use the weapon of the criminal law. And here Devlin uses another analogy: the law of treason. "The justi-

---

[20] Shell-Duncan et al. 2000, 143–145.

[21] Devlin 1959, 129–151.

[22] If Devlin was writing his essay today, he would undoubtedly also stress the fact that most Christians believe that marriage is between one man and one woman. (The prospect of gay marriage was not anticipated by anyone in 1959.)

fication for this [law] is that established government is necessary for the existence of society and therefore its safety against violent overthrow must be secured." By analogy, society is also justified in enforcing its moral code. "The suppression of vice is as much the law's business as the suppression of subversive activities"

Third, Devlin concedes that the rights and interests of the individual should be balanced with those of society's right to enforce its moral code. One consideration is privacy. [W]hen all who are involved in the [immoral] deed are consenting parties..., the public interest in the moral order can be balanced against the claims of privacy." But this is not a "definite limitation" of all private immoral acts such as homosexual encounters, but "a matter to be taken into account" before charges are brought against the participants in the crime.

Returning to the case of female circumcision, all we need to do is to replace the word "Christianity" with the word "Islamic" in the preceding argument and we get the conclusion that there should be no legal prohibition of this practice in Islamic countries. Moreover, Devlin's theory could be used to argue for no relaxation of *any* of the family laws in Islamic countries that support patriarchy and inequality, for example polygamy, sexual segregation, prohibitions of women from driving a car, voting, political activity, going out in public without a head scarf or veil or unaccompanied by a male member of her family, and making her own decision about when and with whom to marry. Devlin's version of moralism would argue that if proscribing female genital circumcision is part of the Islamic moral code, then rules requiring or forbidding acts proscribed by the code cannot be removed without "bringing down" the societies in which the code is dominant. Since these societies have the right to self-preservation, then they have the right to use the criminal law as a means to enforce whatever might threaten their existence. Immoral conduct, even if not harmful to others, is as threatening to the existence of society as acts of treason. Hence, with the possible exception of "lesser acts of indecency" committed in private, all immoral acts should be prosecuted, including parental refusal to have their 5-year old female child circumcised.

Devlin's emphasis is on consequences, "on repairing the damage done to the social order, on avoiding the chaos that can result from puncturing the social fabric of relationships, obligations and expectations."[23] This is what makes his brand of moralism compatible with the moral code of any society, including those dominated by Islamic morality. The emphasis of his liberal critics is on the freedom to choose how we will lead our lives: "morality is objective, persons have human rights, individuals are sacred, and none of this has anything to do with the social or religious setting in which persons happen to find themselves" (Simmons, 59). This is why the choice of a Muslim parent to have her female child circumcised is justified as a matter of family honor in Islamic cultures, but is condemned as a violation of a child's right not to be "mutilated" by Westerners. The child has objective, fundamental rights that are independent of the social setting in which she resides.

If Devlin is not swayed by the counter-example of female genital circumcision/mutilation, then we should look more closely at his argument for moralistic inter-

[23] Simmons 1999, p. 54.

vention in the family. Although it may be true that society needs a moral code to exist, it does not follow from this that it needs the exact moral code it has at any given time. Moral codes change over time, and there is no evidence that when this happens society itself will disintegrate. The change may be at the peripheries of the code, for example, the recent changes in beliefs about the morality of homosexual conduct between consenting adults in private. Devlin offers no proof that these changes would have the same detrimental consequences to society as would a change in belief and attitude about the immorality of killing or injuring others with impunity.

The only defense that Devlin can put up at this point is to fall back on what H.L.A. Hart refers to as Devlin's "seamless web" characterization of a society's moral code.[24] In the same way that a seamless web can crumble if a part of the web is damaged, so society itself could disintegrate if the moral code that holds it together is weakened. Although a single act of victimless immoral conduct that goes unpunished might not damage the social fabric, the decriminalization of all victimless immoral conduct would put so much stress on the fabric that it could pose an irretrievable danger to society.

But again, the burden is on Devlin to prove this. It is an empirical claim for which there is no credible evidence. His argument seems to assume, without proof, that "people will not abandon morality, will not think any better of murder, cruelty, and dishonesty, merely because some private sexual practice which they abominate is not punished by the law." What disintegrates when victimless immoral conduct is decriminalized is not the rest of society's moral code, but the *analogy* of society's moral code to a "seamless web."

5.4 Testing the Limits of Intrafamily Sexual Behavior

The following kinds of intrafamily sexual conduct defined here are either punishable or have been punishable in most states of the United States as either felonies or misdemeanors:

Bigamy is the crime of marrying while still in a valid, undissolved marriage with someone else.

Incest is the offense of having sexual contact with a blood relative, usually a parent, child, sibling, grandparent or grandchild. In the United States the District of Columbia and every state and inhabited territory have some form of codified incest prohibition (felony or misdemeanor).

Adultery is voluntary sexual intercourse of a married person with a person other than the offender's husband or wife. Adultery is a crime in two states (Michigan and Wisconsin), and a misdemeanor in most of states having laws prohibiting it.

[24] Hart 1963. 50–51. Although it is commonly thought that the "seamless web" metaphor was invented by Devlin, it was first used by Hart in his criticism of Devlin.

Polygamy is the condition or practice of having more than one spouse at the same time. Since bigamy is a crime, polygamy would also be a crime if the man in the relationship married a second woman while still in a valid marriage with the first. However, most people in polygamous relationships (one man and two or more women) are either not legally married or the man is legally married to only one of the women with whom he cohabits. Most polygamists who have a first marriage have a "spiritual" or religious ceremony when they cohabit with new "brides." The relationship of cohabitation was made illegal in the state of Utah under a part of its bigamy law that prohibited this practice (defined as "a living arrangement in which an unmarried couple lives together in a long-term relationship that resembles a marriage"). This part of the law was recently struck down by a U.S. federal judge as an unconstitutional violation of the First Amendment (freedom of religion). The Utah attorney general has entered an appeal in the 10th U.S. District Court (*Brown v Buhman*).

The problem in this chapter was set by John Stuart Mill: "What is the nature and limits of the power which can legitimately be exercised by society over the individual." Our concern is with society's use of its legal system to restrain the liberty of its members. Is it justifiable to prevent any or all of the aforementioned types of conduct?

In order to answer Mill's question within the context of some of the theories outlined in the section on liberty-limiting principles (harm-to-others, paternalism and moralism), we need clear definitions of key concepts as well as factual information consistent with the demands of each principle. For example, in asking whether the state can legally prohibit incest under the principle of paternalism, we need to know what constitutes *informed consent* when there is sexual contact between (for example) father and daughter, and if there is consent, the paternalist will inquire whether the contact is potentially harmful to one or both of the participants. We also need to know what kind of harm is predicted. Is it emotional or psychological harm, for example, and how is this to be determined?

If we approach incest from the utilitarian harm-to-others principle, we will want to know what would count as an "other" who is harmed by the incest of two consenting adults. If genetic research supports the notion that inbreeding has untoward genetic consequences, then the harm of incest resulting in pregnancy is harm that presumably is done to future persons and to social groups that do not exist. If a child is born with severe defects due to inbreeding should this constitute a crime on the ground that it causes a public harm? Should the child be allowed to sue her incestuous parents for damages on the ground they negligently caused the child's defects? To put the question another way, should the legal system recognize a right *not* to be born?

The principle of moralism in its simplest form would condemn incest on the grounds that it is regarded as immoral in almost all cultures, especially incest between fathers and daughters, mothers and sons. The question whether incest is harmful to the participants who engage in it is irrelevant, as is the question whether those who engage in incestuous behavior do this voluntarily. Incest is immoral-in-itself and this judgment does not depend on harm or on fault. However, Devlin's version of moralism is concerned with the consequences of a society's failure to criminalize immoral conduct. Therefore, it is as important for Devlin to produce empirical data to prove societal damage as it is for the paternalist to produce data that shows that incest.

The above remarks are only intended to provide a guide to further investigation of the limits of state power over intrafamily conduct. I will leave it to the reader to apply these recommendations when using the principles of harm-to-others, paternalism and moralism in order to determine whether rational, informed adults in consensual relationships should be legally prohibited from engaging in incest, bigamy, adultery and polygamy and other types of intrafamily sexual behaviors.

Questions for Thought and Discussion

1. What does it mean to say "the personal is political?" Is the family political? How would you go about proving that this is either true or false?
2. Explain the relevance of the three liberty-limiting principles discussed in this chapter to justify instances of state intervention in the family. For example, how does the harm-to-others principle limit the liberty of parents in interactions with their own children?
3. Is the state *justified* in prohibiting the kind of conduct described in the definition of incest in Sect. 5.4? Answer this question with specific reference to the liberty-limiting principle you would use in giving either an affirmative or negative reply to the question. What principles would you *not* use in answering this question? Explain.
4. Since bigamy is a crime, polygamy would also be a crime if the man in the relationship married a second woman while still in a valid marriage with the first. Is the state *justified* in prohibiting the kind of conduct described in the definition of polygamy? Answer this question with specific reference to the liberty-limiting principle you would use in giving either an affirmative or negative reply to the question. What principles would you *not* use in answering this question? Explain.

References

Anon. 2016a. Timeline of Abortion Law and Events. http://www.chicagotribune.com/sns-abortion-timeline-story.html. Accessed 27 Mar 2016.

———. 2016b. Birth Control and the Law: Basics. *FindLaw.com*. http://family.findlaw.com/reproductive-rights/birth-control-and-the-law-basics.html. Accessed 27 Mar 2016.

Blustein, Jeffrey. 1982. *Parents and Children: The Ethics of the Family*. New York: Oxford University Press.

Centers for Disease Control and Prevention. 2014. Prevalence and Characteristics of Sexual Violence, Stalking, and Intimate Partner Violence Victimization – *National Intimate Partner and Sexual Violence Survey, United States*, 2011. http://www.cdc.gov/mmwr/prview/mmwrhtml/ss6308a1.htm?s_cid=ss6308a1_e

Devlin, Patrick. 1959. The Enforcement of Morals. In *Proceedings of the British Academy*, XIV, 129–151. London: The British Academy.

Dworkin, Andrea. 1987. *Intercourse*. New York: Free Press.

Find-Law. 2015. *Birth Control and the Law: Basics*. http://family.findlaw.com/reproductive-rights/birth-control-and-the-law-basics.html#sthash.WWV6eVcb.dpuf
Gavison, Ruth. 1992. Feminism and the Public/Private Distinction. *Stanford Law Review* 45: 1–45.
Hart, H.L.A. 1961. *The Concept of Law*. Oxford: Clarendon Press.
———. 1963. *Law, Liberty and Morality*. Stanford: Stanford University Press.
———. 1983. Positivism and the Separation of Law and Morals. In *Essays in Jurisprudence and Philosophy*. Oxford: Clarendon Press.
Hobbes, Thomas. 1651. All editions.
James, William. 1983. *A Review of Women's Suffrage, the Reform against Nature* by Harold Bushnell and *Subjection of Women* by John Stuart Mill. In *Visions of Women*, ed. Linda A. Bell. Clifton: Humana Press.
Keller, Nuh Ha Mim, (ed. and trans). 1987. Reliance of the Traveler, The Classic Manual of Islamic Sacred Law 'Umdat al-Salik by Ahmad ibn Naqib al-Misri (d. 769/1368) in Arabic with Facing English Text, Commentary, and Appendices. Beltsville: Amana Publications. http://wikiislam.net/wiki/%27an,_Hadith_and_Scholars:Female_Genital_Mutilation
Locke, John. 1980. *Second Treatise of Government*, ed. C.B. Macpherson. Indianapolis: Hackett. First published in 1690.
MacKinnon, Catherine. 1987. *Feminism Unmodified: Discourses on Life and Law*. Cambridge: Harvard University Press.
Macklin, Ruth. 1988. Changing Conceptions of Motherhood. *Law, Medicine and Health Care* 16: 35.
Mill, John Stuart. 1979. *On Liberty*. Indianapolis: Hackett. First published in 1860.
Minow, Martha. 1985. Forming Underneath Everything That Grows: Toward a History of Family Law. *Wisconsin Law Review* 4: 819.
Mohr, Richard. 1995. The Case for Gay Marriage. *Notre Dame Journal of Law, Ethics and Public Policy* 9: 216–229.
Morris, Herbert. 1976. *On Guilt and Innocence: Essays in Legal Philosophy and Moral Psychology*. Berkeley: University of California Press.
Norton, Caroline S. 2010. *A Letter to the Queen on Lord Chancellor Cranworth's Marriage and Divorce Bill*. Cambridge University Press.
Okin, Susan Moller. 1989. *Justice, Gender and the Family*. New York: Basic Books.
Olsen, Frances E. 1984. The Family and the Market: The Politics of Family Law. *Law and Inequality* 2(1).
———. 1985. The Myth of State Intervention in the Family. *University of Michigan Journal of Law Reform* 18(4).
Rousseau, Jean-Jacques. 1983. *On the Social Contract*. Indianapolis: Hackett. First published in 1762.
Schoeman, Ferdinand. 1980. Rights of Children, Rights of Parents, and the Moral Basis of the Family. *Ethics* 91: 6–19.
Shell-Duncan, Bettina, and Ylva Hernlund. 2000. *Female "circumcision" in Africa: Culture, Controversy, and Change*. Boulder: Rienner.
Simmons, A. John. 1999. Fault, Objectivity, and Classical Islamic Justice. In *Perspectives on Islamic Law, Justice and Society*, ed. Ravindra S. Khare. Lanham: Rowman and Littlefield.
U.S. Department of Health and Human Services. 2015. Administration for Children and Families, Administration on Children, Youth and Families, Children's Bureau. *Child maltreatment 2013*.http://www.acf.hhs.gov/programs/cb/research-data-technology/statistics-research/child-maltreatment. Accessed 26 March 2016.
Von der Osten-Sacken, Thomas and Thomas Uwer. 2007. Is Female Genital Mutilation an Islamic Problem? *Middle East Quarterly*, Winter: 29–36. http://www.meforum.org/1629/is-female-genital-mutilation-an-islamic-problem
West's Encyclopedia of American Law, Second Edition. 2008. The Gale Group, Inc.

Chapter 6
Family Crime and Punishment

> *"Each transgression may be punished to that degree, and with so much severity, as will suffice to make it an ill bargain to the offender, give him cause to repent, and terrify others from doing the like."*
>
> John Locke, *Second Treatise of Government* (1690)

Abstract What response should the legal system make to intrafamily harm? Should these harms be classified as crimes and punished in the same amount and manner as other criminal acts? Or should there be some other type of response focusing not on the individuals who caused the harm but on the family to which they belong? Questions about the general justification of punishment, the amount and manner of punishment, and alternatives to punishment are central to the philosophy of law. In this chapter we discuss the debate between utilitarians who look to the future by justifying punishment on the grounds of deterrence and retributivists who look to the past by justifying punishment on the grounds of moral blame and desert. We examine this debate through the lens of the crime of sexual abuse of a child by its parent. We then turn to a discussion of therapy as an alternative to punishment in cases of intrafamily crime. Our question is whether there is something about intra-family harm that would make therapy a more just response to those who cause such harms than the response of punishment.

6.1 Public and Private Harms

Crimes are traditionally classified as public harms. This means that the harm is done to an interest of the public (society), as represented by the state. Officials of the state seek out and prosecute (in criminal court) those who commit such harms. If the prosecution is successful, other officials will execute any punishment that is ordered by the court. Crimes are usually classified by their degree of "seriousness." The more serious crimes are called *felonies:* for example, murder, assault, rape,

L.D. Houlgate, *Philosophy, Law and the Family*, AMINTAPHIL: The Philosophical Foundations of Law and Justice 7,
DOI 10.1007/978-3-319-51121-4_6

kidnapping and armed robbery. The less serious crimes are referred to as *misdemeanors*: for example, shoplifting and driving under the influence.

Torts are private harms. Although a function of tort law, similar to that of criminal law, is the prevention of undesirable conduct, a tort is a private harm in the sense that the response to the harm is left up to the person who has suffered the harm. The state participates by providing a neutral forum (civil court) to which the injured person can bring a lawsuit to gain compensation. Torts are often classified by reference to the mental state of the defendant: intentional (for example, wrongful death), negligent (for example, most auto accidents), and strict liability (for example, dog bites[1]).

In some cases, one and the same harm can be both a crime and a tort. In one of the most sensational trials of the late twentieth century the star football player O.J. Simpson was found not guilty of the crime of murder (of his ex-wife and her friend). However, in a subsequent trial in civil court Simpson was successfully sued by the victim's families for the intentional tort of wrongful death, for which Simpson was made to pay millions of dollars in damages.

In this and the next two chapters we will identify and discuss some of the philosophical problems of deciding how society should respond to situations in which *intrafamily harm* occurs. The typical public response to crime is punishment, and the justification of this response is either deterrence or retribution. One question in this chapter is whether either of these theories provide a satisfactory justification for intrafamily crimes, for example, domestic violence (including spousal rape and child abuse), incest, or bigamy. We will also discuss an alternative theory that therapy or rehabilitation (not punishment) is the only justifiable response to crimes that occur within the family.

A second public response to intrafamily harm is illustrated by how cases of child abuse and neglect are treated in family or juvenile court. The response to most forms of child abuse and neglect is not to declare these acts or omissions as criminal, but to transfer them to a family or juvenile court for a *child protection disposition* (for example, in-home supervision of the child by a child protective services team, transfer of the child to foster care, or severance of parental rights). We will defer discussion of this type of response until Chap. 7.

6.2 Intrafamily Crimes: Justifications for Punishment

An intrafamily crime is a crime committed by one or more family members against another member of the same family. Examples of intrafamily crimes include domestic or family violence, bigamy and incest. Domestic violence is a relatively large category that includes spousal abuse, spousal rape, child abuse, child sexual abuse,

[1] Strict liability means that the defendant is liable for damages even if he or she was not negligent (for example, your dog gets out of your fenced yard and bites your next-door neighbor).

and elder abuse.[2] The words "violence" and "abuse" include many different kinds of harm. Here is a quote from the U.S. Department of Justice:

> Intimate partner and family violence, including physical, sexual, and financial abuse, neglect and maltreatment of children, and elder abuse, occurs throughout the country every day. Unlike most other crimes, intimate partner or domestic violence is usually not a sudden, isolated, and unexpected incident. It may involve years of emotional and psychological trauma as well as physical injuries which may become increasingly more severe and occur frequently over time. Exposure to such violence has a devastating impact on all involved, including children living with and experiencing it as witnesses and not direct victims. (DOJ: Office for Victims of Crime)

Although historically it was difficult to prosecute crimes against members of the same family, especially those in which a married woman was the victim of her husband's rape, violence inside the family unit is now taken as seriously as is violence perpetrated by a stranger. Our question is whether this is justified. Should intrafamily violence be regarded as criminal and therefore punishable? If we believe it should be punished, should the kind and amount of punishment be the same as that meted out to nonfamily members who are convicted of the same acts of violence?

There are two traditional approaches to providing a rationale or justification for the practice of responding to crime with punishment: utilitarian and retributive. Both of these approaches or theories provide not only a *general justification* of punishment, but they set standards for determining the *manner* and *amount* of punishment for particular crimes.

6.2.1 Punishment as Deterrence

All versions of utilitarianism start from the premise that our basic moral obligation is to promote the good and prevent the bad, where "good" means happiness or pleasure and "bad" means unhappiness or pain. The good referred to by the utilitarian is *not* the individual's own good, but the greatest amount of good altogether. If a choice is believed to produce both good and bad consequences, then our obligation is to choose the course of action that produces the *greatest balance* of good over bad consequences, making sure to calculate long-term as well as short-term consequences and the number of persons who might be affected by our action.

The idea of punishment implies the intentional causing of pain to the criminal, whether the pain is in the form of community service, a fine, a jail term, forced labor, or execution. Because it involves pain to a designated individual, punishment

---

[2] The state of Texas has a family code [§71.004 (1) – (3) (2005)] that defines all of these instances of domestic violence: An act by a member of a family or household against another member of the family or household that is intended to result in physical harm, bodily injury, assault, or sexual assault or that is a threat that reasonably places the member in fear of imminent physical harm, bodily injury, assault, or sexual assault, but does not include defensive measures to protect oneself; Abuse, as that term is defined by Sections 261.001(1) (C), (E), and (G), by a member of a family or household toward a child of the family or household.

requires justification. According to the utilitarian rationale, the burden is on those who cause the pain to show that this produces more pleasure or happiness than the amount of pain suffered by the wrongdoer. That burden of proof is met by the utilitarian when she proves that punishment of the criminal will at least reduce and at most entirely prevent future crime. It will reduce it either through *deterrence* (of the criminal or those in others who might succumb to the threat of punishment), *incapacitation* (if imprisoned or put to death, the criminal will not have the ability to repeat the offending conduct), and in rare cases, *moral rehabilitation* (the criminal might undergo a change of character and vow never to misbehave again).

According to the utilitarian, the amount of punishment should produce no more and no less pain than the amount necessary to achieve its end: the prevention of future crime through deterrence, incapacitation and rehabilitation. Capital punishment for shoplifting would produce far more pain to a shoplifter than is necessary to prevent future cases of shoplifting, and a few days in jail would produce far less pain to a person who has committed armed robbery than would be necessary to deter future crimes of the same kind.

How does the utilitarian justification of punishment and of amounts of punishment apply to intrafamily crime? The example we will use is intrafamily child sexual abuse, defined as sexual conduct with a child that occurs as the result of force by a family member or in a relationship that is exploitative because of age difference and family membership. Of the nearly 63,000 children who were sexually abused in the U.S. in 2012, about 30% of the perpetrators were family members (American Humane Association 2012). The punishment for this crime can range from a felony lifetime sentence to gross misdemeanor with no jail time, lifetime registration as a sex offender, and termination of parental rights. Here is a typical case:

> Rob and his sister Margaret were sexually abused in childhood. Rob's father abused him on camping trips in the summers when Rob was between the ages of eight and thirteen. The abuse consisted of Rob's father masturbating him and showing him pictures from *Playboy* magazine. Rob hated these episodes and came to hate his father who beat him and made fun of him as gay because he did not get erections when looking at Playboy while his father masturbated him until his penis was sore. Margaret was abused in toddlerhood by her father a few times and by two other men one time each. Both men were family acquaintances. She hardly remembers her father's sexual abuse, but she recalls the smell of beer on his breath, his sense of urgency and fear, his breathing, and the pressure of his penis against her vulva (University of Minnesota 2014, 1–2).

Rob and Margaret's father was eventually convicted of felonious child sexual abuse and spent time in state prison. The general question about whether a utilitarian would recommend that intrafamily child sexual abuse should be punished was answered in the previous chapter. Individual liberty is justifiably restricted by the law when conduct causes harm to others. There is little doubt that children like Rob and Margaret are harmed by a parent who involves their children in sexual activities, whether this is done by force or by exploiting their relationship to the child. There is ample evidence of the physical harm and psychological damage suffered by the child victim: sexually transmitted disease and pregnancy in older female children, and a myriad of psychological disturbances in both younger and older children, ranging from fear of particular people, places or activities to nightmares or sleep disturbances, eating disturbances, and withdrawal from family and friends. Adolescents may suffer from depression, be promiscuous, abuse drugs, run away from home, be suicidal, and have early pregnancies. Hence, the freedom of a parent to direct their child's life is justifiably limited by criminal laws prohibiting the sexual abuse of a child.

How much and what kind of punishment is justifiable? We have seen that this question is about balancing the pain caused to the offender by punishing him against the beneficial consequences of a reduced future incidence of child abuse that we can predict will occur as a result. But how much pain is too little and how much is too much to achieve this benefit? In answer to this question, there are some who would gladly execute all child abusers and others who would charge the offending parent with a misdemeanor and order either a relatively short jail sentence, community service, or payment of a fine. The problem with all of these recommendations is that we have no empirical evidence of how they have affected or will affect future behavior of either the perpetrator or other potential sexual abusers of children. If it is true that highly publicized executions of parents who sexually abuse their own children would bring a significant reduction in future cases, thereby eliminating large amounts of physical and psychological distress, then we would have a convincing argument for making child sexual abuse a capital crime. But these statistics are not now and probably will never be available.[3]

Apart from the empirical problem of determining the amount of punishment sufficient to achieve deterrence, there is the moral problem of possibly sanctioning punishments that are unjust. This is one of the central criticisms of the utilitarian theory of punishment. Here is the kind of counter-example used by the critics. Suppose that a woman wants to divorce her unfaithful husband in order to marry another man. A friend of hers who is a social worker is disturbed about the rising rate of child sexual abuse incidents in the county in which they both live. They hatch a plan that they believe will achieve both of their goals: to rid the woman of her husband and also reduce the rate of child sexual abuse. They contrive to falsely charge the woman's husband with the sexual abuse of their teenage child. The teenager says that she will go along with the scheme (she hates her father because he has confiscated her cell phone). The social worker says she will stand as a witness. They contact the police, the husband and father is arrested, charged with and convicted of sexual abuse of his daughter. His punishment is 30 years in state prison. The trial

[3] The reason that the death penalty for child sexual abuse will never be an option is to be found in the Supreme Court ruling in *Kennedy v Louisiana*, No. 07–343, June 25, 2008. The court declared unconstitutional a Louisiana statute that made it permissible to impose the death penalty for the rape of a child. (La. Stat. Ann. §14:42, West 1997 and Supp. 1998): Writing for the court majority, Justice Anthony Kennedy said "the Eighth Amendment bars Louisiana from imposing the death penalty for the rape of a child where the crime did not result, and was not intended to result, in the victim's death." Kennedy did not use utilitarian reasoning in reaching this decision. Instead, he used the language of retribution when he wrote that the severity of the punishment was not "proportional" to the seriousness of the crime.

and the conviction are heavily publicized in the media. As a result, there is a significant drop in the rate of sexual child abuse allegations in the county.

The critic uses this and like cases to argue that if any theory of punishment could conceivably justify the punishment of an innocent person, then the theory must be rejected. No innocent person should ever be punished, no matter the beneficial consequences that might result from his or her punishment. Because there are possible cases in which punishing an innocent person would produce a greater balance of good over bad consequences than the alternative of not punishing an innocent person, then the utilitarian theory must argue that not only is it permissible to punish an innocent person, but it is obligatory. In sum, the *injustice* of punishing an innocent person trumps any amount of social benefit that might be achieved by doing this.

Utilitarians have several responses to this critique. First, they admit that the theory could justify some cases of punishing the innocent, but contend that this is acceptable. They might say "Far better that we imprison one or two innocent people than that we fail to seize the opportunity to prevent the future sexual abuse of hundreds of innocent children." Second, using the same reasoning, utilitarians might argue that it is *not* unjust to punish the husband in the example above. The concept of justice is so vague and flexible in its every day application that it can be used to achieve this result in the present case.[4] And it could also be said that there is an injustice done to all children if we fail to use every opportunity to protect them from their abusers, including (if necessary) the prosecution of an innocent person. Third, under some versions of utilitarianism, it would be argued that the counter-example of the innocent father is irrelevant. These are the "rule utilitarians" who contend that the theory should be seen as a justification of *rules*, not as a justification of *particular acts* ("act utilitarianism"). One of the rules that would be justified as part of a system of rules is "Only the guilty shall be punished." If asked whether it is justifiable to punish the father for a crime he did not commit, the rule utilitarian would say "No, for the reason given in your question -- he did not commit the crime." Whether it produces net utility to punish the innocent man is as irrelevant as telling an umpire at a baseball game that it would produce net utility to give an underdog team four strikes instead of three when they are at bat. Questions about utility are only legitimately raised when we are evaluating rules and practices, not when we are making a judgment about whether a particular person accused of violating a criminal law is innocent.

6.2.2 Punishment as Retribution

Retributivism is the main alternative to the utilitarian theory of deterrence. Retributivist theory argues that the justification of punishment is to be found in its emphasis on the *essential nature* of the criminal act, not its consequences. If the act

[4] "Not only have different nations and individuals different notions of justice, but in the mind of one and the same individual, justice is not some one rule, principle, or maxim, but many which do not always coincide in their dictates, and, in choosing between which, he is guided either by some extraneous standard or by his own personal predilections." (Mill, *Utilitarianism*, V)

is a moral wrong, then this constitutes a complete justification for punishing the person who performed the act. The utilitarian looks *forward* to the consequences of punishment in order to justify it. The retributivist looks *backwards* in order to determine guilt. If she finds that the person is guilty, then this is logically sufficient for the conclusion that the agent deserves punishment. When the guilty person, the criminal, gets the punishment that he or she deserves, then justice is done.

Suppose that the father in the previous case was guilty of sexually abusing his teenage daughter. The retributivist would argue that the father *naturally deserves* punishment, not because his punishment would deter others, or because punishment will incapacitate him, or because he might undergo a change of character while in prison. Instead, he deserves punishment because of *the immorality of what he did*, and only because of this. A failure to punish would cancel the presumption that what he did was morally wrong. It is logically impossible to be morally guilty of sexually abusing one's child and at the same time not be liable to punishment.

How much punishment to administer depends on the seriousness of the immoral act. The severity of the punishment should be proportional to this. This does not mean that the punishment should be identical to the crime, even though the principle of "an eye for an eye" is deeply etched into the reactive desire of persons when a serious crime is committed. But although capital punishment for the crime of murder nicely fits the demands of the retributive principle, it does not easily transfer to other crimes. How are we to punish the homeless arsonist or the childless kidnapper? It is because of the impossibility of finding a punishment that will serve as the metaphorical "eye for an eye" that led retributivists to the principle of proportionality. This principle states that, "the amount of punishment should be *proportionate* to the moral seriousness or moral gravity of offenses…" (Ten, 154).

Setting aside questions about what it is that makes one offense more or less morally grave or serious than another, let us assume that the sexual abuse of a child is relatively high on the scale of moral seriousness. What standard of severity are we to use in deciding among the various kinds and amounts of punishment, and how are we to know when we have achieved a "fit" with the gravity of the crime? 10 years seems more severe than 5 years in prison because it is a longer period of time. How do we match this to an entirely different standard used for the moral seriousness of an offense, whatever that standard may be? I will leave this question to be answered by the reader, while cautioning her or him not to let their primitive desire for revenge dictate the kind and amount punishment they choose, nor revert to utilitarian calculations about deterrence.

The retributivist thinks it obvious that a parent who sexually abuses his child deserves punishment. But some critics dispute this. They do not see a *natural* connection between wrongdoing and criminal punishment because punishment is a *legal* response to wrongdoing. Legal responses imply the existence of an elaborate system of police, courts of law, prisons, and formal rules of both substance and procedure. The critic demands to know how a moral wrong could logically imply not only the existence of a complex and organized system of punishment, but its application in the instance case.

This question is reminiscent of a similar question asked about the relationship between morality and law in Chap. 2. The traditional theory of natural law proposes a natural or necessary connection between morality and positive law when it proclaims that "an unjust law is not a law." Retributivist theory also argues for a necessary connection between morality and positive law when it proclaims that a failure to punish wrongdoing violates the moral obligation to respond to the demand that the wrongdoer should be given the punishment he or she "deserves." And the same type of criticism made of natural law theory applies to retributivism. The retributivist cannot explain how it is that some morally neutral conduct is justifiably punished by law (for example, carrying a concealed weapon on a university campus), or how it is that there is immoral conduct that some believe should not be legally punished at all (for example, turning down an invitation to dinner with someone you do not like by telling the lie that you will be out of town).

One possible way to avoid these criticisms is to propose another version of retributivism that locates the justification of punishment in the unfair advantage gained by the criminal when he or she violates rules that others follow (Altman, 140). Here is an analogy to clarify this approach.[5] Suppose you are driving your car on a four lane highway and you see a sign directing all traffic to merge into a single lane on the right. You and most other drivers dutifully merge into single file, but you notice that a few cars are using the advantage of the slowed traffic to speed up in order to jump to the front of the line. By analogy, a criminal takes advantage of the restraint of others when she violates the law. The criminal and the driver are cheaters. The driver cheats by taking advantage of other drivers who dutifully merge at the end of the line of cars. The criminal cheats by taking advantage of behavior of those who obey the law.

This version of the retributivist theory answers the critic of the traditional version. It is justifiable to punish morally neutral conduct because such conduct amounts to cheating. The person who carries a concealed weapon on campus takes advantage of the restraint of those who obey the "no guns on campus" law in the same way that a cheater in a game of poker takes advantage of the rule-following behavior of others with whom she is playing.

But the analogy is flawed. Although the restraint of other drivers in the "merge to the right" example makes it possible for some drivers to take advantage of the obedience of others and get to the front of the line, it is not because of the restraint of others that makes it possible for a parent to sexually abuse his own child. There is no unfair advantage he has that *helps* him to sexually abuse his child. Unlike the "merge to the right" example, there is no causal relationship between the obedience of others to the child abuse laws and *him* having an opportunity to abuse his child.

The analogy between criminal conduct and cheating is also flawed. If I hide a card during a game of poker I have violated the rules of the game. This is properly called "cheating." When I cheat I am no longer playing the game of poker, although I disguise this fact from other players. I expect that others will not cheat because this would greatly reduce the chance I have of winning the game. I am in a better posi-

[5] This is a thought experiment shared with me many years ago by Professor Herbert Morris.

tion to win if I am the only cheater. But the rules of law and morals are not like the rules of a game. The persons in society to whom the rules of law and morals apply are not in a competition with each other, as if there were prizes to be won at the end of the day. When a parent sexually abuses his child he has not impaired the chance of others to win a perverse game he is playing with them, nor do other child abusers reduce his chance of winning this alleged game.

A more general criticism is that it is needlessly *redundant* to justify the punishment of child sexual abuse by deriving it from the immorality of "taking advantage of the restraint of others" or the immorality of "cheating." Surely the abuse of a child can stand on its own as seriously immoral behavior whether or not it can successfully be explained as violating some other moral rule (such as the rule prohibiting cheating). Moreover, this reductive attempt seems to diminish the *seriousness* of child sexual abuse. If we are to see child sexual abuse as a kind of cheating, then parental sexual abuse of a child would be seen as no more serious as cheating while playing a card game with her. The only way to avoid this criticism is to grade different instances of cheating from less to more serious. If the alleged cheating of a child sexual abuser is said to be more serious than cheating at cards and we explain this by the greater amount of suffering experienced by the victim of sexual abuse, then we are back to traditional retributivism. It is the suffering of the victim that justifies both the punishment and the amount of punishment meted out to the offender, and *this has nothing to do with cheating*.

6.3 Therapy, Not Punishment

There are some who believe that punishment is not a morally justified response to criminal conduct. They believe this because they believe that persons who commit crimes could not have helped what they did. They say that the persons accused of crime are suffering from a mental disease and the criminal conduct is a symptom of this disease. A criminal can no more have helped committing the crime than a child with measles can help displaying the familiar symptoms: body rash, high fever, muscle aches, sore throat, and runny nose. For the same reason that it would be morally wrong to punish the child for his symptoms, so it is immoral to punish an offender for actions that are symptomatic of a mental disease. Both are helpless victims of their disease and are not responsible for the symptoms they display.

An objection to this analogy is that an adult person with measles, though not responsible for her symptoms, is nonetheless responsible for infecting others. It was her choice to go out in public if she knew she was ill. But this objection does not apply to most cases of mental illness. Mental illness is not an infectious disease, and most persons who are mentally ill are unable to restrain themselves from a display of their symptoms, even if the display involves harming others.

Therefore, on this theory the only morally appropriate response of the legal system to crime is therapy, not punishment. This is how we respond to measles, headaches and heart murmurs, and this is how we should respond to criminal acts. Here are two quotes from leading proponents of this approach:

> Basically, criminality is but a symptom of insanity, using the term in its widest generic sense to express unacceptable social behavior based on unconscious motivation flowing from a disturbed instinctive and emotional life, whether this appears in frank psychoses, or in less obvious form in neuroses and unrecognized psychoses. ... If criminals are products of early environmental influences in the same sense that psychotics and neurotics are, then it should be possible to reach them psychotherapeutically. (Karpman, 9).

> We, the agents of society, must move to end the game of tit-for-tat and blow for-blow in which the offender has foolishly and futilely engaged himself and us. We are not driven, as he is, to wild and impulsive actions. With knowledge comes power, and with power there is no need for the frightened vengeance of the old penology. In its place should go a quiet, dignified, therapeutic program for the rehabilitation of the disorganized one, if possible, the protection of society during the treatment period, and his guided return to useful citizenship, as soon as this can be effected (Menninger, 63–64).

In Chap. 5 we looked at and rejected an *organic* model of the family and its implied recommendation that domestic violence should be treated as a sign of *family* dysfunction (section "Intrafamily harm and the family privacy principle"). We there rejected the organic model because of its disutility. Our main concern is that it could be used to justify a strong version of the Family Privacy Principle which might be used to block coercive state interventions on behalf of thousands if not millions of abused children and adults who have suffered from the violence of a family member. However, if we assume an *individualistic* model of the family and accordingly see domestic violence as a symptom of *individual* dysfunction to be responded to with therapy instead of punishment, then quite different problems emerge. Let us look first at the implications of a therapy system.

"The logic of sickness implies the logic of therapy, and therapy and punishment differ widely in their implications" (Morris, 482). The implications of a system that responds with therapy for those who have sexually abused their own children are these: First, the response to the abusive parent is not for what the parent has done to his child, but for the condition from which the therapist believes the abusive parent is suffering. The emphasis of a therapeutic response is not on the past suffering of the child but on something that is going on in the present: the abusive parent's mental disease. Second, unlike punishment, the aim of therapy is to help the abusive parent, not to harm him or deprive him of something we regard as good (for example, his liberty). Third, with punishment, we speak of proportioning the punishment to the crime. But with therapy, "attempts at proportionality make no sense." It is perfectly plausible to give someone who sexually abuses a child one week of counseling, but "treating for a lifetime within an institution one who has broken a dish and manifested accident proneness" (Morris, 484). All that matters is whether he is cured of what we believe to be the inner condition that caused the aberrant behavior, and this might take one day or a lifetime of therapy. Finally, in a punishment system there is no intervention until a person attempts or commits the criminal act. We do not want to visit the deprivations of punishment on a parent who might only be *thinking* of having sexual contact with her child but who has not yet taken the first steps toward doing this. We do not punish a person who only has immoral thoughts, and we want to allow for a possible change of mind. But in a therapy system there is no reason to wait until the diseased person manifests the symptoms of her disease. If we believe that a parent is suffering from a mental illness that inclines her to sexually abuse her child, then we would be justified in restraining and treating her now rather than wait for her to commit her first act of child abuse.

Should we treat all individuals who commit intrafamily harm as candidates for therapy instead of punishment? First, there is the empirical problem of proof. What evidence do the proponents of a therapy system have that *all* criminals, including all those who harm members of their own family, are "insane" in the generic meaning of this word given by Karpman in the quote above? And what evidence do we have that there are therapies that would change the relevant criminal behaviors? In light of the fact that there is little or no evidence to answer these two questions it would be presumptuous to discard the punishment system for a system of psychological rehabilitation. (It would be as presumptuous as it would be to propose that all certifiably insane people should be punished for the harms they cause while insane.) This is not to deny that there are individual cases in which the person who commits an act of family violence is mentally ill, and confinement for the purpose of therapy is an appropriate response. But there is no evidence to back up the claim that *all* or even a majority of those who commit such acts are mentally ill to the extent that they cannot help what they do.

Second, it is important for the proponent of therapy to concede that there are at least a few cases where the criminal act is an act the criminal *choose*s to commit. If the proponent does not concede this, then his claim that *all* criminal acts are symptomatic of mental disease should be taken as a conceptual claim about the notion of "criminality," But this is clearly not how the concept of criminality is used in either legal or non-legal language. The concept of a criminal act implies nothing about the mental health, reasoning or motivation of the criminal. It is true that a common reaction upon hearing about a parent who sexually abuses his child is to say "That man must have been very sick to have done such a thing." But it is just as common for one to say "That man must be very evil," implying in the latter case that he had a choice to refrain but refused to do this.

If the point about choice is conceded and yet the system is one that responds to *all* instances of domestic violence as suitable for therapy of the perpetrator, then the system is forcing the offender to change "so that he functions in a way regarded as normal by the current therapeutic community."

> We have to change him and his judgments of value. In doing this we display a lack of respect for the moral status of individuals, that is, a lack of respect for the reasoning and choices of individuals. They are but animals who must be conditioned. I think we can understand and, indeed, sympathize with a man's preferring death to being forcibly turned into what he is not. (Morris, 487)

There are many who will not sympathize with the man who freely chooses to sexually abuse his children. They would see no good reason to respect either his reasoning or his choices. But this is to misunderstand Morris's point in the quoted passage. He does not mean that we should show respect for *what* he chooses. Instead, he means that the morally appropriate response of the legal system should be of a kind that displays respect for his *choosing* to do it. The system ought to treat the offender *as a person* (not as an animal), and this is done only by responding to his free choice with punishment, not with therapy.

Questions for Thought and Discussion

1. Suppose it is recommended that *all* intrafamily harms (child abuse, child sexual abuse, spousal rape) should be responded to with therapy, not punishment. Would you support this recommendation? Explain.
2. "The logic of sickness implies the logic of therapy" (Herbert Morris). What does this mean?
3. How should we decide on the *manner* and *amount* of punishment for particular intrafamily crimes (incest, bigamy, polygamy, adultery, child sexual abuse, spousal rape)? Compare utilitarian and retributive responses to this question.
4. What justifies the common practice of excusing persons from criminal liability (punishment) if the harm they caused was unintentional or involuntary? Compare and contrast a utilitarian to a retributivist answer to this question.

References

American Humane Association. 2012. *Stop Child Abuse*. http://www.americanhumane.org/children/stop-child-abuse/fact-sheets/child-sexual-abuse.html. Accessed 28 March 2016.

Bentham, Jeremy. 1931. *The Theory of Legislation*. New York: Routledge and Kegan Paul.

Davis, Michael. 1992. *To Make the Punishment Fit the Crime*. Westview.

Devlin, Patrick. 1965. *The Enforcement of Morals*. New York/London: Oxford University Press.

Feinberg, Joel. 1984. *Harm to Others*. New York/London: Oxford University Press.

Hart, H.L.A. 1963. *Law, Liberty and Morality*. Stanford: Stanford University Press.

———. 1973. *Punishment and Responsibility*. New York/London: Oxford University Press.

Kant, Immanuel. 1965. *Metaphysical Elements of Justice*. Trans. J. Ladd. Indianapolis: Bobbs-Merrill.

Karpman, Benjamin. 1956. Criminal Psychodynamics. *The Journal of Criminal Law and Criminology* 47: 9.

Kennedy v Louisiana, 554 US 407 (2008).

Menninger, Karl. 1959. Therapy, Not Punishment. *Harper's Magazine* (August).

Mill, John Stuart. 1979. *On Liberty*. Indianapolis: Hackett.

Morris, Herbert. 1968. Persons and Punishment. *The Monist* 52: 475–501.

Ten, C.L. 1987. *Crime, Guilt and Punishment*. New York/London: Oxford University Press.

Texas Constitution and Statutes. 2016. http://www.statutes.legis.state.tx.us/?link=FA. Accessed 27 Mar 2016.

University of Minnesota. 2014. Case Studies. *Center for Advanced Studies in Child Welfare*. http://cascw.umn.edu/. Accessed 28 Mar 2016.

U.S. Department of Justice. 2014. *Raising Awareness about Sexual Abuse: Facts and Statistics*. http://www.nsopw.gov/en/Education/FactsStatistics. Accessed 28 Mar 2016.

———. 2016. Office for Victims of Crime. www.ovc.gov. Accessed 27 Mar 2016.

Chapter 7
Child Abuse and Neglect

> *"It is time to abandon the myth that 'the best foster family is not as good as a marginal biological family.' The ability to make a baby does not ensure that a couple have, or ever will have, the ability to be adequate parents."*
>
> Richard Gelles (1996)

Abstract A familiar public response to intrafamily harm is child protection. It is a response that occurs when cases of child abuse or neglect are given over to a family or juvenile court. The court orders a disposition primarily aimed at protecting the child from further harm. The disposition may consist of court ordered home services for the family, temporary transfer of the child to a foster family, or permanent severance of the parent-child relationship. In creating the disposition, a judge will first attempt to determine what is in the child's best interest. This is where philosophical questions arise. What is an interest? How does an interest relate to the concept of a harm? What should count as a child's interests? What interests are best or better than other interests? The answer to these questions often depends on one's conception of the relationship of a child to the family. We look at a distinction between different models or ideals of the family, each of which generates different answers. These answers are closely related to a debate between social welfare professionals over whether it is more important to protect the child or to preserve the family, and to a related debate between those who want to criminalize abusive conduct and those who want to take a therapeutic approach to domestic violence by searching for and correcting its underlying causes.

7.1 Protecting the Child: The Family Court Option

There are three major categories of court cases that result from child abuse and child neglect: criminal, tort and family or juvenile court. In a criminal case, "the alleged perpetrator of child maltreatment is charged with a crime (for example, sexual

L.D. Houlgate, *Philosophy, Law and the Family*, AMINTAPHIL: The Philosophical Foundations of Law and Justice 7,
DOI 10.1007/978-3-319-51121-4_7

assault), and the case proceeds through the criminal courts." In a tort case, "the victim, or a representative of the victim, may be able to sue the perpetrator in a civil action for damages." In Chap. 6 we looked at the justification for responding to intrafamily crime with punishment (Sect. 6.2) and with therapy (Sect. 6.3) But the most common judicial response to child abuse and neglect, whether caused by a person who is or is not a family member, is a family court intervention to *protect the child* from further harm. This is the legal response we shall examine in this chapter.

When the family court option is taken by the state, a two-stage procedure usually occurs: *jurisdictional* and *dispositional*. In the jurisdictional stage, "the court determines if it has subject-matter jurisdiction by deciding whether the facts of the case come within the definition of abuse, neglect, or dependency used in the state as established by statute and court opinion" (*id.*). If the family (or juvenile) court has jurisdiction, then it must decide what *child protective disposition* it should make:

> The court's judgment is sometimes called a *dispositional order*. A number of options are available. Examples: (a) Leave the child with the current parent or other caregiver under the supervision of the child protective services or a child welfare agency and require counseling or other conditions designed to prevent future maltreatment; (b) Place the child in foster care or in an institution. (c) Begin proceedings to terminate the parental rights of the parent so that the child can be adopted (Statsky 2015).

A family court judge will usually ask for the recommendation of Child Protective Services (CPS) prior to making a dispositional choice for an abused or neglected child. CPS will then organize a Child Protective Team (CPT) and assign it to the requested case. Our concern here will be with the dispositional stage of the process

7.2 Two Cases

Let us begin with brief descriptions of two cases, drawn from the extensive social sciences literature on domestic violence.[1] The first is a case of child abuse. The second is a case of child neglect. The difference between the two is that *child abuse* involves harmful acts of *commission*, specifically "serious physical, emotional or sexual mistreatment of a child that is not the result of accident or circumstances beyond the control of the parent or guardian." *Child neglect* involves harmful

[1] "Children are suffering from a hidden epidemic of child abuse and neglect. Last year 3.6 million reports of child abuse and neglect were reported to state and local agencies in the United States involving 6.6 million children (reports can include multiple children). The United States has one of the worst records among industrialized nations – losing more than four children on average every day to child abuse and neglect" (American Society for the Positive Care of Children 2016). The overwhelming number of children who die from abuse or neglect are under the age of four; roughly half are less than a year old. Across the U.S. "about one in three children who die from maltreatment belongs to a family that had previously drawn attention from the attention of child-protective services" (Lepore 2016). See also fn. 22 at 5.3.3.

omissions, specifically "the failure of a parent or guardian to provide the basic needs of a child, including physical needs (e.g. food and shelter), emotional needs, medical needs, and educational needs" (Statsky, 746).

Denise: A Case of Child Abuse. Denise is a recently adopted nine-year-old girl who had been subjected to 226 lashes with a belt for failure to bring home her homework papers. Denise's mother, in addition to doing most of the beating, had attempted to breast feed the nine-year-old, checked her genitals daily for signs of masturbation, and engaged her in games of *Sorry* whenever Denise confessed the impulse to masturbate. The dispositional order was to place the child in foster care, under the supervision of CPS until such time that her mother could be cured of the condition that prompted her abnormal behavior (Newberger and Rosenfeld, 1977: 2087).

Jason: A Case of Child Neglect. Jason was originally removed from his home, at the age of 4 months, following a report of life threatening medical neglect. No relatives were available to take Jason so he was placed in foster care .... Four months after Jason was removed, he began partially supervised overnight and weekend visits [with his mother]. Following these visits the foster parent expressed concerns that the child was being overfed, that he was returning to the foster home with a very dirty diaper area and that there was concern that the child was not receiving medicine... [The agency worker] was also concerned about mother's relationship with Jason. She wrote, "Many times the mother will not initiate any contact with Jason...Most visits, Jason can be found in his walker, with [the mother] sitting, talking on the phone or watching T.V. She rarely, if ever, picks Jason up and even then it is for very short periods. Despite these reports, Jason was returned to his mother. Five months later Jason and his siblings were found in the hall playing with a lighter and gasoline. They were unsupervised and burned themselves. This incident was reported on TV news. A report followed which read, "mother leaves the children alone and will lock them in their room for hours . . . the mother leaves the children in the care of a 12-year-old who drinks and smokes." All of the children, including Jason were permanently removed from their mother on grounds of chronic child neglect, specifically for maintaining a life endangering environment and lack of supervision (Indiana University School of Social Work).

7.3 The Standard of "Best Interests of the Child"

It is not clear how the family court judges in the preceding cases reached their dispositional decision, although we can assume they employed the universally recommended standard of *the best interests of the child.* This phrase implies that the judge is to regard as secondary whatever interests the parents or other legal guardians of the child might have – unless the satisfaction of their interests can be shown to promote the interests of the child. Judges are given great discretion in making dispositional decisions based on the best interests standard, so much so that critics claim that their decisions are often unpredictable and sometimes arbitrary. This is largely because the terms "best" and interests" in the standard is so vague. In deciding what disposition is in the best interests of the child the judge must not only decide what counts as a child's interest but she must also decide which of the many possible interests is "best." It is difficult to see how a judge is going to prevent herself from injecting her own personal views in making this determination in order to avoid the criticism that she is (consciously or unconsciously) promoting the values of her own life experiences, culture and upbringing. Hence, our next question is whether there are any objective criteria that would help the court to make a "best interests" decision.

What was once subjective is believed to be objective if there is a list of interests that have been either codified, or frequently used by a majority of family and juvenile courts over a long period of time[2]. The list of interests will then serve as a precedent and therefore immune to the charge of arbitrariness on the part of the court. For example, 28 states refer to "family integrity and preference for avoiding removal of the child from his/her home" as one of the most important interests of a child (Child Welfare Information Gateway 2013).[3] A second interest is "the health, safety, and/or protection of the child" mentioned in the codes of 19 states. 12 states want assurances that a child removed from his/her home "will be given care, treatment, and guidance that will assist the child in developing into a self-sufficient adult." The statutes of 21 states include more specific interests of the child: "Emotional ties and relationships between the child and his or her parents, siblings, family and household members, or other caregivers" (15 states); "The capacity of the parents to provide a safe home and adequate food, clothing, and medical care" (9 states); "The mental and physical health needs of the child" (8 states); "The men-

[2]The Revised Code of the State of Ohio attempts to clarify the meaning of "best interests of the child" as follows: (1) In determining the best interest of a child …the court shall consider all relevant factors, including, but not limited to, the following: (a) The interaction and interrelationship of the child with the child's parents, siblings, relatives, foster caregivers and out-of-home providers, and any other person who may significantly affect the child; (b) The wishes of the child, as expressed directly by the child or through the child's guardian ad litem, with due regard for the maturity of the child; (c) The custodial history of the child, including whether the child has been in the temporary custody of one or more public children services agencies or private child placing agencies for twelve or more months of a consecutive twenty-two-month period, or the child has been in the temporary custody of one or more public children services agencies or private child placing agencies for twelve or more months of a consecutive twenty-two-month period and, as described in division (D)(1) of section 2151.413 of the Revised Code, the child was previously in the temporary custody of an equivalent agency in another state; (d) The child's need for a legally secure permanent placement and whether that type of placement can be achieved without a grant of permanent custody to the agency; (e) Whether any of the factors in divisions (E)(7) to (11) of this section apply in relation to the parents and child. For the purposes of division (D)(1) of this section, a child shall be considered to have entered the temporary custody of an agency on the earlier of the date the child is adjudicated pursuant to section 2151.28 of the Revised Code or the date that is sixty days after the removal of the child from home. (2) If all of the following apply, permanent custody is in the best interest of the child, and the court shall commit the child to the permanent custody of a public children services agency or private child placing agency: (a) The court determines by clear and convincing evidence that one or more of the factors in division (E) of this section exist and the child cannot be placed with one of the child's parents within a reasonable time or should not be placed with either parent. (b) The child has been in an agency's custody for two years or longer, and no longer qualifies for temporary custody pursuant to division (D) of section 2151.415 of the Revised Code. (c) The child does not meet the requirements for a planned permanent living arrangement pursuant to division (A)(5) of section 2151.353 of the Revised Code. (d) Prior to the dispositional hearing, no relative or other interested person as filed, or has been identified in, a motion for legal custody of the child (section 2151.414)

[3]All of the data in this paragraph about how the best interest's standard is interpreted by the states is taken from this source.

tal and physical health of the parents" (8 states); "[Protection from] domestic violence in the home" (8 states).

What is an interest? Both the opponents and proponents of the best interests standard would probably agree with Joel Feinberg's definition of an *interest* as something which a person *has a stake in* because that person stands to gain or lose depending on what happens to it (Feinberg 1973). Thus, an infant has a stake in being frequently picked up and held by her parents or other caretakers because she stands to suffer psychologically and physically depending on whether or not this simple act is done. Second, an interest is not a preference. A newborn has no preferences, but it makes perfectly good sense to say that she has an interest in being frequently held, as well as being fed, clothed and sheltered. An 8-year-old child may not prefer to eat the vegetables on her dinner plate, but she has an interest in consuming them. The child makes it known to her parents what she prefers, but her parents reasonably claim to know what foods she *needs* to consume.

As argued in Chap. 5, harm involves more than being physically hurt (Sect. 5.3.1). When my uninsured house burns down while I am on vacation and I do not know this until I return home weeks later, I was harmed at the very moment my house burnt down, not at the moment that I found this out. The harm is to my financial status and probably to my emotional state as well (I lost all my family photos). The point is that we have interests other than an interest in being free from physical and emotional pain. Feinberg concludes from examples like this that *harm* is best defined as a *setback to an interest*, that is, a setback to something in which one has a stake. I have an interest in my financial status, and this interest can suffer a setback whether or not I feel am hurt. A woman whose husband is having an ongoing adulterous affair may not know about this for many years. Because she is unaware, she is not hurt by her husband's behavior, but he is certainly harming her interest in (what she believes to be) his loyalty, devotion and faithfulness to his marital vows.

Returning to the "best interests of the child" standard, if we are to call some interests "best" in the sense of being better than others, then we need to rank interests. In addition to the interests mentioned above (family integrity, emotional ties, safe home, security, adequate food, clothing and shelter), other interests of the child might include stability (in living arrangements, schooling, access to relatives and friends), availability of a parent to spend time with the child, equal access to educational opportunities, being raised in a religious or "moral" environment, not being exposed to incidents of domestic violence.

In order to rank these interests, we might take a clue from H.L.A. Hart's minimum content theory of natural law (Sect. 3.7.3). Humans are vulnerable creatures, and human children are especially vulnerable to physical and emotional harm while they are young. This natural fact plus the fact that some parents lack either the will, knowledge or intelligence to respond adequately to childhood suffering (as in the cases of Denise and Jason) explains why a just legal system must not only contain rules prohibiting child abuse and neglect but the standards governing the court ordered disposition of an abused child must have content specifying a physically and emotionally safe environment for the child, protection from accidental injury, and adequate provision of food, clothing and medical care. Without health and security little else matters for a child. Hence, physical and emotional health should count as *fundamental* (or *best*) interests of a child, while an alleged interest in being raised by a parent who is a theist or a heterosexual would be at the bottom of the ranking scale, each of these having little or no relevance to the goal of child protection.

7.4 Using Family Models to Determine the Best Interests of a Child

We earlier distinguished between two models or conceptions of the family: individualistic and organic (section "Intrafamily harm and the family privacy principle"). Let us now expand on this distinction in order to see how they might be used to influence an interpretation of a child's interests that can be used to make decisions at the dispositional stage in a child abuse or neglect case.

In the *individualistic* model of the family the central concepts are the *individual* and the *rights* of the individual family member. In this model, the family is viewed in much the same way that one might view a business partnership. When one person forms a partnership with another we see it composed of individual persons who are basically complete outside the partnership. They use the partnership to fulfill their *individual needs and desires*, and the partnership is at most a useful instrument for the satisfaction of these needs and desires, to be abandoned whenever it fails to achieve this end. And so it is, or should be, within the family, according to the individualistic model. A family is a coming together and creation of independent individuals, each of whom has his own interests, desires, plans, and standards of judgment. The family combines the efforts of its members, but it does not merge the members into a single entity, and the purpose of the family is to see that the interests, needs, and desires of each family member are advanced. Hence, the goods stressed by those who think of the family on this model are individualistic: goods the enjoyment of which do not necessarily involve the participation of others, for example, the goods of food, shelter, clothing, health, security, and aesthetic and intellectual goods.

In the *organic* model the central concepts are the *family* and the *autonomy* of the family. This model of the family is called organic because the family is literally compared to a living organism. In an organism, the parts exist for the whole. Thus, the heart, liver, and lungs of the human body may be conceived as subservient to the interests of the total living organism. Indeed, these bodily parts are viewed as constituted by, rather than constituting the body – for they are basically incomplete apart from the body. Finally, in an organism, we speak of a "proper subordination" of the parts, not "equality," and we certainly do not speak of the separate interests, plans, or purposes of the parts. Each part exists for the whole, not for itself. Parents and children take their existence and their purpose from their participation in the family. In the patriarchal organic model, the father gives the orders that the subordinate family members, wife and children, obey. Yet all family members, including the father, submit to the interests of the unified whole that is the family. Each family member exists for the family, not for itself. The fundamental duty of the family, on the organic conception, is that of taking care of the needs of the family, and far less the satisfying simply of one's own needs. The type of good for children stressed by those who promote the organic conception of the family are the inherently *social goods*, goods whose very enjoyment directly involves relationships with others – for example, the goods of love, friendship, trust, devotion, community, and participation in the life of the family. In general, relationships involving intimacy are goods the pursuit of which are central to the organic conception of the family.

Let's consider some implications of these two models for disposition decisions regarding abused or endangered children. First, if the child protection team (CPT) advising the family court judge assumes an individualistic model of the family as the ideal to be followed, then disposition decisions will be largely based on the notion of rights. This is because the idea of a contract is essential to the model. All family members, as parties to the contract, have rights. These rights are rights against someone, and the persons against whom the rights are asserted have a reciprocal duty or obligation. Moreover, these rights necessarily require third parties to enforce them.[4] Since the child is viewed as an individual whose good is something that (logically) can be attained independently of his participation in the life of the family and since the contract guarantees the child a right to the enjoyment of this good, then the team will not hesitate to intrude into the child-family relationship when necessary to aid the child in the pursuance of this good. That is, the two features of the individualistic model of the family – goods the enjoyment of which are essentially localized in individuals and contract rights to the enjoyment of these goods – suggest a dispositional approach that would have the CPT aggressively intervene when necessary to secure the child's right to physical and psychological health.

Second, dispositional decisions employing an organic model of the family will be based on a consideration of the interests of the entire family when it uses the best interest standard. This is because the child's good or interest is believed to be primarily social. The child's best interests cannot be separated from the interests of the family. If her interests are to be achieved, they can only be achieved by promoting the good of the family. Hence, it is important for the CPT to respect the *integrity of the family* in making treatment decisions. The child is seen as a mere part of an organic whole – a whole in which the natural "ruling" part of the family are the parents. The parents are presumed to know what is best for the child, since the child's good cannot be separated from that of the family and only the parent can know the latter good. However, this presumption can be overridden if it is believed that the harm suffered by an abused or neglected child is not something that the parents or other caregivers can control. In that case, the role of the CPT is to recommend services and family therapy sufficient to cure the underlying condition that led to the abuse of the child.

The tension between organic and individualistic models of the family can be seen in policies recommended by child welfare organizations and pediatricians for the

---

[4] For example, the right of a child not to be abused or neglected is a claim against society that it intervene to protect it against those who would commit these acts or omissions. The three parties are: the child, the state, and those who would injure the child.

disposition of abused and neglected children. There are two sets of policies we examine below, each containing opposing recommendations: Family Preservation vs Child Protection, and Compassion vs Control.

7.4.1 Family Preservation vs Child Protection

The term *family preservation* (sometimes referred to as *family integrity*) has been used since the 1970s to describe a variety of social welfare programs that are intended to provide services to children and families experiencing serious problems that may eventually lead to the placement of children in foster care or otherwise result in the dissolution of the family unit. These programs "shared a common philosophy of family centered services including focusing on family strengths, involving families in determining their case plan goals, serving the entire family, and treating family members with respect" (U.S. Department of Health and Human Services 1995). When applied to family court disposition decisions in cases of child abuse and neglect, the family preservation approach attempts to change the way in which the family functions as a whole.

> Under the original program in Iowa, teams of workers carried a caseload of 10 to 12 families whom they saw in the families' homes for an average of four and one-half months. Both concrete and therapeutic services were provided and the principles of working with families in a respectful and positive manner were emphasized... In Oregon, a family treatment model was used. It relied less on the provision of concrete and supportive services and more on family therapy. Services were provided in an office as well as in the home... Workers carried a caseload of approximately 11 families. Services were provided for 90 days with weekly follow-up services provided for an average of three to five and one-half months.

The family preservation approach to family court dispositions stands in contrast to *child protection* (also referred to as child removal) dispositions that emphasize the health and safety of the abused or neglected child. This approach gets its impetus from a number of family preservation attempts which have led to more abuse and, in some cases, the death of a child. One of the early critics of family preservation was Richard Gelles.

> The essential first step in creating a safe world for children is to abandon the fantasy that child welfare agencies can balance the goals of protecting children and preserving families, adopting instead a child-centered policy of family services. This [child protection] is not a new policy, but rather a return to the policy of the 1960s that established child safety as the overriding goal of the child protection system. It is time to abandon the myth that "the best foster family is not as good as a marginal biological family." The ability to make a baby does not ensure that a couple have, or ever will have, the ability to be adequate parents. The policy of family reunification and family preservation fails because it assumes that *all* biological parents can become fit and acceptable parents if only appropriate and sufficient support is provided (Gelles 1996).

Gelles' criticism is utilitarian and empirical. It is utilitarian in that he bases his rejection on the *consequences* of using family preservation as a dispositional policy. Family preservation should always be seen as a means to an end, not an end in itself.

The end of any policy governing family court dispositions should be the health and safety of the abused or neglected child. Second, it is *empirical* in that the facts do not support family preservation policy as a means to this end. Instead (Gelles claims) it has frequently had the opposite effect of continued abuse and neglect.[5]

7.4.2 Compassion vs Control

Closely related to the policies of family prevention and child protection are two approaches to family court dispositions that might be recommended to the court by the CPT. These approaches are referred to as *compassion* and *control*. To take the compassionate approach is to try to form a helpful professional-parent relationship in order "to understand and to improve the functioning of the abusing family" (Bittner and Newberg, 1981: 205). By way of contrast, the control approach to child abuse cases "refers to the aggressive uses of intervention to limit, and if necessary to punish deviant behavior. It assumes that an individual must take full responsibility for his actions and the State will hold him accountable" (Newberger and Rosenfeld, 1977: 2087). If the advice to the court is to limit the deviant behavior, then the recommended disposition would probably be to remove the child from the home and place her in foster care and/or to terminate parental rights. If the recommendation is to "punish deviant behavior," then abuse of the child would be treated as a criminal case.

The control approach to creating a family court disposition is consistent with the child protection policy. Both would make protection of the child their first priority, and both appear to assume a version of the individualistic model of family relationships. In the case of Denise (Sect. 7.4.1), her case would either be referred to the criminal court to be adjudicated as felonious child sexual abuse, or it would receive a family court disposition order to remove the child from her mother. Some would say that Denise's mother should be treated no differently than the way she would be treated if she had done such things to the child of a stranger, or to an adult. She should be charged with a crime and the case should proceed through the criminal court. If the case remains in family court, removal would probably be the disposition ordered. Since Denise's interests or good can be defined independently of her participation in the life of her family and since her interest in bodily security cannot be guaranteed if she remains in the home, then she should be removed until the court is assured that she will no longer be harmed.

---

[5] Lepore discusses a continuing cycle of scandal and reform in state child welfare departments. The result is a "policy pendulum" between "family preservation (keeping kids with their family of origin) and removal (removing kids from their homes and severing parental rights so that the kids can be adopted). If a child dies while under the watch of the child welfare department, the pendulum will swing toward removal. If the number of deaths goes down as the result of this policy, then complaints are made about the department "breaking up the family" and the pendulum will swing back to a policy of family preservationDOUBLEHYPHEN until there is another child death (Lepore, 49).

The policy of family preservation, based on an organic conception of family relationships, would take a compassionate approach in recommending a disposition in cases of child abuse and neglect. The organic model implies that treatment decisions regarding children are based on a consideration of the interests of the entire family. This is because of the assumption that the child's good or interest cannot be separated from that of the family. If her good is to be achieved, it can only be achieved by promoting the good of the family.

As some experts on child abuse dispositions have stressed, "with child abuse the whole family is disturbed and not each needy member alone" (Terr and Watson, 119). That is, if we assume the organic model of the family, when a parent abuses a child the parent's conduct is to be regarded as a symptom of some pathological condition of the family in the way that high fever, listlessness and spots on the body are symptoms of a pathological condition (e.g. as in measles) of the organic body. Abusive parental behavior toward children diverges from what we regard as normal behavior. Such divergent behavior is viewed as a manifestation of family disease. Parental behavior toward children conforming to what is normal is assimilated to the normal and healthy functioning of bodily organs.

We previously discussed (Sect. 6.3) the analogy of child abuse to symptoms of a disease. First, as just noted, there is something abnormal in both the case of parental abuse of children and a symptom of an organic disease. Second, there are causes for this abnormality such that once we know of them we can explain the abnormality as we can now explain the symptoms of many organic diseases. Parental abuse of their children is looked upon as a happening with a causal explanation rather than an action for which the abusing parent had reasons. Thus, commentators who take the organic approach to understanding child abuse commonly attribute abusive parental behavior to a variety of causes, for example stresses produced by the child (e.g. the child is handicapped, retarded, hyperactive), stresses produced by the parent (low self-esteem, depression, abused as a child, alcoholism, drug addiction, psychiatric illness), and social situational stresses (poverty, unemployment, excess or unwanted children). Underlying these causes are "the social and cultural factors that guide individual behavior" (the acceptability of corporal punishment as a mode of parental discipline of children, violent entertainment in the cinema and on television, or an inequitable, alienating economic system).

If we conceive of parental abuse of children as a symptom of family disease, in the manner just specified, then the child protection team and the court is to respond to a case of abuse, not with the approach of "control," but with that of "compassion," not with punishment, but with therapy. "The logic of sickness implies the logic of therapy" (Morris, 31). And therapy suggests compassion for what the family is undergoing, not resentment for what the parent has illegitimately done to the child. The approach of therapy is not like an approach to an individual who is at fault. The response that the clinician is to make to the family is based not on what the parent has done to the child but is to be directed to the condition, the disease, from which the entire family is suffering. And since the disease is quite complex, with "multivariate origins," the response will tax the abilities of the clinician. Not only must the abused child's injuries be treated, but also such community resources as child care homemaker services and psychological counseling must be utilized in the multidisciplinary treatment of the family. Family preservation becomes the priority of the social worker, not because the family is to be preserved for its own sake, but because the child's best interests cannot be separated from the best interests of the family.

An example of how the organic model influences a clinical approach is the case of an 8-month-old child suffering from a condition called *failure to thrive*. "The child was tiny, emaciated and did not respond to play. There were moderate hip and elbow contractures. Her weight and length were below the third percentile" (Bittner and Newberger 1981, 205). The cause of the child's failure to thrive was the neglect of the mother to provide adequate care. The clinician does not presume that the child's neglect is the fault of the mother. Instead, it is to be seen as symptomatic of family crisis. In the instant case, the crisis was that the mother was unmarried, and her infant was the fourth child of the fourth father. The mother had moved to an alien large city with her children, but she could not get child care, dental care, decent employment or health care, including contraceptive services. She subsequently fell into a state of extreme depression. The disposition ordered by the court reflected and responded to the particular facts of family crisis. A compassionately conducted family assessment permitted identifying a management program, which enabled the child to thrive in her care. On discharge from the hospital, a homemaker came three days a week, a visiting nurse on alternate days. Weekly clinic visits were scheduled. Preschool services were found for her two older children. A social worker gave weekly counseling, which was associated with an increase in the mother's self-esteem. Dental and medical treatment, along with the other elements in the management plan, was coordinated by the social worker. The disposition of this case was quite successful, "At a 5-year follow-up the patient was physically and psychologically normal. Her family, including a new younger brother, was happy and healthy" (*Id.*)

7.5 An Alternative Dispositional Standard

Decisions on whether a child should be removed from the home or whether supportive in-home services should be ordered are the most important ones confronting the family court and the child protection team when making disposition recommendations to the court. Hence, it is important to have clear standards on which to base one's recommendations. My argument has been that the "best interests of the child" standard fails to provide the requisite clarity. The notion of an "interest" employed in the standard is susceptible of wide variation depending especially on whether a child's good or interest is seen as one the enjoyment of which is essentially localized in individuals or whether it is one the enjoyment of which directly involves a communal (organic) relationship. Hence, one and the same case may receive two different, opposed recommendations for disposition depending on which notion of the "child's best interests" one adopts.

We can resolve this difficulty in one of two ways. First, we can choose to retain the "best interests of the child" standard, but rule that only certain kinds of things will count as interests of the child. For example, we might side with the individualistic account and rule that only those things the enjoyment of which does *not* require relationships with other persons are genuine interests. But this seems arbitrary, especially in light of examples like the "failure to thrive" case discussed above (Sect. 7.4.2) which argues for a broader, organic view of a child's interests. Second, we can abandon the "best interests of the child" standard altogether and search for a test to be used in disposition proceedings that does not permit such wide variation in dispositional recommendations.

An alternative standard was suggested many years ago by the National Institute for Juvenile Justice and Delinquency Prevention (Flicker 1982: 156). The standard recommends that a child should not be removed from the home unless the court finds that:

(a) The child has been adjudicated as abused or neglected; and,
(b) The court finds that removal is necessary in order to protect the child from further harm *of the type precipitating adjudication*; and,
(c) The court finds that there is a placement available in which the child will not be harmed in a manner which would constitute the same or another basis for family court jurisdiction.

I will call this the *jurisdictional interests* (*JI*) standard. The major difference between this and the *best interests* (*BI*) standard is that *JI* attempts to protect those interests and only those interests (or prevent those harms and only those harms) *over which the court has jurisdiction*. Thus, suppose that emotional or psychological harm is a basis for family court jurisdiction under the laws prohibiting child abuse. Consider again the case of Denise. Under most state codes, a sufficient condition for calling her case one of child abuse is that Denise is the victim of "sexual conduct harmful to her mental, emotional, or physical welfare, including conduct that constitutes the offense of continuous sexual abuse" (Texas Family Code, 261.001).[6]

[6](1) Under the Texas Family Code, "abuse" includes the following acts or omissions by a person: (A) mental or emotional injury to a child that results in an observable and material impairment in the child's growth, development, or psychological functioning; (B) causing or permitting the child to be in a situation in which the child sustains a mental or emotional injury that results in an observable and material impairment in the child's growth, development, or psychological functioning; (C) physical injury that results in substantial harm to the child, or the genuine threat of substantial harm from physical injury to the child, including an injury that is at variance with the history or explanation given and excluding an accident or reasonable discipline by a parent, guardian, or managing or possessory conservator that does not expose the child to a substantial risk of harm; (D) failure to make a reasonable effort to prevent an action by another person that results in physical injury or that results in substantial harm to the child; (E) sexual conduct harmful to a child's mental, emotional, or physical welfare, including conduct that constitutes the offense of continuous sexual abuse of a young child or children, indecency with a child, sexual assault, or aggravated sexual assault; (F) failure to make a reasonable effort to prevent sexual conduct harmful to a child; (G) compelling or encouraging the child to engage in sexual conduct, including compelling or encouraging the child in a manner that constitutes an offense of trafficking of persons, prostitution,

Now once having decided in (a) that there is a basis for family court jurisdiction, then the court must decide (b) whether removal of Denise from the home is necessary to prevent recurrence of the sexual abuse. If the child protection team finds that this is likely, then under part (c) a dispositional order of the court should be one that aims at preventing a recurrence of the specific harm for which it intervened in the first place. If it fails to design a disposition that is likely to prevent recurrence of the sexual and emotional harm, then one wonders why the court had jurisdiction to intervene in the first place. Finally, there is no need to make further inquiries about Denise's "best interests." The only relevant interest is her emotional and psychological well-being, that is, the very interest that was violated and which prompted the adjudication under the child abuse statute. This is what will guide and should guide the court in creating a dispositional order.

This is not to deny that there are a number of types of disposition that the court might design to prevent recurrence, including both court ordered services as well as temporary removal. If it is clear from the evidence that there is a probability of recurrence of the abusive incident, then the family court disposition might require the abused child's parent(s) to accept certain services (day care, homemaker services, psychiatric counseling, case worker visits) before it takes the next step of ordering removal from the home. Many child protective service professionals are inclined to accept the preference for the home and the family, but only because "a child is most apt to thrive in the custody of those who have cared for her since birth" (Goldstein, Freud and Solnit, 32-34). I would caution against basing this preference on an original right of the parents to the care and custody of their children. Parents have the legal right to make decisions regarding child management only because child development research has established that children are more likely to achieve proper growth and development through continuous relationships with a "psychological" parent. Hence, the preference for leaving the child in the home while ordering services for the family is based on concern for the well-being of the child, not on any right to well-being of the family.

Finally, before any child is removed from his home, the court must find that there is a placement in fact available in which the child will not suffer further (legally defined) abuse (Mnookin, 615). Thus, there would be little point in removing a child from a home in which, say, she has been sexually abused if, as a result of removal she might be harmed again in a way that causes her to display one of those symptoms of emotional harm that would normally serve as a basis for intervention, e.g. untoward aggressive behavior, severe anxiety, depression, or withdrawal.

In closing, it should be noted that we have not touched on a question that some might regard as the most important: what harms to the child should constitute a basis for family court jurisdiction? In attempting to construct a standard to guide the court in making post-adjudicatory removal decisions, it is assumed that the court has a clear standard for the scope of its jurisdiction. Where the standard for family

---

or compelling prostitution; (H) causing, permitting, encouraging, engaging in, or allowing the photographing, filming, or depicting of the child if the person knew or should have known that the resulting photograph, film, or depiction of the child is obscene, or pornographic.

court jurisdiction is couched in such vague language as "parental immorality" or "lack of proper parental care", then using the standard for removal I have suggested above, the court is allowed to order removal in cases in which some might argue the child has suffered no specific physical or psychological damage, and might be much worse off through being separated from his parents. The way to guard against this unhappy result is to review the standards for family court jurisdiction, a review in which we should be quite clear about the moral principles guiding us in a determination of the kinds of interests of the child the juvenile court thinks that it would protect. These principles were critically discussed in a previous chapter (Sect. 5.3). It seems clear from that discussion that any standard we might suggest for the dispositional phase of a juvenile court proceeding are defensible only if we can also defend, on moral grounds, clear standards for determining what is to count as child abuse.

Questions for Thought and Discussion

1. Explain the difference between *family preservation* and *child protection* policies of child welfare agencies. How would you defend these policies? Is it possible to find a compromise between these two approaches to family intervention?
2. What is the difference between the approaches of *compassion* and *control* when a CPT responds to a case of child abuse or neglect? What problems arise in recommending either of these approaches in a dispositional order to a child protection team?
3. What is the difference between an *individualistic* and an *organic* model of family relationships? How does the choice of a model influence an interpretation of the best interests of the child standard in fashioning a dispositional order for a child who is found to be abused or neglected?

References

American Society for the Positive Care of Children. 2016. *Statistics and Facts about Child Abuse in the U.S.*http://americanspcc.org/child-abuse-statistics/. Accessed 7 Apr 2016.

Bittner, S., and E. Newberger. 1981. Pediatric Understanding of Child Abuse and Neglect. *Pediatrics in Review* 2: 7.

Child Welfare Information Gateway. 2013. *Determining the Best Interests of the Child.* Washington, DC: U.S. Department of Health and Human Services, Children's Bureau. https://www.childwelfare.gov/topics/systemwide/laws-policies/statutes/best-interest/. Accessed 28 Mar 2016.

Feinberg, Joel. 1973. *Social philosophy*. New Jersey: Prentice-Hall.

Flicker, Barbara Danziger. 1982. *Standards for Juvenile Justice: A Summary and Analysis,* 2nd edn. American Bar Association. Institute for Judicial Administration. Cambridge, MA: Ballinger.

Gelles, Richard J. 1996. *The Book of David: How Preserving Families Can Cost Children's Lives*. New York: Basic Books.

Lepore, Jill. 2016. Baby Doe: A Political History of Tragedy. *The New Yorker*. 1 February, 46–57.

Mnookin, Robert. 1973. Foster Care—In Whose Best Interest? *Harvard Educational Review* 43: 613.

Morris, Herbert. 1968. Persons and Punishment. *The Monist* 52: 475.

Newberger, E., and A. Rosenfeld. 1977. Compassion vs Control: Conceptual and Practical Pitfalls in the Broadened Definition of Child Abuse. *Journal of the American Medical Association* 237: 19.

Ohio Revised Code, Title 21, XXI, Chapter 2151, Juvenile Court.

Statsky, William P. 2015. *Family law: The essentials*, 3rd ed. Stamford: Cengage.

Terr, V., and B. Watson. 1968. The Battered Child Rebrutalized: Ten Cases of Medical Legal Confusion. *American Journal of Psychiatry* 124: 10.

Texas Family Code, Title 6, Subtitle E, Chapter 261, Subchapter A.

U.S. Department of Health and Human Services. 1995. Review of Family Preservation and Family Reunification Programs. https://aspe.hhs.gov/basic-report/review-family-preservation-and-family-reunification-programs. Accessed on 31 Jan 2016.

Chapter 8
Family Torts and Remedies

"The flames which [tort] litigation would kindle on the domestic hearth would consume in an instant the conjugal bond, and bring on a new era – indeed an era of universal discord, of unchastity, of bastardy, of dissoluteness, of violence, cruelty, and murders."

J. Woodward (1858)

Abstract In this chapter we define the concept of a tort and explain the distinction between tort and criminal liability. We introduce the doctrines of parental and spousal immunity that are still used in some jurisdictions to shield parents and spouses from lawsuits brought against them by a child or spouse. We begin the chapter by asking general and particular questions about tort law and its application to injuries occurring in the family. The general questions are: What is the general aim of tort law? Why are certain types of conduct classified as torts and other kinds of conduct are not torts? Responses to these questions refer to principles governing the just allocation of costs when a person has suffered an injury. In the section on intrafamily immunities we distinguish between several variations of the extent to which parents and spouses have historically been immunized, and we will determine whether any of these immunities can be morally justified. Finally, in those cases in which a parent or spouse has no immunity and is a defendant in a tort action for negligence, then they must prove that their act or omission that led to the tort was not a violation of legal duty. This raises the final normative question of the chapter. Under what standard of care should a jury be instructed to decide whether the defendant is or is not negligent? Should the defendant's conduct be judged by an objective standard (for example,"the reasonable parent") or should the jury use a subjective standard and inquire only about what the defendant honestly believed?

L.D. Houlgate, *Philosophy, Law and the Family*, AMINTAPHIL: The Philosophical Foundations of Law and Justice 7,
DOI 10.1007/978-3-319-51121-4_8

8.1 Tort Liability and Remedies

In his 1690 work *Second Treatise of Government*, John Locke distinguished between "the crime which consists in violating the law," and "injury done to some person or other, and some other man receives damage by his transgression: in which case he who hath received any damage, has, besides the right of punishment common to him with other men, a particular right to seek reparation from him that has done it" (§10). Locke was referring to violations of the law of nature, but the distinction he makes between a crime and the "injury done to some person or other," which gives the injured person the right to seek reparation for the harm, is what we today refer to as the distinction between *crimes* and *torts*.

Crimes and torts are both types of prohibited harm. Criminal laws prohibit public harms and tort laws prohibit private harms. The word "public" means that the harms are seen as harms to society. The word "private" refers to harm suffered by the particular person or persons who have been injured. If the criminal court finds the accused wrongdoer to be guilty, then the response is punishment. If a civil court finds that the defendant (the tortfeasor) has violated a legal duty (a tort), then the response of the court is an award for the plaintiff (the person who has brought the lawsuit) in the form of a judgment of liability, usually requiring the defendant to compensate the plaintiff financially.[1]

Tort law is a small but growing part of family law. Family torts can be divided into two main categories: *intrafamily torts* in which spouses and other family members bring tort actions against each other and *extrafamily* torts in which one or both spouses sue a non-family member for a tort that has seriously harmed one of them or their child (Statsky, 417). In this chapter our main concern is with intrafamily torts.

There are two ways in which liability is distributed by *intrafamily* tort law: *vicarious liability* and *fault liability*. *Vicarious liability* is liability that is "imposed on a person because of the conduct of another, based solely on the status of the relationship between the two. The person liable is not the person whose conduct led to the liability" (Statsky, 424–425). Most states have *parental liability laws* that make parents vicariously liable for the torts of their children. If a 10-year-old child throw a baseball through the neighbor's window, then the parents of the child are (vicariously) liable for the damage.[2] If a teenager using the family car for a family purpose

---

[1] "On rare occasions, a plaintiff may also be awarded *punitive* damages, defined as damages in excess of compensatory relief. In other cases, a plaintiff may obtain an *injunction*: a court order preventing the defendant from injuring her or from invading one of her property rights (perhaps harmlessly" (Coleman and Mendlow).

[2] In California, the relevant statute says: "Any act of willful misconduct of a minor that results in injury or death to another person, or in any injury to the property of another, shall be imputed to the parent or guardian having custody and control of the minor for all purposes of civil damages." The statute goes on to state that the custodial parent or guardian is jointly liable, along with the minor, for any damages resulting from the minor's willful misconduct, for an amount not to exceed $25,000 for each wrongful act. (California Civil Code section 1714.1)

(rather than a business purpose) and negligently injures someone, then the parent who owns the car is vicariously liable.

Fault liability is liability imposed on a person because of a violation of a legal duty not to injure negligently, recklessly, or intentionally. For example, in some states one spouse can sue the other for *negligently* or *recklessly* failing to disclose the existence of a venereal disease, which was passed on to the victimized spouse. Another example of fault based intrafamily liability is for an injury to a child caused by the parent's *negligent* operation of a motor vehicle. An example of an *intentional* intrafamily tort would be a case of marital rape in which the offending spouse is sued for the tort of battery or the tort of intentional infliction of emotional distress.

Fault liability is significantly different from criminal liability. Criminal liability can be defeated by an excuse, for example, "I was not at fault: I did it by mistake." But in tort, you can be held liable "even if you are morally faultless, that is, even if your conduct is not morally blameworthy, even if you have a complete excuse for what you did" (Coleman and Mendenhall, 2010). But there is still a way to avoid fault liability. You can *justify* the act or omission that led to the harm by showing that you took the precautions that any reasonable person would have taken under the same circumstances. For example, A, while exhibiting his new handgun to B, not realizing that the gun is loaded, pulls the trigger of the gun. The gun goes off, killing B. A is not criminally liable – he did not know the gun was loaded. But A can still be held liable in tort for the death of B – unless he can justify his failure to check the gun prior to displaying it to his friend.

Not all harms committed within the family are allowed as the basis of a claim in tort. If a teenager is disciplined by a parent who "grounds" her for one week for poor grades at school, she may be harmed by this, but she has no claim in tort to repair her frustration at not being able to go out at night with her boyfriend. This is because parents have no legal duty to refrain from using discipline in raising their children, including the use of nonexcessive corporal punishment.

Second, in some states intrafamily torts cannot be brought because an *immunity* exists for those who have caused the injury. An immunity is "an exemption from what a person enjoys from the normal operation of the law such as a legal duty or liability, either criminal or civil" (Duhaime 2016). In the history of American tort law there have been two kinds of immunity extended to families: *interspousal* and *parental.* The names of these immunities are sufficiently descriptive: a person is immune to liability for injuries negligently caused to a spouse, and parents are not liable for injuries negligently caused to their children. If John drives a car while inebriated and crashes the car, injuring his wife, his child, a friend and the friend's child, he is liable for injuries caused to the friend and her child. But under early versions of the parental immunity doctrine he is exempt from liability for injuries caused to his wife and their child.

"I have an immunity" is only one of two possible responses a defendant might make to a suit for liability. In the immunity cases the parent who injured his child or spouse means by this "Even if I was at fault for what I did *I have no legal duty* to act otherwise." Another different but common response a parent or spouse might make is "*I have a legal duty* to act faultlessly, but I was not in violation of the duty – I was not at fault." This is the response of justification mentioned above: "I was not at fault (negligent) because my act or omission met the standard of care required by the court under the circumstances."

In the remainder of this chapter we will begin by asking general philosophical questions about tort law. If an injury is a tort only if it violates a legal duty, then how should we determine what injuries to protect? Under what conditions should an immunity be granted to a class of persons who would otherwise be liable? What principles ought to govern the allocation of costs when a person has suffered an injury? We will then turn to specific questions about parental and spousal immunity and the more general question about the limits of legislating intrafamily torts: Is there sufficient justification for the tort laws of some states that immunize spouses and parents from liability when these persons have negligently injured their spouse or child? Finally, we will ask about the "reasonable person" standard used in determining whether behavior in the family has been negligent. Should these standards be objective (using a "reasonable parent" as a standard of care), or subjective (using only the subjective beliefs of the parent at the time of conduct as the standard)?

8.2 Philosophical Questions About Torts and Tort Remedies

When a legislative body is considering whether to enact a statute making a particular kind of conduct tortious, part of their aim is identical to the aim of creating a criminal statute: to reduce the incidence of undesirable conduct. The difference is that the aim of a tort statute is accomplished by treating certain individual interests as *rights*. These rights are reciprocal with a *legal duty* that is created by the statute. For example, if Betty is removing shingles from her roof and throws them on to the public sidewalk below, Betty has a legal duty to take reasonable precautions before she discards the old shingles. Everyone passing underneath the roof has a right that she takes these precautions. The second way that the aim is accomplished is by giving the right-holder the power to protect his rights and obtain compensation if his rights are infringed by undesirable conduct that has been marked as a violation of a legal duty.[3] Third, the power of the right-holder to protect his rights and obtain compensation can only be achieved by the state maintaining, and probably subsidizing a tort system and an institutional framework, including courts, to give effect to it (Honore, 94).

Is the state justified in marking conduct as tortious and attaching to it the right of the injured person to compensation? In support of this answer Honore provides an argument having a hypothetical for its first premise: "If the state is justified in making conduct criminal and attaching to it penalties that may include prison, it must also be justified in marking conduct as tortious and attaching to it the lesser sanction

[3] Locke traces this power to the natural right of self-preservation. If I have this right, then I must also have the power to appropriate from the person who has caused my loss whatever is needed to restore myself to the position I was in prior the loss.

of compensation" (77). If we affirm the antecedent of this premise, then we get the conclusion that the state is justified in maintaining a tort system. But we should notice that we could rewrite the consequent (in italics) of the premise as follows: "If the state is justified in making conduct criminal and attaching to it penalties that may include prison, *then it must also be justified in reclassifying all tortious conduct as criminal and attaching to it lesser criminal penalties*." In other words, we can all agree that the state must have the right and duty to minimize undesirable conduct, but this does not imply making some conduct criminal and other conduct tortious. Nor does it imply that the "lesser sanction" *must* be compensation. We need another argument to establish these conclusions.

Honore writes that the state is *probably* justified in subsidizing a tort system with an institutional framework. He uses this qualifier because of sensitivity to the political objection that it may not be a proper use of state resources to subsidize private rights in this way. The answer to the objection is that the alternatives are even worse. If the state charges a fee for the cost of judicial enforcement or closes the courts to all tort claims, then it would weaken or give up an important technique for lessening undesirable conduct. Fees for the cost of judicial enforcement may be out of reach for all but the well-to-do, thereby raising moral questions about the fairness of the tort system. Closing the courts to tort claims would leave it up to the individual to pursue his own claims against alleged wrongdoer without judicial support. John Locke endorsed such pursuits, but only in his imagined "state of nature." He also had a warning about it. If you seek reparation from someone who you believe has harmed you, then this person may not share your belief, or she may not want to provide a remedy. If you decide to secure a remedy by "force, or the declared design of force" (Locke, III, §19), then she may interpret this as a threat to cause her harm. She may respond in kind. Since there is no common authority to whom you and she can appeal to settle your differences, you are both in a "state of war." The only way to avoid this unfortunate result is for all persons to subject themselves "to the fair determination of the law; because then there lies open the remedy of appeal for the past injury and to prevent future harm" (§20).

If the aim of a statute creating a tort is (in part) to reduce the incidence of undesirable conduct, then we are left with the question "What constitutes undesirable conduct for the purposes of making it tortious?" The answers to this question are as diverse as some of the answers given to a similar question about criminal conduct: "What constitutes undesirable conduct for the purposes of making it criminal?" We could call conduct undesirable for the purposes of making it a tort because the tortious conduct causes harm to others, it is non-harmfully offensive to others, or it is non-harmfully immoral.[4] There are few who would dispute a proposal to make only harmful conduct tortious, especially if the damage is obvious to any observer. Proposals to make non-harmful offensive conduct tortious meets more resistance

[4] The conduct that *could not* qualify as a tort is conduct that is *harmful to oneself*. If the use of heroin is prohibited only because it might cause harm to the user, then the user can be made liable to criminal punishment, but the conduct could not constitute a tort because those who violate the law cannot sue themselves for damages.

because of skepticism about the existence of damage, whether permanent or temporary. The usual cases are those involving emotional distress. If it rises to the level of trauma, then recovery may be available. In this case, offensiveness, as emotional trauma, would fall under the harm-to-others principle (Sect. 5.3.1).

Proposals to make immoral conduct tortious are quite rare. Common law cases in England include conduct relating to prostitution and extra-marital cohabitation. However, in these cases *the injury* was not considered a tort. Instead, relief for an injury was denied to the plaintiff because the conduct in which he was injured was considered immoral (Dyson 2014). This consideration is relevant to the question "What are acceptable grounds for *exempting* conduct from tort liability?" but it has no bearing on the question "What are acceptable grounds for *placing* conduct under rules of tort liability?"

In our discussion in Chap. 5 about the grounds for making immoral-but-non-harmful conduct criminal we considered Patrick Devlin's recommendation that enacting such laws might have the beneficial effect of rescuing society from disintegration. Devlin argued that (a) there is a public morality, and (b) society could not exist without shared ideas on what types of acts are immoral, and (c) these shared ideas must be protected by making immoral behavior prohibited by law. Although Devlin's remarks were intended to apply to criminality, there is no reason why they should not also be applied to tort. If tort laws share with criminal laws the aim of deterring undesirable conduct, and some of the conduct is believed to be undesirable because it is immoral, then the immorality of conduct would constitute sufficient grounds for making it tortious. The problem with this proposal is locating plaintiffs who could convincingly argue that certain kinds of immoral conduct causes damage for which they ought to be compensated. If the conduct is of a kind mentioned by Devlin (homosexual behavior, prostitution), then it would be presumed to damage the social fabric of society itself, of which the plaintiffs and all others who wish to join in the lawsuit are a part. In that case, a successful suit for damages could conceivably bankrupt the relatively small population of tortfeasors by bringing compensatory relief for damages to all citizens. Other problems with Devlin's proposal have already been critiqued in Chap. 5 (Sect. 5.3.3).

8.3 Theories of Justification for Tort Remedies

What justifies the person whose rights have been infringed in claiming compensation from the wrongdoer? According to Tony Honore,

> It is not enough to show that the state is entitled to take steps to minimize undesirable behavior and to give individuals the power to protect their rights and obtain compensation if they are violated. It must also be shown that *some principle or principles of justice* entitle the right-holders (tort-plaintiffs) to sue the wrongdoers (tort-defendants) for compensation. For though the state may be entitled to designate certain interests as rights and certain sorts of conduct as wrongs, it cannot thereby make it *just* for the right-holders to sue the

wrongdoers for compensation. It cannot by fiat create a principle of justice linking the two (Honore, 1997, my emphasis).

The problem is whether we can find independent principles of justice that adequately justify tort claims against tort-defendants. Three of the most discussed principles in tort theory are: *Corrective justice*, *retributive justice* and *distributive justice*. We will discuss these principles in the context of the torts of intentional or negligent interference by a parent with her child's personal or real property. The relevant law directs that the child is to be treated as a person with a right to property, and he has the consequent right to protect his property and get compensation if the right is infringed.[5] Let us imagine a case in which a ten-year-old child inherits ownership of a valuable painting that is to be kept in his mother's house until he reaches the age of 18 years, at which point the boy might choose to sell the painting to pay for his college tuition. The child's mother loans the painting to a friend. The friend's house catches fire, destroying all of its contents, including the boy's painting. The child sues his mother for compensatory damages of $100,000.

8.3.1 Corrective Justice

Corrective justice requires that those who have violated the legal duty not to injure (harm) must repair the wrongful losses caused by their conduct. The duty to repair arises from a violation of the duty not to injure.[6] Any concern about whether or not one is morally to blame for the loss one has caused is irrelevant. It is only the *outcome* of the defendant's conduct that is relevant. Is the outcome a loss "incident to the violation of the victim's right not to be injured–a right correlative to the wrongdoer's first-order duty not to injure"? (Coleman and Mendenhall). If the reply to this question is affirmative, then the wrongdoer must put the matter right, even if she is not at fault.

Putting the matter right... is a concept that may (according to the circumstances) require the harm-doer to restore something to the person harmed, or to repair a damaged object, or (when the unharmed position cannot be restored, as it usually cannot) to compensate the harm-sufferer. Compensating in turn means doing something conventionally regarded as

[5] "At common law a parent (unlike a husband in the case of his wife) has no right to or in (or even a right to use) property of any kind of his minor child." McCurdy (1960), citing *Pollard v. Pollard*, 207 Ala. 270-272, 2 So. 488 (1922). Under certain circumstances a parent might apply the child's property toward the child's support. *Linton v. Walker*, 8 Fla. 144 (1858) 8. *Estate of Tetsubumi Yano*, 188 Cal. 645, 206 Pac. 995 (1922) 9. *Edmunds v. Mister*, 58 Miss. 765 (1881).

[6] Corrective justice appears to be Locke's position when he writes that "he who has suffered the damage has…this power of appropriating to himself the goods or service of the offender, by right of self-preservation..." (Locke, §11). The right that one has to preserve his own life justifies a right to do what is necessary to achieve this, including the power to "appropriate" from the one who caused the harm whatever "goods or services" are necessary to put the sufferer in the same position he was in prior to the loss.

restoring the harm-sufferer to his unharmed position. "Compensate" is used to cover whatever may be done to make good the loss when reparation is not literally possible... (Honore)

In the case of the minor child cited above, the child's mother has a legal duty not to loan her child's painting to anyone. She may not have known that she had this duty, and she may plead that she had no intention of putting the painting at risk of damage. Under the principle of corrective justice, this appeal is pointless. Her duty to repair the loss is a direct result of the loss itself, not her ignorance of the law, her negligence in loaning the painting, or even her lack of any intention to put the painting at risk of damage. She cannot replace the painting, but she can be required to provide sufficient compensation to make good on the loss.

8.3.2 Retributive Justice

The principle of retributive justice says that the blameworthy *deserve* to suffer. When one person intentionally, recklessly or negligently causes harm to another, they are blameworthy. It is because of the blameworthiness of tortfeasors that they deserve the pain of retribution by being forced to pay (to "make up") for the damage they have caused.

Retributive justice differs from corrective justice in this important respect. It asks whether the harm or injury caused by the plaintiff is something for which he is morally to blame. Corrective justice concentrated entirely on causal responsibility *for the outcome*, the actual loss, not the defendant's moral responsibility (blameworthiness). Second, according to retributive justice the first order duty in tort (as it is in crime) is *to do harm to the wrongdoer*. In criminal cases, this is done for the purpose of restraint. In tort, it is done for the purpose of reparation. In both cases, the harm done to the criminal or tortfeasor must be "proportionate" to the transgression.[7] The second order duty in tort is to adjust the harm done to the wrongdoer so that it completely repairs the loss suffered by the victim. The sanction should not be disproportionate to the harm or damage caused to the plaintiff for which the sanction is imposed.

By way of contrast, the duty of repair in corrective justice is like a debt payment. As a debt payment it can be paid by third parties. For example, you can purchase insurance to guard against the burdens of tort liability (Coleman and Mendenhall). Retributive justice does not characterize the harm to the tortfeasor as payment of a debt. It is *a sanction that involves reparation* and this burden can only be borne by

[7] In the state of nature, when one person violates the law of nature (for example, by damaging his property), then "*one man comes by a power over another*; but yet no absolute or arbitrary power, to use a criminal, when he has got him in his hands, according to the passionate heats, or boundless extravagancy of his own will; but only to retribute to him, so far as calm reason and conscience dictate, what is proportionate to his transgression, which is so much as may serve for *reparation* and *restraint*; for these two are the only reasons, why one man may lawfully do harm to another, which is that we call punishment" (Locke, §8).

the wrongdoer as a public acknowledgement of his moral responsibility. It is his burden and only his burden. Hence, it cannot be transferred to a third party. This would mitigate or perhaps even eliminate the harm to the tortfeasor that is an essential part of the process of retribution.

Let's see how retributive justice deals with the example of the minor child and his painting. First, although the mother is responsible for the loss of the painting, she may not be entirely blameworthy. Blameworthiness has much to do with the mental state of the person prior to or during the time at which the injury, harm or damage was caused. Her ignorance of the law regarding her duty not to loan, give away or sell her child's property may not get her much sympathy, but she may be able to show that she was not in violation of a legal duty – because she was not negligent when she loaned the painting to her friend – after all, no reasonable person could have predicted that the painting was at risk of being lost in a house fire. Hence, the degree of her moral blame for the loss of her child's painting is less than it would be if she had intentionally destroyed the painting.

It is at this point that we see the weakness of the retributive principle. It appears to justify an unjust distribution of the cost of a loss by linking it to the degree of blame of the person who caused the loss. In the instant case this principle seems to justify the conclusion that the mother need only pay part of the cost of the damage because she did not intend nor was she negligent about the outcome of loaning it to her friend. This result, based as it is on her degree of blame, is an injustice to her child. Second, because of the punitive element of retributive justice, the mother cannot shift the cost of compensation to a third party. She must bear the cost alone. If she cannot afford to pay the cost, then this result is an even greater injustice to her child. Third, her legal duty is to not loan the painting. It is not her property. It is her child's property. She *has* violated this legal duty. The duty is *not* "Don't loan the painting negligently." It is "Don't loan the painting – it is not yours to loan." Hence, it is irrelevant that she did not intend, nor was negligent or reckless about the outcome of loaning the painting to her friend.

8.3.3 Distributive Justice

Distributive justice is justice in the distribution of resources. For example, if we notice that children living in wealthy communities have far more educational resources than children living in poor communities we might say that this distribution of resources is unjust. Similarly, if a judge declares that the burden of paying for losses after an accident should be borne entirely by the injured person and not by the person who injured her, then we might also say that this distribution (of burden) is unjust. The question begged in both cases is: What constitutes an unjust distribution? Should desert play a role, that is, should the losses be distributed entirely on the basis of who deserves to shoulder the cost of the loss? Egalitarians propose that participants in the distribution of burdens should do so according to the concept of equality. This prompts questions about what equality demands. Should it diminish existing disparities in holdings? Should it respond to the needs of both the plaintiff and defendant? In sum, the distributive approach sees tort law as "the locus for distributing burdens (and benefits) caused in the process of involuntary interaction in a private setting, and considerations of desert (both positive and negative), merit, needs, and equality all serve to help decide how the loss should be allocated, and to whom" (Keren-Paz. 2007, 17)

For example, in the case of the mother who is sued by her child for the damage caused to his painting, the principle of distributive justice is not of much help until we know the considerations that will guide us in the distribution of the burden of loss that the mother has caused by loaning her child's painting. If we use desert as the sole consideration, then it would seem that the child deserves to have his loss compensated because his mother is at fault for the damage. If we use equality to decide how the loss should be allocated, then we need information about such matters as the financial circumstances of both the plaintiff and defendant. Suppose that the child not only inherited the painting, but he also inherited several million dollars that are in a trust for his use when he reaches the age of majority. His mother inherited nothing and as his guardian and custodian she has no resources for compensating her child for the loss of the painting. An egalitarian version of distributive justice would tell us not to add to the mother's burden by requiring her to give compensation to her child. Corrective justice, on the other hand, ignores this disparity and requires only that the person who suffered the harm (the child) be restored to his unharmed position. The balance that existed prior to the damage must be restored, even if we are convinced that the distribution of benefits and burdens between mother and child prior to the damage is unjust.

8.4 Intrafamily Torts and Immunities

There are two categories of harms to family members caused by the commissions or omissions of another member from which the latter have historically been immunized from liability: parental and spousal. Each category has gone through different stages from the earliest cases when both parents and spouses had extreme (full) immunity until contemporary stages when most states have abrogated (eliminated) these immunities. We will describe these stages while considering typical cases before turning to possible justifications for granting full or partial immunity.

8.4.1 Parental Tort Immunity

The doctrine of parental and spousal immunity has gone through several phases. I will follow legal tradition and label these phases as *extreme*, *moderate*, and *abrogated.*

Stages of Parental Tort Immunity

In the *extreme* cases, the exemption from liability for a parent who has injured his child is absolute in the sense that the fault from which the parent is exempt from liability includes intentional, reckless and negligently caused injuries. In the first case that created the doctrine in the United States a married, but unemancipated minor tried to sue her mother for wrongful confinement in an insane asylum (*Hewlett v Hewlett*). The Mississippi Supreme Court refused to recognize the daughter's cause of action against her mother, reasoning that

> [t]he peace of society, and of the families composing society, and a sound public policy, designed to subserve the repose of families and the best interests of society, forbid to the minor child a right to appear in court in the assertion of a claim to civil redress for personal injuries suffered at the hands of the parent. The state, through its criminal laws, will give the minor child protection from parental violence and wrong-doing, and this is all the child can be heard to demand.

Later cases involving intentional parental torts also fall into the "extreme" category. In *Roller v. Roller* the Supreme Court dismissed a suit for civil damages brought by a fifteen-year-old girl against her father, who had been convicted of raping her. The Roller court asserted two reasons for adopting the parent-child immunity doctrine. First, the court indicated that if a child were to recover a judgment from his or her parent, such parent could inherit the "very property which had been wrested by the law from him" in the event of the child's death. Second, the court emphasized the injustice that could occur if an injured child recovered damages from his or her parents and imperiled the financial welfare of other family members.

In cases of *moderate* parental immunity, a child is allowed to bring a lawsuit against a parent if the tort is intentional, but not if it is negligent. The immunity doctrine is revised to include only negligence and recklessness in the definition of "fault." For example, in a Connecticut case, a parent was sued by his child for injuries caused when he jumped from a burning building with her in his arms. Here are the background facts: The defendant (Farricelli) and his former wife (Ascuitto) divorced in 1990 when their daughter Ariana was less than two years old. The parents shared legal custody. The mother had sole physical custody, but the father's visitation rights increased as the child grew older. (The closeness of the relationship between father and daughter was not in dispute.) In August 1994, a fire broke out in the father's home when Ariana was visiting. To escape the fire in his home he jumped from a second story window carrying his daughter Ariana in his arms. Both suffered injuries when they fell to the ground below. The mother filed an action on Ariana's behalf, alleging that her injuries resulted from her former husband's negligence concerning electrical wiring, smoke detectors, and handling of a burning cigarette in his home. She made no allegation as to his leap from the burning building (Hardy 1999). According to the court majority, the parental immunity doctrine barred the daughter Ariana's negligence action. In reaching its ruling, the court majority the Court held: (1) The alleged negligent acts did not constitute breach of a duty owed the general public; (2) They involved the father's exercise of parental discretion as part of his supervisory duties. These are deserving of protection from court interference; (3) An element of family harmony survived the divorce, and (4) The availability of insurance did not support abrogating the doctrine of parental immunity.

Another kind of moderate parental immunity includes supervisory duties but excludes injuries caused to a child in automobile accidents. For example, in 1987 the North Carolina Court of Appeals refused to apply parental immunity when they ruled that an unemancipated minor child who sustains injuries due to a parent's negligent operation of a motor vehicle can maintain a cause of action against the parent for damages (Falk 1457). The court's reasoning was that transporting a child was not within the ambit of the normal supervisory duties of a parent. Hence, in North Carolina and many other states negligent driving is no longer included as a fault from which a parent can escape liability in a lawsuit for compensation.

The legal concept of *abrogation* means "abolished" or "revoked." Hence, the third and final phase of parental immunity is its demise. Here is one of many late 20th century cases announcing abrogation. In April of 1980 Al Shearer and the passenger in his car, Mary Shearer, were involved in a motor vehicle accident in Cuyahoga County, Ohio. Mary Shearer was pregnant at the time of the accident and in July, 1980 she gave birth to Al's daughter, Cynthia Shearer. One month later, Al and Mary became husband and wife. However, the marriage did not prevent Mary and her daughter Cynthia from filing suit against husband and father Al for personal injuries they allegedly sustained in the April accident. Both claims were dismissed by the county civil court. Mary's was dismissed on the ground of interspousal immunity ("A spouse cannot sue his or her spouse for designated torts"). Her daughter Cynthia's suit was dismissed on the grounds of parental immunity ("Children and parents cannot sue each other for designated torts"). The Appeals Court for the county affirmed the lower court ruling, but on a motion to the Ohio Supreme Court to certify the record, the rulings were reversed and remanded. Both the parental and interspousal immunity doctrines were abolished in Ohio (*Shearer v Shearer* 1985).

Instead of refuting the traditional policy reasons for upholding that doctrine, the *Shearer* court adopted an empirical analysis by examining the current experience in states without the parental immunity doctrine. The court noted that "states without parental immunity showed that those states reported no greater incidence of family disharmony than did states which retained the doctrine." The court concluded that "to sustain the parental immunity doctrine, in the face of overwhelming evidence that no empirical justification exists for it, would be a violation of due process for those it barred from bringing suit" (Vardiman, 30).

Justifications of Parental Tort Immunity

The philosophical question to ask is normative. What is the moral justification for giving immunity to a parent whose intentional or negligent conduct has caused injury to her child in circumstances in which immunity would not be extended to a person who is not the parent of the child?

The first point to make is that most of the principles of justice (Sect. 8.3) offered in support of tort remediation apply to parental torts. When there is a loss (harm to the child) caused by the parent, then under the principle of corrective justice (Sect. 8.3.1) the wrongdoer (the parent) must "put the matter right," even if she is not at fault. If there is a degree of moral blameworthiness for the harm caused by the parent, then under the principle of retributive justice (Sect. 8.3.2) the child deserves reparation and the parent owes this moral debt in proportion to the degree of moral blame. The principle of distributive justice (Sect. 8.3.3) will also apply if *desert* is used as the standard for distributing the cost of the loss suffered by the child. Under this standard the parent deserves to pay for the loss (she owes a moral debt) and the child deserves to be paid. But if we use *equality* to decide how the loss should be allocated between parent and child, then we need information about such matters as the financial circumstances of both parent and child.

The second point is that the usual justifications for parental tort immunity are traceable to the discredited Family Privacy Principle discussed at (Sect. 5.3.1). Utilitarian defenders of an organic conception of family relationships claim that granting immunity to parents promotes the social goods of "family unity and harmony among its members." They might support this claim by submitting evidence that family unity is best achieved when members are left to their own devices and are allowed to work through internal family problems without outside interference. Hence, extending an immunity to an injured child's parent will achieve this purpose.

Even if this is factually true (and there is little evidence for this claim), it seems clear that the bad consequences of a child bearing the full cost of his or her loss by granting tort immunity to parents would far outweigh good consequences secured thereby. It is highly improbable that family harmony would improve to such an extent that the amount of instances of internal family harm would drop if there was no social intervention to help victims of child abuse, spousal abuse or intimate partner sexual violence. Our conclusion (at Sect. 5.3.1) was that there is no utilitarian rationale for endorsing the Family Privacy Principle. When we ask questions about harm to others we must concentrate our attention on the individual members of the family who are harmed, not harm to the family (where "family" is a term applied to an independent organic entity).

8.4.2 Interspousal Tort Immunity

The origins of interspousal tort immunity are quite different from that of parental tort immunity. At common law women who married suffered an extraordinary change in their legal status. Their husbands acquired the right to any property they brought into the marriage, including the right to earnings. Married women could not enter into contracts, file claims, be sued, or transfer any real property. The reason for this was partly Biblical (the man and woman become "one flesh" upon marriage), but it was also legal. As previously noted (Sect. 5.3.2), William Blackstone enunciated it in the eighteenth century as *the doctrine of coverture*: "By marriage, the husband and wife are one person in law; that is, the very being and legal existence of the woman is suspended during the marriage, or at least is incorporated and consolidated into that of her husband, under whose wing, protection, and cover, she performs everything" (*Commentaries*, 442). The idea of a single identity (coverture) formed the basis for preventing one spouse from acquiring a tort cause of action against the other. (Tobias, 364). If the married man and his wife were one, then she could no more sue him than she could sue herself for damages. Hence, potential interspousal personal injury suits "were unknown at common law" (Tobias). The lack of adjudication did not change until the 25-year period of 1840–1875 when the Married Women's Property Acts were enacted in every jurisdiction.

> The Married Women's statutes were important because they provided a basis for recognizing personal injury actions between husband and wives. The typical legislation authorized a married woman to "maintain an action in her own name, for damages, against any person...for any injury to her person and character the same as if she were sole." The statutes, therefore, made it plausible to contend that coverture had been destroyed and independent legal status bestowed or, at least, that common-law disabilities had been removed or indicia of legal personality provided, so that interspousal tort litigation should be permitted. (Tobias, 373 citing N.Y. Laws of 1862, Ch. 172, § 3)

We will use the same classification scheme of distinguishing phases of tort immunity as employed in the previous section "Stages of parental tort immunity".

Stages of Interspousal Tort Immunity

The cases decided in the first stage of interspousal tort immunity, like the first stage of intrafamily tort immunity, were *extreme*. After passage of the Married Women's Property Acts the earliest cases to test the willingness of civil courts to rule favorably on interspousal torts involved intentional harms inflicted by the defendant. In the first case a wife was not allowed to maintain an action for assault and battery inflicted by her husband upon her (*Longendyke v Longendyke* 1863), and in a second case a wife could not maintain an action against her husband for a slander uttered by him (*Freethy v Freethy*1865). Courts espoused many policy reasons for these decisions. One familiar justification was "fear that allowing personal injury claims would create, or exacerbate preexisting, marital disharmony" (Tobias, 390). One mid-19th century jurist (quoted in the epigraph) went further when he colorfully predicted that "the flames which litigation would kindle on the domestic hearth would consume in an instant the conjugal bond, and bring on a new era – indeed an era of universal discord, of unchastity, of bastardy, of dissoluteness, of violence, cruelty, and murders" (*Ritter v Ritter*1858). A second justification was legislative intent. When legislatures passed the Married Women's Property Acts, it was argued that there was no intention to permit tort actions between spouses. Privacy considerations were also at the forefront of their concern. By allowing domestic disputes to be fought in the courtroom would reveal to the public the reality of the patriarchal family and "a husband's control over his wife's body." One can understand why jurists would conclude that such intervention in "the most delicate area of the sacrosanct institution of marriage" could not have been what state legislators intended (Tobias, 396).

The *moderate* stage of interspousal tort immunity began in the early part of the twentieth century when intentional torts were brought as a cause of action (Tobias, 409, fn. 245).[8] For example, in Florida interspousal tort claims were statutorily authorized for battery. "The common law doctrine of interspousal tort immunity is hereby abrogated with regard to the intentional tort of battery, and the ability of a person to sue another person for the intentional tort of battery shall not be affected by any marital relationship between the persons" (Laws of Florida, Ch. 85–328). The Florida legislature was responding to a shocking 1984 case in which Joyce Waite and other members of her family were attacked by her husband with a machete, inflicting substantial injuries upon them. He subsequently was convicted of several crimes, including attempted murder. Joyce Waite divorced him. Later, she filed suit seeking a recovery of damages against a home-owner's insurance policy. On the husband's motion, the trial court dismissed the cause as being barred by the doctrine of interspousal immunity (*Raisin v Raisin* 1979). The decision was reversed on appeal. The Appeals Court reasonably held that "the doctrine of interspousal immunity no longer is applicable when the public policy reasons for applying it do not exist" (*Waite v Waite*).

The policy reasons included "disruption of marital harmony." But it was clear to any reasonable jurist that marital harmony will not be decreased merely because of the addition of a lawsuit for the various types of personal injury at issue. Another reason for changing the immunity doctrine is that successful lawsuits for intentional interspousal torts could serve as a form of punishment and thus could have a deterrence effect on future interspousal behavior (Tobias, 411). And to the recommendation of earlier courts that had upheld the immunity doctrine on the ground that the more serious torts (such as battery) would best be pursued as crimes and/or as grounds for divorce, it was replied that "criminal prosecution and marital dissolution provided little redress to injured wives" (see, for example, *Louisville & N.R. Co. v Johnson* 1920 and cases cited therein).

Justifications of Interspousal Tort Immunity

In the final stage a majority of states had *abrogated* (eliminated) the doctrine of interspousal tort immunity. This was accomplished by the end of the twentieth century. When the Supreme Court of Florida began its case review with the question: "Does the doctrine of interspousal immunity remain a part of Florida's common

[8] Citing *Johnson v. Johnson*, 201 Ala. 41, 44, 77 So. 335, 338 (1917); *Fitzpatrick v Owens*, 124 Ark. 167, 177, 186 S.W. 832, 836 (1916); *Brown v. Brown*, 88 Conn. 42, 49, 89 A. 889, 892 (1914); *Gilman v. Gilman*, 78 N.H. 4, 5, 95 A. 657, 657 (1915); *Crowell v. Crowell*, 180 N.C. 516, 524, 105 S.E. 206, 210 (1920); *Fiedler v. Fiedler*, 42 Okla. 124, 129-30, 140 P. 1022, 1025 (1914) (styled as *Fiedeer v. Fiedeer* in 140 P. 1022); *Prosser v. Prosser*, 114 S.C. 45, 47, 102 S.E. 787, 788 (1920).

law?" the answer was a resounding "No." Here is a portion of Justice Harding's concurrence with the majority decision in the Court's review of *Waite v Waite* (1992):

> The abrogation of the doctrine of interspousal immunity will not damage what the marital relationship is designed to be — a special relationship between partners who share love, common interests, concerns, hopes, and endeavors. As the majority notes, if one of those partners commits a wrong against the other, the injured party should not be foreclosed from bringing an otherwise meritorious claim just because he or she is married to the wrongdoer....
>
> The Legislature has already statutorily abrogated the doctrine with regard to the intentional tort of battery. Section 741.235, Fla. Stat. (1991). Florida law also permits a spouse to file a criminal complaint against a spouse, to seek an injunction for protection from that spouse's violence, and to sue in equity over property interests. If the preservation of marital harmony is the compelling reason for maintaining interspousal immunity as to other personal tort actions, then that rationale should apply with equal force to these legal actions that the law permits one spouse to maintain against the other. Certainly, it is difficult to make any rational argument for interspousal immunity as to these permitted legal actions. Yet, such actions are just as likely, if not even more likely, to foster marital discord than are the personal tort actions that are barred by the doctrine of interspousal immunity.
>
> Moreover, if the overriding concern is to prevent fraud or collusion by spouses in bringing such an action, then the remedy should be to expose the fraud rather than to discard all the honest claims along with the bad ones. As the majority notes, legal devices exist to detect possible collusion or fraud whether the parties are married or not. Thus, this policy does not warrant the continuation of the interspousal immunity doctrine.
>
> Although the doctrine of interspousal immunity is one of long standing in Florida, fourteen of the thirty-two states that have completely abrogated the doctrine did so before 1970. ...In fact, Connecticut abandoned the doctrine nearly eighty years ago. The thirty-two states that have abrogated the doctrine have not suffered any adverse effects from that decision. Nor have they found any credible evidence that marital relationships have been negatively impacted in those states, or that the insurance industry has been brought to its knees by a proliferation of fraudulent suits.

Central to the Florida court's justification for eliminating the interspousal tort immunity is that it fails to bring about any good consequences that would outweigh the bad. When the court says that there is no "rational argument" for this immunity it means that there is no sound argument based on utility. We can add to this that there is also no sound argument based on an appeal to justice. If we believe that the principles of justice (Sect. 8.3) apply to those cases in which a person injures his or her child, then we will get a similar result when we apply these principles to interspousal torts.

8.5 Summary: Limits of Tort Intervention

We have earlier defined an immunity as "an exemption that a person enjoys from the normal operation of the law such as a legal duty or liability, either criminal or civil" (Duhaime 2016). The civil legal duty in this case is that of all persons to refrain from intentionally, recklessly or negligently causing harm or injury to one another. The early immunity doctrines traditionally called for the release of parents and spouses from this duty when their conduct is within the context of the parent-child or marital relationship.

In the court's decision in *Ascuitto* (above), the ruling was that liability for the loss suffered by the child due to the negligent conduct of the parent shall be borne by the child and shall not be transferred to the parent. Recall that liability in tort is *fault liability*. Liability is imposed on a person because of a violation of a *legal duty not to injure negligently, recklessly, or intentionally*. Unlike the rules of criminal law, liability in tort law is *built into* the definition of the legal duty. The principle of corrective justice requires those who *without justification* violate this legal duty "to put the matter right" by assuming liability for what they have done. There is no question that the father's conduct harmed his child when he jumped from the window with her in his arms. His negligence was not the leap from the burning building, but his failure to repair the electrical wiring, install smoke detectors, and safely handle burning cigarettes in his home. These are the omissions that constitute a violation of legal duty.

This leaves us with the question whether the father's conduct was "without justification." According to the court's interpretation of the parental immunity doctrine, the father *was justified* in failing to take the preventive steps noted above. Although he might have been negligent in not making his home environment safe from fire, this is part of his "discretion" in carrying out his "supervisory duties" as a parent. As a parent he has no legal duty to make his house fire proof. How he maintains the home environment is a private matter and immune from state intervention. Therefore (using the reasoning of the court), the parental immunity doctrine does not violate the principle of corrective justice. The cost of reparation for the loss of her injuries shall remain with the child and will not transfer to the child's father.

Why should injuries due to a parent's negligent operation of a motor vehicle maintain a child's cause of action against the parent for damages (as in *Shearer* above), but not a parent's negligence to provide a fire safe home environment? The standard answer is that negligent operation of a motor vehicle is not a discretionary part of a parent's supervisory duties.[9] Another answer is that allowing a child to successfully sue her parent for a negligent tort disturbs the peace, repose and harmony of the family.

> [T]he peace of society, and of the families composing society, and a sound public policy, designed to subserve the repose of families and the best interests of society, forbid to the

---

[9] Other courts using the *Ascuitto* rationale to justify parent-child immunity include e.g. *Barlow v. Iblings*, 261 Iowa 713, 718, 156 N.W.2d 105, 107-08 (1968); *Luster v. Luster*, 299 Mass. 480, 481, 13 N.E.2d 438, 439 (1938), overruled in *Sorensen v. Sorensen*, 369 Mass. 350, 339 N.E.2d 907 (1975); *Small v. Morrison*, 185 N.C. 577, 584, 118 S.E. 12, 15 (1923).

minor child a right to appear in court in the assertion of a claim to civil redress for personal injuries suffered at the hands of the parent (*Hewlett v George* 1891).[10]

These answers beg the questions "What should count as *justification* for parental conduct that would otherwise be classified as a tort?" "What should determine the dividing line between private and public in intrafamily matters?" and specifically "Why should maintenance of parental discipline and promotion of family harmony take precedence over and trump the moral principle of corrective justice?"

Putting aside the factual questions about the truth of the claim that allowing children to sue their parents for negligent torts will endanger parental discipline or the harmony of the family, the moral claim that precedence should be given to the twin values of parental discipline and family harmony has no foundation. We can acknowledge that the ability of a parent to supervise the conduct of her child and the maintenance of peace and harmony in the family are desirable goals, but there is no evidence that the greater good for families or for society will be achieved by pursuing these goals at the expense of denying corrective justice for the injured child. Moreover, the burden of proof for this is not on those who advocate for corrective justice. It is on those who argue that it is more important (has greater social utility) to support parental supervisory control over the child or to maintain family harmony. No evidence has been presented to show they have met this burden. Until this burden is met we can conclude that the parental immunity doctrine should be abolished. No child should bear the cost of her own injury when she is injured by the conduct of a parent.

Arguments for retaining the interspousal immunity doctrine that are still being used in twenty-first century cases are preservation of marital harmony and the fear that married couples would engage in fraud and collusion in order to cheat insurance companies. Let us look at both of these in light of the principles of justice outlined earlier. First, corrective justice states very simply that those who have violated the legal duty not to injure or otherwise harm must repair the wrongful losses caused by their conduct. The legal duty has fault built into its definition. The duty is to *not to faultily* (that is, intentionally, recklessly or negligently) *harm or injure others*, and if one does so, then one has an obligation to repair the loss one has caused. There is nothing in the principle that explicitly or implicitly says that it does not apply to those who are in a marital relationship. Let us assume the facts in *Waite v Waite*. The husband has intentionally and seriously injured his wife. It is safe to assume that the peace and tranquility of their marital relationship has been disrupted by this heinous act. In fact, we can go further and maintain that there is not even the

[10] *Hewlett* involved a married, but unemancipated minor daughter who tried to sue her mother for wrongful confinement in an insane asylum. The court refused to recognize plaintiff's cause of action against her mother. Other courts have used the Hewlett rationale to justify parent-child immunity. See *Thomas v. Inmon*, 268 Ark. 221, 223, 594 S.W.2d 853, 854 (1980); *Pedigo v. Rowley*, 101 Idaho 201, 202, 610 P.2d 560, 561 (1980); *Barlow v. Iblings*, 261 Iowa 713, 722, 156 N.W.2d 105, 107-08 (1968); *Small v. Morrison*, 185 N.C. 577, 579-80, 118 S.E. 12, 13 (1923); *Chaffin v. Chaffin*, 239 Or. 374, 382, 397 P.2d 771, 775 (1964).

vestige of harmony that remains in the relationship. Nor could anyone reasonably expect that the relationship could be repaired by making the husband immune to liability. The important point is that the immunity doctrine implies that maintenance of the marital relationship is more valuable than the value of corrective justice for the individuals in the relationship. The idea seems to be that a marital relationship should be protected by the courts regardless of the quality of particular relationships, and regardless of the existence of a suit for remedy by a plaintiff whose case would be allowed to proceed if she were not married to the defendant. This is not only hypocritical in light of liberal rules regarding no-fault suits for divorce, but no arguments are presented to show why a marital relationship, no matter how poisonous it is, should provide immunity to the wrongdoing spouse in situations in which other kinds of intimate relationships (friendship, cohabitation) would never be allowed to qualify for the same treatment.

8.6 Standards of Care in Intrafamily Negligence Torts

In the introduction to this chapter I mentioned a second response that a parent or spouse might make as a defense to a charge of negligence. If immunity to tort liability is not available in their jurisdiction, then the defendant parent or spouse might argue "I was *not* in violation of the legal duty not to act negligently because I was not negligent." In such cases the defendant must show to the court's satisfaction that the act or omission that led to the harm met the standard of care required by the court.

In tort law the duty is "ordinary care" under all circumstances, and this duty varies with changing circumstances. The standard is that of the "ordinarily prudent or reasonable person." In order to help members of a jury to discover what a reasonable person would have done if in the same circumstances as the defendant, in many early cases the court said that a reasonable person might be what the persons on the jury believe *they* would have done if they were in the defendant's place (Duxbury, 42). The difficulty with this instruction is that it begs the question "Why should a member of the jury use his or her own conduct as a standard for what an ordinary prudent and reasonable person would do?" The answer is (probably) that jury members would not be on the jury unless the judge and attorneys for the defendant and plaintiff believed they were paradigms of reasonableness and prudence.

However, the substitution of an ordinary member of the jury for the reasonable and prudent person does give us some idea of what the standard of care would be like. The word "prudence" connotes that such a person cannot be mentally defective. And yet even this presents problems. If mentally defective persons do their best, then this would be legally irrelevant. Their conduct will not be held to the standard of what a mentally defective person would do, but what a prudent and reasonable person would do. This raises a question of fairness. Is it fair that the legal consequence of the fool's folly should be visited upon the fool? After all, we do not blame a mentally defective person for their aberrant conduct as we do those who are of average intelligence.[11]

Similar difficulties arise when we examine the question of the physical characteristics and capabilities of the prudent and reasonable person. If the defendant has one leg, is blind, experienced a blow on the head, suffered a heart attack or paralysis, then these are all facts which are considered relevant to a question of negligence under current law. We do not require that a blind or deaf defendant should have taken the precautions that a person of normal or average physical capacity would have taken in the same circumstances.

8.6.1 *Objective and Subjective Standards of Care*

The underlying problem is whether the court should be using an objective standard to determine what constitutes the duty to use due care. An *objective* standard is one that requires that the defendant's behavior should be evaluated against a standard of what care an imagined *prudent or reasonable person* would have taken in the individual defendant's situation. A *subjective* approach, on the other hand, would argue that the defendant's's honest beliefs about the amount and kind of care he or she should take are all that should count.

Consider the example of a parent who leaves a loaded handgun in her bedroom in a drawer of her bedside table. Her 7-year-old child finds the gun while playing in the bedroom. The gun goes off while in his hand and the bullet strikes his 5-year-old sister who is sitting nearby. The sister dies.

The subjective standard for determining negligence requires only that the parent honestly believed that her 7-year-old child would not play with the gun (for example, because she had ordered him not to enter her bedroom when she was not there and he had always obeyed her orders). The objective standard would counter that the parent's honest beliefs are irrelevant. The law should examine only what a reasonable person would have believed about the danger of keeping a hand gun in a place accessible to a young child.

Those who defend the subjective approach "claim that it is fairer to individuals than the reasonable-person approach. Its fairness stems from the fact that it better reflects the actual blameworthiness or culpability of the individual." (Altman, 125). If the parent honestly believed that a loaded handgun kept out of sight in a bedroom drawer does not pose a hazard to her children, then she cannot be justifiably blamed for the death of her daughter. "[Her] perspective thus determines the extent to which [she] is to blame and so should determine how the law imposes its duties and liabilities on [her]" (Altman, 125).

---

[11] Nor do we blame young children for behavior that we find negligent if done by an adult. In a recent incident in California a 2-year-old toddler pulled a gun from his mother's purse while the mother was shopping. The gun went off, and the bullet struck his mother, killing her. This is a tragic but perfect case of avoidable ignorance (*Washington Post* 2014).

The problem with this defense of the subjective approach is in the premise that "it better reflects the actual blameworthiness or culpability of the individual." This defense can be challenged. The actual blameworthiness of the child's mother is that she did not take reasonable steps to *confirm* the false belief that led to the harm. Even if it is true that she had an honest belief that the handgun did not constitute a hazard, the belief itself was false and she could have taken steps to discover this. It is the reasonable *avoidability* of her false belief that constitutes her blame, not the possibility that she might not be honest in saying that she *had* this belief.

There have been several revisions suggested by theorists designed to accommodate the concerns of the subjective approach to negligence. One suggestion is that we pitch the standard of care very low so that only certain very elementary precautions need be taken in order to qualify those who (like the parent in the handgun example) might have very different experiences and very different perspectives arising from those experiences than what we would expect from the reasonable and prudent person. However, even then it may well be the case that there will still be some individuals who, through lack of intelligence, powers of concentration, poor memory, or even sheer physical clumsiness, will not be able to meet even a minimal objective standard of care (Hart 1961, 29–49).

Perhaps a more serious difficulty with individualizing the reasonable person standard is that it may require us to excuse certain individuals of average intelligence and physical ability (like our parent) who we usually would not consider to be exempt from blame. Suppose that the parent is a person of relatively low intelligence who has grown up in a rural area where almost all families have guns in the home. She and others from that area have a long experience and ingrained habit of safe handling of guns. The experience dates from childhood. This parent subsequently moves to the suburbs where she buys a home. She buys a handgun for protection, and places it in the drawer of the table next to bed so she will have quick access to it. She does not give much thought to where she has placed the gun except to tell her children not to enter the bedroom. If the objective standard of the reasonable and prudent person becomes so broad as to include the kind of low level of intelligence, care and precaution that this person takes with her handgun, then it would be a defense for almost *anyone* to show that they have taken sufficient care to prevent childhood accidents and deaths by gunshot.

Another way of individualizing the objective reasonable person standard is to render such incapacitating factors as low intelligence, infancy, blindness, susceptibility to heart attacks or stroke, as part of the "circumstances" or situation in which the reasonable and prudent person might find himself. Suppose that your car, stopped in traffic at a stop light is struck in the rear by my car. I testify that I suffered a heart attack and, although I did not lose consciousness, the pain was so great that I forgot to press the brake. Under the suggestion that we should consider such incapacitating factors as a heart attack as part of the circumstances in which the reasonable and prudent person may find herself, the question directed to the jury would be: "What would a reasonable or prudent person have done if, like the defendant, that person had suffered a heart attack?" The problem with this question, of course, is that members of the jury with no experience of what happens during a heart attack could only guess at what a reasonable person would do in these circumstances.

Their confusion would only be compounded by expert witnesses testifying on both sides of the question, some saying that a reasonable person would not be distracted, and others saying the opposite.

The suggestion that incapacitating factors be made part of the circumstances has absurd consequences when being a child, being of low intelligence or mental defectiveness are included among the circumstances in which a reasonable person might find herself. The nonsensical question directed to the jury would be: "What would a reasonable and prudent person have done (what precautions would such a person take) if, like the defendant, he or she is a child (or is an adult with the IQ of a 5-year-old)?"

8.6.2 H.L.A. Hart's Two-Question Proposal for Determinations of Negligence

It is the desire to accommodate the subjectivist insistence that we treat all persons in a fair and just manner that gives rise to the preceding variations of the reasonable person standard of care. Another attempt to accommodate the fairness objection is H.L.A. Hart's recommendation that the jury should be instructed to distinguish two questions when attempting to determine whether a defendant should be made liable for negligence: (D1) What would a reasonable person with normal capacities have done in these circumstances? (D2) Could the defendant with his or her capacities have done that? Hart writes that "reference to such factors as lunacy or disease should be made in answering only the second of these questions" (Hart 1961) If the answer to the second question is negative, then there is no liability for negligent behavior. Suppose a small child drowns in a private swimming pool at his home because his father was watching a football game on television instead of watching out for his child. After the tragedy he explains "I did not pause to think about what I was doing. I should have not have been watching television." If we apply Hart's dual question proposal to this case, the first question (D1) is answered by saying "A reasonable parent in similar circumstances would have taken the simple precaution of shutting off his phone while his child was in or near the swimming pool." The answer to the second question is affirmative: "The defendant could have (had the ability to) take this precaution."

8.6.3 Objections to Hart's Proposal: Standards of Care for Children

In American law, the standard of reasonable conduct for a parent is measured against the standard of the reasonable and prudent person. But the precautions expected of a child are determined by a standard that takes into account "subjective factors such as intelligence and experience."

> In this sense the standard is less strict than for adults, because children normally do not engage in the high-risk activities of adults and adults dealing with children are expected to anticipate their "childish" behavior. In many states children are presumed incapable of negligence below a certain age, usually seven years. In some states children between the ages of seven and fourteen years are presumed to be incapable of negligence, although this presumption can be rebutted. Once a person reaches the age of majority, usually eighteen years, she is held to adult standards of conduct. One major exception to the rules of negligence exists with regard to children. If a child is engaging in what is considered an "adult activity," such as driving an automobile or flying an airplane, the child will be held to an adult standard of care. The higher standard of care imposed for these types of activities is justified by the special skills required to engage in them and the danger they pose to the public (Legal Dictionary entry for "Negligence").

Hart's two question approach would lead to the exculpation of most children for their torts of negligence (except those engaging in adult activity). It is thus consistent with rulings in U.S., English and Canadian courts regarding the liability of children. But there are exceptions. Consider the case of a 13-year-old boy who "playfully" threw nitric acid at a young girl who was innocently passing by, causing lifelong scars (*Pollock v Lipkowitz* 17 DLR 3d 766 [1970, MBQB]). Hart's first question (D1) is about the behavior expected of a reasonable *adult,* not a reasonable child of the same age and experience. Assuming that a reasonable and prudent person with normal capacities can be expected to know enough about nitric acid not to throw it at anyone, Hart's second question (D2) would be whether a child of 13 could have known about the effects of nitric acid and restrained himself from throwing it at the innocent girl. If children of this age can reasonably be thought to have some knowledge and experience of chemistry and chemical reactions, then we might give an affirmative answer to D2. But it seems clear that children of this age and experience cannot be expected to have this knowledge. Although the ruling in this case was to find for the plaintiff, Hart's affirmative answer to D2 would find for the defendant.

8.6.4 An Alternative Approach: Sub-categorization

To summarize the previous discussion: (1) an objective standard of negligence disregards the particular physical and mental abilities of the defendant. It does this by imposing the abilities of a hypothetical reasonable person who is placed in the same circumstances as the defendant. The conduct of the defendant is compared to the imagined conduct of the reasonable person in order to determine liability. (2) The problem with the objective standard is that liability *is sometimes imposed where there is no fault* on the part of the defendant. (3) Because the subjective standard uses only the honest beliefs of the defendant about the circumstances that existed at the time of their alleged wrongful conduct, liability is sometimes not imposed when there is fault on the part of the defendant. (4) H.L.A. Hart's solution to the stand-off between the champions of the objective and subjective standards for determining negligence is to retain the reasonable person standard while at the same time making an accommodation for actual fault by requiring the court to ask and answer a second question: "Could the defendant *with his or her capacities* have done what a reasonable person would have done in these circumstances?" The advantage of Hart's solution is that it would relieve young children and many of those with mental disabilities of any liability because they are without fault.

The solution is to repair Hart's two-question approach by making a change in the first question that he requires the jury to answer. The change is to make the category of "reasonable person" less broad by "taking account of the differences in experience and perspective to which the law should be responsive" (Altman 2001, 127). This can be done by adding more specific categories. In fact, there is ample precedence for this in such legal subcategories as age (children) and physical disability (deafness, blindness). We do not hold children, the deaf or the blind to the "reasonable person with normal abilities" standard when determining negligence. It is a small step from this to adding other subcategories, for example, mental illness, mental retardation, certain other developmental disabilities, cognitive impairments, and traumatic brain injury.[12]

Some have argued that the problem with this proposal is that it would open up "a host of irresolvable controversies over what subcategories to use" (Altman 2001, 128). How would we avoid a slippery slope that leads us to adopt such categories as gender, race or economic class? Should we adopt a special category for parents of young children? Would this category include any precautionary measures that we would not expect any reasonable person to know? Would the controversies over new categories lead us all the way back to the original subjectivist proposal that blame or fault in determinations of negligence should be predicated only on what the defendant honestly believed at the time of the (alleged) wrongful conduct?

What is needed is an account of what subcategories to use and why. But we have already found this account in the argument for creating subcategories for children, and the physically disabled. A 13-year-old child is held to the standard of what a child of the same age would do when in the same circumstances, because it is *not*

---

[12] Mental illness and other types of mental disability would present different problems for my proposal, but none that are impossible to resolve. The main problem is how to frame the two questions that we want to put to the jury. Consider the example of a woman with the paranoid delusion that God is controlling her automobile. She crashes into another car, causing injury to its occupant. If schizophrenia and acute paranoia are within the legally approved subcategory of mental disability, then the question (E1) that the court should ask the jury to answer would be "What precautions should we require of schizophrenics and acute paranoiacs about driving automobiles?" Suppose that the jury's answer to this question is: "Don't drive." The next question (E2) is whether the defendant could have restrained herself from driving a car. The answer to this question begs another: "Was her mental illness foreseeable?" If the answer to this question is negative, then she could not have restrained herself from driving her car. But if there is no forewarning of an onset of a delusion, then while she is in the hallucinatory state of believing that God is controlling the vehicle, then the answer to E2 is negative. If these mental aberrations were not constant, the jury could infer she had knowledge of her condition and the likelihood of a hallucinationDOUBLEHYPHENjust as one who has knowledge of a heart condition knows the possibility of an attack. In that case, the answer to E2 would be affirmative and she would be liable. In both of these possible answers to E2 the guiding moral principle is "no liability without fault."

fair to hold the 13-year-old to an adult standard of reasonableness. A blind person is held to the standard of what persons with the same disability would do in the same circumstances, because it is *not fair* to hold the blind to a standard of what a sighted person would do. And "fairness" in these cases is based on *fault*. In order to insure that fault is the guiding concern the court should also require that the defendant must show that she could not have conformed her conduct to the precautionary behavior required of persons in the sub-category. In order to make this clear, consider the following changes I would make in Hart's two question formula. In place of D1 and D2, we will require the court to ask the following questions of the jury:

(E1) What would a person in the legally approved subcategory [for example, a child, a deaf person] have done in these circumstances?
(E2) Could the defendant with his or her capacities have done that?

In an example discussed earlier we imagined a deaf person struck by a train while crossing the railroad tracks in his car (Sect. 8.4.1). Assuming that deafness is in a legally approved subcategory, then in order to determine contributory negligence of the defendant, the jury will be asked to answer E1: what precautions should we require of a deaf person in these circumstances? Let us assume that the jury would answer this question by requiring that a deaf person should take the precaution of taking a careful look up and down the tracks before she ventures across. If it is determined that the defendant did not do this, then we must ask the second question E2: Could the defendant have done that? That is, was there any impediment *other than* her deafness that prevented her from taking the necessary precautions? If the answer is negative, then we can attribute at least partial fault to her for the injuries she suffered, and the jury should find for the plaintiff.

Lastly, the phrase "legally approved subcategories" mentioned in E1 are those subcategories that are approved for use by the courts in the jurisdiction in which tort case decisions are made. Whether gender, race or economic class should also be adopted as subcategories depends upon whether it can be successfully argued that there are clear standards of care for persons in these categories that significantly differ from the reasonable person standard. I have serious doubts that an argument can be successfully made for this proposition, but I will defer an analysis and criticism of these arguments until Chap. 11.[13]

Questions for Thought and Discussion

1. What is the distinction between a crime and a tort? Describe an example of both, and explain how they compare and how they differ.
2. How would you choose between the principles of justice (corrective, retributive, distributive) discussed in Sect. 8.3?
3. What immunities have existed in tort law for parents and spouses? What arguments have been or might be given to justify these immunities? How would you assess these arguments?

---

[13] "Extensive sub-categorizing would entangle the law in a thicket of controversies that could not be settled except by the greater political might of one side or the other" (Altman, 128).

4. What is the difference between objective and subjective standards of care in determining whether a defendant should be made liable for a tort? Give an example of an objective standard of care and explain what it is that makes it objective rather than subjective. Does H.L.A. Hart's two-question approach resolve the debate between objectivists and subjectivists?

References

Coleman, Jules and Mendlow, Gabriel. 2010. Theories of Tort Law. In *The Stanford Encyclopedia of Philosophy*, ed. Edward N. Zalta.http://plato.stanford.edu/archives/fall2010/entries/tort-theories/.

Dumaine. 2016. *Legal Dictionary*. http://www.duhaime.org/LegalDictionary/.

Duxbury, Neil. 1995. *Patterns of American Jurisprudence*. Oxford: Clarendon Press.

Dyson, Matthew. 2014. *Unravelling Tort and Crime*. Cambridge: Cambridge University Press.

Falk, Beth Ann. 1987. Survey of Developments in North Carolina Law, 1986: North Carolina Retains Its Partial Parent-Child Immunity Doctrine. 65 *North Carolina Law Review* 1457.

Florida, Laws. 1993. Twitle XLIII. Chapter 741. Marriage, Domestic Violence. http://www.leg.state.fl.us/statutes/index.cfm?App_mode=Display_Statute&URL=0700-0799/0741/0741ContentsIndex.html. Accessed 28 Mar 2016.

Freethy v Freethy (1865) 42 Barb. 641 Hardy, Benjamin H. 1999. Parental Immunity. *ORL Research Report*. 99-R-0667 June 4, 1999. http://www.cga.ct.gov/ps99/rpt/olr/htm/99-R-0667.htm.

Hewlett v Hewlett 68 Miss. 703, 9 So. 885 (1891).

Honore, Tony. 1997. The Morality of Tort Law: Questions and Answers. In *The Philosophical Foundations of Tort Law*, ed. David G. Owen. Oxford: Oxford University Press.

Locke, John. 1980. *Second Treatise of Government*, ed. C.B. Macpherson. Indianapolis: Hackett. First published in 1690.

Louisville & N.R. Co. v Johnson, 201 Ala. 611 (1920).

Raisen v. Raisen, 379 So.2d 352 (Fla. 1979), modified, Sturiano v. Brooks, 523 So.2d 1126 (Fla. 1988).

Ritter v. Ritter, 31 Pa. 396, 398 (1858). Tobias (*supra*) notes that *Ritter* was not a tort case (442, fn 419).

Roller v Roller 37 Wash. 242, 79 P. 788 (1905).

Tobias, Carl. 1989. *Interspousal Tort Immunity in America.* 23 *Georgia Law Review* 359.

Vardiman, Martha. 1986. Case Note: Ohio Abolishes Intrafamily Immunity:*Shearer V. Shearer,* 18 Ohio St. 3d 94, 480 N.E.2d 388 (1985). *University of Cincinnati Law Review 55.*

Washington Post. 2014, December 30. Toddler Accidentally Shoots and Kills His Mother. http://www.washingtonpost.com/news/post-nation/wp/2014/12/30/toddler-accidentally-shots-and-kills-his-mother-in-idaho-wal-mart-police-say/

Part III
Marriage, Children and the State

Chapter 9
Family Contracts: Marriage and Divorce

> *"Marriage is a coming together for better or for worse, hopefully enduring and intimate to the degree of being sacred. It is an association that promotes a way of life, not causes; a harmony in living, not political faiths; a bilateral loyalty, not commercial or social projects. Yet it is an association for as noble a purpose as any involved in our prior decisions."*
>
> J. Wm. O. Douglas *Griswold v Connecticut* (1965)

Abstract Legal marriage is a type of contract that confers a status on those individuals who marry. In this respect it substantially differs from the traditional idea that legal duties arising under contract law should be self-imposed by individuals, not dictated by the public in the form of a contract which everyone is required to enter if they wish to achieve the status of "married person." This status consists of non-changeable terms about the indefinite duration of the contract, support obligations of spouses, the distribution of property, and the amount of taxes paid to federal, state and local government. One reason that unmarried persons might see this status as a desirable choice is that marriage has considerable economic benefits that are not enjoyed by unmarried co-habiting couples. One of the central questions of this chapter is whether this distribution of benefits between married and unmarried couples is justifiable. We look at several principles of just distribution in an attempt to answer this question. Another important part of this chapter is about the description and evaluation of gendered marriages in which laws in earlier times dictated specific roles for husband and wife. Third, and perhaps of most relevance in contemporary family law are questions about access to marriage. In this context, we examine both the 2015 Supreme Court decision overturning state laws prohibiting same-sex marriage, and the arguments given in the public debate about same-sex marriage prior to this decision. We will next look at some of the alternatives to traditional marriage such as private contracts and a recent proposal called "minimal marriage" which uses state regulation only to recognize and promote caring relationships between the parties to the marriage, regardless of number and gender. Our concluding discussion is about the exit rules enabling divorce or dissolution of a marriage in which we ask whether the rules for dissolution should be neutral with respect to moral and religious beliefs.

L.D. Houlgate, *Philosophy, Law and the Family*, AMINTAPHIL: The Philosophical Foundations of Law and Justice 7,
DOI 10.1007/978-3-319-51121-4_9

9.1 A Conversation About Marriage: Past and Present

A friend once told me that he and his cohabiting partner did not want to get married because "we do not want the government to regulate our relationship." Their reason for this was the fear that government regulation would result in the *depersonalization* of their relationship. They were afraid that they might come to look on each other as persons bound by a business contract instead of seeing each other as friends and lovers. He said "It is more likely that legal marriage will damage our relationship than help it."

I explained to my friend that for most of Western history, neither the state nor the church interfered with marriage. But I added that this would probably not change his fears about depersonalization. Marriage in those times was a private contract between two families. "The parents' agreement to the match, not the approval of church of state, was what confirmed its validity" (Coontz, A27). If my friend had been born in the tenth century, he and his partner would certainly have objected to the parental approval requirement on the grounds that neither he nor his partner had a right to refuse the match. If he had been born in the thirteenth century when the Catholic Church decreed that a "licit" marriage must take place in church, then his objection would have been that marital rights and obligations of husband and wife were determined not by him and his partner but by the Church. If they had children out of wedlock, then the children would be declared illegitimate. If they were to wed, then the wife would have inheritance rights only if their marriage was approved by the Church. And because marriage under Canon Law was considered a sacrament and an indissoluble bond, the Church could not grant a divorce.

It was not until the sixteenth century that the secular courts of European states intervened and began to require that marriages be performed under auspices set by the legal system. At first this "was an attempt to prevent unions between young adults whose parents opposed their match" (Coontz, A27). In the early history of the United States, marriage law was used to exert control over those allowed to marry (for example, laws prohibiting interracial marriage), and those allowed to end a marriage (for example, by setting "fault" conditions for those who wanted to divorce a non-consenting spouse).

If we jump forward to the twentieth century we begin to see the marriage license as a pathway to special benefits that were not extended to the unmarried. For example, the newly enacted Social Security Act of 1935 provided survivors' benefits with proof of marriage. "Employers used marital status to determine whether they would provide health insurance or pension benefits to employees' dependents. Courts and hospitals required a marriage license before granting couples the privilege of inheriting from each other or receiving medical information" (Coontz, A27). These were seen as considerable benefits available only to married couples.

One year after my friend had announced that he and his cohabiting partner would never marry I ran into him at the grocery store. He told me that they were recently married. When I asked what brought about this change of mind, he replied: "Health insurance. The health benefits that we could obtain just by being married were much less expensive than the insurance we could obtain as unmarried persons." The prospect of realizing these economic benefits of marriage trumped his earlier concern about possible damage to a valued personal relationship.

9.2 Traditional Marriage: Rights, Duties and Benefits

The phrase "marriage law" refers to the complex set of rules that comprise the legal union of two persons as spouses with designated rights and obligations to each other. The basic elements of a marriage are: (1) the parties' legal ability to marry each other. For example, if a person is under the minimum age required for marriage in the state in which they reside, then they cannot marry. (2) Mutual consent of the parties, as determined (for example) by the absence of compulsion; and (3) A marriage contract as required by law.

The marriage contract differs from other contracts in that it confers a *legal status* ("married" and "spouse") on the persons who enter into this union in much the same way that birth of a child confers the legal status of "parent" on the biological mother and father. The word "status" means that the rights and duties are set by the state and cannot be altered by the individuals in the legal relationship. For example, the term of the marriage contract is indefinite. Persons who legally marry cannot insert a clause that their marriage will terminate at a particular time in the future ("in 10 years, with an option to renew"). Any such stipulation would not be recognized as legally valid. And (to give a second example) a marriage contract cannot stipulate that one of the spouses will have no obligation to support the other spouse or to pay child support. These obligations are unalterable components of legal marriage.

The Family Code of the state of California says this about the duties and reciprocal rights of support:

> Upon marriage, each spouse enters into an agreement to support the other. Each spouse is committed to using whatever resources are available for this purpose. If there is not adequate community property to provide support for your spouse, you are expected to expend your own separate property to support your spouse. (Fam. Code, § 4301.)

California also has rules for married persons regarding the distribution of property:

> If you lived in California during your marriage, everything you or your spouse own is either "community" or "separate" property. Unless you and your spouse agree otherwise, all property in or out of the state that is acquired by you and your spouse through either of your labor or skills during the marriage is community property. Each spouse owns one-half of all community property. This is true even if only one spouse worked outside the home during the marriage and/or the property is held in the name of only one spouse. (Fam. Code, § 125.)[1]

[1] Common-law states now allow the divorce court to distribute the spouse's property between them on a doctrine known as "equitable distribution." This is not equivalent to equal distribution, but it is still regarded as just and fair (in times past common-law property was property owned by the spouse who earned or had title to it).

And there are complex federal and state rules regarding taxation when married:

> When you are married, you may file a "joint" tax return with your spouse, or a "married filing separate" tax return. State and federal tax laws are complicated. Various tax decisions will be of special importance to you because you are married. Tax issues of particular concern to married couples include "joint" and "separate" filing (Rev. & Tax Code, §§ 17045 and 18521), inheritance and estate tax planning, homestead rights, and your possible liability for tax fraud committed by your spouse. (Rev. & Tax Code, § 18531.)

If a person is told that they need to establish that they are or have been legally married, they might be trying to obtain some other objective such as: pension benefits or social security benefits as the surviving spouse; assets as the spouse of a deceased person who has died without leaving a valid will; recovery for the wrongful death of a spouse; entrance into the United States or avoidance of deportation as a result of being married to a U.S. citizen. Each of these objectives signals a benefit that comes from being married.

There are several philosophical (normative) questions to ask about the rules of marriage. In this chapter we will discuss (a) whether married couples ought to be entitled to benefits not provided to unmarried single or cohabiting adults, or be subjected to burdens they did not have prior to marriage; (b) whether marriage ought to be "gendered" by practices such as coverture (in which a woman's legal identity disappears into that of her husband upon marriage), and male "head of family" rules; (c) whether marriage law ought to be structured in such a way that some persons are allowed to marry (for example, *two* persons of the *opposite* sex) and others are not (for example, two persons of the *same* sex or *three* persons of the same or opposite sex); and (d) whether the so-called "exit rules" for dissolving a marriage should be conditioned on anything other than the desire of one spouse to terminate the marriage.

9.3 Justice and the Distribution of Marital Benefits and Burdens

In its 2004 report, the U.S. General Accounting Office wrote that there are 1,138 benefits, rights and protections provided on the basis of marital status in Federal law (*Defense of Marriage Act*, GAO-04-353R). The report does not mention any burdens or loss of rights and protections by virtue of one's marital status. However, the burdens are relatively few in number, pertaining largely to the assumption of a portion of debts that one of the spouses might bring into the marriage, and to other obligations that are reciprocal to some of the rights of the marital relationship, for example, the duty to support the other spouse by using "whatever resources are available for this purpose."

Our question is about the *justice* of this distribution of rights and obligations in the population of married and unmarried cohabiting couples. In answering this question there is no need to look at each and every benefit and burden. That would not only be tiresome but unnecessary. Our task is to enunciate a general principle of distribution that will satisfy the demands of justice and then apply it to a few cases for illustration.

The focus will be on principles designed to cover the distribution of benefits and burdens of economic activity among married and unmarried cohabiting individuals in society. Government has the primary role in the distribution of economic benefits and burdens by virtue of creating, changing and revoking laws and policies. These changes have distributive effects. To quote Lamont and Favor

> Almost all changes, whether they regard tax, industry, education, health, etc. have distributive effects. As a result, every society has a different distribution at any point in time and we are becoming increasingly more adept at measuring that distribution. More importantly, at every point in time now, each society is faced with a choice about whether to stay with current laws, policies, etc. or to modify them. The practical contribution of distributive justice theory is to provide moral guidance for these constant choices. (Lamont and Favor, 2014)

As previously noted in our discussion about the distribution of losses in tort law (Sect. 8.3), there are several moral principles that have been defended in the literature as the best principles to guide the state in the distribution of benefits and burdens. We shall examine three of the most prominent principles, using marriage rules on tax policy as our illustrative case: Egalitarian, Difference and Utilitarian.

9.3.1 Egalitarian Principles

Egalitarianism makes the dual assumption that (a) all persons are morally equal and (2) the best way to give effect to this ideal is to create laws and policies that give every person, married or unmarried, the *same level* of material goods and services. Money is an index for the value of material goods and services. Therefore, any policy that confers tax breaks on married persons that it does not give to the unmarried (or vice versa)[2] would seem to violate the egalitarian principle of distribution. Some policies involve burdens, for example, making a married person liable for tax fraud committed by a spouse but not making that same person liable for the tax fraud of a cohabiting person to whom she is not married.

One of the problems with the egalitarian principle is in the word *level.* How do we specify and measure levels when distributing material goods and services? Are amounts of money the best index? If you prefer apples and I prefer oranges, but apples are three times the cost of oranges, then an income tax policy that taxes us equally, whether married or not, would put you in a worse financial position than you would be under an alternative system in which we would swap apples and oranges.

---

[2] In the current U.S. system, single-income married couples usually benefit from filing as a married couple because of income splitting, while dual-income married couples are often penalized in comparison. This is commonly referred to as "The Marriage Penalty."

This criticism of egalitarianism does not seem relevant to the moral question about whether married couples should be put in an advantageous or disadvantageous position relative to similarly situated cohabiting unmarried couples through discriminatory tax policy. Even if we had the same set of preferences for apples and oranges the injustice of distributing these goods on the basis of marital status would be as obvious as it would be if we did this distribution on the basis of race, gender or ethnicity. By the same line of reasoning, if we adopt a system of taxation that is progressive or regressive while at the same time giving special preference to persons on the basis of marital status, then the injustice of this form of discrimination would still be apparent.

"Why should the mere performance of a marriage ceremony provide a tax break for the persons getting married?" According to the egalitarian principle, the answer is that it should not.[3] If we want to promote equality, then it would seem that a system of taxation would be neutral with respect to marital status. It would also strive to achieve equality in its treatment of taxpayers, irrespective of marital status, and it would correlate tax liability with the taxpayer's ability to pay. A system of taxation that uses one tax rate schedule and also uses the individual as the basic tax unit would satisfy these criteria. One advocate of an egalitarian tax structure argues that this system would also remove

> The built-in-bias towards the single income married taxpayer by applying the same rate structure to income earners, *whether married or single*. Adopting a single rate structure also adheres to the principle of progressivity since individual taxpayers with the same taxable income would be taxed in the same rate bracket regardless of their marital status. (Mess, 1979)

9.3.2 *The Difference Principle*

In *A Theory of Justice* John Rawls proposes the following two principles of justice:

1. Each person has an equal claim to a fully adequate scheme of equal basic rights and liberties, which scheme is compatible with the same scheme for all; and in this scheme the equal political liberties, and only those liberties, are to be guaranteed their fair value.

[3]A common justification for the tax benefit provided to married taxpayers is that "marriage increases family responsibility and necessitates the lower tax liability" (Oldman and Temple 1960). The problem with this rationale, however, is that the benefit is given to all married taxpayers, irrespective of any actual increase in responsibilities, such as the existence of children. Rather, the mere performance of a marriage ceremony provides the tax break. (Mess, 87) "A woman married to a man for just 9 months gets Social Security survivor's benefits when he dies. But a woman living for 19 years with a man to whom she isn't married is left without government support, even if her presence helped him hold down a full-time job and pay Social Security taxes. A newly married wife or husband can take leave from work to care for a spouse, or sue for a partner's wrongful death. But unmarried couples typically cannot, no matter how long they have pooled their resources and how faithfully they have kept their commitments." (Coontz, A27, quoting Kotlikoff).

2. Social and economic inequalities are to satisfy two conditions: (a) They are to be attached to positions and offices open to all under conditions of fair equality of opportunity; and (b), they are to be to the greatest benefit of the least advantaged members of society.

The Difference Principle is stated in part 2(b). Because it deals with possible economic inequalities, this is the principle on which we should focus in determining what would constitute a just system of taxation. Economic inequalities produced through a system of taxation can be justified but only if they can be shown to "to be to the greatest benefit of the least advantaged members of society." The Difference Principle prescribes economic inequality up to that point where the absolute position of the least advantaged can no longer be raised. Hence, those who believe that the tax system should give preference to married couples have the burden of proving that this provides the greatest benefit to the least advantaged members of society. There is no evidence that this burden has been met.

To take this discussion in another direction, it has been argued that the Difference Principle does not require commitment to any particular tax system at all.

> The Difference Principle, which demands that economic inequalities are justifiable only if they benefit the least advantaged, can be satisfied through the combination of a wide variety of institutions, of which the tax system is only one. Inequalities in taxation that fail to benefit the most disadvantaged may be outweighed by other economic arrangements and provisions that benefit those who are worst-off. Only a tax system that burdens exclusively the poorest group would be foreclosed on account of the difference principle, because that scheme of public finance would necessarily entail some redistribution, in the form of public goods at least, from the worst-off to the better-off. (Surging, 2004)

If the state raises sufficient resources to provide a social minimum for the least advantaged members of society, then this is consistent with any number of tax schemes, including those that give reduced tax rates to married persons, giving reduced taxes rates to unmarried couples, or giving the same rates to both — as long as this has no detrimental effect on the least advantaged. In sum, the difference principle says nothing about taxation schemes that benefit one group rather than another unless that scheme "would necessarily entail some redistribution, in the form of public goods at least, from the worst-off to the better-off" (Surging).

9.3.3 Utility-Based Principles

Traditional utility-based principles are motivated by the idea that what is of primary moral importance is the level of happiness of people, where "happiness" is defined as pleasure and the absence of pain (Mill). Happiness is the only thing that has intrinsic value and all other things are good or desirable only because they are a means to happiness. The goods mentioned in previously discussed theories (material equality and the level of good for the least advantaged) have only instrumental value, that is, they are only valuable insofar as they affect utility.

Hence, all distributive questions are ultimately settled by how the distribution affects utility. The principle for distributing economic benefits for utilitarians is to distribute them so as to maximize the greatest amount of happiness for the greatest number of people. The utility function for such a principle has a relatively simple theoretical form which requires choosing the distribution which maximizes the arithmetic sum of pleasure over pain, adjusted for the intensity of these experiences. To accommodate uncertainty with respect to outcomes the function can be modified so that expected utility is maximized.

How does this apply to a proposed taxation scheme that benefits married couples? In order to answer this question one would have to show that such preferential treatment would increase the happiness not only of those who are married but of *all* persons in the general population, including unmarried cohabiting couples, unmarried single adults, and children. This is first of all an empirical problem, involving an enormous amount of data collection. But there are preliminary questions that must be answered. Presumably a long-term longitudinal study would be required where data is gathered for the same subjects repeatedly over a period of time. How would the study be set up? What kind of data is relevant? How would we know whether an increase or decrease in overall happiness had been specifically caused by the taxation scheme? To make things even worse for utilitarians, *each* taxation scheme would have to be examined in order to determine the distribution of benefits and burdens yielded by the scheme. Three other factors would be involved in this process: "the identity of each person in the distribution (if individuals' utility functions differ); the utility of each person from the goods and services distributed to them; the utility of each person from the policy itself." The size of the information requirements makes this task almost impossible to achieve the desired goal (Lamont and Favor).

In addition to the empirical problem, the standard normative criticism of utilitarian distributive principles is that they could be used to justify distributions that commonsense morality would regard as unjust. For example, it might be argued that utilitarianism could conceivably justify a taxation system based on race in which a racial minority is taxed at twice the rate of all others in the population. It is logically possible to imagine a scenario in which this scheme would maximize overall utility, but it does so by requiring (not asking) individuals who are in the minority to sacrifice their happiness for the happiness of others. It is immoral to make some people suffer or be sacrificed so that others may gain.

Utilitarians reply to this criticism by *defending* the rules of common-sense morality, arguing that such rules maximize utility. The rule that prohibits non-consensual sacrifice would be among this set of rules. Hence, the counter-example fails. Utilitarians would not justify the enactment of a taxation scheme that discriminates on the basis of race. However, this reply does not satisfy the objectors. They will counter with the argument that it is logically possible to imagine a system, justified by utility, that would contain a rule that prohibit non-consensual sacrifice, but also containing an exception permitting such sacrifices "when the circumstances require it". The circumstances, of course, would be those in which utility is maximized by these non-consensual sacrifices.

None of the preceding distributive principles (egalitarian, difference, utility) provide a justification for the common practice of distributing taxes in a manner that gives tax benefits (breaks) to married couples while denying the same benefits to the unmarried. However, this has not been an exhaustive analysis of all distributive principles. We have not discussed libertarian or desert-based or feminist principles. It is doubtful that these principles would provide the desired justification. *Libertarians* would be critical of any governmental tax scheme other than one that protects property rights. This would disqualify any taxation system that benefits any individual on the basis of marital status. *Desert-based theories* distribute economic benefits on the basis of what persons deserve. These theories differ primarily according to what they identify as the basis for desert. Aristotle proposed virtue or moral character. Locke proposed labor as the best basis deserving a reward. Locke's proposal prompts the question whether marriage is a form of labor or work activity deserving compensation in the form of tax benefits, or is marriage its own reward? Liberal *feminists* believe that a proper recognition of the position of women in society requires that women be given the same rights as men, and that these rights should primarily protect their liberty and their status as equal persons under the law. "Thus, government regulation should not prevent women from competing on equal terms with men in educational, professional, marketplace and political institutions" (Lamont and Favor). The same principle applies to taxation schemes. If a liberal feminist were to endorse any scheme it would be one that used the individual not the married couple as the basic tax unit in order to better protect equal rights.

9.4 Legally Gendered Marriage

A gendered marriage is one in which the legal system defines family roles and most property rights on the basis of gender. For example, there was a time in U.S. history in which a married woman could not make her own will, own property, make a contract in her own name, be a juror, vote, sue someone (and be sued), execute a deed, or keep her own earnings (Sects. 4.1, 5.3.2). "The legal status of a woman was called *coverture*, whereby her legal existence for many purposes merged with (was covered up by) that of her husband." (Statsky 2015). The married woman disappeared from the legal landscape. Of course, this situation could be reversed. A marriage could be gendered to disadvantage the husband in such a way that he could not perform any of the aforementioned actions and have his legal existence covered up by that of his wife.

Is there an argument for gendered marriage that would favor the wife over the husband or the husband over the wife? On what factual and moral basis would one construct such an argument? The moral basis would involve constructing a justification for unequal treatment under the law. Everyone can agree with the formal principle that persons who are similar should be treated the same and those who are different should be treated differently. What we want to know about is the material principle of relevance that would be used. People are justifiably treated differently when the differences between them are *relevant* to the purpose of the law. If the purpose of serving as a juror in a criminal trial is to determine guilt or innocence, then it is justifiable to exclude minor children from the juror pool on the ground that they are relevantly different from adults pursuant to the purpose of serving as a juror. They lack the degree of intelligence and understanding required for making a rational decision about guilt or innocence. Is there an equally relevant basis for excluding married women or any adult women from some family or public roles?

It was once thought that women were by nature unsuited not only for jury duty, but also for all of the other activities noted above. This idea was clearly pronounced by Justice Bradley of the U.S. Supreme Court when he concurred with the majority decision that the State of Illinois did not violate the U.S. Constitution by prohibiting women from the practice of law.

> Man is, or should be, woman's protector and defender. The natural and proper timidity and delicacy which belongs to the female sex evidently unfits it for many of the occupations of civil life. The Constitution of the family organization, which is founded in the divine ordinance as well as in the nature of things, indicates the domestic sphere as that which properly belongs to the domain and functions of womanhood. The harmony, not to say identity, of interest and views which belong, or should belong, to the family institution is repugnant to the idea of a woman adopting a distinct and independent career from that of her husband. So firmly fixed was this sentiment in the founders of the common law that it became a maxim of that system of jurisprudence that a woman had no legal existence separate from her husband, who was regarded as her head and representative in the social state, and, notwithstanding some recent modifications of this civil status, many of the special rules of law flowing from and dependent upon this cardinal principle still exist in full force in most states. One of these is that a married woman is incapable, without her husband's consent, of making contracts which shall be binding on her or him. This very incapacity was one circumstance which the Supreme Court of Illinois deemed important in rendering a married woman incompetent fully to perform the duties and trusts that belong to the office of an attorney and counselor. It is true that many women are unmarried and not affected by any of the duties, complications, and incapacities arising out of the married state, but these are exceptions to the general rule. The paramount destiny and mission of woman are to fulfill the noble and benign offices of wife and mother. This is the law of the Creator. And the rules of civil society must be adapted to the general constitution of things, and cannot be based upon exceptional cases. (*Bradwell v. State of Illinois*1873)

It was not until 1971, nearly 100 years after *Bradwell* that the Court would use the Equal Protection Clause of the Fourteenth Amendment to overturn this decision by rejecting gender-based distinctions (*Reed v. Reed,* 1971). This and a later decision (*Craig v Boren*, 1976) contradicted the factual basis of Justice Bradley that "a married woman [is] incompetent fully to perform the duties and trusts that belong to the office of attorney and counselor." The de-genderization of family law in the twenty-first century is a testament to the almost universal acknowledgement that there are no differences between women and men relevant to the purpose of any of the legally protected tasks of everyday life (making a will, owning property, make a contract in one's own name, serving as a juror, voting, suing someone (and being sued), executing a deed, and keeping one's own earnings).

9.5 Access to Marriage

Not everyone can marry. A man who is married to one person (man or woman) cannot concurrently marry a second person. That would be bigamy. Children under a certain age cannot marry (eligible persons must be 18 years or older unless a judge or parent consents to the union). Polygamous marriages are illegal (under bigamy law). People who lack the mental capacity to enter into a contract cannot marry. Blood relatives closer than third cousins cannot marry (first and second cousins can marry if they are elderly or cannot conceive).

Disputes about access to marriage have been argued at two levels. For most of the nation's history arguments about whether same-sex couples should be allowed to marry have been confined to public debate. The debate has been essentially over the *morality* of granting one group of competent, consenting adults access to marriage while denying it to other equally competent and consenting adults. As the late Justice Scalia wrote, this public debate, although often loud and contentious, was a good thing. It "displayed American democracy at its best":

> Individuals on both sides of the issue passionately, but respectfully, attempted to persuade their fellow citizens to accept their views. Americans considered the arguments and put the question to a vote. The electorates of 11 States, either directly or through their representatives, chose to expand the traditional definition of marriage. Many more decided not to. Win or lose, advocates for both sides continued pressing their cases, secure in the knowledge that an electoral loss can be negated by a later electoral win.

The second and more recent level of the debate about same-sex marriage has been waged in the courts over the question whether the Constitution might *require* the States to license and recognize marriages between two people of the same sex. The U.S. Supreme Court answered this question in the affirmative on June 25, 2015 when it invalidated all state laws prohibiting same-sex marriages (*Obergefell v Hodges*, 2015).

Before we look at the majority and minority arguments in arriving at this historic decision, let us examine some of the reasons why legislators, scholars and many citizens have resisted making any change in their state laws prohibiting same-sex marriages.

9.5.1 The Public Debate

Let us assume for purposes of argument that the dissenting voices on the Supreme Court had prevailed in the *Obergefell* decision. We shall suppose that a majority of justices agreed with the late Justice Scalia that a decision to declare all state prohibitions on same-sex marriage "robs the people of the liberty to govern themselves." The hypothetical question we shall instead ask is this: If the democratic process in the state houses had *not* been halted by the decision in *Obergefell*, what would be adequate *moral* grounds that an individual citizen or legislator might give in support of the position that same sex couples should *not* be given access to legal marriage?

Not surprisingly some of the grounds for denial are quite similar to the grounds once used to justify denying *interracial couples* the right to marry (Sect. 2.2.2). It has long been argued that there are relevant differences between same-sex couples and opposite-sex couples that would disqualify the former from consideration for marriage. The same kind of argument about relevant differences was found in earlier debates about interracial marriages. In both sets of cases we are told that as long as we understand that the differences are relevant, then the demands of justice have been met.

Is this true? Have the demands of justice been met when access to marriage is denied to same-sex couples? The principle of justice is a combination of a *formal* and a *material* principle. The formal principle simply says "Treat like cases alike and treat different cases differently." Unfortunately, this principle gives us very little direction when our task is to distribute burdens and benefits among a population. If I decide to give high grades only to students with blue eyes, then I have met the demands of the formal principle — all blue eyed people are being treated alike and all non-blue-eyed people are treated differently — but the use of eye color as a basis for grading student performance is (quite obviously) unjust. Why? The answer is that the color of a student's eyes is *not relevant* to determining his or her final grade. Hence, we need to supplement the formal principle of justice with a material principle that tells us what factors make two or more cases relevantly alike or relevantly different. In the grading case, the relevant factors most teachers employ are student performance on examinations, term papers, and in-class participation. The relevance of these factors is to the *purpose* of the course: learning the material or skills that are being taught, whether it is moral philosophy, the history of Ireland, or riding a bicycle.

Skin color, race and ethnicity are now believed to be as irrelevant to the purposes of marriage as is eye color, height and weight. Can the same argument be made for same-sex couples? Is there an argument that would convince us that gender is relevant to the purpose of marriage in a way that race is not?

The word "relevant" applies to purposes, goals and aims. Several types of purpose have been mentioned for the institution of marriage: legitimizing fornication and lust, procreation, rearing children, exploiting tax breaks and other governmental benefits provided to married persons, eligibility for naturalization, beneficiary of spouse's health insurance, and of course achieving "equal dignity in the eyes of the law." The first purpose (legitimizing fornication) makes the dual assumption that (a) sexual intercourse between consenting, adult unmarried persons is immoral, and (b) immoral behavior can be made moral by making it lawful. Both assumptions are suspect. The former assumption requires an argument to show what it is about extramarital sex that makes it morally wrong, and the second assumption cuts too wide a swath: it implies the absurdity that we can make it morally permissible to assault, rape or kill by making these acts legally permissible. Finally, even if we are convinced that an important purpose of marriage is to legitimize fornication, then surely this purpose would also apply to same-sex couples. What was previously immoral (extramarital intercourse of unmarried same-sex couples) could be made moral by giving them access to legal marriage.

Of course this result will be resisted by those opposed to same-sex marriage. Their resistance is due to the age-old claim, enunciated earlier by Thomas Aquinas, John Locke and other natural law philosophers that the natural purposes of "conjugal society" (marriage) are procreation and child-rearing (section "Natural law and paternal power"). This has been challenged by those who argue that procreation and child-rearing can be and has been done just as well by same-sex couples as it is by opposite-sex couples. And if it is replied that same-sex couples do not have the biological resources to procreate solely from their own bodies, it only needs to be pointed out that this can also be said of infertile couples and elderly couples beyond the age of successful procreation. If the sole purpose of marriage is procreation, then we should either withdraw the opportunity to marry from all of these groups or withdraw it from none. Finally, Locke correctly points out that there are other purposes of marriage than procreation. Locke maintained that an important purpose is the opportunity marriage provides for giving and receiving the "care and affection" to each other necessary for their "mutual support and assistance" (VII, 78). Although he limited his discussion to opposite-sex couples, and although this purpose can just as well be achieved outside of marriage, it is a justification that easily extends to same-sex marriages.

It follows that there is no sound argument for the conclusion that the gender of the persons who wish to marry is relevant to any of the announced purposes of marriage, whether that purpose be to legitimize sexual conduct by bringing it within the umbrella of marriage, procreation for the purpose of bearing and raising children, or providing persons with the opportunity to engage in a caring relationship. Hence, it is an injustice to deny same-sex couples access to marriage and to the economic and social benefits that are conferred on those who are legally married.

It is often pointed out that if the preceding arguments justify same-sex marriage, then they also justify polygamy. A group of three or more persons of the same or different sexual preferences can and do procreate and rear the children they bear. They also are capable of long-term loving and caring relationships with one another. Why, then, shouldn't these groups also have access to legal marriage, provided that their relationships are consensual? This argument is usually presented as a counter-example, forcing us to see what is believed to be an unwelcome consequence of the claim that marriage should permitted for same-sex couples. It is unwelcome partly because polygamy is believed to be unnatural, and partly because of the fear that women might be exploited and that children born into the marriage would be neglected. But exploitation assumes vulnerability and a lack of options. If this assumption can be defeated, then there seems to be no justification for prohibiting such arrangements. Child neglect has to do with the lack of resources rather than a lack of will, and this could be corrected in serious cases by the government help to which they would be eligible as a result of legal recognition of polygamous marriage.

The other factor justifying unequal treatment of those who might want access to marriage is actual or potential harm-to-others. If there is the probability that the consequence of allowing a particular group of people's access to legal marriage would be harmful to others, then it would not be unjust to deny the access. Denial of access on grounds of consanguinity is an example. Marriages of blood relatives in some populations have a higher probability of defective births than marriages of persons who are not blood related in the same populations who are not blood related.[4] The "other" who is harmed in these cases would be the defective newborns who suffer from nervous system and heart problems. Another kind of harm is largely economic. The health and welfare system and the taxpayers who fund the system would bear the costs of treating the defective infants whose births could have been avoided were it not for the cultural practice of consanguinity. However, since there are many other "avoidable" practices leading to financial burdens on the community (obesity, smoking), it would be unfair to choose between denying treatment to defective infants while providing it to persons suffering from the consequences of bad and avoidable habits.

9.5.2 The Constitutional Debate

The cases that prompted Supreme Court review in *Obergefell v. Hodges* were from four states that defined marriage as "a union between one man and one woman." Fourteen same-sex couple and two men whose same-sex partners had died petitioned the Court with the claim that the relevant laws of these states "violate the Fourteenth Amendment by denying them the right to marry or to have their marriages lawfully performed in another State, given full recognition."

Justice Kennedy wrote the majority decision ruling that the State laws are constitutionally invalid "to the extent they exclude same-sex couples from civil marriage on the same terms and conditions as opposite-sex couples." In reaching this conclusion Justice Kennedy demonstrated that the reasons why marriage is regarded as a fundamental right under the Constitution applies "with equal force to same-sex couples" (B III). He derives this conclusion from "the Court's relevant precedents," each of which points to "a principle in the Court's jurisprudence." The first principle is inherent in "the concept of individual autonomy." Decisions concerning marriage are like choices concerning contraception, family relationships, procreation and child-rearing, "all of which are protected by the Constitution" (id.) The second principle is the protection of a two-person union "unlike any other in its importance to the committed individuals." Only the right to marry can "dignify couples who wish to define themselves by their commitment to one another." Third, the right to marry "safeguards children and families, and thus draws meaning from related rights of childrearing, procreation, and education." Finally, marriage is "a keystone of our social order," recognized long ago in Court decisions stating that marriage is "the foundation of the family and of society, without which there would be neither civilization nor progress … a great public institution giving character to our whole civil polity" (*Maynard v. Hill*, 1888).

[4] Marriage to a blood relative accounted for nearly a third (31%) of all birth defects in babies of Pakistani origin in Bradford, England. The study involved 13,500 babies delivered in the Bradford Royal Infirmary between 2007 and 2011. (Bosely 2013).

All of these principles taken together give us "a better informed understanding of how constitutional imperatives define a liberty that remains urgent in our own era" (*Obergefell*, B III). Same-sex couples seek in marriage the same legal treatment as opposite-sex couples, "and it would disparage their choices and diminish their personhood to deny them this right." Hence, the right of same-sex couples to marry is part of the *liberty* promised and guaranteed to all by the Fourteenth Amendment.

Justice Kennedy also argued that the right of same-sex couples to marry is derived from the Fourteenth Amendment's guarantee of the *equal protection of the laws*. Marriage is a contractual relationship between persons which creates rights and duties with respect to one another, as defined in most state laws. It is a contract that once entered into, provides for mutual support, property, taxes, and inheritance and many other economic benefits. Justice Kennedy described these benefits at length in his decision for the *Obergefell* majority.

> Just as a couple vows to support each other, so does society pledge to support the couple, offering symbolic recognition and material benefits to protect and nourish the union. Indeed, while the States are in general free to vary the benefits they confer on all married couples, they have throughout our history made marriage the basis for an expanding list of governmental rights, benefits, and responsibilities. These aspects of marital status include: taxation; inheritance and property rights; rules of intestate succession; spousal privilege in the law of evidence; hospital access; medical decision-making authority; adoption rights; the rights and benefits of survivors; birth and death certificates; professional ethics rules; campaign finance restrictions; workers' compensation benefits; health insurance; and child custody, support, and visitation rules. (*Obergefell v Hodges*, 16)

The central benefit denied to same-sex couples by laws that deny them access to marriage is the loss of "*equal dignity* in the eyes of the law":

> No union is more profound than marriage, for it embodies the highest ideals of love, fidelity, devotion, sacrifice, and family. In forming a marital union, two people become something greater than they once were. As some of the petitioners in these cases demonstrate, marriage embodies a love that may endure even past death. It would misunderstand these men and women to say they disrespect the idea of marriage. Their plea is that they do respect it, respect it so deeply that they seek to find its fulfillment for themselves. Their hope is not to be condemned to live in loneliness, excluded from one of civilization's oldest institutions. They ask for equal dignity in the eyes of the law. The Constitution grants them that right. (*Obergefell v Hodges,* 33)

There is no doubt that laws prohibiting same-sex marriage are "in essence unequal" because they deny "all the benefits afforded to opposite-sex couples." This denial "works a grave and continuing harm" by depriving them of the opportunity to enter into the only kind of relationship that would afford them such substantial benefits.

These two considerations, one based on the Fourteenth Amendment's promise of liberty and the other of equal protection, leads Kennedy to the conclusion that the right to marry is a fundamental right, "and under the Due Process and the Equal Protection Clauses of the Fourteenth Amendment couples of the same sex may not be deprived of that right and that liberty."

Justice Scalia's dissent to the majority decision was both blistering and predictable. In arguments reminiscent of the *textualist* approach to interpreting the

Constitution (Sect. 4.1) Scalia wrote that the Court has "no basis for striking down a practice that is not expressly prohibited by the Fourteenth Amendment's text" (I). He next used an *originalist* theory of constitutional interpretation (Sect. 4.4.1) by arguing that "*the People's* understanding of 'liberty' — at the time of ratification or even today" was ignored by the majority, who instead chose to focus on four principles and traditions in order to reach the conclusion that the states should be prohibited from defining marriage as an institution consisting of one man and woman.

> This is a naked judicial claim to legislative—indeed *super*-legislative—power; a claim fundamentally at odds with our system of government. Except as limited by a constitutional prohibition agreed to by the People, the States are free to adopt whatever laws they like … A system of government that makes the People subordinate to a committee of nine unelected lawyers does not deserve to be called a democracy.

Justice Roberts in a separate dissent said that none of the precedents cited by the Court majority were relevant to this case. For example, in *Loving v. Virginia* (388 U.S. at 12) the constitutional challenge was to *racial restrictions* on the right to marry. The *Loving* decision that struck down these restrictions left intact the definition of marriage as a union of one man and one woman. The decision says "nothing at all about a right to make a State change its definition of marriage." Roberts also questioned the relevance of the majority opinion that expanding marriage to include same sex couples would "pose no risk of harm to themselves or third parties." This observation about the harm principle "may or may not be attractive moral philosophy," but it has no place in the courtroom: The Court should be "guided by law, not any particular school of social thought" (Roberts, dissent, II, B, 4).

Although the Supreme Court decision satisfied a steadily increasing majority of Americans who thought that same-sex marriages should be valid,[5] there were many who continued to resist the decision on religious grounds by declaring either that the decision was itself invalid (the decision contravened the laws of God) and/or that individual state officials had no moral duty to comply.[6]

9.6 Alternatives to Traditional Marriage

In a 2007 New York Times op-ed, Stephanie Coontz recommended that "it's time to revert to a much older marital tradition. Let churches decide which marriages they deem 'licit.' But let couples — gay or straight — decide if they want the legal protections and obligations of a committed relationship" (Coontz A27). The churches can set their own rules about who can marry, but the state should not set any barriers

---

[5] 60% of those polled in 2015 said that same-sex marriages should be valid, a 33% increase from polls taken in 1996. http://www.gallup.com/poll/117328/marriage.aspx

[6] A county clerk in Kentucky recently denied a marriage license to a same-sex couple on the day after she lost an appeal to have the Supreme Court delay its decision in *Obergefell v Hodges*. The reason she gave for denying the license was that she was "acting under the authority of God's law." http://www.nytimes.com/2015/09/02/us/same-sex-marriage-kentucky-kim-davis.html

for competent adults who wish to marry. Marriages both in and out of church would be recognized as legal marriages. The only difference is that *the state* can no longer set requirements prohibiting marriage between (for example) persons of the same sex.

Coontz offers one solution to the problem of setting marriage requirements but she does not resolve the problem about the injustice of a system of benefit distribution in which married couples are given preferential treatment. Nor does Coontz answer the complaint of my unmarried friend who proclaims he will never marry because he does not want a third party (the state or an employer) to regulate his personal relationships (Sect. 9.1). Although he eventually married in order to receive the benefits offered to married couples, he remains convinced that he was unjustly "forced" to do this by a legal and commercial system that manipulates the rules in favor of those who are married.

There are several solutions other than removing existing barriers to same-sex marriage. The state could completely abolish legal marriage, replace legal marriage with private contracts, or offer a form of legal marriage that would support caring relationships between two or more persons of any gender or sexual preference ("minimal marriage").

9.6.1 Contract Law and the Abolition of Legal Marriage

One recommendation is to get the state entirely out of the marriage business by leaving marriage to the church and to private arrangement. When the state constructs the rights and obligations of marriage it inevitably does so in order to promote its own ideas about what is appropriate for love, intimacy and sex. These ideas may not be shared by every member of a diverse society. If we believe that the state should not promote particular religious, philosophical, or moral views in its laws and policies, then it should practice complete neutrality about how people behave in intimate relationships. This can only be accomplished when the state ceases to regulate such relationships. It should allow consenting adults who wish to cohabit to choose those arrangements they prefer. If they are religious, then they may prefer to be bound by the precepts of their religion. But their religious marriage will have no legal consequences and the state will not intervene in any future dispute the couple might have.

9.6.2 Marital Contracts as Private Contracts

This leads to a second, related solution: private contracts. The traditional view of private contracts between individuals is that the duties arising under contract law should be self-imposed, not imposed by society "through the judges who fashion and enforce the common law of contracts" (Altman, 120). Courts have long recognized that the traditional marriage contract is "unlike any other contract" (Okin,

122–123) because it creates a status, that is, relationship which cannot be changed by the persons in the relationship. But "all other contracts may be modified, restricted, or enlarged, or entirely released upon the consent of the parties" (Weisbrod, 779–780). The solution is to "allow marriage to be regulated like any other legal relationship between adults—by *freedom of contract*" (Brake, 154). The state will no longer define the terms of marital contracts, nor place burdensome qualifications on who shall be allowed to create them. They can be created by same-sex couples or polygamous groups of any number. Private contracts impose no standards of behavior on individuals other than those they wish to impose on themselves and no one has any obligations that they did not accept for themselves. The marital contract as a private contract may contain terms that look like the terms of traditional marriage but which, unlike traditional marriage can be modified and cancelled at any time upon the consent of the "married" couple.

9.6.3 Minimal Marriage

A third solution, recently offered by Professor Elizabeth Brake, retains the role of the state in marriage, but it does so by giving marriage a legal framework that does not endorse or promote any controversial moral or religious norms. She calls this framework "minimal marriage."

> Minimal marriage allows individuals to select from rights and responsibilities exchanged within marriage and exchange them with whomever they want, rather than exchanging a predefined bundle of rights and responsibilities with only one amatory partner … The central idea is that individuals can have legal marital relationships with more than one person, reciprocally or asymmetrically, themselves determining the sex and number of parties, the type of relationship involved, and which rights and responsibilities to exchange with each. (156–157)

Brake calls it minimal because it has "far fewer state-determined restrictions than current marriage" (157). For example, as with private contracts, minimal marriage contains no legal barriers to same-sex or polygamous marriages. It is minimal in a second sense. Any restrictions on marriage "are the most extensive that can be justified within political liberalism" (134). Political liberalism "prohibits policy and legislation, at least in important matters of justice, from being based solely on controversial moral or religious norms—they must also be justifiable by public reason" (135).

> Public reason requires that in deciding public matters citizens must give reasons which they could reasonably expect those with different conceptions of the good (views of what is good or valuable) drawn from different comprehensive moral, philosophical or religious doctrine to accept.... In the political sphere, public reason allows the giving of reasons from within comprehensive religious, philosophical, or moral doctrines *only if* a justification that respects public reason is also available[7] (Brake, 136, my italics)

[7] "Thus, Martin Luther King's use of Christian themes in his speeches met this standard because his calls for racial equality could also be justified through public reason," but "legislation such as the Marital Rape Exemption or laws or private policies requiring female schoolteachers to resign on marriage is ruled out" (Brake, 136 and 139).

Under the constraints of public reason, Brake argues, "the reasons given for marriage law or policy on the basis of comprehensive religious, philosophical, or moral views" are precluded. This means that the *legal* definition of marriage must be justified *without* appeal to these comprehensive doctrines. Minimal marriage meets this requirement. "No more extensive or restrictive law than minimal marriage is consistent with political liberalism" (Brake, 167).

We still don't have an answer to my friend's question: Why does the state need to get involved in any personal (or caring) relationships? Why won't private contracts between those who want to cohabit give them all of the assurances about property division and other matters that anyone would want or need?

Brake's answer to the first question is that in an ideal liberal egalitarian society, minimal marriage would consist only in rights that recognize and support *caring relationships.*

> Caring relationships may include friendships, urban tribes, and care networks as well as polyamorous or monogamous different-sex relationships. Care, broadly construed, may involve physical or emotional care-taking or simply a caring attitude (an attitude of concern for a particular other). Parties to such a relationship know and are known to one another, have ongoing direct contact, and share a history (160).

Minimal marriage *recognizes* caring relationships (for example) by giving status designation for third parties, burial rights and bereavement leave, and it *supports* caring relationships by creating immigration rights (eligibility for spousal immigration) and spousal care-taking leave. The rationale for all of these is determined by their essential support of caring relationships.

Not only is minimal marriage of benefit to those who are either in or intend to be a part of a caring relationship, but (Brake argues) "a liberal state is *required* to provide legal supports for caring relationships" (Brake, 160).

> These supports, or minimal marriage rights, are juridical rights designed to support caring relationships. They protect such relationships through entitlements facilitating relationship maintenance and by giving their members a way to signal to the institutions shaping their lives (employers, government, hospitals, states, and so on) which relationships should receive these protections (Brake, 160).

Hence, the answer to my friend's question is that he may want state involvement in his personal (caring) relationship with his cohabiting partner because this could be to the benefit of both of them. Minimal marriage will create no conflict between his desire to maintain a personal relationship with his spouse and the rights he and his spouse will gain.

However, those who wish to enter a minimal marriage should be forewarned that they will not receive many of the current traditional marriage rights such as health care and basic income.

> Law should not assume dependency between spouses, because this presumes that they order their relationship according to a particular comprehensive doctrine, so most marital entitlements to direct financial assistance would be eliminated (except for those, such as in-state tuition eligibility, whose primary purpose is to enable relationship maintenance). Because the state would not assume dependency, property arrangements would be contractualized, allowing parties to decide property division, alimony, and inheritance, and to set

conditional terms and specify penalties for default. Some "insurance" provisions—particularly those that reflect the significant relationship between the spouses in the case of death—would be maintained" (Brake 162).

Glaringly absent in this discussion of private contracts and minimal marriage is any mention of the rights and welfare of children or the legal duties and rights of their parents. This is because such rights and duties have largely been separated from marriage. Whether married or unmarried the legal parent of a child has a duty to support that child. A parent can divorce his spouse but not his child. Thus, whether or not a parent is involved in a traditional marriage, has a private co-habitation contract with another person or multiple persons, or is in a minimal marriage with state benefits, none of this is relevant to a determination of their legal duties as parents. There are several reasons for this. First, parenting obligations are between parent and child, not between parent and parent. Securing parental obligations independent of marriage "protects children in high-conflict marriages and marriages that end in divorce." Second, separating parenting and marriage frameworks allows providing benefits associated with marriage to children of single parents living outside of marriage. (Brake, 149). Third, the valuable political goal of getting society to recognize their direct responsibility to vulnerable children is best achieved by separating it from marriage than by having such help mediated through marriage.

9.6.4 Assessing the Alternatives to Traditional Marriage

The proposal that state-sponsored (traditional) marriage should be abolished is supported by the argument that it "cultivates injustice and discrimination through promoting divisions between men and women, different racial groups and different socio-economic classes" (N. McKeever, 9210). However, as Brake points out, that marriage has had this consequence is a contingent fact about it. There is no reason why it could not be reformed in a way that eliminates any injustice. Second, if marriage were abolished it would leave the process of marriage in the hands of institutions, mainly religious, who could deny entry to certain groups of people, thus fostering discrimination (Brake, 123).

The second proposal that argues for both abolition of traditional marriage and replacement of it with private contracts eliminates a key feature of legal marriage. A private contract could not be used to require public authorities to recognize the foreign marriage of a U.S. citizen to a non-U.S. citizen and thus to allow immigration of the non-citizen. Nor can a private contract between a couples require an employer to give leave-time to care for a sick or dying spouse.

Finally, Brake's proposal for minimal marriage does not entirely avoid the criticism that it unjustly distributes benefits to (minimally) married persons while not providing the same benefits to those who are not married. Brake's main justification for preferential treatment is that caring relationships are a "primary good." This means that 'they are all-purpose goods that people are assumed to want whatever their plans' and are 'essential to the development and exercise of the moral powers and to the pursuit of varied conceptions of the good' (173–174). Hence, state support for them is justifiable within a Rawlsian politically liberal framework. However, if care is the basis of state support, then, if the politically liberal state supports some caring relationships, it must support them all, including the caring relationships of cohabiting but unmarried individuals (those who want to avoid even a minimal marriage). "Distributing health care and other benefits through marriage … unjustly excludes the unmarried and subsidizes the married at their expense… Why should single taxpayers and employees subsidize spousal health insurance and other benefits?" (Card, 192). To deny unmarried couples and single persons the benefits given to those who are minimally married is an obvious injustice.

Second, the recommendation that all personal or caring relationships should be treated the same under marriage law seems to cut too wide a swath. Most people have friends that they see once or twice a year and they may not have any communication with some of their closest friends for several years. None of this diminishes their friendship or the fact that they would respond to any requests for help if the situation demanded it. But there is no commitment with our friends that we "share a life" with them, nor are we expected to organize our life plans around our friendships. This is quite different from how we behave in romantic relationships.

> Your partner has a right to be involved in any of your life decisions that will affect the quality of your shared life. For example, if you are in a long-term romantic relationship it would be unreasonable of you to decide to move to Australia without consulting your partner, but you need not (typically) consult your friends. This is true even if you are in a serious romantic relationship with someone you do not care for, such as in an arranged marriage… Unless you have made an explicit commitment to share a life with your friend, it would generally seem unreasonable for her to expect to spend a considerable amount of time with you and for you not to move to a different city in order to stay near her. This is because our concept of friendship only includes a shared life in a very minimal way, if at all. Indeed, sometimes one of the things we value about friendship is its relative lack of burdensome obligations (McKeever).

The point is that it is important to distinguish between caring relationships, especially for the purpose of marriage. Serious romantic relationships have a distinctive feature which may make them more suitable candidates for marriage in general than friendships. They typically involve greater commitment to sharing a life than friendships do. Perhaps it is this commitment to a shared life within the broader context of a caring relationship that should be legally recognized, not the mere fact that two or more people consider themselves to be friends.

9.7 The Exit Rules

If college roommates in the United States in the year 1950 decided that they no longer wanted to room together, then there were no legal barriers to the termination of their relationship. It was their joint decision to room together and it was up to them to go their separate ways. They did not have to go to court and file papers requesting that their roommate relationship be put to an end. If one of the roommates wanted the relationship to continue and the other did not, then there is nothing he or she could legally do to force the other to stay. He could try to persuade, cajole, even beg the other to continue on as his roommate, but he could not require this.

But if the relationship of a man and a woman in the same year (1950) was *marriage* then their joint decision to exit the marriage was decidedly not "up to them." The prevailing law required that some kind of fault on the part of one of the partners had to be established. "Marriages could not be terminated unless there was evidence of serious wrongdoing by one of the spouses" (Statsky, 127). The fact that they no longer wanted to be married was not a sufficient reason for a court to grant a divorce. One court in the 1950s said this: "Testimony which proves merely an unhappy union, the parties being high strung temperamentally and unsuited to each other and neither being wholly innocent of the causes which resulted in the failure of their marriage, is insufficient to sustain a judgment" (Statsky, 243, citing *Rankin v Rankin*, Pennsylvania 1956).

It is no wonder that the Latin phrase for divorce is *divorce a vincula martimonii* — "divorce from the chains of marriage." The usual response of couples who wanted to break the chain tying them together was for both spouses to lie to the court in order to make it appear that fault grounds for divorce existed.[8]

If one spouse wanted to divorce and the other did not, then the prospects of obtaining a judgment for divorce were even worse. The only way that one had a chance at divorce was to prove fault on the part of the unwilling partner, for example, adultery, cruelty or desertion. If there was no evidence of fault or evidence could not be manufactured, then the unhappy partner had to remain married.

The lies and deceit that characterized much of the divorce proceedings in the United States came to a halt in 1969 when California enacted the first system of *no-fault divorce*. The words "no fault" mean that there is no requirement to prove any marital wrongs that might have precipitated the divorce. Other states soon followed, and at this writing no-fault grounds exist in every state. One result of this revolution in marriage law was not only that people seeking divorce no longer had to lie about their wrongdoing, but the divorce rate dramatically increased. "In the years between 1970 and 1996, the number of divorced people living in the country more than quadrupled, from 4.3 million to 18.3 million" due at least in part to the fact that the large number of couples who had been trapped in unhappy marriages could now obtain a relatively easy divorce.

The transition to no-fault divorce has not diminished the influence of the legal system. Although most divorce cases are uncontested, there is still great deal to

[8] Statsky quotes one attorney who commented that for decades New York's divorce system was "built on a foundation of winks and falsehoods. If you wanted to split quickly, you and our spouse had to give one of the limited number of allowable reasons–including adultery, cruelty, imprisonment or abandonment–so there was a tendency to pick one out of a hat ... One legendary ploy involved listing the filing lawyer's secretary as the partner in adultery (which may even have been true in a few cases)" (Statsky, 127–128, citing Elizabeth Gilbert, *Eat, Pray, Love,* 2006:30).

adjudicate in the contested cases, including alimony (spousal support), property division, child custody, and child support.

Moral philosophers and philosophers of law have not had much to say about divorce and its legal consequences. This may be due to the fact that they do not detect a moral problem about either the act of divorce or contemporary divorce law. In this section we will (briefly) correct some of these omissions by asking the following two normative questions: Is there a justification for state involvement in divorce? In particular, why should the state intervene in divorce but not intervene when persons choose to terminate other close relationships (for example, private roommate contracts)? Second, if we want to embrace the liberal principle that the rules of both marriage and divorce should be perfectly neutral and not promote controversial moral and religious norms, then we need to ask whether there are any neutral liberal principles that are being ignored. For example, if there is evidence that divorce rules might allow some individuals to take advantage of their spouse's economic vulnerability or rules that fail to prevent divorcing couples from ignoring probable emotional harm caused to their young children by the divorce, then we need to ask how a just legal system should respond to these harms.

9.7.1 Divorce and the Vulnerability of Women

To return to the roommate example (Sect. 9.7), the state does not intervene in either the entrance into or the exit from their relationship. They are free to create a contract that sets a date for termination of their relationship and to share the expenses of rent, furniture, and groceries. They are also free to alter the contract at any time by mutual consent, or (as in most cases) to may choose to have no formal contract at all.

Those who support private contracts in lieu of marriage (Sect. 9.6.1) argue that this is how it should be with suits for divorce. There is no need or justification for the state to intervene and set special requirements and regulations for exiting from (dissolving) a private marriage agreement — as long as each person is treated equally. Spouses should be free to set a termination date for their marital relationship as well as set their own rules of support for each other during their marriage. They should also be free to decide how their property will be divided, whether one of them will receive alimony payments from the other, and who shall have custody of their children in the event of a divorce. Because consent is of primary consideration in a contract, the husband or wife must make a full and accurate disclosure of assets during negotiations for the agreement, and not lie about assets. They must also refrain from any fraud or duress.

There is some support for this position from the traditional view of private law. That view promotes the basic idea that a contract is a self-imposed obligation which leaves individuals free to decide the terms of their agreement and to determine the conditions under which either or both shall be released from these terms. The role of the state should only be to enforce the terms of the contract in case of a conflict about its interpretation or application. The state has no business imposing any non-contractual duties based on the public good or social need in their relevant statutes. All contracts, including contracts-in-lieu-of-marriage, as part of *private* law should be kept separate from politics and public law.

One objection to spouses determining their own property division upon divorce through individual contract is that some women bargain with their husbands from a disadvantageous position. Many women become economically vulnerable during marriage. They "subordinate their economic independence to child care and household work" (Brake 193, citing Okin). This puts them at a disadvantage post-divorce and "this is compounded by the greater likelihood that children will remain with the mother after the divorce, bringing her greater financial costs." If the wife has limited job skills and she signs a separation agreement with a property division giving her husband marital assets that provide her with far less than she needs to avoid becoming a public charge, this would be an unjust outcome. By contrast, just outcomes are *guaranteed* through current state-mandated divorce laws regulating division of property. "Insofar as women are likely to become economically vulnerable in marriage, they will be better protected economically by mandatory property division and alimony than by contractualization" (Brake, 194, citing Minow and Shanley).

A response to this objection can be found in the practices of some courts when they consider the validity of *separation agreements*.[9] Suppose that a naive woman with little business acumen signs an agreement that gives her $15,000 cash and her husband gets marital assets totaling $500.000. The terms of this agreement could be declared *unconscionable* by the court ("shocking the conscience by heavily favoring one side due to the absence of meaningful choice and the highly unequal bargaining positions of the parties" Statsky 176). The agreement will be declared invalid. By analogy, contractualization of marriage should not end in an unjust settlement in the event of a dissolution. A process is available to protect those who might have entered into a divorce settlement from an unequal bargaining position.

Another way to establish the invalidity of a private contract is to show that there was *overreaching* on the part of one of the spouses, that is, he or she took advantage of the other's vulnerability, "especially by deception" (Statsky 176). In both this and the previous case, the court protects the spouse in a way that ensures that he or she gives full and voluntary consent to the final divorce agreement. At the same time, if there has been full disclosure of assets and debts, no fraud, no unconscionable agreement and both parties had the opportunity to seek independent advice before they signed, most courts will presume that the separation agreement is valid and enforceable, even if one of the parties has regrets or if the contract appears to others to be a bad bargain. In such cases it can no longer be argued that the distribution of property was the result of an unjust procedure or that the outcome itself was unjust.

[9] These are pre-divorce agreements by married persons who have separated. They can cover support, custody, property division and other terms of their impending divorce. The divorce court must approve the terms of the separation agreement if the spouses want a divorce based on the separation agreement. (Statsky, 168).

9.7.2 Divorce and the Vulnerability of Young Children

A second and more serious objection to both types of divorce (those regulated by mandatory rules of the state *and* those governed only by the terms of a private contract-in-lieu of marriage) is that both appear to ignore the emotional harm caused to young children by the separation and divorce of their parents. If we are serious about the role of the harm-to-others principle (Sect. 5.3.1) in resolving normative debates about the limits of the law, then we should certainly be concerned about the potential harmful effects of marital dissolution on non-consenting others, especially if the "others" are young children.

The concern about possible harm suffered by the children of divorce was first mentioned in the West by the philosopher Bertrand Russell and the author and journalist Rebecca West. In his bestselling and controversial book *Marriage and Morals* (1929) Russell commented on the high rate of divorce in America which he attributed primarily to "extremely weak" family feeling. He regarded easy divorce "as a transitional stage on the way from the bi-parental to the purely maternal family," and he observed that this is "a stage involving considerable hardship for children, since, in the world as it is, children expect to have two parents, and may become attached to their father before divorce takes place." In characteristically strong language, Russell concluded that "parents who divorce each other, except for grave cause, appear to me to be failing in their parental duty" (Russell, 239).

Russell's concern was echoed by Rebecca West in an article she wrote in 1930 for *The London Daily Express*. West wrote "the divorce of married people with children is nearly always an unspeakable calamity." She gave several reasons for this:

> It is only just being understood, in the light of modern psychological research, how much a child depends for its healthy growth on the presence in the home of both its parents … If a child is deprived of either its father or its mother, it feels that it has been cheated out of a right. It cannot be reasoned out of this attitude, for children are illogical, especially where their affections are concerned, to an even greater degree than ourselves. A child who suffers from this resentment suffers much more than grief: he is liable to an obscuring of his vision, to a warping of his character. He may turn against the parent to whom the courts have given him, and regard him or her as responsible for the expulsion of the other from the home. He may try to compensate himself for what he misses by snatching everything else he can get out of life, and become selfish, and even thievish. He may, through yearning for the unattainable parent, get himself into a permanent mood of discontent, which will last his lifelong and make him waste every opportunity of love and happiness that comes to him later (West, 1930).[10]

Let us assume that (1) there is ample evidence that children whose parents divorce while they are young are more at risk of suffering short-term and/or long-term psychological distress and social harm (for example, anxiety, depression, withdrawal, difficulties in school achievements, peer relationships, and handling of

[10] Rebecca West, "Divorce," *The London Daily Express*, 1930.

aggression) than are children who grow up in intact marriages.[11] If we couple this fact with the following premise, (2) Parents have a duty to behave in ways that do not cause harm to their children, then we derive this conclusion: (3) it is morally wrong for the parents of young children to divorce.

I will call this the Harm-to-Children Argument or HCA. HCA is similar in structure to moral arguments used to condemn child abandonment and various forms of child abuse. When we think of child abuse, we usually think of cases in which children have suffered severe physical injury or death as a result of parental behavior. But some child abuse statutes recognize emotional or psychological harm. Thus, the New York Family Court Act defines "impairment of emotional health" as

> a state of substantially limited psychological or intellectual functioning in relation to, but not limited to such factors as failure to thrive, control of aggressiveness or self-destructive impulses, ability to think and reason, or acting out or misbehavior, including incorrigibility, ungovernability or habitual truancy…

If we think that parental behavior that causes or is likely to cause the kind of emotional or psychological harm specified in the preceding statute is morally wrong, and if we think that some children have been harmed by the divorce of their parents, then it would appear that divorce is wrong for the same reason that parental behaviors causing the psychological and behavioral conditions noted in the New York statute are wrong.

Faced with the conclusion of HCA, there are a number of ways in which divorced parents of young children might attempt to defend themselves against the charge that it was morally wrong for them to divorce.

Divorce and Emotional Abuse

First, it may be objected that the preceding analogy between divorce and child abuse is misplaced. Some boys whose parents divorce while they are young may very well suffer, but their suffering never rises to the minimum level of suffering required by legal standards for determining emotional abuse.

The response to this objection is that HCA does not argue that divorce *is* child abuse. Legal definitions of child abuse and neglect are formulated solely to deal with the problem of the conditions under which the state may justifiably intervene in the family to protect the child. HCA says nothing about state intervention, nor does it recommend any change in the laws regulating divorce. Instead, HCA is an

---

[11] "Boys suffer more from divorce than girls because they understandably identify with their father, and in most cases of divorce it is fathers who leave the family home. When fathers leave they have much less contact with their children than they had with them prior to the divorce. "One large survey in the late 1980s found that about one in five divorced fathers had not seen his children in the past year, and less than half of divorced fathers saw their children more than several times a year. A 1981 survey of adolescents who were living apart from their fathers found that 52% had not seen them at all in more than a year; only 16% saw their fathers as often as once a week. Moreover, the survey showed fathers' contact with their children dropping off sharply with the passage of time after the marital breakup" (Popenoe 1996).

argument about the morality of divorce. It argues that some divorces arc wrong *for the same reason* that child abuse is wrong. The reason that some divorces are wrong is that they cause or are likely to cause emotional harm to the children of the divorcing parents. Whether the emotional harm suffered by children whose parents divorce rises to the level of severity required by the child abuse standards of some states is beside the point. The point is whether some children whose parents divorce suffer emotional harm, *not* whether they suffer the kind or amount required by the courts to recognize a child abuse petition for purposes of court-ordered intervention.

Treating Symptoms of Emotional Distress

The second objection to HCA is that so long as parents aggressively treat any symptoms of emotional harm that their children may suffer post-divorce in order to minimize the deleterious effects of the divorce, then they have done nothing wrong by obtaining the divorce. What *would* be wrong would be to ignore the symptoms and to leave them untreated.

This argument has the following structure: It is not wrong to divorce; it is only wrong to divorce and do nothing to minimize its bad effects on children. But consider the following counterexample: so long as I secure medical treatment for my child after 1 have engaged in risky behavior that resulted in his leg getting broken, then I have done nothing wrong in putting my child at risk. The reason that we resist this conclusion is that we do not think it justifiable to engage in behavior that puts the lives and health of our children at risk in the first place. This is why we think it morally incumbent on us not to smoke when children are in the house, to put them in restraining seats when we have them in the car with us, and do countless other things to minimize their chances of injury in and out of the home. It is simply not enough to announce that one is prepared to treat a child's injuries after they occur. We demand that parents take steps to prevent the harm *before* it occurs.

Hostile Family Environments

The third objection to HCA takes advantage of a "loophole" suggested by the Bertrand Russell. He proposed it as an exception to his general claim that parents who divorce violate their parental duty. Russell's loophole is that the divorce might be justified if it was done for "grave cause." A grave cause exists when it is established that (a) the children will suffer less post-divorce emotional distress than they will suffer if the marriage of their parents remains intact; and (b) during the marriage, the parents could not control those behaviors that cause their children to suffer emotional harm. For example, Russell mentions insanity or alcoholism as possible candidates for grave cause justifications for divorce because in both cases the affected parent may be unable to prevent himself from engaging in behavior detrimental to his child's welfare.

"Grave cause" is probably the most common of the rationales that parents will offer to justify their divorce. Some of the studies of the psychological effects of divorce show that the adverse effects observed in children were often seen prior to the divorce as a result of a hostile family environment. One commentator has concluded from this that the transition, through divorce, from an intact two-parent family to a single-parent family can no longer be objected to on the grounds that divorce is bad for children.

However, the preceding data only establishes the first of the two conditions that are together sufficient for a grave cause justification for divorce. That is, although a hostile family environment may cause a child to suffer as much or more than he or she would suffer from the divorce of her parents, it does not follow that the divorce is justifiable. In order to establish the existence of a grave cause, the parents must also prove that they could not control the "hostile family environment" that caused their children to suffer. Russell has the best rejoinder to those parents who claim that they were helpless to control the marital behavior that caused emotional distress in their children:

> The husband and wife, if they have any love for their children, will regulate their conduct so as to give their children the best chance of a happy and healthy development… To cooperate in rearing children, even after passionate love has decayed, is by no means a superhuman task for sensible people who are capable of natural affections … As soon as there are children it is the duty of both parties to a marriage to do everything that they can to preserve harmonious relations, even if this requires considerable self-control (Russell, 236).

In other words, to say that one had no choice but to obtain a divorce in order not to expose one's children to marital discord is to make the extraordinary assumption that one could not control one's behavior. It is analogous to the contention of a cigarette smoker that he had to abandon his child in order to save her from the physical effects of his second hand smoke. The point is that we are as capable of controlling the behavior toward our spouse that causes distress in our young children as we are capable of not smoking in their presence.

The Primacy of Children's Interests

Finally, it may be objected that HCA puts far too much stress on the rights and interests of children, ignoring the legitimate needs of the parents. Surely, it might be said, the desires, projects, and commitments of each parent which give them reasons to divorce in the pursuit of ends that are their own may sometimes outweigh those reasons not to divorce that stem from the special non-contractual obligations that they have to nurture their young children.

This objection assumes a version of the Family Privacy Principle (section "Intrafamily harm and the family privacy principle") by recommending that a barrier be established between the decisions of the divorcing parents and the *parens patriae* duty of the state to prevent harm to children. FPP recommends that parents should be left alone to make their own decisions about whether their family should be left intact or dissolved. *Parens patriae* invokes the harm principle and the power of the state to protect the best interests of children.

To the objection that parental desires to be free to pursue their own interests, regardless of the deleterious effects on the health of their children it can be replied that if it is permissible for parents to divorce for these reasons, then one wonders what it would mean to say that they have an obligation to protect and nurture their children. How can one be said to have an *obligation* to protect and nurture her young child if it is permissible for her to perform an act that risks harming the child for no other reason than that she wants to pursue her own projects? This empties the concept of parental obligation of most of its content. Parents of young children who divorce for no other reason than that they find their marriage unfulfilling and believe that this is justifiable seem to me to be parents who lack an understanding of what it is to have an obligation to their children. They must believe that they can treat their own children as they would treat any other child. In the case of children other than our own, most of us would acknowledge that the effect on these children of what we do counts for something. But even if it were proved to me and my spouse that (e.g.) the children of our next-door neighbor will suffer emotionally as result of our divorce, we would not think that this puts us under an obligation to cancel or delay our separation. If we did delay it, this would be an act of charity, not an obligation. But with our own children, things are otherwise. Our children exert an "ethical pull" on us not exerted by the children of others. Benevolent acts toward our children become perfect duties within the context of the family, and as such they outweigh parental desires to pursue their own projects when these come into conflict. This is surely part of what it means to become a parent.

Let us assume that Russell is correct in contending that many of the divorces of parents who have young children are morally unjustifiable when the reason for the divorce is similar to one or more of the reasons commonly given by parents, for example "We have grown apart," "We have become different persons than we were when we first married," "We are profoundly unhappy with one another," "We want to pursue a single lifestyle again," or "I found someone else with whom I would much rather live." For those parents who are capable of exercising self-control over their negative emotions (spite, anger, jealousy), Russell's argument is that none of these reasons rises to the level of a grave cause.

Now it may be objected that even if these considerations establish that parents who divorce for such reasons are wrongfully violating a *moral duty* to their children, this does not establish that the state should place a *legal* burden on the parents of young children to prove that their divorce will not cause them emotional harm. We have yet to provide empirical evidence that the children of divorce suffer the kind or amount of harm required to establish a violation of the harm principle. We do not know with any certainty that all or even most of the children of divorce suffer from the emotional damage indicated in the New York statute mentioned above (Sect. 9.7.2). But even if the evidence does not establish this, it might be sufficient to at least put a temporary brake on a divorce action, at least to give parents pause to reflect on the effect that their divorce might have on their children and how they can alleviate potential future emotional impairments.

Questions for Thought and Discussion

1. Is the distribution of rights and obligations in the population of married and unmarried cohabiting couples a just or fair distribution? What principles of just distribution should would you use in answering this question?
2. Is there any substantial difference in the arguments given by the majority in *Obergefell v Hodges* than those arguments given by the majority in *Loving v. Virginia*? Explain.
3. What do you think Elizabeth Brake means when she says that traditional marriage encourages and even promotes controversial moral and religious views? Can you give some examples of this? Should marriage laws be neutral with regards to moral and religious views or should it promote some of them and not others? Explain.
4. What should be the "exit rules" for those couples who want to dissolve their marriage? Should they include the rule that no one should be allowed to divorce a non-consenting spouse unless they can show that the spouse is somehow "at fault" (for example, that the spouse is an adulterer, or has been physically or emotionally abusive)? Should they include a rule that parents of young children cannot separate or divorce until their children are old enough not to be emotionally damaged?

References

Aquinas, Thomas. *Summa Theologica.* I–II. q. 94.

Bosely, Sarah. 2013. Marriages of First Cousins Doubles Risk of Birth Defects. *The Guardian, U.S. Edition.*http://www.theguardian.com/science/2013/jul/04/marriage-first-cousins-birth-defects

Bradwell v. State of Illinois, 83 U.S. 141–142 (1873)

Brake, Elizabeth. 2012. *Minimizing Marriage: Marriage, Morality and the Law*. New York: Oxford University Press.

Coontz, Stephanie. 2007. Taking Marriage Private. *New York Times.* 26 November. A27. http://www.nytimes.com/2007/11/26/opinion/26coontz.html?_r=1&

Craig v Boren, 429 U.S. 190 (1976)

Lamont, Julian and Favor, Christi. 2014. Distributive Justice. *The Stanford Encyclopedia of Philosophy*, ed. Edward N. Zalta.

Locke, John. 1980. In *Second Treatise of Government*, ed. C.B. Macpherson. Indianapolis: Hackett.

McKeever, N. 2012. Review of Elizabeth Brake: *Minimizing Marriage: Marriage, Morality and the Law* in *Res Publica: A Journal of Moral, Legal and Social Philosophy*. 19:9210.

Mess, Michael A. 1979. For Richer for Poorer: Federal Taxation and Marriage. *Cath U L Review* 28: 87.

Obergefell v Hodges, 576 U.S. __ 2015.

Oldman and Temple. 1960. Comparative Analysis of the Taxation of Married Persons. *Stanford Law Review.* 12: 585.

Popenoe, David. 1996. The Vanishing Father. *The Wilson Quarterly*. 14.
Russell, Bertrand. 1929. *Marriage and Morals*. London: George Allen & Unwin.
Statsky, William P. 2015. *Family Law: The Essentials*. 3rd ed. Stamford: Cengage Learning.
Surging, Linda. 2004. Theories of Distributive Justice and Limitations on Taxation: What Rawls Demands from Tax Systems. *Fordham Law Review* 72: 5.
West, Rebecca. 1926. Divorce. *Forum*. 76: 161–170.
———. 1930. Divorce. *The London Daily Express*.

Chapter 10
Children, Parents and the State

"Students in school as well as out of school are "persons" under our Constitution. They are possessed of fundamental rights which the State must respect, just as they themselves must respect their obligations to the State."

J. Abraham Fortas, *Tinker v Des Moines School District* (1969)

"Juveniles, unlike adults, are always in some form of custody ... Children, by definition, are not assumed to have the capacity to take care of themselves."

J. William Rehnquist *Schall v Martin* (1984)

Abstract In this chapter we discuss both the moral and constitutional conception of children's rights. The moral conception has been debated since the seventeenth century by Thomas Hobbes, John Locke, John Stuart Mill and Herbert Spencer. All except Spencer accept the idea that children have none of the so-called "liberty rights" possessed by adults. This idea is reflected in state laws denying such rights to children, including the right to freedom of expression when at school. But in a series of Supreme Court cases beginning in 1967, the U.S. Supreme Court declared that children are persons who are possessed of fundamental rights that the state must respect. Included among these rights is the right to freedom of expression. In this chapter we consider several Supreme Court cases introducing this right and later restricting its scope because of its inevitable conflict with another idea: children are human beings who are always in custody of their parents, of the school they attend, or ultimately of the State. We conclude the chapter by discussing several theories that attempt to resolve the dilemma of conceiving children as both persons with fundamental rights and as human beings who are always in some form of custody.

L.D. Houlgate, *Philosophy, Law and the Family*, AMINTAPHIL: The Philosophical Foundations of Law and Justice 7,
DOI 10.1007/978-3-319-51121-4_10

10.1 The Custodial Status of Children

In the context of family law, the word "child," is equivalent in meaning to "minor," or "juvenile," that is, a person who is younger than the legal age of majority (18 years in most U.S. states). As a minor, the law imposes on the child a certain *status* or bundle of rights and obligations. It is this status to which Rehnquist refers (in the epitaph above) when he says that "juveniles, unlike adults, are always in some form of custody." There are several types of custody, but the type to which Justice Rehnquist undoubtedly refers is *legal custody*. Legal custody gives a parent the right to make long-term decisions about the raising of a child, and about key aspects of the child's welfare — including the child's name, place of residence, education, medical care, dental care, nutrition, and religious instruction. These rights are reciprocal with a parental obligation to do most of these things, under threat of child neglect laws. For example, although parents have no duty to provide their children with a religious education or fashionable clothing, they must provide them with adequate food, shelter and clothing, and the child has the reciprocal right to receive these benefits.

Because of their legal status as children, their rights and obligations are imposed by law, not by consent or contract. When children attain the age of majority, they will be able to decide for themselves where they shall live, what food they shall eat, whether or not to seek medical care, and when and where to attend school But as children, these options are not available. Why is this? Is there a justification for the legal concept of a child as someone who is (by definition) always in custody? What is it about children (in the non-legal sense of this word) that leads us to conclude that all persons under the age of 18 should be in custody and (therefore) legally incapable of making adult decisions? Second, what is the constitutional basis for the unequal treatment of children under the law? How is it possible for the Supreme Court to stipulate both that children are "persons with constitutional rights" (Sect. 4.3.1) and also assert that children are persons who are always in custody?

10.2 Philosophical Theories on the Status and Rights of Children

Modern philosophers have given a wide variety of answers to the first of these questions. There are some who would discard the word "custody" and replace it with the word "ownership." Others have swung to the opposite pole, agreeing not only that the word "custody" should be discarded, but urging that it be replaced by the word "freedom," arguing that children should be free to make the long-term decisions that are now possessed by adults. There is a third group of philosophers who take the middle-ground by promoting the idea that although children are not property, any rights granted to them should not conflict with the basic custodial duties of their parents. We begin our analysis by clarifying the legal concept of a "right" before we look at each of the preceding proposals.

10.2.1 A Typology of Rights

W.N. Hohfeld (1920, 60) distinguished differing kinds or types of rights in terms of the relationship between right-holders and right-regarders. These relationships are signified by the words "claim," "liberty," (or "privilege") "power," and "immunity."

First, a right "in the strictest sense" of this word is a *claim* that one individual (the right holder) has on another (the duty bearer) to do or forbear from some act. Should the claim be in force or exercised, and the act or forbearance is not done, it would be moral or legal, other things being equal, "to use coercive measures to extract either the specific performance … or compensation in lieu of it." For example, to say that children have a right to be provided with food, clothing and shelter, is to say that the child has a claim on others (the duty bearers) to provide him with these things, and if they do not do this, then the child can use coercive measures to achieve this end. The class of mandatory rules mentioned in Chap. 1 create rights understood as claims (Sect. 1.2).

Second, some rights are *privileges* or *liberties*. Thus, if it is said that an adult, but not a child under the age of 16 years, has a right to obtain a driver's license from the Department of Motor Vehicles, this means that she is *at liberty* (or has the *privilege*) to obtain a license. To have a privilege, then, is to be excluded from the claims of another that you do or refrain from doing some act that others are required to do or refrain from doing.

Third, some rights are *powers*. To say that an adult, but not a child has the right to marry is to assert that she lacks the power to alter her legal relationship with another from unmarried to married. The power-conferring rules mentioned in 1.2 create rights that have this function.

Fourth, we sometimes say, using the language of rights, that children have an *immunity* from having certain of their rights or claims (such as the right to an inheritance after the death of a parent) subject to willful alteration by others who say they have the power to do this. We might express this by saying that the child has a right that not to have her legal relationship with her parent altered (as stated in the will).

Examination of these rights-relationships indicates the following contrasts and comparisons. A privilege is a freedom *from* the claim of another. If you have the privilege to drive an automobile, then no one has a right [claim] to prevent you from doing this. An immunity is one's freedom *from* the power or control of another as regards some legal relationship. If you have an immunity not to testify against your spouse in a court of law, then you are free from the power of the court to command said testimony.

10.2.2 Parents as Owners of Children: Thomas Hobbes

The seventeenth century philosopher Thomas Hobbes would have been astounded at any proposal that would grant legal rights (of any type) to children, including the right to life (the claim not to be killed by another). According to Hobbes, children have only duties of obedience to their parents and *no rights* at all.

> Children, therefore, whether they be brought up and preserved by the father, or by the mother, or by whomsoever, are in most absolute subjection to him or her, that so bringeth them up, or preserveth them. And they may alienate them, that is, assign his or her dominion, by selling, or giving them, in adoption or servitude to others, or may pawn them for hostages, kill them for rebellion, or sacrifice them for peace, by the law of nature, when he or she, in his or her conscience, think it to be necessary. (*The Elements of Law* 23.8).

The idea that parents have absolute authority over their children did not originate with Hobbes. It is to be found in Roman law under the ancient principle of *patria potestas* ("rule of the father"), which originally gave to the male head of the Roman family the right to punish by death any family member, including his children of any age.

This is a far cry from the parent-child relationship of custodianship or caretaker. Hobbes recommends a relationship that is akin to that of master and slave in which the child, like a slave, is seen as the property of the parent, to be sold to others if this is what he wishes, or even to kill the child if he should rebel against parental commands. The only difference between the child and a slave is Hobbes' surprising claim that the child *consents* to the absolute dominion of his parent-owner.

> The right of Dominion by Generation, is that which the Parent hath over his Children; and is called PATERNALL. And is not so derived from the Generation, as if therefore the Parent had Dominion over his Child because he begot him; but from the Childs Consent, either express, or by other sufficient arguments declared. (2:20)

Express consent is either verbal or written. Since it is absurd to argue that a newborn child has given his express consent to the dominion of his parents, Hobbes must rely on the idea of "consent by inference," or what is now called "tacit consent."

> Signs by Inference, are sometimes the consequence of Words; sometimes the consequence of Silence; sometimes the consequence of Actions; sometimes the consequence of Forbearing an Action; and generally a sign by Inference, of any Contract, is whatsoever sufficient argues the will of the Contractor. (*Leviathan* 1:14)

Suppose that a man is hungry and, without saying a word or entering into a written agreement, accepts food from another person who silently hands it to him. We might safely infer that the hungry man (the Contractor) accepts the food because he wants it (this is his will). We might also infer that he consents to taking the food, although we have no grounds for saying that he consents to anything else (for example, to pay for the food, or to be obedient to the person who gives him the food).

But none of these conjectures about tacit consent applies to the infant who suckles at her mother's breast. The infant does not know what she is doing, nor can we infer that she wishes to obligate herself to the future dominion of her mother. There is nothing about the infant's behavior that would lead us to infer that she consents to anything at all. And has been pointed out by some of his critics (King 74), Hobbes contradicts himself on this point in an earlier discussion about the inability of children to enter into a covenant:

> Over naturall fooles, children, or mad men there is no Law, no more than over brute beasts, nor are they capable of the title of just, or unjust, because they had never power to make any covenant, or to understand the consequences thereof … (*Leviathan* 2.26)

If children cannot make covenants because they do not "understand the consequences thereof," then there is no basis for Hobbes' extraordinary claim that children are human property because they have given their tacit consent to be treated as such.

10.2.3 The Perfect Freedom of Children: Herbert Spencer

At the opposite end of the spectrum of philosophical positions on the rights of children is the egalitarian theory that says that the child "has claims to freedom—rights, as we call them—co-extensive with those of the adult." This position is here represented by the nineteenth century social philosopher Herbert Spencer:

> The fullest endowment of rights that any being can possess, is perfect freedom to exercise all his faculties. And if each of two beings possesses perfect freedom to exercise all his faculties, each possesses complete rights; that is, the rights of the two are equal; no matter whether their faculties are equal or not. For, to say that the rights of the one are less than those of the other, because his faculties are fewer, is to say that he has no right to exercise the faculties he has not got! —a curious compound of truism and absurdity. (Spencer, Pt. II, Ch. XVII).

Applied to children and the intellectually disabled, this means that their claim-right to make and act on their own decisions cannot be abridged on the grounds that they are not as intelligent or experienced as the average adult. The child who wants to cross the decrepit bridge (section "Intrafamily harm and the family privacy principle") possesses "perfect freedom" to exercise the mental faculties she possesses regardless of how these faculties would compare with those of an adult. Her right to "exercise her faculties" by making a decision to cross the bridge is equal to the right of an adult to make the same decision. These rights are not less because her ability to reason is less than that of an adult reasoner. Spencer's argument, quite simply, is that everyone has a right to make decisions on the basis of whatever reasoning abilities they have, not on the basis of an objective standard of intelligence extracted from the ability of average adult reasoners.

Spencer echoes John Locke's much earlier claim that the state all men are naturally in is "a state of perfect freedom to order their actions, and dispose of their possessions and persons, as they think fit." Spencer also agrees with Locke's claim that every man has "an equal right … to his natural freedom, without being subjected to the will or authority of any other man." (*Second Treatise*, 54) However, it is apparent that Spencer would immediately part ways with Locke if he had read this sentence: "Children, I confess, are not born *in* this full state of equality, though they are born *to* it." (55) Locke here contradicts Spencer's major premise that the child, like all human beings, possesses perfect freedom to exercise all his faculties. Locke argues that children are born *in* a state of subjection, not in a state of freedom. "Their parents have a sort of rule and jurisdiction over them, when they come into the world, and for some time after." This is a temporary condition: children are born *to* a full state of equality because the age and reason they eventually attain will "loosen the swaddling clothes" of the bonds of their subjection. It is only then that they will achieve what Spencer refers to as "perfect freedom."

The difference between these two natural law philosophers is to be found in their different claims about the nature and origin of perfect freedom. Spencer argues that a child has perfect freedom at birth. Locke denies this, saying only that children will achieve freedom over time. Neither of these philosophers provide an argument to support their respective claims beyond appeals to Biblical interpretation. Spencer says that the law is a Divine ordination "rooted in the nature of things." The law says that "every man has freedom to do all that he wills, provided he infringes not the equal freedom of any other man," and it applies "as much to the young as to the mature." (Spencer, 172).

Locke also invokes God and the natural law in his argument for the opposite conclusion. The parents of the child have a God-given obligation "to take care of their off-spring, during the imperfect state of childhood" (Locke, 58). As for Spencer's claim that the child has a perfect freedom at birth, Locke's reply might be that freedom does not truly exist where there is no *reason* or *understanding* to direct the will:

> … for God having given man an understanding to direct his actions, has allowed him a freedom of will, and liberty of acting, as properly belonging thereunto, within the bounds of that law he is under. But whilst he is in an estate, wherein he has not *understanding* of his own to direct his *will*, he is not to have any *will* of his own to follow; he that *understands* for him, must *will* for him too; he must prescribe to his will, and regulate his actions … (58).

The natural law is "promulgated or made known by reason only." As reason needs the will to carry out its commands, so the will requires reason (understanding) to know the natural or moral law and direct the will according to prescriptions of the law. Hence, "he that is not come to the use of his reason, cannot be said to be under this law; and Adam's children, being not presently as soon as born under this law of reason were not presently free" (57). In these sentences Locke is relying on a theory of the mind first announced by Plato. In *Republic* the character Socrates distinguishes anger "without calculation" from calculations about "better and worse." His example is "small children" who "are full of spirit right from birth, while as far as rational calculation is concerned, some never seem to get a share of it while the majority do so quite late" (441a–b). A small child does not have the ability to make a calculation about better and worse when she attempts to run into the street while chasing a ball. A free act occurs only when it is grounded on understanding. The small child lacks this faculty. Hence, it is absurd to say that we have interfered with her "perfect freedom" when we restrain her from running into the street.

10.2.4 Parents as Temporary Custodians: John Locke and J.S. Mill

Both John Locke in the late seventeenth century and John Stuart Mill in the mid-nineteenth century, rejected the Hobbesian theory of children as property and both would have rejected Spencer's theory of the moral equality of adults and children. Although operating from completely different moral foundations, the theories of Locke and Mill regarding children's rights and obligations are surprisingly similar.

Locke's Children

One year after the death of Thomas Hobbes, and 100 years before the birth of Herbert Spencer, John Locke posited a relationship between parent and child that was much different from the Hobbesian theory of consensual slavery and the Spencerian theory of full equality. As noted in the previous section (Sect. 10.2.2), Locke argued that parental power derives not from consent but from the natural duty of parents to preserve, nurture and educate their children. Parents have a right to control their children's behavior, not because the child has consented to this but because the parents *need* the right of control in order to carry out their God-given duty to protect the child from harm and to provide her with food, shelter and education. And they must exercise this control because children are not capable of regulating their own behavior. If a child lacks "the understanding of his own to direct his will," then giving him the liberty to regulate his own actions would be positively dangerous:

> To turn him loose to an unrestrained liberty, before he has reason to guide him, is not the allowing him the privilege of his nature to be free; but to thrust him out amongst brutes, and abandon him to a state as wretched, and as much beneath that of a man, as theirs. This is that which puts the authority into the parent's hands to govern the minority of their children. (*Second Treatise*, §63)

Hence, the power that parents have to bring up their children not only derives from the obligation to protect and care for them, but this obligation is reciprocal with the natural right of children "not only to a bare Subsistence but to the conveniences and comforts of Life, as far as the conditions of their Parents can afford it." Parents are temporary custodians or caretakers of their children, not owners and certainly not their equals. This is a far cry from both Hobbes' contention that children have no rights at all and Spencer's claim that children's rights are co-extensive with the rights of adults.

Mill's Children

As with Locke, Mill's remarks about children were also incidental to a larger project. In Locke's case it was to distinguish political and paternal power. In Mill's writings, his ultimate aim was to give an account of the justifiable extent of political or state power over the liberty of the individual:

> The object of this Essay is to assert one very simple principle … That principle is, that the sole end for which mankind are warranted, individually or collectively, in interfering with the liberty of action of any of their number is, self-protection. That the only purpose for which power can be rightfully exercised over any member of a civilized community, against his will, is to prevent harm to others.

In Chap. 5 we referred to this as the *harm-to-others principle* of justifiable interference with individual liberty (Sect. 5.3.1), and compared it to the principle of *paternalism* (Sect. 5.3.2) which Mill explicitly rejects:

> His own good, either physical or moral, is not a sufficient warrant. He cannot rightfully be compelled to do or forbear because it will be better for him to do so because, in the opinions of others, to do would be wise, or even right … Over himself, over his own body and mind, the individual is sovereign (*On Liberty*, Ch. I).

Although Mill soundly rejects paternalistic interference with the liberty of adults, he does not reject this type of interference with the liberty of children:

> It is, perhaps, hardly necessary to say that this doctrine is meant to apply only to human beings in the maturity of their faculties. We are not speaking of children, or of young persons below the age which the law may fix as that of manhood or womanhood. *Those who are still in a state to require being taken care of by others, must be protected against their own actions as well as external injury …* (*On Liberty*, Ch. I, my emphasis).

The reason Mill gives for excluding children from the doctrine of individual liberty is that they are "not capable of being improved by free and equal discussion." It is assumed that they will eventually attain this capacity (when they reach the age of majority). As soon as they attain it, they will be "guided to their own improvement by conviction or persuasion, [and] it is no longer justifiable to compel them to their own good … " (*On Liberty*, I).

Mill does not specifically discuss issues concerning the extent of parental power over children, except to say that their state or condition requires that they be taken care of by others. But we can assume from his writings on individual liberty that he would endorse Locke's position that parents are justified in exercising control over their children for purposes of protection and preservation. Mill only departs from Locke when he states that he foregoes "any advantage which could be derived to my argument from the idea of abstract right, as a thing independent of utility" (*On Liberty*, Ch. I) Mill regards utility, not natural rights, as "the ultimate appeal on all ethical questions; but it must be utility in the largest sense, grounded on the permanent interests of man as a progressive being." He contends that all of us have a permanent interest in both mental and moral self-improvement. It is the development of this interest that justifies giving adults the most extensive liberty that is consistent with their not using this liberty to harm others. But it is also this that tells us not to interfere with those behaviors that might cause harm-to-oneself. When we pull back the man who is about to cross over a decrepit bridge that he does not know is about to collapse, we do this without making any *real* infringement of his liberty; because liberty consists in doing what one desires, and he does not desire to fall into the chasm below. But once apprised of the danger, if he should continue to walk onto the bridge, we cannot "forcibly prevent [him] from exposing himself to it." "[N]o one but the person himself can judge of the sufficiency of the motive which may prompt him to incur the risk" (*On Liberty*, Ch. I).

If it is a teenage girl who is about to walk over a decrepit bridge that she has been told might soon collapse, we *can* justifiably judge "the sufficiency" of her motive and forcibly restrain her. The justification for restraining her is to be found not in the foolishness of her decision, but in the fact that she is not yet capable of being persuaded to do otherwise by a free and equal discussion with her about her options. Hence, she can be restrained at least until the time that she achieves this capability. Her mental and emotional condition is like that of a delusional man standing on the top of a building who believes that he can jump off and safely fly to the ground. We can justifiably restrain this man until he regains his ability to think rationally and weigh the benefits and risks of what he is about to do. We can restrain the girl now so she can live to make autonomous choices when she becomes an adult.

10.2.5 Criticisms of Locke and Mill

There are several criticisms that have been made of these accounts of the psychology and the rights of children, two of which we will mention here. Let's start with Mill and his decrepit bridge example. If we reasonably assume that the girl who is about to walk over the bridge does not want to be seriously injured, then *as a child*, she is either "chronically or episodically thoughtless or merely inexperienced" (Turner, 145). If children are *episodically* (that is, occasionally) thoughtless then this does not mark a relevant difference between children and adults. Adults (like the delusional man) are also episodically thoughtless, and we do not use this as a basis for *permanent* interference with their liberty. So it must be *chronic* thoughtlessness that marks the difference for Mill between childhood and adulthood. He must believe that children are chronically uncontrolled risk-takers, even though they want to avoid death and injury. Although this might be true, it is an empirical remark which Mill does not support with evidence. Moreover, if true it does not mark an unassailable difference between children and adults. There are "extreme" sports which are known to have a high rate of participant death but which continue to attract adult newcomers.[1] We might attempt to persuade, even beg them not to

[1] We do not make it illegal to engage in BASE jumping, despite the relatively high rate of death and injury. "BASE jumping sees participants leap from a cliff, bridge or even skyscraper and quickly deploy their parachutes before reaching the ground, wingsuit flyers – a subsection of BASE jumpers – don a winged suit that allows them to control their movement and swoop like a bird of prey, reaching speeds of up to 200 mph in the process. Only last year, three leading lights of wingsuit flying died after jumping from a helicopter over Lütschental in Switzerland. In 2013, stuntman Mark Sutton, who skydived into the Olympic opening ceremony at the start of London 2012, was killed after crashing into a ridge near Martigny at the Swiss-French border. In a report published in 2007, a study of the results of 20,850 BASE jumps between 1995 to 2005 at the Kjerag Massif in Norway revealed that during this 11-year period there had been 82 nonfatal accidents (1 in every 254 jumps) and 9 fatal accidents (1 in every 2317 jumps)" (Soreide et al. 2007).

participate, but Mill tells us that we are not justified in forcing the willing adult to not take such risks. But if we are not justified in forcibly preventing this group of adults from risking their lives, then why is it permissible to use the relevant characteristic (chronic thoughtlessness) as a justification for denying liberty rights to children?

Second, Mill and Locke seem to recognize that psychological maturation is gradual. That is, a child gains the ability to reason and achieves knowledge about the world through a continuous and cumulative passage from childhood into adulthood. And yet neither philosopher contends that one should be given legal rights in a gradual way, with different rights being granted at different times in the psychological maturation process. Both see the granting of rights as an "all-or-nothing affair." When the child becomes an adult at 12:01 am on the day he comes of legal age, he immediately quits "parental authority, inherits property, becomes a citizen, and assumes political obligation at a single stroke" (Archard, 95). Mill and Locke do not appear to acknowledge the relevance of the fact that a young person of 17 years is psychologically much less like an infant of 1 year or a young child of 9 years, and much more like an adult of 21.

10.3 Constitutional Theories About the Rights of Children

David Archard (quoted above) rightly contends that the question which we must answer is: How can we consistently think of children as *both* on the way to being adult reasoners *and* as having a legal status that is less than that of the adult?

Imagine the following scenario. Gloria, a 19-year-old student at the University of California, Berkeley, takes part in an on-campus event sponsored by her political club. The purpose of the event is to drum up student support for legislation in the State Assembly that would legalize the sale and use of small amounts of marijuana. Gloria climbs up on a ladder and displays a humorous banner that says "LET'S GET HIGH." She and her friends collect hundreds of signatures on a petition to be delivered later in the day to legislators. The event concludes without incident. No one protested the content of the banner display, nor did anyone claim that some students might be encouraged to use illegal drugs after viewing the banner.

Gloria's (imaginary) experience when displaying her banner bears a remarkable contrast with what actually happened at a high school-sanctioned event in Juneau, Alaska in 2002. Joseph Frederick, a senior at Juneau-Douglas High School, unfurled a banner saying "BONG HiTS 4 JESUS" during the Olympic Torch Relay that was passing through town. Frederick's attendance at the event was part of a school-supervised activity. The school's principal, Deborah Morse, saw the banner and told Frederick to put it away, as she was concerned it could be interpreted as advocating illegal drug activity. After Frederick refused to comply, she took the banner from him.

Frederick originally was suspended from school for 10 days for violating school policy, which forbids advocating the use of illegal drugs. The school superintendent upheld the suspension, explaining that Frederick was disciplined because his banner appeared to promote illegal drug use in violation of school policy. Joseph filed a lawsuit alleging that the school board and Morse had violated his First Amendment rights. The Ninth Circuit agreed that although the banner expressed a positive sentiment about marijuana use, Joseph's First Amendment right to freedom of speech was violated because the school punished him without demonstrating that his speech threatened substantial disruption. The school district appealed this decision to the U.S. Supreme Court. A 5–4 majority endorsed the action taken by the school principal and reversed the Ninth Circuit decision. In *Morse v Frederick* (127 S. Ct. 2618, 2622, 2007), Chief Justice Roberts held that the Juneau school officials in this case did not violate the First Amendment by confiscating the pro-drug banner and suspending Frederick. Schools may take steps to safeguard those entrusted to their care from speech that can reasonably be regarded as encouraging illegal drug use.

A student at a public university in the U.S. would not be ordered by the university president to take down a banner like the one displayed by Joseph Frederick, nor would any threat be made to suspend the student if he or she did not comply. In fact, if an attempt were made to suspend a student under these circumstances, then it would probably be the university president, not the student who would face the threat of suspension or even dismissal. These facts prompt the following question: "What explains this difference in the way that public high school and university students are treated when they express their political, moral or religious opinions?"

The relevant legal differences between Gloria (the university student) and Joseph Frederick are (1) Joseph's legal status as a *minor* and (2) the fact that he displayed his banner at a *school-sponsored and supervised event.* The word "minor" means "being under the age of legal adulthood," that is, under the age of *majority*. Joseph is legally dependent on his parents or legal *guardians.* As such, they are his *custodians* in the sense that they have the dual right to his care and to control his behavior. When Joseph is at a school sponsored event the right to his care and control is temporarily transferred to his teachers and others who supervise his education. If Joseph runs away from home or is persistently truant from school, then his care and control is ultimately transferred to other agents of the State under the doctrine of *parens patriae.*[2] As the Supreme Court put it in an earlier case "[J]uveniles, unlike adults, are *always in some form of custody* ... Children, by definition, are not assumed to have the capacity to take care of themselves" (*Schall v Martin,* 467 U.S. 265).

What is confusing about the preceding quote from *Schall* is that it comes long after the *Tinker* decision (first discussed at Sect. 4.2.2) in which the Court declared that "...students in school as well as out of school are persons under our Constitution. They are possessed of fundamental rights which the State must respect." (393 U.S. 503). The children in this ground-breaking case were wearing armbands at school to symbolically express their moral and political views about the Vietnam War. Although the Court acknowledged that the State and school authorities have "comprehensive authority … to prescribe and control conduct in the schools," the Court also said that they cannot exercise this authority unless the child's conduct "materi-

[2] Literally "parent of the country." In this context it refers to the state's role in protecting children.

ally and substantially interfere[s] with the requirements of appropriate discipline in the operation of the school" (*id.*, 629). Because the children in *Tinker* did not disrupt any operation of the school, the Court found that their suspension violated their First Amendment rights to freedom of expression.

10.3.1 Socially Inappropriate Speech: Bethel v Fraser

Seventeen years after *Tinker*, a more conservative Supreme Court held that administrators could punish a student for his political speech at a local high school (*Bethel v. Fraser*, 1986). During an assembly at Bethel High School in Washington State, Matthew Fraser delivered a speech nominating a fellow student for elective office. He used "elaborate, graphic, and explicitly sexual metaphor[s]" (*id.*, at 678). For this, Fraser was suspended for 2 days. He challenged the suspension.

The District Court concluded that the punishment violated Fraser's First Amendment right to freedom of speech, and said that the school's policy on speech was "constitutionally vague and overbroad." (*id.* 679). The Court of Appeals concurred, holding that Fraser's speech was "indistinguishable from the [protest] armbands used [by school children] in *Tinker*. In reversing, the U.S. Supreme Court applied a "balancing test" to students' free speech rights.[3] On the one hand, students have "the undoubted freedom to advocate unpopular and controversial views in schools and classrooms." On the other hand, society has a "countervailing interest in teaching students the boundaries of socially appropriate behavior" (*id.*, 681) While *adults* have the right to use "offensive form[s] of expression to make a political point," the same liberty is not necessarily available to juveniles in public school, according to the Court (478 U.S. 682). Public schools have the right to "prohibit the use of vulgar and offensive terms in public discourse." (*id.* at 683). Because Fraser's speech "glorified male sexuality," it was "acutely insulting to teenage girl students" while "undermining the school's basic educational purpose," and was therefore constitutionally impermissible.[4]

Concurring in the result, Justice Brennan agreed that the school district had the right to restrict the student's speech because he used "disruptive language" (*id.* 688–689). Justice Marshall, dissenting, observed that the school district offered no evidence that the speech in any way disrupted the educational process at the high school (*id.* 689, n.2)[5] Justice Stevens, also dissenting, argued that the speech did not

[3] "A constitutional doctrine in which a court weighs an individual's rights with the rights or powers of the state." (Fisher, 19).

[4] 478 U.S. at 683 and 685. The following excerpt from Fraser's speech was at the center of the controversy: "I know a man who is firm—he's firm in his pants, he's firm in his shirt, his character is firm...Jeff Kuhlman is a man who takes his point and pounds it in... He doesn't attack things in spurts—he drives hard, pushing, and pushing until he finally succeeds. Jeff is a man who will go to the very end—even the climax for each and every one of you."

[5] 478 U.S., at 689, n. 2.

fall into the category of "conduct" regulated by the school's disciplinary rule (*id.* 690).[6] Indeed, the district's rules of conduct contained no "unequivocal prohibition against the use of 'indecent language'" (*id.*694).

The Appeals Court had suggested that there is no relevant difference between the facts used by the Supreme Court in *Tinker* to extend free speech rights to school children and the facts used by the Court in *Bethel*. Expressing one's political opinion by wearing black armbands is a form of speech. It is only a short step from the Tinker children's non-verbal expression of a political opinion to Fraser's speech nominating a fellow student for elective office. The only differences suggested by the Court majority were that Fraser's speech violated the boundaries of "socially appropriate behavior." And yet the language used by Fraser did not qualify under any legal standard as "obscene,"[7] nor was there any evidence that the speech was found to be disrupting or insulting by any of the students who heard it.

Let us assume that we know what types of speech are "socially inappropriate." Why should children be denied the right to express themselves in this way? A possible justification is their *status* as children and the *context* of the public school setting in which they express their views. As a child, Matthew Fraser is under the custodial supervision of his parents and, by extension, of the public school that he attends. Since his parents have the right to regulate his speech at home, the Court concluded that his teachers have the right to regulate his speech while he is at school.

What has changed in the years between the decision in *Tinker* and the decision in *Bethel* is a change in the conception of the child from "a person who has fundamental rights" to "a person who is always in some form of custody." As a result, the *Tinker* standard for deciding children's constitutional rights has been substantially changed by the Supreme Court. Persons in custody may have the right to express their moral, religious or political views, but they cannot express them in ways that are offensive or socially inappropriate. They are under the control of custodians who are allowed to dictate the content of their speech in ways that would never be allowed in the case of adults.

10.3.2 "Reasonable" Censorship of Children's Speech: Hazelwood v Kuhlmeier

Two years after the *Bethel* decision, the Supreme Court once more acted to change a child's First Amendment rights (*Hazelwood v Kuhlmeier* 484 U.S. 1986.). The principal of a Missouri high school deleted two pages of a student newspaper to which he objected. One of the stories was about three Hazelwood students' experience with pregnancy and the other discussed the impact of divorce on students at the school (*id.* 263). The principal believed that although false names had been

[6] 478 U.S., at 690.

[7] Standards of obscenity were set in *Roth v. United States* 354 U.S. 476 (1957), and *Miller v. California* 413 U.S. 151 (1973).

provided in the pregnancy story, the pregnant girls might be identifiable from the text *(id.)*. Furthermore, he felt that discussion of birth control and sexual activity was inappropriate for younger readers.

While the District Court sided with the school district, the Court of Appeals did not (607FSupp1450 1985). School officials were only allowed to censor the articles if publication could have resulted in tort liability to the school, the appellate court held (484 U.S.266).

In *Hazelwood* v. *Kuhlmeier*, the Supreme Court reversed the appellate court and noted that rights of students are "not automatically coextensive with the rights of adults in other settings."(*id.*) Even though the district policy stated that the student newspaper accepted "all the rights implied by the First Amendment," school officials were entitled to regulate the contents of the publication "in any reasonable manner" (*id.* 269–70). The Court also favorably noted Justice Black's dissent in *Tinker* in which he argued that the Federal Constitution does not compel teachers, parents, and elected school officials "to surrender control of the American public school system to public school students"(*id.*). The Justices believed that restricting publications to take into account the "emotional maturity of the intended audience" on sensitive topics was within the principal's powers. Administrators may "exercise editorial control" over student newspapers "so long as their actions are reasonably related to legitimate pedagogical concerns"(*id.* 272–273). Censorship would be forbidden only when the restriction "has no valid educational purpose" (*id.* 273).

In dissent, Justice Brennan took note that the majority approved of press censorship "that neither disrupt[ed] class work nor invade[d] the rights of others"(*id.* 275). The Court in *Tinker* had acted to protect student speech unless it "materially disrupt[ed] class work or involve[d] substantial disorder or invasion of the rights of others"(393 U.S. 503.). In Brennan's view the "mere desire to avoid the discomfort and unpleasantness that always accompanies an unpopular viewpoint … or an unsavory subject" does not justify suppression of student speech in a high school (484 U.S 260, 280–81). Furthermore, *Tinker* does not permit school officials to act as "thought police" to restrict publication on "potentially sensitive" topics (*id.*285, 287).

It is against this background that the Supreme Court made its decision to further alter (some would say "erode") the right of school children to freedom of expression in *Morse v Frederick*. Not only is student speech *not* protected speech when it is disruptive (*Tinker*), socially inappropriate (*Bethel*), or about a sensitive topic (*Hazelwood*), but student speech is also not protected if it might be construed by other students as promoting illegal behavior. Most important in each of these decisions is that there is no mention of the central reason for the custodial status of children: to prevent them from doing harm to themselves.

10.4 The Supreme Court's Dilemma of Classification

A dilemma occurs when one is given a choice between two or more alternatives, each having an unwanted outcome. In the thirty-year history of its rulings on the constitutional speech rights of children, the Supreme Court appears to be struggling with a "dilemma of classification" where the alternatives (between which it believes it is forced to choose) are two different ways of classifying children. Either children are to be regarded as persons with fundamental rights that the state must respect, or they are to be regarded as non-persons who are always in some form of custody. If children have fundamental rights, then the problem it immediately faces is how the Court can justify the different treatment that children receive under the Constitution. If both children and adults are "persons," then it seems to follow that they should have the same set of constitutional rights. On the other hand, if children are classified as non-persons who are always in some form of custody, then there appears to be no basis for granting them *any* constitutional rights.

Each of these classification schemes has consequences that the Court has not been willing to accept. The *Tinker* court was not prepared to accept the consequences of treating children as persons by *granting* them full constitutional rights, and the *Bethel*, *Hazelwood* and *Morse* courts had no desire to embrace the consequences of classifying children as non-persons in custody by *denying* them all of the rights that adults take for granted under the Constitution.[8] We are to presume that a child can still wear a black-arm band to school to make a symbolic political protest, and she can still give a speech to her classmates about her political beliefs, as long as the speech is "socially appropriate."

When faced with a dilemma, the usual tactic is to attempt to find other alternatives in the hope that at least one of them will not have an unacceptable consequence. In the remainder of this chapter we will critically examine three alternatives to the Supreme Court's two conflicting classifications of children. Each provides a unique interpretation of the idea of children's constitutional rights that attempts to make this idea consistent with the widely held belief that children are and should be under the control of their parents or the State.

The alternative theories are these: (1) Children's constitutional rights are rights of a scope that is more *limited* than the scope of adult constitutional rights of the same name (e.g. the right to freedom of speech). (2) Children's constitutional rights are rights that can be *outweighed* by important familial or State interests which do not outweigh adult rights of the same name. (3) Children's constitutional rights are *rights-in-trust*, that is, rights which children possess but which, in some cases, they are justifiably prevented from enjoying.

[8] For example, the *Bethel* court continued to assert that children have the constitutional right to express their political opinions in public school.

10.4.1 Limited Scope Rights

In 1980, the authors of a lengthy note on "The Constitution and the Family" in the *Harvard Law Review* wrote that there were two reasons why a child may not be entitled to the full constitutional protection that an adult would receive under similar circumstances:

> First, a child may possess a constitutional right of lesser magnitude than an adult possesses. This might be the case if the values animating a given constitutional provision were not as applicable to children as adults. Second, the state may be able to assert interests to support its treatment of children that it could not assert with respect to adults. This would be the case if the state's treatment of children fell within its police power or *parens patriae* power while the treatment of identically situated adults did not come within this category (Developments, 1358).

I suppose that what is meant by the phrase "right of a lesser magnitude" is that the *scope* of the right may be smaller for children than for adults. Consider, for example, First Amendment rights. The scope of First Amendment rights is not unlimited either for adults or children; that is, the courts have never guaranteed anyone a "right" to say anything, any time, any place. But the Supreme Court has set more limits on First Amendment rights for children than it has for adults. On the Harvard interpretation of what it means to say that children have the constitutional right of freedom of speech, both children and adults *have* the right to free speech, but the *scope* of free speech is narrower for children than the range of speech for adults. To say that a child has the right to free speech means something quite different than what it means to say that an adult has this right. Neither an adult nor a child can use the First Amendment to justify a speech act of defamation, fraud, incitement to riot, or solicitation to crime. But a child in school has the further restriction of refraining from speech that uses "vulgar and offensive terms [to make a political point] in public discourse" (478 U.S. 683).

One advantage of the Harvard approach is that it is consistent with Justice Blackmun's assertion that "minors, as well as adults, are protected by the Constitution and possess constitutional rights."[9] Second, the Harvard approach also explains how

[9] *Planned Parenthood of Central Missouri v. Danforth*, 428 U.S. 52, 74 (1976). The Court declared unconstitutional part of a Missouri abortion statute requiring an unmarried minor female to acquire the consent of her parent(s) or guardian(s) in order to have an abortion performed (unless a physician, in order to save her life, certifies the abortion). Justice Blackmun, delivering the majority opinion, famously wrote, "Constitutional rights do not mature and come into being magically only when one attains the state-defined age of majority. Minors, as well as adults, are protected by the Constitution and possess constitutional rights." In this case the relevant right is the "right of personal privacy, or a guarantee of certain areas or zones of privacy…(which) encompass a woman's decision whether or not to terminate her pregnancy." Blackmun conceded that although the Court "long has recognized that the State has somewhat broader authority to regulate the activities of children than of adults," upon examining whether there is any "significant state interest" in conditioning an abortion on the consent of a parent, he found that there is none. Parental interest in the termination of a child's pregnancy "is no weightier than the right of privacy of the competent minor mature enough to have become pregnant." The right of privacy was again invoked in *Carey* v. *Population Services International.* In this case, which reached the Supreme Court in 1977, the

a child can have a constitutional right but also be regarded as subject to the custody and control of his parents or the State. The function of the right is to set a limit to what a custodian can demand of the child who is under his control. For example, even though the scope of a child's free speech right is narrower than that of an adult, its scope is sufficiently large that a child cannot be prevented by her public school custodians from advocating a view that is merely unpopular or controversial (*id.* 681).

However, there are several disadvantages of the Harvard interpretation of the constitutional rights of a child. First, I am not at all sure that when Blackmun wrote that minors are protected by the Constitution, he meant that the Constitution protects a set of rights having a different scope than the scope enjoyed by adults. This seems clear from his ruling in a previous children's privacy case in which he said *without qualification* that a minor seeking an abortion has the "right of personal privacy, or a guarantee of certain areas or zones of privacy [which] encompass a woman's decision whether or not to terminate her pregnancy" (428 U.S. 60). He did not say or imply that this right was in some way different than an adult woman's right of personal privacy.

Second, the Harvard approach gives us *two* sets of constitutional rights, one for adults and the other for children, where the difference between rights in each set having the same name is a difference in their scope. Why not a third, fourth and even more sets of rights for other classes of persons? The question that is begged by the Harvard approach is: What are the criteria for deciding whether a given class of persons should have rights of the same or of a different scope than persons of another group or class?

Third, I have a more general concern about the very idea of constitutional rights of the same name having varying scopes. Suppose, for example, that John, a U.S. citizen, has the right to give a public speech about his dissident political beliefs, but Mohammed, a citizen of Iran, does not have this right. However, Mohammed does have the right to talk publicly about controversial non-political topics. I believe that we would characterize this situation by saying that John has the right to freedom of speech, but Mohammed does not. It would be not only odd, but also misleading to say that Mohammed has the right to freedom of speech but his right has a narrower scope than John's. This is because we understand the very concept of a constitutional right to freedom of speech to include political expression. Where it does not

---

Court overturned a New York law prohibiting the distribution of non-prescriptive contraceptives to minors under the age of 16 years. Justice Brennan, writing for the majority, declared: "In a field that by definition concerns the most intimate of human activities and relationships, decisions whether to accomplish or to prevent conception are among the most private and sensitive." The Court rejected the Attorney General's argument that New York had a legitimate interest in protecting morality by casting doubt on his contention that limiting minors' access to contraceptives substantially discourages early sexual behavior. Moreover, the Court concluded, "It would be plainly unreasonable to assume that the state has prescribed pregnancy and the birth of an unwanted child or the physical and psychological dangers of an abortion as punishment for fornication."

include political expression, we would reasonably conclude that the right to freedom of speech does not exist.

For example, in *Bethel* v. *Fraser*, the Supreme Court said that although adults have the constitutional right to use "offensive form[s] of expression to make a political point," the same liberty is not necessarily available to juveniles in public schools (*id.* 675). But if this right is not available to juveniles, then we should conclude not that children in school have a constitutional right to freedom of speech that is narrower in scope than the adult right to freedom of speech, but that *children in school do not have the constitutional right to freedom of speech at all*! There is *one* right to freedom of speech in the Constitution, and it includes the right to use offensive forms of expression to make a political point.[10]

10.4.2 Rights-to-Be-Balanced

A second interpretation of the concept of constitutional rights of children is the "interest-balancing" approach. This interpretation is suggested in the second part of the Harvard position quoted earlier: "the state may be able to assert interests to support its treatment of children that it could not assert with respect to adults." During the 1970s, the Court frequently prefaced their decisions about the rights of children by implying that the question before them is to what extent a child's acknowledged constitutional rights should be "outweighed" by the State's interest in protecting them from harm. In Justice Blackmun's decision about the privacy rights of children alluded to earlier, he conceded that the Court "long has recognized that the State has somewhat broader authority to regulate the activities of children than of adults" (*id.*). Hence, the Court must be prepared to weigh the right of privacy of the competent minor against her parent's interest in the possible termination of her pregnancy.

This is troublesome. In *Roe v Wade*, the Court ruled that the decision to abort one's pregnancy comes within the scope of the constitutional right of privacy. Once having pronounced abortion to be within the area of constitutional protection it is no longer open to the Court to "weigh" that protection against other considerations (for example, strengthening the family unit, protecting the mother from harm). The Constitution says that its guaranteed rights, once correctly determined "always have

---

[10] Before turning to an examination of the next concept of children's rights, we take a brief look at the Harvard claim that a child may possess a constitutional right of lesser magnitude than an adult possesses if "the values animating a given constitutional provision were not as applicable to children as adults." Although we can accept the implication that this may be the best way to interpret the Constitution it is not clear why the values relevant to the amendments should not be as applicable to older children as to adults. On the basis of what criterion are we to decide this? In the case of free speech, it might be said that the "animating value" is the value of knowing the truth. That is, when speech is free, we are more likely to make progress toward discovery of the truth than we are when speech is restricted. But why should this value not be as applicable to high school students as it is to college students or other adults? This question remains unanswered.

more weight than any possible combination of opposing interests, public or private" (Feinberg 81, citing Frantz 1438). If the Court proclaims that a child has the constitutional right of privacy, then it cannot "weigh" or "balance" this right against family or other interests any more than it can do this in the case of an adult. The real focus of the debate in the Court should not be over the question whether in the case of children the right of privacy is to be outweighed by the State's interest in protecting them from harm (that makes no sense), but over the question whether children ought to be granted the constitutional right of privacy *at all.*

We should reach the same conclusion when we turn to the right of free speech. *Once the scope of the constitutional right has been determined* through precedent-setting court decisions, it is not to be weighed or balanced against other interests. Thus, we can presume from previous decisions of the Court that the right to freedom of expression does not include the right to defame the reputation of others, to shout "fire" in a crowded theater when there is no fire, or to publish military secrets. These decisions inform us about the scope of the constitutional right. Once this is determined the Court is barred from "balancing" the right of free speech against other possible interests, for example the interest in not being made to feel uncomfortable, or hearing speech that is socially inappropriate, or hearing speech that might encourage one to obtain or use illegal drugs. This is part of what it means to say that someone has a constitutional right. Whether it is possessed by adults or children, the right of free speech, is "fundamental" *within its defined scope*, and is not to be balanced or weighed against other concerns or interests.

10.4.3 Rights-in-Trust

There is a distinction between *having* a right and *exercising or enjoying* a right. In the same way that property law allows us to speak of individuals possessing a *future interest*, so in constitutional law we might speak of children possessing the right to be treated as a person, although complete enjoyment of this right might be justifiably postponed (Morris, 49–50). There are two situations in which this might occur. (1) Situations in which a child is clearly incapable of exercising a constitutional right, and (2) situations in which a child, though capable of enjoying the right, might damage his future ability to exercise his rights if he is allowed complete enjoyment of his rights now. Let me explain by discussing these situations in more detail.

(1) A small child might be regarded as a person under the Constitution with the right to freedom of religious choice, even though she presently lacks the cognitive capacity to form or express such beliefs. Of course, the usual objection to this characterization is that possession of the capacity to exercise a right is a necessary condition for possessing it. That is, it has been argued that if a small child lacks the capacity to pray, attend church services, and promulgate her faith to others, then surely it makes no more sense to say that she has the right to do these things than it would be to say this about the family dog.

But there is a significant difference between the child and the family dog. The child is a person. She will eventually become an adult able freely and in an informed way to choose, and who will be prepared to assume responsibility for her choices. Hence, to say that the infant *qua* person has the right of religious expression could only be construed as a *right in trust*. That is, it is best interpreted as the right to have her future options kept open until she is a fully formed self-determining adult capable of creating her own opinions about religion and making public expression of her beliefs.

When we attribute moral or legal rights to children who are clearly not yet capable of exercising them, these are rights that are to be *saved* for the child until he or she is an adult. Moreover, these rights can be violated "in advance," so to speak, before the child is even in a position to exercise them. Legal philosopher Joel Feinberg has observed, " the violating conduct guarantees *now* that when the child is an autonomous adult, certain key options will already be closed to him. His right while he is still a child is to have these future options kept open until he is a fully formed self-determining adult capable of deciding among them …" (Feinberg 1980, 126). For example, an infant of 2 months has the right to walk freely down the public sidewalk, even though she is not yet capable of enjoying this right. What then could it mean to say that she has the right to freedom of movement? The answer is that it is a right-in-trust. It is a right to be saved for the child until she gains the ability to walk. One would violate this right now by cutting off her legs, making it physically impossible for her to ever be capable of self-locomotion at some future time.[11] By analogy, a young child has the right of free expression even though she cannot yet speak. Her right is a right-in-trust and we are under a constitutional obligation not to interfere with her development of the future ability to exercise this right.

(2) What about older children who are clearly capable of exercising and enjoying at least some constitutional rights? For example, in *Bethel* v. *Fraser,* no one doubted that 17-year-old Matthew Fraser had the cognitive and emotional ability to form and express his own political opinions. The ground for his suspension from high school was not his incapacity to advocate an unpopular and controversial opinion, but that his speech was "acutely insulting" and "disruptive," grounds (by the way) that would never be recognized by the Court as a basis for prohibiting adult speech.

Older children, like Mathew Fraser, though competent, are still under the control of their parents, school administrators, and ultimately, the State. Is there any way of reconciling their status as individuals-in-custody with their status as "persons" under the Constitution?

My suggestion is that the personhood of older children, like that of younger children, can also be understood as a right-in-trust, with this important difference, that

[11] A more realistic example of how a right-in-trust can be violated is the practice in some cultures of female genital mutilation. In this case, the relevant (violated) right is the right to sexual freedom. Although a young girl is not capable of sexual pleasure, her parents could violate her right to sexual freedom *now* by mutilating her genitals, making it physically impossible for her to enjoy herself sexually when she becomes an adult.

the grounds for postponing an older child's enjoyment of his fundamental rights are nearly identical to the grounds for postponing an adult's enjoyment of the same.

Nearly, but not quite identical. The older child is still under the custodial control of his parents. However, the fact that the older child is competent to exercise his constitutional rights severely limits what his parents or the State can do to him while he is in their custody. The point of reminding us that the older child is a person is that this places strict limits on the kind and degree of legitimate interference by his custodians. To be specific, the child's custodians must provide conditions for the child to become an adult who is able freely and in an informed way to make choices, that is, to become autonomous. Hence, any interference in the child's attempt to exercise his rights is justifiable only if it can be proved that this is necessary to protect his future autonomy. For example, in the *Fraser* case, if evidence had been presented that would have shown that when high school students give offensive speeches, they put at risk their future ability to exercise their free speech rights, this would have constituted sufficient grounds for postponing Fraser's right to give his speech. It is only under this limitation that his custodians could argue that they are respecting Mathew as a person.

Employing the distinction between having a right and enjoying a right and the related notion of a right in trust, I am suggesting the following three-part theory of the constitutional rights of older children. First, because children are persons, they have the same set of constitutional rights possessed by adults. Second, primarily because they are still under the custody and control of their parents or the state, the full enjoyment of their constitutional rights may sometimes be postponed. However, third, the child's exercise of a right can be postponed only if when there is evidence that exercising the right *in the present* will damage that child's *future* autonomy. Restrictions on an older child's enjoyment of his rights for any other reason (e.g. because the exercise of his rights might offend or disrupt the peace and quiet of others) are simply unjustifiable.

Finally, I believe that this theory solves the dilemma about children's constitutional rights which I outlined earlier. The question was: How can children be said to be "persons under our Constitution" with the "fundamental rights which the State must respect" and at the same time be regarded as individuals who are "always in some form of custody"? The answer is that younger children are persons in the sense that they have the right to be provided with the opportunities and conditions assuring their full enjoyment of their constitutional rights when they acquire the characteristics of adult persons. Full enjoyment of their rights may be postponed until this is accomplished. But this also explains the sense in which children are always in some form of custody. The child's right to be treated as a person is a right-in-trust. The child's parents, the school and the State are the trustees charged with the duty to help children develop into fully autonomous adults capable of enjoying their constitutional rights.

As the child grows older and acquires more and more of the intellectual abilities of a fully autonomous adult, then the obligation to respect her choices and to place upon her the responsibility for the choices she makes becomes even stronger. This is reminiscent of the criticism of Locke and Mill about their failure to account for the inconsistency between acknowledging the *gradual* development of a child's psychological maturation and their defense of the practice of granting legal rights to a child *suddenly* upon reaching a certain age. It is interesting that Justice Blackmun did notice this disparity when he wrote that constitutional rights "do not mature and come into being magically only when one attains the state-defined age of majority." If children have constitutional rights before the age of majority, then we need an explanation of how this is consistent with custodial interventions preventing the exercise of these rights. The theory we propose is that the only ground that the custodian of an older minor can use to justify postponing the exercise of her right to be treated as a person is when postponement is necessary to assure the child's development into a fully autonomous adult.

I shall call this the *Rights-in-Trust Theory* of children's constitutional rights" because it is a theory about the conditions under which a person can be justifiably denied the *exercise* (enjoyment) of a right that they legally have or hold. One objection to the theory is identical to the objection that I launched against the "balancing" theory of children's constitutional rights discussed earlier, namely that the very idea of protecting speech or other activity as a constitutional right excludes the possibility of ever weighing it against other interests. For example, once having pronounced abortion to be within the area of constitutional protection for a female minor, it is no longer open to the Court to "weigh" that protection against other considerations (for example, strengthening the family unit, or protecting the young mother from harm). How, then, can the Court consistently maintain the position that a child's enjoyment of a constitutional right to freedom of speech might be legitimately postponed when there is evidence that exercise of the right will damage the child's future autonomy? Am I not suggesting that the Court "balance" the child's interest in her future autonomy against the exercise of her constitutional right?

The reply to this objection is that a temporary interference with a person's liberty for the purpose of protecting their future ability to act autonomously is not a case of balancing one interest against another. Let me refer once again to John Stuart Mill's "decrepit bridge" example in which he said that we could seize and turn back a person attempting to cross an unsafe bridge "without any real infringement of his liberty." Analogously, if we postpone a child's exercise of his constitutional rights because there is a substantial risk that his exercise of those rights at this moment might prevent him from ever exercising them again, we have not "balanced" one interest against another. To use Mill's words, we have not infringed on his liberty, "for liberty consists in doing what one desires," and (we might reasonably assume) the child does not desire to cripple his future ability to exercise his rights.

Questions for Thought and Discussion

1. In what ways do the theories of Hobbes, Locke, Mill and Spencer about the rights of children compare and and in what ways do they differ?
2. Why does Mill say that the principle of paternalism justifies adult interference with the behavior of children, but it does not justify adult interference with the liberty of other adults?

3. What is Mill's "decrepit bridge" example designed to prove? How does it apply to interventions in the behavior of children? Is the distinction between episodic and chronic thoughtlessness relevant to answering these questions?
4. If intellectual and emotional maturation is gradual, why is this fact not reflected in legislative decisions about when a child becomes an adult? Should children gradually receive more adult liberty rights as they get older, or should they not get any liberty rights until they achieve the designated legal age of adulthood?
5. Is it possible for a child to be both a human being who is always in some form of custody and at the same time be regarded as a person possessed of the First Amendment right to freedom of speech?

References

Bork, Robert. 1990. *The Tempting of America*. New York: Free Press.

Developments in the Law. 1980. The Constitution and the Family. *Harvard Law Review* 93: 1358.

Feinberg, Joel. 1973. *Social Philosophy*. Upper Saddle River, NJ: Prentice-Hall, 81 (citing Frantz, Laurent B. 1962. The First Amendment in the Balance. *Yale Law Journal*, LXXI. 1438).

———. 1980. Child's Right to an Open Future. In *Whose Child? Children's Rights, Parental Authority and State Power*, ed. W. Aiken and H. LaFollette. Totowa: Littlefield, Adams & Co.

Fisher, Louis. 1990. *American Constitutional Law*. New York: McGraw-Hill.

Friedman Ross, Lainie. 1998. *Children, Families and Health Care Decision-Making*. Oxford: Clarendon Press.

Hobbes, Thomas. 2008 [1640]. In *The Elements of Law, Natural and Politics*, ed. G.C.A. Gaskin. Oxford University Press.

Hohfeld, Wesley N. 1920. *Fundamental Legal Conceptions as Applied in Judicial Reasoning and Other Legal Essays*. New Haven: Yale University Press.

Locke, John. 1980 [1690]. (ed.) McPherson, C.B. *Second treatise of government* Indianapolis: Hackett. First published 1690.

Mill, John Stuart. 1979. In *Utilitarianism*, ed. George Sher. Indianapolis: Hackett.

Morris, Herbert. 1979. Persons and Punishment. In *On Guilt and Innocence: Essays in Legal Philosophy and Moral Psychology*, ed. Herbert Morris, 49–50. Berkeley: University of California Press.

Soreide, K., et al. 2007. How Dangerous is BASE Jumping? An Analysis of Adverse Events in 20,850 Jumps from the Kjerag Massif, Norway. *J Trauma* (62): 1113–1117.

Spencer, Herbert. 1851. Social Statics: or, The Conditions Essential to Happiness Specified, and the First of them Developed, London: John Chapman. http://oll.libertyfund.org/titles/273#Spencer_0331_350 Last Accessed 8 Oct 2015.

Part IV
Contract and Property Disputes Arising from Alternative Birth Methods

Chapter 11
Surrogacy

> *"Public policy has always been that children should remain with and be brought up by both of their natural parents."*
>
> J. Harvey Sorkow, *In re Baby M* (1988)

> *"The judge said Mrs. Johnson [the surrogate mother] was a 'genetic stranger' to the baby and did not acquire genetic rights to claim parenthood through her surrogacy."*
>
> *New York Times* (1990)

Abstract It has long been assumed that the woman who carried and gave birth to a child is its legal mother, possessed of all moral and legal rights to custody. And if she is married when she gives birth, then it is presumed in law that her husband is the child's father. But recent scientific and technological changes in Assisted Reproductive Technology (also known as ART), coupled with the practice of surrogacy, have led many to challenge these assumptions. We here consider the case of a woman who gestates or gives birth to a child while serving as a surrogate for a married couple who hired and paid her for the "job" of being inseminated with a pre-embryo grown in vitro from their genetic contributions. The surrogate carries the fetus to term, and she is expected to deliver the child to the couple when it is born. If the surrogate refuses to comply, she has a long history of precedent cases supporting her gestational claim to custody of the newborn child. In this chapter we will discuss the normative underpinning of the principle that gives preference to the gestational or birth mother. Why should the state prefer her to other claimants for custody, for example, those who claim a right to the child on the grounds of their genetic relationship to the child, or those whose claim is based on an existing contract for the gestational services of a surrogate? In this discussion we will look at several different answers from the perspective of natural law, Kantian and utilitarian ethical theories.

L.D. Houlgate, *Philosophy, Law and the Family*, AMINTAPHIL: The Philosophical Foundations of Law and Justice 7,
DOI 10.1007/978-3-319-51121-4_11

11.1 The Internal Oracle of Justice

In his 1861 essay *Utilitarianism*, John Stuart Mill expresses skepticism about the oft-repeated claim that if we take "Justice" for our rule then "its application to any given case could leave us in as little doubt as a mathematical demonstration" (Mill 54) Mill's counter-examples to this claim include the familiar controversies over the justice of punishment, the justice of fixing particular amounts of punishment, the justice of giving "superior remuneration" to persons who have talent or skill, and the justice of taking a higher percentage of taxes from those who have higher incomes. In each case Mill shows with devastating ease that there is considerable dispute when questions of justice are asked:

> Not only have different nations and individuals different notions of justice, but in the mind of one and the same individual, justice is not some one rule, principle, or maxim, but many which do not always coincide in their dictates, and, in choosing between which, he is guided either by some extraneous standard or by his own personal predilections (Mill 54).

If justice is a standard "which the mind can recognize by simple introspection of itself, [then] it is hard to understand why that internal oracle is so ambiguous." Why do so many things appear both just and unjust "according to the light in which they are regarded"? If Mill were alive today, he probably would add to his stock examples of the ambiguity of our internal oracle the controversies in family law about the "justice" of the judicial and legislative responses to new birth technologies.

Beginning in the late Twentieth century we have witnessed several instances of what one judge has referred to as "[the] technological fragmentation of the procreative process" (*In re C.K.G*, 2005). There are new words and acronyms to describe the fragmentation. Assisted Reproductive Technology (ART) is a general title for all the technologies that help a woman to become pregnant. The most common ART method is in vitro fertilization-embryo transfer (IVF-ET), a technology involving surgically removing eggs from a woman's ovaries, combining them with sperm in a laboratory, and returning the resulting pre-embryo to the woman's body.[1] The pre-embryo may also be transferred to the uterus of a surrogate (another woman who will carry and deliver the resulting child to another). Some embryos resulting from IVF are cryopreserved: stored at sub-zero temperatures for later thawing and use.

ART has made possible the birth of thousands of babies in the U.S.A. to infertile couples who would otherwise not have been able to have a biological child. Cryopreservation has made family planning much easier for couples who want to have children at a future time in their life that is more amenable for child rearing. But these technologies are moving much faster than the law. The first set of legal problems we shall discuss arise not from ART per se but from post-ART surrogacy contracts in which there is a custody dispute between the surrogate mother and the couple for whom she agreed to carry and deliver the newborn child. The second

---

[1] Other ART methods include gamete intrafallopian transfer (GIFT), zygote intrafallopian transfer (ZIFT), and frozen embryo transfer (FET). http://www.sart.org/sart_assisted_reproductive_technologies/ Accessed 15 March 2016.

problem, to be discussed in Chap. 12, arises when there is a disagreement between a husband and wife who file for divorce before all their frozen embryos are used. The disagreement is about what should be done with the embryos. In both the surrogacy and the cryopreservation cases "courts are increasingly faced with legal issues for which there are no precedents" (Statsky 2013, 596).

11.2 Two Surrogacy Cases

There are two kinds of surrogacy, illustrated by the cases discussed below. The first case (*Baby M*) is an example of a legal controversy arising from *traditional surrogacy* in which a woman, using her own egg, becomes pregnant for someone else. The surrogate is gestationally *and* genetically related to the child because she uses her own egg, carries and gives birth to the child. The second case (*Johnson v Calvert*) illustrates a dispute arising from *gestational surrogacy* in which a woman, *not* using her own egg, becomes pregnant for someone else.

11.2.1 In re Baby M *(1987)*

In one of the most highly publicized family law cases of the late twentieth century the New Jersey Superior Court in Bergen County awarded to her biological father sole custody of a child born pursuant to a "surrogate mother contract," and terminated the parental rights of her natural mother. William Stern, a 41-year-old biochemist from Tenafly, and his wife, Elizabeth, a 41-year-old pediatrician, had agreed to pay Mary Beth Whitehead, a married woman, $10,000 to be artificially inseminated with Stern's sperm and bear them a child. The terms of the contract stipulated that Mrs. Whitehead agreed to relinquish all of her parental rights to and the custody of any child conceived, and to consent to the Sterns' adoption of any such child. However, after the child was born, Whitehead refused the money and later refused to surrender the infant. The Sterns were granted temporary custody of the child after police located Mrs. Whitehead, her husband, and the baby in Florida, moving from relative to relative.

After a lengthy trial, culminating in March 1987, Judge Harvey R. Sorkow awarded full custody of the infant to Mr. Stern, stripping Mary Beth Whitehead of all legal parental rights. Sorkow ruled that the surrogacy contract was valid under New Jersey law, and that it may specifically be enforced, because the child's best interests will be served by such remedy. Immediately after handing down his ruling, Judge Sorkow conducted a private adoption ceremony, decreeing Elizabeth Stern is the legal mother of the child. (Sorkow, *Family Law Reporter* p. 2019).

On February 3, 1988, the New Jersey Supreme Court unanimously overturned most aspects of Judge Sorkow's ruling. Surrogate motherhood contracts were held to be illegal, the parental rights of the baby's mother, Mary Beth Whitehead-Gould (now remarried) were restored and the order permitting Elizabeth Stern to adopt the child was ruled invalid. The only part of the lower court judgment that remained standing was the decision to grant custody to Mr. Stern (New Jersey Supreme Court, *New York Times*, 1987, pp. 1, 14).

11.2.2 Johnson v. Calvert *(1993)*

Mark and Crispina Calvert, a married couple, desired to have a child, but could not accomplish this because Crispina's ovaries were not capable of producing eggs. In 1989, after hearing about the Calvert's plight, Anna Johnson offered to serve as a surrogate for the Calverts. The Calverts and Anna signed a contract providing that an embryo created by the sperm of Mark and the egg of Crispina would be implanted in Anna and the child born would be delivered to Mark and Crispina as "their child." Anna agreed that she would relinquish all parental rights to the child in favor of Mark and Crispina. In return, Mark and Crispina would pay Anna $10,000 in a series of installments. The embryo was implanted 4 days after the signing of the contract.

Ultrasound tests soon disclosed that Anna was pregnant, but unfortunately, relationships between the Calverts and Anna started to deteriorate. Two months prior to the infant's birth, each party filed lawsuits seeking a declaration that they were legal parents of the child. At trial, the court ruled that (1) Mark and Christina were the child's "genetic, biological and natural" mother and father, (2) Anna had no "parental" rights to the child, and (3) the surrogacy contract was legal and enforceable against Anna's claims.

The California Court of Appeal affirmed, and the Supreme Court of California granted review. The court immediately noted that the state allows that both gestational and genetic evidence can be used to establish the existence of a parent-child relationship. The relevant statutes do not say what a court must do when the two kinds of evidence lead to conflicting results. In the present case, Anna is the gestational mother and Crispina is the child's genetic mother. However, the court noted a relevant difference between the two claimants: whereas Crispina "affirmatively intended the birth of the child," she never intended to donate the embryo to Anna. Therefore, the court affirmed, declaring that Crispina is the "natural mother" (legal mother) of the child under California law.

11.3 The Biological Preference Principle and the Language of Surrogacy

What is the justification for the traditional principle that says that the natural mother and her husband are to be regarded as the legal parents of a newborn child? The New Jersey Supreme Court notes that "our policy has long been that to the extent possible, children should remain with and be brought up by both of their natural parents." In Baby M Judge Sorkow apparently ignored this policy, saying instead that the only legal concepts that "attach to surrogacy arrangements are contract law principles and parens patriae concepts for the benefit of the child." (Sorkow, *Family Law Reporter*, p. 2019). Acknowledging that an "agreement between parents is inevitably subservient to the considerations of the best interests of the child," he then determined that Baby M should be placed in Stern's custody and that specific performance of the contract is thus appropriate; in short, Judge Sorkow suggests that any right that a birth mother might have to a child can be weighed and balanced against the merits and demerits of an alternative placement where a surrogate contract exists. What, if anything, is wrong with this approach to child custody decisions? What are the grounds for choosing a principle that gives the birth mother an absolute right to her child rather than a doctrine that allows the presumption for the birth mother to be overridden by such considerations as a contract and the best interests of the child?

First, we need to define the terms we will use in the remainder of this chapter. A *natural mother* is a woman from whose uterus the child was gestated and born. She is also referred to as the *gestational* or *birth mother*. A *genetic parent* is a person from whose reproductive material (sperm or egg) the child was produced. A *biological parent* is a person who is either a genetic parent or a natural mother or both. A *legal parent* is a person on whom the law confers or imposes certain rights, privileges, duties, and obligations with respect to a particular child; especially, a person on whom the law confers the rights and obligations of custody. An *intended parent* is "a person seeking to raise a child as its legal parent and who enters an agreement with a woman to become pregnant, to give birth to a child, and then to relinquish all parental rights to the couple, who will then adopt the child." (Statsky, 603). A *surrogate contract* is an agreement in writing between intended parents and a woman who consents to become pregnant, to give birth to a child, and then to relinquish all parental rights to the intended parents.[2] Finally, a *surrogate mother* is any woman who consents to the aforesaid terms of a surrogate contract.

Children born during the course of a marriage are legally presumed to be the legitimate offspring of the married couple. To challenge this presumption successfully, state laws commonly require the husband to affirmatively disown the child and present evidence in court proving beyond a reasonable doubt that he is not the genetic father. At present there is no method by which the natural (gestational) mother can disown a child born to her by proving to a court that she merely served as a gestational donor, carrying a fetus that genetically "belongs" to others. The assumption has always been that the gestational mother is the legal mother of a newborn child, and her husband is its legal father. In both the case of the natural mother and her husband, there is the further assumption that they are the child's genetic parents,

[2] The strong version of a surrogate contract would be one in which the terms of the contract stipulate that the aforesaid woman agrees to relinquish to the married couple, immediately after the child's birth, all parental rights to and custody of any child conceived, and to consent to the adoption of any such child. A weak version of a surrogate contract would be one that provides for a certain time period (e.g., six months) in which the natural mother could change her mind.

although the husband is permitted to present evidence that will rebut this. Let us extract from this the following principle: In a contest for custody between a biological parent and one who has no biological relationship to the child, the state should prefer the biological parent. That is, when deciding who shall be granted the status of legal parent, the state should always prefer the biological parent to all other contestants. I shall call this the Biological Preference Principle (BPP).

It should be noted that the word "biological" in the BPP is ambiguous. If "biological" means "gestational," then the court in both of the previous cases should prefer the surrogate mother. If it means "genetic" then the court should prefer Mr. Stern and Mary Beth Whitehead in *Baby M*, and it should award sole custody to the Calverts in *Calvert v Johnson*. If the BPP demands both a gestational and genetic relationship between parent and child, then only Mary Beth Whitehead should have custody of the baby. However, the BPP offers no resolution to the custody dispute in *Calvert* because no party to the dispute can claim the dual relationship required under this interpretation.

The central question we will attempt to answer in this chapter is, "Is there an adequate justification for the BPP under either interpretation?" Answers to this question, I shall show, involve some of the major ethical theories and illustrate, once again, the fundamental division in philosophical ethics between natural law and utilitarian ethical theories. But first, we need to get clear about the traditional rules of contract law and the accompanying rules regulating recovery when a contract has been breached.

11.4 Traditional Rules of Contract Law

The traditional view of a contract is to be found in the way that it treats legal duties. Unlike the duty in tort to exercise due care in one's relations with other people, all duties under contract law are self-imposed by the individuals who create the contracts. Thus, contract law did not impose on Mary Beth Whitehead or any other woman a duty to become a surrogate mother. She had no prior duty to become pregnant and give the newborn child to a couple who have told her that they will pay her $10,000 to be artificially impregnated with the husband's sperm. But she does have the power to *impose a duty on herself* by entering into a legally binding contract with a couple for this purpose.

The second feature of contract law is that the traditional rule for recovery when there is a breach of a contract says that the person who reneged on their obligation (the contractor) should be required to give to the other (the contractee) an amount that would leave them as well off as if they had kept the contract. This is quite different than the rule for recovery in tort which says that the negligent person who caused the injury has a duty to give to the victim an amount that reflects the actual harm done. In the previous example, if there is a breach of the contract by the surrogate mother (she does not hand over the newborn to the married couple), then she must return to them any money they had paid for her service. If the couple breaches the contract by failing to pay for the surrogate's services during her pregnancy, then they can be made to pay the $10,000, as promised. This amount would restore the surrogate to the position she would have been in if not for the breach.

But what happens if the couple pays the $10,000 but also decide that they no longer want to raise this child because it has a physical deformity. They refuse to take the infant. Where does this leave the surrogate mother? How does the court restore her to a position she would have been in if not for the breach? Suppose the surrogate insists that the position she would have been in means "no child" (in addition to receiving the $10,000 promised for her services)? If she decides to keep the child, the expenses she will incur for raising the child until it reaches the age of maturity will be far more than $10,000.[3] Should the couple who reneged on the contract be made to pay this amount? The traditional view on recovery gives no clear answer, although it appears to ignore actual damages suffered by the surrogate mother.

Rules of recovery are not set in stone. Self-imposed obligations should not be seen as the only basis of contract law. The obligations we find in the common law contain considerations of social policy that have been used by the courts as alternative rules for recovery when a contract is breached (Altman 2001, 121). One of these alternatives is *reliance-based.* This means that a way of measuring damages is to consider the costs or the harm suffered by the victim of the breach *as a result of his or her reliance* on the contract.[4] In the preceding example, the woman who agreed to be a surrogate *relied* on the couple for whom she gave birth to a child to not only pay her $10,000 but to also take the (special needs) newborn into their custody. As noted above, if she keeps the child instead of putting it up for adoption, then the costs of child rearing will be considerable. It would be unjust to require her to assume these costs without her having consented to this. She would not have done this had she known that there was a possibility that the couple might renege. Social policy, it can be argued, should always rest on the bedrock of social justice. Let us now look at what philosophers of law might instruct us about how social policy should inform the construction of laws regulating or even forbidding the practice of surrogacy.

11.5 Natural Law

In Chap. 2 we used John Locke's writings about parental power as an example of a natural law approach to evaluating the validity and content of the positive law of family relationships (Sect. 2.3.1). Although Locke had much to say about the obligations

---

[3] A middle-income family with a child born in 2013 can expect to spend about $245,340 ($304,480 adjusted for projected inflation*) for food, housing, childcare and education, and other child-rearing expenses up to age 18. This does not include the cost of raising a special needs child, nor does it include the cost of a higher education. *United States Department of Agriculture* (2013).

[4] In this respect, reliance-based damages "are like the damages given the victim of tortious conduct such as negligence" (Altman, 122).

of a parent to a young child who had not yet reached the age of maturity, he never considers the question whether biological parents have a moral right to the sole custody of their newborn children. Locke would undoubtedly respond affirmatively to this question, but there is no text to support this. Hence, we will have to construct an argument from other sources in Locke's writings.

An argument for the BPP using Locke's famous remarks about private property is one possibility. Thus, it might be argued that since the male sperm and the female egg are, respectively, part of the man's and the woman's body, then nobody but they have the right to a child that results from the union of sperm and egg, the product of their genetic material. Second, another possibility is to focus on gestation. The woman who bears (gestates) the child in a normal case of insemination and gestation can argue that since she has done the "work" or "labor" of carrying the fetus for the nine-month gestation, she has a right to it once it is born. The notion of labor refers primarily to in utero nurture. At the time of birth, only the birth mother can claim that it is her body that has nurtured the fetus until its birth. This would be a parallel to Locke's famous argument about establishing property rights: since people have property in their bodies and their labor is also their property, then anything with which they mix their labor becomes their private property (Locke 1983, Ch. IV). The parallel is this: since the gestational mother provides the fertilized egg the place to develop and grow (her body has nurtured the fetus), then she has a right to the fetus and the newborn that results from this development, either because such a right derives from her prior property rights in the product of her body and its labor; or because such rights are required, in justice, as a return for her labor.

This Lockean argument appears to support the Biological Preference Principle but only when the biological relationship between parents and child is gestational. Merely providing the genetic material that leads to the existence of an embryo as its product is not sufficient to make the embryo one's property. Thus, if I give you the seed to grow a plant and you subsequently dig a hole, plant and grow a vegetable, the vegetable is the product of your labor. It thereby becomes your property, not mine. By analogy, if a man provides the sperm to inseminate a woman to whom he is not married, the Lockean property argument does not support a claim that he might make for custody of the child.

There are two problems with the Lockean natural rights justification of BPP. First, the argument fails to establish that there is any necessary connection between biology and rights. Imagine a society in which tasks are divided between child procreators and child-rearers because of genetic traits that make persons unsuitable for one or the other tasks. In this society persons who are fertile have a hormone that causes them to be violent toward children immediately after birth; the infertile persons have no such hormone. There is surely no contradiction in holding that those who procreate in this society should not be given custody of the children they beget. Hence, having a biological relationship to a child is not sufficient to establish that one ought to be given the rights of custody.

There is a second and perhaps more serious difficulty with the natural rights approach. The theory gives us no plausible way of deciding between situations in which there is a conflict of rights. Suppose that a non-biological contestant for the custody of a particular child has entered into a contract with one of its biological parents for the custody of their child once it is born. According to natural rights theory, each person is free to act as he or she chooses, as long as the rights of others are respected. It follows that contracts for the sale of sperm or for the rental of a womb pose no special problems, if both parties agree. Adults who enter into such agreements are seen as free, contracting individuals. Each has a duty to the other to keep the terms of the agreement. Even if it is established that the genetic material donor or the gestational donor have rights to the child, if they freely entered into a contract with another for the custody of the child after it is born, they have "alienated" any right that they initially had to the child. If someone argues that gestational (or surrogate) mother contracts should not be honored because no one can alienate their natural right to their own biological product, they simply beg the question. That question is whether the (natural) right to enter into contracts with others takes precedence over the (natural) right (if there is such a right) to the biological product of one's own body. To this question, natural rights theory provides no plausible answer. In the language of John Stuart Mill, our internal oracle of justice provides only ambiguity.

11.6 Utilitarian Concerns

An interesting feature of the natural rights argument is the claim that custody rights are an "essential" feature of one's biological relationship to a child. That is, one's status as a biological parent entails the inherent right to power over that child. And yet the argument fails to make clear how the normative relation of custody follows from the genetic and gestational connection between biological parent and child. How do biological facts about procreation logically entail moral and legal conclusions about custody rights?

Utilitarians attempt to make this connection by reference to the attainment and maximizing of goods; yet they often differ over what good results should be emphasized. Some will emphasize the good of individual family members (for example, the best interests of the child, or the good of the biological parents), whereas others will emphasize general good consequences (such as the good of the community or the state).

11.6.1 Best Interests of the Newborn Child

When the good of specific individuals is stressed in making decisions about the initial placement of a child at birth, there may be a dispute between utilitarians over whose interests should be of dominant concern. If the interests of the child are dominant, decisions about the child's custody are made solely in terms of advancing his or her interests. In divorce child custody disputes between two biological parents the court must take multiple factors into consideration prior to making a custody determination: parental stability in living arrangement, schooling, access to relatives and friends; availability to spend time with the child; existing emotional relationships; parental career choice; actual or threatened abuse of one member of a family by another member. Some of these factors will not be relevant to a dispute over whether a biological or surrogate parent will prevail (for example, existing emotional relationships). Other factors will be of primary concerns. For example, let us assume that the sole interest of a child in being placed with a particular adult who will serve as his custodian is in not being abused or neglected. That is, custody will be granted only to those who are not potential child-abusers. Biological relationships will be relevant, but only to the question whether this is a predictor of future abusive behavior toward the child. In this regard, the biological parent might be in a worse position for custody than others. There is evidence that biological parents are five times more likely to abuse their children than non-biological, adoptive parents (LaFollette 1981, 194).

Of course, children have interests other than freedom from neglect and abuse. Recent child psychology has identified the child's perception of being loved and wanted as a crucial factor in his or her present and future psychological development (Goldstein et al. 1973, 17). If it can be established that biological parents are also psychological parents, that is, that they are more likely than other candidates for initial custody rights to rear the child in such a way that the child feels both loved and wanted, then there is at least a prima facie case for making the biological parent the legal parent. And yet there seems to be no evidence to support this claim. Of course, most biological parents can be expected to feel affection for and desire the healthy development of their children. But this does not prove that non-biological custodians do not derive as much satisfaction from rearing children as do biological parents, nor does it establish that children reared by non-biological custodians do not feel as loved and wanted by them as do children reared by their genetic and gestational parents (Purdy 1987, 39).[5]

It follows from the above considerations that a utilitarian argument based entirely on the best interests of the child cannot establish that initial placement of a child at birth should be with the biological parents. There is no evidence that the child is at less risk of being abused and neglected by the biological parents than other possible candidates for custodian, and there is no evidence that the newborn child has a greater chance of receiving love and a feeling of being wanted from the biological parents than from other persons.

[5] It should be stressed at this point that in a custody dispute between a biological parent and a psychological parent the determining test in most states is whether the biological parent is *unfit*, not whether it is in the best interests of the child to have the biological as his or her parent. "Unfit" means that the parent has been abusive or neglectful. If it is determined that the biological parent is not unfit, then they will be awarded custody even if it is in the child's best interests to be placed with the psychological parent (Statsky, 253).

11.6.2 Interests of Parents and State

Let us turn now to a consideration of the interests of those persons who are candidates for the role of child custodian. If we restrict our attention to their interests, can we arrive at a criterion that will guide the state in making custody decisions when a child is born? In particular, is there any reason to prefer the child's biological parents to other persons who would like to have custody of the child?

Both biological and non-biological candidates for child custodian may have certain economic and psychological interests in common. Thus, both may hope that the child they rear will provide support in the parent's old age. Perhaps more important, the child will provide a new bond of love for the child-rearer, and will return the love that he or she gives to the child. Some benefits of child rearing, however, can be realized only through rearing one's own biological child. These are satisfactions realized through rearing a member of one's own bloodline, or achieving a kind of immortality by having one's genetic type persist through the child and his or her descendants. These may be irrational desires, but they appear to be quite common. In addition, according to some child psychologists, the satisfaction of raising one's own biological child is a form of the natural parent's self-love. "Normally the physical facts of having begotten a child or given birth to it have far-reaching psychological meaning for the parents as confirmation of their respective sexual identities, their potency and intactness."[6] Biological parents have a psychological investment in rearing their own children that is not present in the non-biological parent. This does not mean that non-biological parents are not interested in or are not pleased by the healthy development of their adopted children. It means only that they do not receive the same kind of satisfaction that is received by the biological parent.

Finally, there is an argument based entirely on the interests of the child's gestational parents. This argument was presented in Chap. 3 when we used H.L.A. Hart's suggestion to look for a "simple truism" about human nature that would make it contingently necessary to have a rule assigning presumptive custody of a newborn child to its biological parents (Sect. 3.7.3). One writer has argued that a gestational mother has "contributed more of herself" and therefore has a "greater biological investment and interest in" the child who has developed in her womb than any other person who might wish to be the child's custodian.[7] This is the "simple truism" about which utilitarians should be sensitive in constructing moral rules and laws regarding child custody. Rules and laws regarding child custody should have a minimum content based on these truisms. One truism is that all newborns require protection and care. They are helpless at birth and from years beyond birth. The other truism is that "during pregnancy many – perhaps most –expectant parents form a poignantly embodied, but also emotional, intimate relationship with their fetus," a bond established during the lengthy period that the fetus is in utero" (Gaeus, 2012, 444). Indeed,

---

[6] *Ibid.*, p. 17.

[7] George J. Annas, "Redefining Parenthood and Protecting Embryos: Why We Need New Laws," *Hastings Center Report*, October 1984, 51.

gestational mothers and their partners are known to move through a grieving period when they give over the child to a donee parent in much the same way that parents mourn the loss of a child who dies at birth. We should be aware of these maternal and paternal interests and take account of them when we do our utility calculations.

We have, then, strong utilitarian reasons for allocating rights of custody of a child at birth to its gestational parents. The argument is based entirely on the peculiar interests of these parents in rearing their own children, not on any interest of the children. It should be noted that the argument derives most of its force from its appeal to the interest of the birth mother (gestational parent), for only she can refer to herself as the nurture-parent at birth.[8] Nonetheless, it is clear that birth mothers and their partners would undoubtedly experience more happiness and far less misery under a system that grants them custody of their own children than (say) under a system that awards custody solely on the basis of what candidate for custodian is most likely to promote the best interests of the child. Although the former system may produce less aggregate happiness in those persons who would have enjoyed rearing a child awarded to its biological parent, the amount would (on balance) be a great deal less than the amount of unhappiness that would be produced under the latter system. Finally, the utilitarian argument in favor of the BPP becomes much stronger once we realize that any other basis for determining the custody of children at birth would put excessive discretionary power over everyone's lives in the hands of the state. For example, if we decide to place children on the basis of the child's "best interests," then the vagueness of this criterion would permit decision-makers to make custody determinations that would inevitably lead to conflict and dispute between claimants. The problems that we now see in custody disputes between divorcing parents would be replicated every time a child is born.

11.7 Exceptions to the Biological Preference Principle

Should the presumption in favor of awarding custody of a child at birth to its natural mother and her husband be "conclusive and irrebuttable" (Annas 1984, 51) or should we allow it to be overridden under certain carefully defined conditions, for example, by evidence that the natural mother had entered into a surrogate contract?

The arguments in the preceding sections give us a fairly strong utilitarian basis for BPP. However, these arguments establish a conditional rather than an absolute right of a birth mother and her husband to the child at the time of its birth. The biological parents are not to be awarded custody of the child under any and all conditions, for in some cases the parents may not be able properly to care for the child

[8] I owe this observation to Professor Sara Ann Ketchum, who has written two excellent, unpublished papers on surrogate motherhood: "Selling Babies and Selling Bodies: Surrogate Motherhood and the Problem of Commodification" and "New Reproductive Technologies and the Definition of Parenthood: A Feminist Perspective."

(for example, the parent is too young or is mentally defective) and thus will not fulfill the role of nurture-parents. Consequently, the BPP should stipulate that biological parents should be awarded initial custody of their child at birth only if they meet certain minimal standards of child rearing. These standards will stipulate that the birth mother and her husband (if she is married) can be predicted to be nurture-parents to the newborn child. The burden for establishing that this cannot be predicted shall be placed on the state. This conditional right is all that can be supported by the utilitarian argument. The important question, to which I now turn, is whether the existence of a surrogate contract should be allowed to provide an additional factor that will override the presumption in favor of the BPP.

If we generalize from Judge Sorkow's ruling in the lower court decision about Baby M, the result is that the gestational mother is the legal mother of the newborn child unless she has entered into a properly executed surrogate contract.[9] Perhaps the strongest argument for permitting this modification to current law is that it gives childless couples a lawful means, other than adoption, to acquire children. Infertile couples will benefit most from this type of reproduction. They will now have an opportunity to have a child that is in part genetically theirs, an opportunity heretofore available only to fertile couples. Moreover, we provide women who wish to aid infertile couples the legal means to achieve this goal through recognition of their contractual relationship. In this way, both the gestational donors and the infertile couples are able to achieve individual goals and to make predictions about the future (such as who will have custody of the child) that are more accurate than the predictions they would be able to make if such contracts were declared invalid and unenforceable. The ability to make accurate predictions about the future provides another (utilitarian) argument for regulating (and thus legalizing) surrogate contracts. Judge Sorkow noted that with an increasing number of surrogate births, legislation would prevent a great deal of future harm to society, the family and the child.

> Some of the issues that need legislative [action] are: establishing the standards for sperm donors, legitimacy of the child, rights of the biological father's spouse, rights of the biological mother's spouse, rights of the two biological actors as to each other and to the child, qualifications for the surrogate, [whether] compensation to the surrogate is to be allowed, concerns regarding the imperfect child. Many questions must be answered; [and] answers must come from legislation. If there is no law then society will suffer the negative aspects of this alternative reproduction vehicle that appears to hold out so much hope to the childless, who make up a substantial segment of our society (*Family Law Reporter*, p. 2019).

It has been argued in rebuttal that "there is no need for state legislatures to rush to adopt measures to make this practice [surrogacy] any easier." (Capron, sec. H). If we leave things as they are—with the traditional rule that a woman who bears a child is presumed to be its legal mother—then the status quo will create uncertainty in the minds of those infertile couples that wish to hire a surrogate. "The element of uncertainty that the traditional rule had created for surrogacy contracts may well

[9] As of 2010 approximately 16 states had laws regulating surrogate motherhood. Most states are either silent about it or they explicitly refuse to recognize surrogacy contracts http://www.thesurrogacyexperience.com/surrogate-mothers/the-law/u-s-surrogacy-law-by-state/

discourage people from entering into them, which in my view, is all to the good." (Capron, id.). It is interesting that the author of the preceding remark makes no attempt to rebut Judge Sorkow's suggestion, quoted above, that state regulation of surrogate contracts could head off the harmful consequences of private, unregulated contracts. These consequences might be disputes of the kind that we have witnessed in the Baby M case, disputes over the custody of a newborn who is born mentally or physically defective, or future disputes between the child and all parties to the surrogate contract over the child's inheritance rights.

The final utilitarian argument for making a surrogate mother contract an exception to the BPP is an argument from the utility of giving persons as much freedom to enter into contractual relationships with others as is consistent with social welfare. The argument is similar to pro-choice arguments in the abortion debate that begin with the premise that a woman has the right to do as she wishes with her own body. She can only be prohibited by law from doing those acts that would cause harm to others, but "over herself, over her own body and mind, a woman is sovereign" (paraphrasing Mill 1979, Ch. IV). The state cannot prohibit a woman from entering into a surrogate contract on the grounds that it thinks that such decisions are unwise or even immoral. This would be paternalistic interference with a woman's liberty, and all such interference, utilitarians argue, produces more misery in the long run than happiness. The only question that a utilitarian will allow us to entertain is whether such practices are truly voluntary and whether they involve harm to others, for example, harm to the children born of surrogacy contracts. If we can settle these questions in the negative, then there is no justification for state interference. The rationale is to be found in the high utility value of maximizing a person's opportunity to exercise her liberty. The freedom to contract with a married couple to serve as a surrogate mother, like the freedom to use artificial methods of contraception and the freedom to choose whether to have an abortion, can be viewed as just another example of a woman's attempt to gain the right to do as she wishes with her own body.

If this much good can be achieved through legal recognition of surrogate mother contracts, then why not permit them; that is, why not allow the existence of a surrogate mother contract to provide an additional factor that will to allowed to defeat the presumption in favor of the BPP? There are two remarkably different answers to this question, one based on utilitarian factors not yet mentioned, the other based on Kantian concerns about the moral prohibition on "selling babies and selling bodies."

11.8 Utilitarian Objections to Surrogate Mother Contracts

Utilitarians who have thought about reproductive technologies list a number of evils that, they claim, are or will be produced by the general practice of hiring women to serve as surrogate mothers. They fall into three categories: harm to the natural or surrogate mother, harm to the infant, and harm to third parties. I shall here consider only the first two categories.[10]

First in line is the argument that the gestational mother will be exploited. Lower- and middle-class women will bear most of the burden of surrogacy, for it is they who will sign such contracts out of economic necessity. Judge Sorkow's reply was that "the surrogate has an opportunity to consult, take advice and consider her act and is not forced into the relationship." (Sorkow 2019). The fact that one performs a service out of economic necessitude does not mean that one is exploited. A woman is exploited only if she has no reasonable alternative to performing the type of wage-earning labor that she has chosen to perform. In fact, many of those women who enter into surrogate contracts report that they perform this service to help infertile couples, not to make money, and those who do it for the money have options that offer far better working conditions and a higher wage.

Another bad effect of surrogate mother contracts involving the natural mother is that she may suffer emotionally from the act of giving up her infant. Most women become nurture parents during their pregnancy; that is, they become emotionally attached to the fetus they are carrying, and they will suffer more psychological stress from giving up the newborn than would any other potential custodian of the child, including the male sperm donor, upon learning that they will not be allowed to adopt it. Although the psychological "investment" of the gestational parent in her newborn is the factor I have singled out as tipping the scales in favor of the BPP, we do not yet have sufficient empirical data on matters such as the amount of psychological stress that would be suffered by a surrogate mother required to honor her contract and hand over her newborn, how long her anguish can be expected to last, and the effect that this might have on her future psychological health. And yet this is precisely the sort of information we need if we are to do the sort of "balancing" of good and bad consequences of surrogate mother contracts required by the principle of utility. Finally, it is important to realize that less than 1 percent of surrogate mothers have changed their minds about giving up the child to the sperm donor. Although additional facts may persuade us to modify surrogate contracts to provide for a period in which the birth mother could change her mind, one wonders whether the entire justification for this modification should rest on our desire to satisfy the emotional needs of such a small number of women.

Will the newborn child suffer any short- or long-term harm from being the object of a valid surrogate mother contract? As indicated above, there is no empirical basis for concluding that a child will be any better off being raised by its gestational mother than by non-biological custodians. What does appear to be crucial to a child's development is that the child perceives that he or she is loved and wanted by

[10]Third parties who might be harmed include other children of the surrogate. "How secure can they feel when they learn that their brother or sister has been traded for $10,000? If the price is right, are they for sale, too? Conversely, might the situation breed resentment in some children that they weren't taken from their family and adopted by other, more affluent, parents?" (Capron, *op. cit.*, p. 5). Since the author presents no evidence to support a claim that there is psychological harm of either type suggested (insecurity, resentment), it would be presumptuous to make his queries into data for utility calculations.

at least one adult on a continuous basis during the formative years. The evidence that we have from the long history of adoption shows that this can be accomplished by adoptive parents as well as by the child's natural mother and her husband.

11.9 Kantian Objections: Selling Babies and Renting Bodies

The preceding discussion would be regarded as largely irrelevant to one group of philosophers. Those who adhere to Kantian principles, as these are stated in various versions of the Second Formulation of the Categorical Imperative, contend that commercializing reproduction is morally objectionable, not because of its consequences in terms of social or individual harm, but because it involves treating people as means rather than as ends, as objects rather than as persons (Kant 1959, pt. II). Utilitarian considerations are as out of place here as they would be in discussions about the morality of baby selling. According to the Kantian, the sale of an infant is wrong because this involves treating the newborn as a mere commodity and this is also why we should think that a contract to gestate and hand over a newborn at birth to its genetic father cannot be permitted.

There are two ways of avoiding the Kantian objection. First, we can admit that it is wrong to sell babies but deny that surrogate mother contracts are contracts to sell babies. This is what Judge Sorkow did. He contended that the $10,000 that the Sterns paid to Mary Beth Whitehead was payment for her services, not payment for the baby. "The money to be paid to the surrogate is not being paid for the surrender of the child to the father… The biological father pays the surrogate for her willingness to be impregnated and carry his child to term. At birth, the father does not purchase the child. It is his own biological genetically related child. He cannot purchase what is already his" (Sorkow 2017–2018).

Judge Sorkow begs the question when he writes that the child whose custody Mr. Stern is vying for "is already his." Baby M is the child of William Stern only in the sense that she is his genetic product, but not in the sense that he is the legal parent of the child; it is up to the court to determine the latter relationship. Judge Sorkow cannot assume the conclusion that he is to determine in his ruling.

11.9.1 Selling Babies

The New Jersey Supreme Court rejected Judge Sorkow's attempt to classify the surrogate mother contract as a contract for services, contending instead that "this is the sale of a child, or at the very least, the sale of a mother's right to her child, the only mitigating factor being that one of the purchasers is the father" (2014). It is not clear to me from reading the decision in this case whether the New Jersey Supreme Court would employ the Kantian objection to baby-selling. Let us suppose that it does. Is the Kantian argument sound? Should we object to baby- selling, and thus to surrogate mother contracts, on the (Kantian) ground that this involves treating the infant as a mere object instead of as a person?

The answer to this question is negative. First, if what makes it wrong to give up a child under the provisions of a surrogate contract is that this involves treating the infant as an object, then it must also be wrong voluntarily to relinquish one's custody rights to a child under any circumstances whatever. A woman who gives up her newborn child for adoption because she does not want to interrupt her career can also be accused of treating it as an object. This may be a conclusion that some may wish to embrace, but I can discern no rush to legally prohibit the practice of voluntary relinquishment of parental rights. But, second, we reach this unsatisfactory conclusion because of the vagueness of the phrases "treating as a person" and "treating as an object." Under the ordinary interpretation of these phrases, it is logically impossible to treat an infant as a person. For Kant, a person is a moral agent, one who possesses an autonomous will. This means that one has the capacity to formulate purposes, plans, and policies of his own and to carry out his decisions without undue reliance on the help of others. Since newborns do not possess an autonomous will, they cannot be conceived of as moral agents or persons (Houlgate 1980, 50, 52). Therefore, the failure to treat a newborn as a person cannot be what is wrong with the sale of an infant; and if a surrogate contract is the sale of an infant, this cannot be what is wrong with surrogate contracts. We must look elsewhere than to Kantian ethics if we wish to find a moral objection to these practices.

11.9.2 Renting Bodies

Although, as mentioned above, Judge Sorkow begs the question when he writes that because the infant is the product of William Stern's sperm it is "already his," I find that it is certainly logically possible to conceive of a surrogate mother contract as a contract for services. The woman who agrees to be a gestational mother contracts for the use of her womb for a nine-month period, and although she (usually) provides some of the material (the egg) from which the infant is produced, it is still the case that she has contracted to perform the service of gestation. Consider the following analogy. If a woman contracts to rent her garage so that someone can grow orchids therein with the understanding that he (not she) keeps the orchids when they are grown, the contract is not for the sale of orchids, even if she has donated some of the materials used in growing them.

The difference between the surrogate contract and the orchids-in-the-garage case is that in the former case the birth mother is presumed in law to be the legal parent of the child. Hence, the "services" that she provides to the sperm donor can only be accomplished when she signs over her right to the child. It is this act of assigning her rights that makes the case look more like baby selling than mere womb rental. However, this is to miss the point of what is wanted by those who are attempting to achieve legal recognition of surrogate contracts. If surrogate contracts are declared to be legally enforceable then according to the agreement between contracting parents and the surrogate mother, the contracting parents (the sperm donor and his wife) are to be considered in law as the child's parents from the moment of its birth. In this case, there would be no need for the surrogate to "sign away" the child to those for whom she has provided the service.

As far as I can tell, there is no logically decisive reason for refusing to think of surrogate contracts as contracts for services. But this does not mean that there is an end to the Kantian objection. A consistent Kantian is not only morally compelled to object to the practice of selling babies, but she will also press objections to legal recognition of any practice that involves "renting" one's body or a part of one's body to another. The argument is that to rent one's body to another is to treat one's body as part of another person's domain by granting the other rights to one's body. Thus, by signing a surrogate contract, Mary Beth Whitehead had granted William Stern the right to the use of her womb for a nine-month period so that he could "grow" a child therein. But, according to the Kantian, to treat one's body as a part of the domain of another is to treat oneself as less than a person and this is in itself morally wrong. Hence, the Kantian would object to the surrogate mother "service" contract on grounds identical to those she would use to object to voluntary slavery contracts. A person, a being with a rational will, cannot alienate one's own autonomy, for it is autonomy that serves as the defining condition of personhood.

But once again the Kantian argument fails. There may be grounds for objecting to surrogate "womb rental" contracts, but they cannot be those of the argument just noted. First, the phrase "treating oneself as a person" is intolerably vague. The contrast is usually made with the equally vague phrase "treating oneself as merely a means." Suppose that I sign a contract to pose as a model for a painter or a photographer. The contract is for a nine-month period. The painter or photographer has the right to the limited use of my body for several hours a day, placing me in different poses, requiring that I maintain that pose for long periods, and perhaps even requiring that I maintain a certain diet and exercise program during this period so that I maintain the appropriate body tone. I assume that none of us would see anything morally objectionable about this agreement, so long as we are assured that my consent was voluntary and informed. It is not entirely clear to me, however, that the Kantian could reach this conclusion given the criteria already used to condemn a surrogate "service" contract. According to the Kantian, by renting my body to the painter/photographer I am treating my body as part of his or her domain; I am giving her a right to the use of my body and thus I am treating myself as less than a person.

I conclude, then, that unless the Kantian can give us an alternative interpretation of the phrase "treat oneself as a person," the argument sweeps much too broadly, compelling one to condemn not only the practice of women using their bodies to produce babies for others but also using their bodies for any commercial purpose whatever. The reason that I think most Kantians would not want their arguments to sweep this broadly is because of another Kantian concern, namely autonomy, a value that is extolled even more highly by them than it is by the utilitarian. The reason that a Kantian would regard it as impermissible to prohibit a person from contracting with another for the limited use of his or her body (say, as a model) for a certain period of time is that this would place the state in the uncomfortable position of paternalistically declaring that it (the state) knows what is good for women better than they know this themselves. Even if the state is omniscient with respect to the interests of its citizens, the Kantian would object that as persons we have fundamental autonomy rights, especially the right to make self-regarding decisions (decisions that concern only ourselves), even where such decisions might be thought to be foolish, risky, or would be characterized as decisions that involve treating ourselves "as part of another's domain." I conclude that a Kantian cannot consistently condemn surrogate contracts where such agreements are considered as contracts for services on the ground that they imply or involve the practice of a woman treating oneself as less than a person. Again: there may be good reasons for prohibiting such contracts, but they cannot be the reasons produced by the Kantian.

Questions for Thought and Discussion

1. In *Baby M*, the surrogate mother who gave birth to the child had a genetic relationship to the child. In other cases, the surrogate mother had no genetic relationship to the child she was carrying. (She was a "genetic stranger" to the newborn child). Should the biological relationship of the surrogate mother to the newborn have any relevance to settling a dispute over custody between the surrogate mother and the couple with whom she had a surrogacy contract? Why?
2. Is there a natural right to have a child? Is this an absolute right or does it have exceptions (for example, can a person procreate as many children as he/she wants or should there be a limit placed on the number of children any one person or couple can have? What kind of persons should we not allow to procreate? Why?)
3. Some of those opposed to surrogacy contracts have argued that they violate basic moral principles involving exploitation of women, the selling of children, and the rental of a woman's body. Are any of these arguments sound? Should surrogacy contracts be completely banned? If not, what kind of regulation is needed?
4. John and Mary are a married couple who plan to have three children after both finish college and start their careers. They want to space the birth of each child at least two years apart. Should any limits be placed on the means they use to do this? For example, should they be allowed to use artificial contraception devices or pills? Should they be allowed to use the "morning after" pill? Should they be allowed to use abortion as a method of birth control?
5. How should the courts determine damages when surrogacy contracts are breached by a couple who try to back out of a contract with the birth mother when it is discovered that the newborn has a serious birth defect? Should the couple pay all of the costs of raising the child until it reaches the age of 18? Explain.

References

Altman, Andrew. 2001. *Arguing About Law*. 2nd ed. Belmont: Wadsworth.

Annas, George J. 1984. *Redefining Parenthood and Protecting Embryos: Why we Need New Laws*. October: Hastings Center Report.

New Jersey Supreme Court. 1988. Decision in *In re Baby M. New York Times,* Feb 4.

Department of Agriculture. 2013. Parents Projected to Spend $245,340 to Raise a Child Born in 2013. *Press Release No. 0179.14*. http://www.usda.gov/wps/portal/usda/usdahome?contentid=2014/08/0179.xml&contentidonly=true Accessed 11 Oct 2016.

Gheaus, Anca. 2012. The Right to Parent One's Biological Baby. *The Journal of Political Philosophy* 20(4): 432–455.

Goldstein, J., et al. 1973. *Beyond the Best Interests of the Child*. New York: Free Press.

Houlgate, Laurence D. 1980. *The Child and the State*. Baltimore: Johns Hopkins University Press.

In re Baby M. 217 N.J. Super. 313 (1987), 525 A.2d 1128.

In re C.K.G. 173 S.W. 3d 714, 721 (Tenn. 2005).

Johnson v Calvert. 5 Cal. 4th, 84, 81 P.2d776, 19 Cal. Rptr. 2d 494 (1993)

Kant, Immanuel. 1959. *Foundations of the Metaphysics of Morals,* Lewis White Beck. Trans. New York: Liberal Arts Press. First published in 1785.

LaFollette, Hugh. 1981. Licensing Parents. *Philosophy and Public Affairs*.

Locke, John. 1983. McPherson, ed. *Second Treatise of Government*. Indianapolis: Hackett. First published in 1690.

Mill, John Stuart. 1979. *On Liberty*. Indianapolis Hackett. First published in 1861.

Purdy, Laura M. 1987. *The Morality of the New Reproductive Technologies*. Winter: Journal of Social Philosophy.

Sorkow, Judge Harvey M. 1987. In re Baby M, Family Law Reporter. April 7, vol. 13.

Statsky, William P. 2013. *Family Law: The Essentials*. 3rd ed. Stamford: Cengage Learning.

Chapter 12
Frozen Embryos

> *"We would not enforce an agreement that would compel one donor to become a parent against his or her will ... forced procreation is not an area amenable to judicial enforcement."*
>
> J. A. D'Annunzio *M.B. v J.B.* (2000)
>
> *"An in vitro fertilized human ovum exists as a juridical person."*
>
> Louisiana Health Law LA-RS 9 §121 (1986)

Abstract The philosophical and normative questions raised in this chapter are raised in disputes between divorcing couples over the disposition of previously frozen embryos stored in a cryopreservation facility for future use. We examine several court cases in which judges have made explicit and implicit references to rights and interests: for example, a person's right to procreate, a right not to procreate and the interests of future persons. We will discuss whether these concerns might lead to legislation placing justifiable limits on relevant pre-divorce contracts created before decisions are made about in-vitro fertilization and storage.

12.1 Divorce and Cryopreserved Embryos

In the previous chapter we discussed the first of two normative problems arising from Assisted Reproductive Technology. The second problem emerged after the invention and use of cryopreservation technology. Cryopreservation is generally defined as "the process of cooling and storing cells, tissues, or organs at very low temperatures to maintain their viability." In the cases to be discussed below, pre-embryos have been cooled and stored at a temperature below the freezing point. This permits high rates of survivability of the embryos upon thawing. The normative problems occur when there is a disagreement between a husband and wife who file for divorce before all their frozen embryos are used. Their disagreement is about the final disposition of the embryos.

L.D. Houlgate, *Philosophy, Law and the Family*, AMINTAPHIL: The Philosophical Foundations of Law and Justice 7,
DOI 10.1007/978-3-319-51121-4_12

In a series of cases over the past few years, state supreme courts in Tennessee, New York, Massachusetts, and New Jersey have made groundbreaking decisions settling disputes between divorcing couples over the custody and disposition of frozen embryos. When the frozen embryo cases first came before the state courts there were no relevant statutes and no previous cases on which judges could rely in developing arguments for their decisions. Hence, as so often happens in these situations, the courts fell back on time-tested political and/or moral considerations to reach their conclusions. These are often disguised as principles of social or public policy. And it is here where Mill's warning about our dependence on an "internal oracle of justice" is relevant (Sect. 11.1). Absent statutory law and precedent, is it possible to provide non-arbitrary reasons for awarding custody of frozen embryos to one party rather than the other?

12.2 Four Cases

In *Davis v. Davis* (1992), a divorce case that eventually found its way to the Supreme Court of Tennessee, the wife sought custody of the embryos so that she could donate them to another couple for implantation. Declaring that embryos are entitled to "special respect because of their potential for human life," the court recognized that the husband and wife both had legitimate interests in the future of the frozen embryos. The wife wanted to become a genetic parent but her husband had an equally strong interest in avoiding this. She wanted to procreate and he did not. The court regretted the fact that there was no pre-divorce agreement between the couple regarding disposition of the embryos. Therefore, the court balanced the equitable interests of the two parties and concluded that the husband's interest in avoiding parenthood outweighed the wife's desire to become a genetic parent through donation of the embryos to a childless couple.

In the 1998 case of *Kass v. Kass* the Supreme Court of New York issued its first decision in a dispute over the disposition of frozen embryos. The couple in this case was arguing over the custody of five frozen, stored embryos created five years earlier during their marriage. Now divorced, the woman wanted the embryos implanted, claiming that this was her only chance for genetic motherhood. Her former husband objected to the burdens of unwanted fatherhood, claiming that he and his wife had a prior agreement that in the event of a divorce the embryos would be donated to the IVF program for approved research purposes. The court observed that agreements "should generally be presumed valid and binding, and enforced in any dispute between [the donors]." Therefore, the court enforced the agreement that provided that the frozen embryos be donated to the IVF clinic.

In *A.Z. v. B.Z.* (431 Mass. 150,725 N.E.2d 1051, 2000), the Massachusetts Supreme Judicial Court ruled in the first case ever to come before it involving a dispute over the custody of frozen embryos. In this case, the husband and wife already had twins as a result of IVF. Moreover, they had signed a standard contract at the fertility clinic stating that if they were ever to separate, any fertilized eggs should be "returned to the wife for transfer to the uterus." However, after their divorce, the man wanted the contract declared unenforceable. The trial court, which heard the suit, agreed on the ground that "the wife's desire for more children achieved through IVF is significantly outweighed by the husband's interest in avoiding procreation." When the case was appealed, the Massachusetts high court affirmed the lower court decision. In its ruling, the court implicitly rejected the recommendation of both the Tennessee and New York court that the existence of a pre-IVF agreement regarding disposition of the embryos should be determinative. The court argued that "even had the husband and the wife entered into an unambiguous agreement between themselves regarding the disposition of the frozen embryos, we would not enforce an agreement that would compel one donor to become a parent against his or her will." A contract that forces an individual to procreate is a contract that violates public policy.

Finally, in a case that was appealed to the New Jersey Supreme Court in 2001, a man wanted seven frozen embryos donated or, perhaps, implanted in a future spouse. He maintained that his former wife agreed when they underwent IVF during their marriage, that any unused embryos from the process would be frozen for donation to other childless couples. But the woman, insisting that she does not want to become a biological parent against her will argued that her prior agreement should not be enforced. Instead, she wants the embryos destroyed or used for research (J.B. v M.B. 783 A.2d 707 (2001).

12.3 *A.Z. v. B.Z.*: A Closer Look

Each of these cases raises important questions. We begin by taking a closer look at the arguments presented by counsel and by the lower court in the Massachusetts case when it first came to trial. Since *A.Z. v. B.Z.* is the most recent case decided by a state high court, almost all of the issues presented in the earlier cases were re-introduced here. We can avoid needless repetition by focusing on this case and bring in relevant considerations from other cases as needed.

For ease of identification, I will refer to A.Z. as "Allan" and B.Z. as "Betty." Betty's attorney presented a number of arguments in her behalf. First, she claimed that preventing Betty from using the remaining embryos is unjust because it violates her fundamental right to bear children. Second, in order to counter any fears of Allan arising from his paternity, Betty promised that she would not seek child support from him, nor would she require him to have contact with the child. Third, because she is now 45 years old and the medical risks of implantation at her age are considerable, Betty claimed that this was her last chance to become pregnant. Fourth, because the embryos have been frozen for 8 years, this may be the last opportunity for a successful implantation before they lose viability. Fifth, Betty argued that she went through much more pain and suffering than did Allan during the invasive fertility treatments, and this should give her a stronger compensatory claim to the embryos.[1]

Allan's counsel disputed Betty's claim to the embryos, contending that justice is entirely on his side in his attempt to prevent her from using them to attempt procreation. First, Betty already has two children produced from the frozen embryos. Thus, her desire to have more children from the same source diminishes in significance when weighed against Allan's desire that he not procreate. Second, if Betty wants a large family, then she can always adopt. And if she wants more of her own biological children, she can go through IVF again, using another man's sperm. Third, although not specifically raised at the trial, Allan might claim that he as much of a right to refuse having a biological child with a woman who is no longer his wife as he would have if the woman were a stranger.[2] Moreover, Allan could argue that he has a compelling privacy or liberty interest in avoiding procreation. He wants to be able to control the conditions under which he enters into intimate or personal relationships with others. If Betty were allowed to procreate, using the disputed embryos, then (despite her protestations to the contrary) there would be no guarantee that the child would not pursue Allan for money or personal contact when he or she becomes an adult. Finally, Allan might also want to avoid the guilt that he believes he would inevitably feel if he did not contribute to the child's physical and emotional support.

12.4 The Right to Procreate

Some of the preceding arguments make straightforward appeals to the rule of justice or (indirectly) to the related notion of rights in order to support their conclusion. Our question is whether any of these arguments are sufficiently plausible that we can make a clear choice between Allan and Betty's claims to custody when these claims are supported solely by an appeal to justice.

First, if we accept Betty's claim that she has a fundamental right to bear children, does it follow that depriving her of the custody of the frozen embryos has violated this right? There is a distinction, familiar to political and legal philosophers, between positive and negative rights. "A positive right is a right to other persons' positive

[1] Betty's lawyer, Gretchen Van Ness, said, "I've seen what the man goes through and what the woman goes through for fertility treatments, and the woman goes through so much more. There's surgery; it's incredibly demanding. My client suffered from infections and nausea, she lost both Fallopian tubes. That's major! I understand why people say there should be equality between the sexes on this issue but that ignores how much more invasive IVF treatment is for women." (Coles, 1999:37)

[2] In *Davis* v *Davis* (842 SW2d 588, 604), decided by the Tennessee courts in 1992, there was no written agreement between the Davises about their frozen embryos. Upon divorce, it turned out that neither of them wanted custody. The wife, however, did not want them destroyed. She wanted them donated to a surrogate. The husband did not. The court found in the husband's favor, arguing he had a right to refuse having a biological child with a stranger.

actions; a negative right is a right to other persons' omissions or forbearances. For every positive right we have, someone else has a duty to do something; for every negative right we have, someone else has a duty to refrain from doing something" (Feinberg, 1973:59). It has often been pointed out that there is no right to bear children if this means that we have a positive right to the use of another person's body in order to procreate. Nor is there a right to bear children if this means that infertile couples have the positive right that others *provide* them with the means to bear children, for example, the money and/or the technology to bring about a pregnancy through IVF and transplantation. But this is not what Betty is claiming. She is not asking for the use of another person's body, nor is she asking for charity. She is prepared to pay the clinic's fee for the embryo transfer. In her case, "the right to bear children" is the negative right not to be interfered with by others in her attempt to have a child by implanting the embryos.

It may be objected that by granting ownership of the embryos to Allan, the court is not preventing Betty from bearing a child. It is only preventing her from having a child that will be the product of one of *these* embryos. She has a right to bear children, but she has no right to bear the particular children that these embryos will become if they are implanted. But that is like saying if you prevent me from leaving my office by locking the door, then my right to liberty has not been violated because I can always choose to climb out the window. The fact that Betty has an alternative way to achieve her goal of bearing a child does not imply that denying her use of these embryos is not a violation of her right to bear children. Someone who walked into the clinic and discarded the contents of the petri dish prior to fertilization would violate this right. And someone who discarded the contents of the dish immediately after fertilization, thereby preventing her from implanting the embryo, would also violate it. And this is exactly what she is claiming. Her right to bear children via embryo transfer is violated by a decision of the court to grant custody of the embryos to her former husband who will subsequently order the embryos destroyed.

The right to bear children is not an absolute right. For example, it may be limited to protect innocent people, and in particular, children. Thus, it is plausible to argue that a married couple does not have the right to bear a child if they know in advance that the child will be born with HIV infection and will suffer chronic hospitalization and early death because of a progressively deteriorating immune system. Nor do they have the right to bear a child if they know in advance that the child will probably be neglected or abused (e.g. both of them are alcoholics). In other words, birth may sometimes be unfair to the child, and this places a limit on our right to bear children. But again, none of these conditions reflect Betty's situation. The birth of a child from one or more of the embryos will not be unfair to the child. There is no evidence that the child will be born with a serious physical defect, or that Betty will neglect or abuse the child.[3]

[3] A second limit on the right to bear children is probable harm to others as a result of the child's birth. Under certain rare conditions, bearing a child may detrimentally affect the interests of other persons. For example, in some areas of the world there is only enough food to maintain existing children at the minimum level required for survival. Providing food to newborns in such circumstances puts all other children at risk of malnutrition and death. Childbirth, in these cases, is not an occasion of joy, but an occasion of sorrow.

12.5 The Right not to Procreate

Although it cannot plausibly be argued that the future child will be harmed if Betty gives birth from one of the frozen embryos, Allan might point out that *he* will suffer harm. He has an interest in not procreating and this interest will be detrimentally affected (harmed) if Betty gives birth to a child that is partly his biological product. In fact, he asserts this interest as a right. Allan maintains not only that he has an important interest in not procreating a child from one of the disputed embryos, but also that he has a fundamental right not to procreate.

12.5.1 Interpretations of the Right not to Procreate

There are several interpretations of "the right to not procreate." The interpretations are as diverse as the methods of preventing procreation listed below in Table 12.1:

Except for those who accept the prohibitions of religious law, most would agree that men and women have the right to method A1 and A2 respectively: preventing procreation either by abstaining from sexual intercourse or by practicing contraception. Second, although women have the right to method B3, men have no right to method B4, forcing an abortion on the body of a woman, even if the embryo is biologically related. That is, a man's right to not procreate is limited by the location of the embryo. If the embryo is in the body of the woman (*in-utero*), then no one can invade her body and force her to expel the embryo.[4]

Methods C, D and E are relatively recent because the methods of procreation to which they refer were not technologically feasible until the 1970s. For example, because it is now possible to begin the process of procreation *ex-utero* by donating sperm or eggs for *in vitro* fertilization, we can now speak of *not* procreating by C5 and C6. That is, forbearing or refraining from making these kinds of donation. Moreover, we believe that we have a right to C5 and C6, i.e. it would be a violation of our right to bodily autonomy (the equivalent of rape) to forcibly take a man's sperm or a woman's eggs.

Methods D and E contemplate the existence of an *ex-utero* embryo. In these cases, sperm and eggs have been donated, they have been placed in a petri dish and fertilization has occurred. A woman has the right to D7, that is, she under no obligation to implant an embryo in her body, even if the embryo is biologically hers and even if she is "responsible" for its existence, that is, even if she created it with the

[4] In a recent California case, a genetic father demanded that the hired surrogate abort the three fetuses she was carrying, explaining that he only wanted one child—citing financial concerns. The surrogate (a "genetic stranger" to the fetus) refused and the children were born (seven weeks premature). The surrogate is now suing the father for custody of all three newborns. She is contesting a provision of California law which gives parental rights to the intended parents in a surrogacy agreement. (Langford 2016)

Table 12.1 Some methods of avoiding or preventing procreation

	Female	Male
A	**1.** Abstaining from sexual intercourse; using natural or artificial contraception	**2.** Abstaining from sexual intercourse; using natural or artificial contraception
B	**3.** Abortion of an *in-utero* embryo or fetus	**4.** Forcing a woman to abort an *in-utero* embryo or fetus
C	**5.** Forbearing from the donation of one's eggs to be used for IVF	**6.** Forbearing from the donation of one's sperm to be used for IVF
D	**7.** Forbearing from the implantation of a biologically related *ex-utero* embryo in one's own body	**8.** Preventing the transfer of a biologically related *ex-utero* embryo to the body of the female egg donor
E	**9.** Preventing the transfer of a biologically related *ex-utero* embryo to the body of a third-party gestational surrogate	**10.** Preventing the transfer of a biologically related *ex-utero* embryo to the body of a third-party gestational surrogate

intention of implanting it.[5] Moreover, despite a recent law passed by the Louisiana state legislature declaring *ex utero* embryos to be "juridical persons", no court can force a woman to proceed with an implantation. If a woman has the right to expel an *in utero* embryo during the first trimester of a pregnancy, then she surely has the right to refrain from the implantation of an *ex utero* embryo.

If a man had the physical means to gestate an embryo, then we would not hesitate to say that he had a right equivalent to the woman's right to method D7. But since men do not yet have this ability, the closest equivalent is D8, which is, preventing a woman from implanting an *ex-utero* embryo that is biologically his. Moreover, D8 has close parallels to the methods described in E9 and E10. The difference is that in E10 the male sperm donor prevents the transfer of the embryo to an unrelated surrogate (that is, a woman who is not biologically related to the embryo), and in E9 the female egg donor prevents the transfer of the embryo to the uterus of another woman.[6]

12.5.2 Application to Legal Decisions

The question whether men and women have the right to the respective methods of preventing procreation described in D8, E9 and E10 is central to all of the court cases mentioned above. And the answer to this question has been unanimously negative.

[5] Suppose she does implant it. Does this change her moral relationship to the embryo? For example, once implanted, does she now have any obligation she did not have prior to implantation? Does she have an obligation to gestate the embryo until it grows to the point that it can survive outside of her body? For a discussion about the alleged right of an embryo to the "use" of a woman's body, see Judith Thomson, A Defense of Abortion, *Philosophy & Public Affairs*, Vol. 1, no. 1 (Fall 1971).

[6] E9 describes the fact situation in *Davis v Davis* and E10 duplicates the fact situation in the most recent case from New Jersey.

First, according to the court in *AZ v BZ*, the right not to procreate by preventing implantation of an *ex-utero* embryo is interpreted as or is derived from the right not to enter into intimate relationships with others. The court declared that pre-IVF contracts giving custody to a spouse who wants the embryos implanted are unenforceable. "[I]ndividuals shall not be compelled to enter into intimate family relationships, and… the law shall not be used as a mechanism for forcing such relationships when they are not desired" (5).

The phrase "intimate relationship" is significant in the context of child rearing. It is part of the definition of the concept of "psychological" or "social parent." There is a distinction between becoming a biological (or natural) parent and becoming a psychological (or social) parent to a child. The biological parents are those who physically produce the child. In the case of the female, the biological parent is the child's gestational and genetic mother. In the case of the male, the biological parent is the child's genetic father. A psychological parent, on the other hand, has an intimate relationship with the child. He or she "is one who, on a continuing, day-to-day basis, through interaction, companionship, interplay, and mutuality, fulfill the child's psychological needs for a parent, as well as the child's physical needs" (Goldstein, 1973: 98).

In ethics, the right to enter or not enter into an intimate relationship with another person is derived from the general right of self-determination, the right to develop one's own life goals and to pursue them. We have the right to develop our own friendships, marital and parent-child relationships. It is on this basis that Allan asserts a right to prevent his former wife from implanting the remaining embryos: he does not want an intimate relationship with another child. However, Betty has assured the court that she would not seek child support from Allan, nor would she require him to have contact with the child. Of course, Allan is dubious about her ability to prevent the child from contacting him when the child becomes an adult, but Allan should have no doubt about his ability to prevent himself from becoming the child's psychological parent. Allan's biological child cannot enter into an intimate relationship with him unless he willingly reciprocates her attempts to initiate the relationship. Hence, it is entirely up to Allan whether he wishes to become the child's psychological father when she is born.[7] To put it another way, if there is a right not to be forced into intimate relationships with others, this right is not threatened by the enforcement of a contract that compels a man to become a mere biological father.

Is there anything left of Allan's claim that he has a right to prevent the implantation of an *ex-utero* embryo in Betty's uterus? I believe that there is. The right might be derived from the right of bodily autonomy, the right to control one's body and the

[7] This conclusion is consistent with Professor Laurie Schrage's claim that "in consenting to sex, neither a man nor a woman gives consent to become a parent, just as in consenting to any activity, one does not consent to yield to all the accidental outcomes that might flow from that activity" (*Opinionator*, NY Times 2013). By analogy, in consenting to having pre-embryos frozen, one does not consent to become a parent by having them implanted after a divorce, nor does one consent to have them donated to others.

use of a product of one's body, including the right to alienate that product (to waste or destroy it). Suppose that Allan has provided his sperm and Betty has provided her ripe eggs to the fertility clinic. Before fertilization takes place, Allan changes his mind. He decides that that he does not want a child. He wants his sperm destroyed, that is, he wants to use method D6. I believe that most of us would agree that he has a right to do this. But if this is true, then he also has a right to D8, that is, a right to prevent Betty from implanting any egg that has already been fertilized. The mere fact that fertilization has now taken place in a petri dish is not significant. If you believe that Allan has the right to have his sperm destroyed immediately prior to fertilization, then he also has the right to have the fertilized egg (the embryo) destroyed. In sum, Allan's right to D8 and the corresponding right to the methods described in E9 and E10 are instances of the general right to control and consent to the use of a product of one's own body.

Of course there are limits to the right to control (and alienate) a product of our body. The product of our body must at least be extra-corporeal. If the embryo has already been implanted in Betty, Allan cannot order an abortion performed on her in order to destroy the embryo (he does not have the right to method B4). She has a fundamental right not to have her body invaded by others without her consent. Any attempt to perform an abortion on her without her consent would rightly be regarded as an assault.

Another limitation on the right to control a product of our body is that control must be necessary in order to protect ourselves from probable harm. Unless we can prove that we will suffer harm as a consequence of loss of control, then we do not have a right to control how a sperm, an egg, or even an embryo is used. In order to prove this, consider the following analogy. Suppose that an unmarried man makes an anonymous donation of sperm to a sperm bank. Prior to the donation he signs an agreement giving control of future use of the sperm to the clinic. He understands that it will probably be used to fertilize an egg. The clinic promises that his identity will not be made known to the child or to the child's mother. If he later changes his mind on the ground that he does not want his sperm used to procreate, I do not see any moral or legal problem in holding him to his contract. He has waived his right to the future use of his sperm and *because his donation is anonymous*, keeping him to his agreement will cause him no harm. His right to privacy (the right to control information about his identity) is not threatened. He may become a biological father, but he will never know his biological child and she will never know him.

Let us carry this case one step further. Suppose that the sperm he has donated has recently been placed in a petri dish with an egg provided by an anonymous female donor. Fertilization has just occurred. He walks into the clinic and demands that the contents of the dish be discarded. Once again, his demand would be rejected by the court, and rightly so. He has signed a valid agreement giving the fertility clinic control over the use of his sperm, his bodily product. If we do not think it wrong for the court to reject his demand to destroy his sperm before fertilization has taken place, then I do not see how it could be wrong for the court to destroy the contents of the petri dish after fertilization has taken place. Once again, the reason for this is the anonymous nature of his donation. He will suffer no harm through the birth of a child from the implantation of the embryo. And here lies the relevant moral difference between this case and divorce custody disputes over frozen embryos. In the case of Allan and Betty, there are no guarantees that the child will never know that Allan is her biological father. If the frozen embryo is given to Betty and a child is born, then Allan is not only a biological father, but his right to the privacy of his identity has been threatened, with all the possibly deleterious consequences mentioned earlier (e.g. the emotional burden of guilt, possible future claims for child support, inheritance, etc.). Although Allan can decide whether or not he wants to enter into an intimate relationship with his child, it is the fact that he might need to make a future difficult choice that is out of his control. The very existence of a newborn child places on him a psychological burden that he wants to avoid. He may have to make the emotionally difficult choice of whether to become a psychological parent to the child. It is *the decision to become intimate*, not the intimacy that will cause him harm.

It follows that there is a right to control the products of one's body, including one's sperm, egg, and the resulting embryo, but only when the product is extra corporeal and when control of the extra corporeal products is necessary to prevent harm to an important individual interest. The fact that an embryo, if implanted, will become one's biological child is not sufficient to establish a right to control and custody. One must also show that the implantation of the embryo will create an unavoidable burden (emotional, financial, etc.) on the non-consenting parent.

Finally, there are some extra-corporeal products of our body that we have no right to waste or destroy, e.g. our biological children. My biological child is a product of my body, but I have no right to kill my child. And there are some who would argue that since an embryo, if implanted, will become a future child, it has the right not to be destroyed. These suggestions will be discussed in a later section. At this point the argument is only that Allan can make a plausible claim for custody of the frozen embryos on the ground that he has a right not to procreate, where this is interpreted as a right to consent to what happens to his bodily products, with the limitation that (a) the bodily product must be extra corporeal, and (b) the product of his body might be used in ways that could cause him harm.

12.6 Appeals to Utility

The upshot of preceding discussion is that both Allan and Betty have at least one principle of justice that appear as plausible if not true: the principle (invoked by Allan) that says that it is unjust to deprive someone of his right not to procreate, and the principle (invoked by Betty) that says that it is unjust to deprive her of the right to procreate, interpreted as the right not to be interfered with by others in the attempt to bear a child. Assuming that the application of these principles to the particular case is accurate, and if Allan and Betty are not compelled to take into consideration any other maxim of justice than the ones they have selected, then we can declare each of them to be triumphant. To apply Mill's observation here, "each, from his own point of view, is unassailable, and any choice between them, on grounds of justice, must be perfectly arbitrary …" (Mill, 1979:56–57).

Mill was convinced that the only way to reach a decision in cases of ethical conflict is by appeal to the principle of utility. He argues that we need to look at both the good and the bad consequences of each alternative course of action, weigh or balance the consequences and then choose the act that produces the greatest *net utility* (the greatest balance of good over bad consequences. This method appears to be part of the basis of Judge Nesi's decision in *A.Z. v. B.Z.*). When he wrote that "the wife's desire for *more* children achieved through IVF is significantly outweighed by the husband's interest in avoiding procreation" (my emphasis).[8] The judge implies that there is a coherent way of measuring and comparing interpersonal utilities, but if there is a way to do this, then it is not revealed in his decision. Why is Betty's *desire* for more children "significantly outweighed" by Allan's *interest* in avoiding procreation? If she had no children, then would we say that her desire for one child would be outweighed, but not significantly outweighed by Allan's interest? Does a desire for children diminish in weight proportional to the more children that you have? If I want three children, but I've only got two, does my desire for a third child weigh less than a desire for a second child when I've only got one (or a desire for a first child when I've got none)?

Similar questions can be raised about the process of determining the weight of an interest. Allan maintains that he has an interest in avoiding procreation that is weightier than Betty's desire to procreate a third child. We can safely assume that the probable emotional and financial setbacks from the birth of a third biological child are what give strength and weight to Allan's interest in avoiding procreation. If so, then Betty can counter that she will suffer emotionally by being deprived of the opportunity to have another child that is the biological product of her and Allan's embryo, despite Allan's protestations that this is irrational.[9]

Let us assume, then, that both Allan and Betty will be harmed if the other is granted custody of the stored embryos. Let us also assume that it is irrelevant to determining the weight of Betty's desire that two children have already been produced from the stored vials. This being the case, then unless we are given further information it is not at all clear whose interest is weightier. We do not know, for

---

[8] Judge Nesi also seems to imply that it is *not unjust* to deny someone more than she needs of a desirable commodity (babies, cars, food, money, etc.), especially if having it will detrimentally affect the interests of others. If you've already got something of what you need, and having more will affect the interest of someone else, then it is not unjust to deny you more. It is Judge Nesi's belief that since Betty has her *fair share* of children then her desire to have another child should have less weight than her husband's desire that he not procreate. Of course, this interpretation of Judge Nesi's argument falters on the absurd assumption that there is a "fair share" of children allotted to each of us.

[9] We can imagine Allan contending that it is irrational for Betty to want his child even while divorcing him. However, there may be perfectly good reasons for Betty wanting his child, for example, she may want a child with Allan's physical characteristics. Moreover, even if we still think that Betty's desire is irrational, this does not make it any less a desire which, if not satisfied, produces misery in the person who has it.

example, the *strength* of Betty's desire for more children or the *weight* of Allan's interest that he not procreate. Nor can we predict the amount and duration of her happiness or the amount and duration of Allan's misery if she succeeds in having children.

I conclude that the court has no coherent basis for deciding which of the two competing desires and interests is "weightier." Contrary to Mill's assertions, appeals to consequences and to the principle of utility to decide who should get custody of a frozen embryo when its "parents" divorce appear to be as unhelpful as appeals to moral rights and the rules of justice.

12.7 Non-discretionary Standards

We seem to be at an impasse. Neither of the traditional approaches to the resolution of ethical dilemmas are of much help in resolving disputes over who should get custody of frozen embryos when a couple divorces. Both approaches lead to judicial decisions that appear to be arbitrary, in the sense that the opposite decision granting custody of the embryos to the other party in the dispute could have been just as well grounded.

Whenever there is an impression of arbitrariness in judicial decision-making, legislators have sometimes responded by removing discretion from judges. For example, a law might be passed that requires fertility clinics to destroy frozen embryos in the event of a divorce between the couple that produced them. Alternatively, legislators might decide that the embryos should always remain in the custody of the woman (Andrews, 1986:357), and/or that she must attempt procreation with the remaining embryos (Note, 1993: *CLR* 305; Comment, 1992: *UMLR* 803). In either case, dispute settling would be automatic.

The problem with nondiscretionary standards is that they beg all of the questions with which we have been dealing. Why ought the embryos to be destroyed if there are situations in which at least one of the parties to the divorce wants to use them to procreate (as in the case of Allan and Betty)? Why ought the embryos to be given to the woman if there might be men who would like to use a surrogate for the purpose of procreation? Legislative answers to these questions are likely to be seen as just as arbitrary as the ruling of judges who are given discretion to make custody decisions.

12.8 Pre-IVF Contracts

Another solution is for the state to require, *as a condition for IVF treatment*, that couples create their own agreement on the disposition of remaining embryos in the event of a divorce or separation. The fertility clinic had asked Allan and Betty to sign an agreement giving custody to Betty in the event of a divorce or separation.

The court declared the contract unenforceable. However, if it been upheld, it is important to recognize that the terms of the agreement were entirely dictated by the clinic, requiring in all cases that custody should be granted to the woman. Once again, an important moral question was begged: Why should a contract give automatic preference to one of the parties in a potential custody dispute?

The pre-IVF contract I wish to discuss here differs in the important respect that *the couple seeking IVF, not the fertility clinic*, dictate its terms, including such important matters as the final disposition of remaining embryos and whether or not it will be relevant that other children have been successfully produced from previous transplantations. The fertility clinic can advise them on the terms of their contract, but the decision about disposition is entirely theirs. They may decide that the remaining embryos be destroyed, be given to the woman, or be given to the man.

This would be the parents' "last friendly agreement" about the custody of any frozen embryos in the event that they should divorce. The agreement is always open to renegotiation at any time before or after the birth of any children from the IVF treatment, and even before or after any divorce. They need not be held to the original contract if *both* parties want to change its terms. Its effect would be to assure that, if the parents did divorce and could not then agree on custody, this agreement would exist between them and the court would hold them to it.[10]

This is the approach to the solution of embryo custody disputes that was favored by both the Tennessee and the New York courts referred to earlier. In *Davis v. Davis*, the Tennessee court stated that although there was no agreement between the donors regarding disposition of the embryos, such agreements "should be presumed valid and should be enforced." (597). In *Kass v. Kass,* the Court of Appeals of New York agreed with the Tennessee court position. Pre-IVF contracts between donors "should generally be presumed valid and binding, and enforced in any dispute between [the donors]." (597) While recognizing that it is difficult for donors to anticipate the future of their relationship, the court concluded that such agreements minimize misunderstanding, maximize procreative liberty, and provide needed certainty to IVF programs.

There are other arguments in favor of encouraging and enforcing pre-IVF agreements about the disposition of frozen embryos in the event of a divorce or separation. First, this solution is consistent with John Stuart Mill's contention that the state should not interfere with the self-regarding affairs of individuals. They should be left free to make their own private arrangements. Of course, by requiring that couples applying for IVF enter into a binding agreement on the disposition of remaining embryos in the event of a future divorce or separation, we are in effect forcing them to be free. This may be seen as paradoxical, but surely part of the value of freedom is that one takes responsibility for one's choices. To require that donors

[10] In *Kass v Kass*, the New York Supreme Court affirmed the judgement of the New York Court of Appeals enforcing an agreement of the parties that provided for donation of their frozen embryos to the IVF program for approved research purposes. They noted that the court "unanimously recognized that when parties to an IVF procedure have themselves determined the disposition of any unused fertilized eggs, their agreement should control." (*Id.*,at p. 554).

keep to their last friendly agreement about the disposition of frozen embryos is to require that they take responsibility for this decision and not throw it onto the courts.

And this suggests a second rationale. By keeping custody decisions out of the courts, we achieve a significant decrease in litigation. This may adversely affect the economic interests of some law firms, but it is a highly desirable consequence in light of today's crowded court calendars and the heavy financial and emotional toll that lengthy custody battles take on those who wage them.

12.9 Limits on the Content of Pre-IVF Contracts

Two limits have been proposed for pre-IVF contracts: no contract should require that someone be forced to procreate against their will, and no contract should ignore the status of the future personhood of the embryo.

12.9.1 Forced Procreation

I mentioned at the outset of this paper that the Massachusetts High Court rejected the recommendation of both the Tennessee and New York court that pre-IVF agreements should always be enforced. The court argued that such contracts violated "public policy" on the ground that they "would not enforce an agreement that would compel one donor to become a parent against his or her will." (Sect. 12.3).

This is an important objection to the preceding proposal. It is part of a more general objection that there are legitimate limits upon freedom of contract that are posed by the rights of the parties to the contract. Suppose that a couple's pre-IVF contract provides that, in the event of a divorce, any frozen embryos should be carried to term in the mother's womb. Such an agreement cannot be binding on her, even if she did voluntarily enter into it, because it would infringe upon a right that cannot be waived by contract. A woman has a fundamental right not to procreate and she cannot be held to a prior agreement that says that will gestate and attempt to bring to term one or more of the remaining embryos.

The solution to the problem posed by the court's objection is not to abandon the idea of a "last friendly agreement," but to require that pre-IVF contracts be fashioned in a way that is consistent with fundamental rights, legitimate interests, and public policy. The question is whether we can come to some agreement about the nature of these rights and interests. Mindful of Mill's warnings about the difficulty of deciding ethical dilemmas by appealing to rights, and the warnings of Mill's non-utilitarian opponents that the application of the principle of utility does not always lead to unambiguous ethical conclusions, what restrictions should we place on pre-IVF contracts? One restriction has already been mentioned. No contract shall compel a woman to procreate. She cannot be required to undergo transplantation of the frozen embryos. Her constitutional right to *terminate* a pregnancy implies a right not to *begin* a pregnancy. Therefore, simply by an appeal to the right to privacy guaranteed under the U.S. Constitution, we can unambiguously declare that no pre-IVF contract shall require a woman to transplant, gestate and bring to term one of her own embryos.

However, in *A.Z. v. B.Z.*, the court did not contemplate forced intrusions on the body of the woman. Instead, by "the right not to procreate," they meant "the right not to enter into intimate relationships." The individual who they decided had this right was the former husband. Of course, the wife could be forced to enter an intimate relationship with a child in a parallel way. Suppose, for example, she enters into a pre-IVF agreement with her husband giving custody of the embryos to him in the event of a divorce. She discovers that instead of ordering the destruction of the embryos he wants to have them implanted in a surrogate who has agreed to carry them to term. Can his former wife be held to the contract, or should the contract be declared unenforceable on the ground that she has a non-waivable right not to procreate?[11]

I had earlier argued that the right not to enter into intimate relationships does not apply. I had argued this on the ground that it is up to us to decide whether or not to become a psychological parent to a child. If Betty gives birth to a child from one of the embryos, then Allan becomes the child's biological father, but he can avoid having an intimate relationship with the child. In general, a pre-IVF contract can always contain language guaranteeing that the other party need not be a part of the child's life.

However, the question before us is different. Assuming that there is a right not to enter into an intimate relationship and that it applies in this and other cases, is this right fundamental in the sense that it cannot be waived through a pre-IVF contract? Let me offer a definition of "fundamental." A right is fundamental when it is not open to the court to "weigh" the protection afforded by that right against other considerations. A fundamental right always has more weight than any possible combination of opposing interests, public or private.[12] For example, I cannot contract with another person to become her slave, even if this would promote everyone's interests.

Is this how we understand the right not to enter into intimate relationships? If it is, then like the right to liberty, the court should not be able to weigh or balance it against any competing private or public interests. But in fact, this is not how the legal system understands the right not to be forced into an intimate relationship with a child. For example, the object of a paternity suit is to compel a man suspected of being the biological father of a child to take a blood test in order to determine whether he is in fact the father. "Today, it is the public policy of most states that a determination of paternity through a judicial proceeding is in each child's best interests, absent some compelling reason why the issue of paternity should not be

[11] As far as I am aware, no cases based on this factual circumstance have yet appeared before the courts, but the situation is certainly possible, and as has happened so often in the history of American law, a case will appear with precisely this set of facts.

[12] This is the definition of "fundamental right" described at Sect. 10.4.2.

determined."(Kramer, 362) The threat to a man of an intimate relationship with the child is not compelling. He cannot resist the blood test on the ground that he has a right not to be put in the emotionally difficult position of choosing whether or not to become the child's psychological parent.

It follows that the right not to procreate, understood as the right not to be compelled to enter an intimate relationship, is not a fundamental right. Hence, it can be waived by a pre-IVF contract. That is, the interest in keeping a person to a contractual agreement giving custody of embryos to a partner who wants to use them to procreate can conceivably outweigh his or her interest in not procreating.

12.9.2 Interests of Future Persons

The final limitation on the content of a pre-IVF contract that I want to discuss derives from the suggestion that such contracts should contemplate the interest of the future child that the embryo will become if implanted and brought to term. In U.S. law, the embryo has no legal status. Hence, there is no obligation on the part of the court to take into consideration the best interests of the embryo when reaching a custody decision. It has neither the negative right not to be killed, nor the right positive right to a woman's uterus. And yet, as I indicated in my introduction, the embryo is not mere property. The embryo has the potential to become a future person. What if the pre-IVF contract provides that, in the event of a divorce, the woman should have the embryos to do with as she wills, but after the divorce the man claims that she is a chronic alcoholic. He contends that if she implants an embryo, then there is a high probability that she will damage it during pregnancy in such a way as to cause fetal alcohol syndrome in the child that the embryo will become, if it lives. By way of analogy, if a couple drew up a contract prior to marriage providing that, in the event of a divorce, the woman should get custody of any children, most states will not allow such an agreement to be binding upon divorce (Kramer, 1994:92–93). The reason for refusing to enforce such pre-marital contracts is that in child custody disputes there is a third party involved, namely the child. The court may determine that placement in the mother's custody is not in the child's best interests.[13] But if the best interest of the child standard is supposed to make the child's welfare paramount in child custody disputes, this should be no different when an IVF agreement involves bringing into existence a future child.

I find this argument entirely convincing and I would support placing a corresponding limit on pre-IVF contracts. However, there are two difficulties with this proposal, both involving possibly unacceptable consequences. First, if we say that no pre-IVF contract will be enforced that threatens damage to the embryo, then don't we also have to say that no placement shall be made that threatens death to the

[13] For example, "[c]urrent substance abuse, addiction to drugs or alcohol, and the like will almost always result in the parent not having such problems being awarded custody of the child or children in dispute." (Kramer, 69).

embryo? If we decide to adopt a policy that prevents the destruction of an *ex-utero* embryo, then we must extend this to the protection of all *in-utero* embryos. I don't believe that this follows. We cannot harm the future child by discarding or destroying an embryo. If the embryo is discarded, then there will be no future child. If there is no child, then there is no subject of harm. I can no more harm a future child by discarding an embryo than I can harm a future child by discarding the contents of a petri dish before fertilization takes place or by using artificial contraceptives to prevent conception during sexual intercourse.

The second consequence is practical. If courts are directed to consider the best interests of the future child in making embryo custody decisions, then all of the standards now used to determine best interests in divorce child custody disputes must be employed, e.g. the quality of the home environment and the nature of parental guidance that can be offered, the character and reputation of the parties involved, the ability to provide for the continued emotional and intellectual needs and development of the child; the potentiality of maintaining natural family relationships; and material opportunities affecting the future of the child. Courts also consider parental fitness, including moral fitness; love and affection of the parent for the child, and past conduct affecting the child's needs.

The problem is that these factors are so vague that the judge has virtually unlimited discretion when awarding custody. The judge must determine whether the child-rearing conduct of one of the disputants will be superior to the other, and this assumes that the judge has a defensible concept of what counts as "good" parenting and the correlative concept of the child's "best interests." It also implies that the judge can obtain the empirical information needed to make accurate predictions about the child's future with either parent. In short, the best interest standard forces judges to answer what most would regard as unanswerable, predictive questions.

I acknowledge this practical difficulty, but I see no way to avoid considering the best interests of the future child in making frozen embryo decisions. If a future child can suffer future harm as a result of being placed with a particular custodian while still in an embryonic state, then we have an obligation to prevent or minimize the probability of harm.

Questions for Thought and Discussion

1. Suppose that a husband and wife file for divorce before all their frozen embryos are used. How should we refer to the relationship between them and the embryos? Should we call it "custody" or "ownership"? Does it matter which one of these terms we use? Does the term we use have any moral or legal relevance for a dispute between them about what should be done with the embryos? (Suppose that the husband wants them destroyed, but she wants them kept alive so they can be implanted at some future time).
2. In *Davis v Davis* the wife wanted to donate the frozen embryos to a childless couple. The husband was opposed to this. He wanted the embryos destroyed. They had no prior agreement about the disposition of any of the unused embryos in the cryopreservation facility. Nor were there any existing statutes in their state to help the court decide what to do. How would you decide this case, and why?

3. A statute in Louisiana specifies that a human embryo is a fertilized "human" ovum "with certain rights granted by law." This applies both to frozen embryos and *in vitro* fertilized human ova prior to implantation or freezing. In both cases, the statute declares that the embryo is a juridical person which shall not be intentionally destroyed. What impact would the Louisiana statute have on settling disputes between divorcing couples about the disposition of their frozen embryos?
4. Should ART and cryopreservation technologies be regulated? In 2009, a single mother of six children gave birth to eight additional children (octuplets) after undergoing IVF (in vitro fertilization and transfer of the resulting embryo to the uterus). Should there be a restriction on the number of embryos that can be transplanted in one patient? Should other regulations of fertility clinics be put in place? (For example, to prevent mix-ups in which one woman's fertilized egg is mistakenly implanted in another woman, or one man's sperm is used to fertilize the wrong woman's egg?)

References

Andrews, N. 1986. The legal status of the embryo. *Loyola Law Review* 32: 357–409.

Coles, J. 1999. The custody battle for an embryo. *The Times* (London), 1 December.

Feinberg, Joel. 1973. *Social philosophy*. Englewood Cliffs: Prentice-Hall.

Goldstein, Joseph, Anna Freud, and Albert J. Solnit. 1973. *Beyond the best interests of the child*. New York: The Free Press.

Kramer, Donald E. 1994. *Legal rights of children*. Vol. 1. New York: McGraw-Hill.

Langford, Cameron. 2016. After fighting abortion demand, surrogate mom demands custody. *Courthouse news service*. February 4. http://www.courthousenews.com/2016/02/04/after-fighting-abortion-demand-surrogate-mom-demands-custody.htm Accessed 5 April 2016.

Mill, J.S. 1979. Utilitarianism. Indianapolis: Hackett, 1979. First published in 1861

Shrage, Laurie. 2013. Is Forced Fatherhood Fair? *Opinionator*. *New York Times* 12 June. http://opinionator.blogs.nytimes.com/2013/06/12/is-forced-fatherhood-fair/ Accessed 30 Mar 2016.

Thomson, Judith. 1971. A defense of abortion. *Philosophy & Public Affairs* 1(1): 47–66.

Part V
Alternative Approaches to the Philosophy of Law

Chapter 13
Critical Legal Studies and Feminist Jurisprudence

"If you want to know the law and nothing else, you must look at it as a bad man, who cares only for the material consequences which such knowledge enables him to predict."

J. Oliver Wendell Holmes (1897)

Abstract The theories about the relationship between law and morals discussed in Chaps. 2 and 3 and theories of constitutional interpretation in Chap. 4 by no means exhaust the available legal theories that have been prominent in the philosophical literature. In the debates about the validity of laws pertaining to the family and family relationships one will find not only variations of legal positivism and natural law theory, but approaches to the law that attempt to determine how legal decisions are made by judges. What is legal reasoning and how does it differ (if at all) from moral and political reasoning? How does a judge begin the process of legal reasoning? Is her choice of a guiding principle based on the self-evident nature of the principle, as would be recommended by natural law, or is it to be found in whatever policies and practices promote the general welfare, such that we can say "The law is whatever the judge says that it is"? The latter approach to legal reasoning, first developed in the United States in the 1920s and 1930s, is Legal Realism. It was a reaction to an earlier theory now called Legal Formalism. Another theory, influenced by Legal Realism and originating in the 1970s, is Critical Legal Studies. A fourth, partly influenced by both Legal Realism and CLS, is the radical version of Feminist Legal Theory. We will discuss these in order.

13.1 Formalism and Legal Realism

A word of caution before we proceed. There is a distinction between the common law on the one hand and statutory and constitutional law on the other. The common law is *judge-made* law, that is, law that has been developed in the course of time from the rulings of judges, as opposed to *law* embodied in statutes passed by

L.D. Houlgate, *Philosophy, Law and the Family*, AMINTAPHIL: The Philosophical Foundations of Law and Justice 7,
DOI 10.1007/978-3-319-51121-4_13

legislatures (*statutory law*) or *law* embodied in a written constitution (*constitutional law*). Common law in the United States, originally inherited from Great Britain, is also known as "case-law" or "case-precedent."

The distinction is important because the debate between *formalism* and *realism* is largely contained within the common law. It is not about constitutional interpretation nor the interpretation of federal and state statutes. It is a debate that is both descriptive and prescriptive, that is, it is a debate about how common law cases are and ought to be decided. The theory known as Legal Formalism (also referred to as "formalism") contends that cases are and should be decided deductively from the legal principles found in the common law. In American law schools this led to the "case method" of legal study in which "the student was to confront and analyze the opinions written by judges deciding particular disputes in order to extract from them the fundamental principles of law" (Adams 2013, 102). The guiding source of this approach was a desire to make the study of law a scientific discipline, much like the approach a student would take to the study of biology or sociology. But formalism had a prescriptive side as well. The student of law and the legal professional should not only discover the abstract principles of law (descriptive), but she *ought* to use the results of her research to guide her own legal opinions and recommend these legal principles to others (prescriptive).

The theory known as Legal Realism (also referred to as "realism") rejects all of this. The word "Realism" in the title is important. The realist wants to know what judges and the courts *really* or actually do when they make decisions in the common law cases that come before them. What the realists discovered is that judicial decisions in common law cases are not deductions from a coherent set of rules and principles (as suggested by natural law proponents), nor are they the commands of a sovereign power (as suggested by legal positivism). What, then, is the law? Oliver Wendell Holmes answered this question by using the thought-experiment of "the bad man," mentioned in the epigraph to this chapter. Suppose that a bad man in the late nineteenth century wants to know if he can beat his wife without getting arrested. He discovers that he will not suffer this material consequence. This is all he wants and needs to know about spousal abuse law. He can predict that he will not be dragged into court and prosecuted for abuse if he beats his wife. He can be said to "know the law" because the law is no more than "the prophecies of what the courts will do in fact, and nothing more pretentious" (Holmes 1897).

Richard Posner attempts to sort out the debate between formalism and realism by giving both of these theories "a precise sense" that differs from the meaning used by the original nineteenth century American legal formalists and the later realists. "I want [formalism] to mean the use of deductive logic to derive the outcome of a case from premises accepted as authoritative" (Posner 1986: 181). On the basis of this meaning, a commentator will be able "to pronounce the outcome of the case as being correct or incorrect, in approximately the same way that the solution to a mathematical problem can be pronounced correct or incorrect" *(id.)*. "Realism," by way of contrast, means "deciding a case so that its outcome best promotes public welfare in nonlegalistic terms; it is policy analysis." A "realist" decision, therefore, "is more likely to be judged sound or unsound than correct or incorrect" (*id.*)

The model of deductive logic used by Posner is the classic syllogism "All men are mortal. Socrates is a man; therefore, Socrates is mortal." Applied to legal decision-making, the first or major premise is a concept or definition, and the second or minor premise is a factual statement. To illustrate, let's recall the discussion of the *Baby M* case at (Sect. 11.2.1). The Supreme Court of New Jersey overturned the lower court's decision in favor of the married couple who had hired the surrogate or birth mother. The concept used in their major premise is the common law principle that the legal mother of a child is its birth mother. The factual statement in the minor premise is that the surrogate, not the married woman who hired the surrogate, gave birth to the child. Therefore, as a matter of a valid deductive inference, the surrogate is the child's legal mother. The same logical process also supports the court's decision to give custody to the natural father on the ground that the legal father of a child is the child's biological father. Using a combination of formalism (the use of deductive logic to derive an outcome) and realism (a major premise based on policy analysis), we get the following argument:

Major premise:	The legal mother of a child is its birth mother.
Minor premise:	The surrogate is the birth mother of Baby M.
Conclusion:	(Therefore) The surrogate is the legal mother of Baby M.

Posner points out that "the choice of premises is critical, and that is where public policy comes in" (182). Why decide for the birth mother and the natural (biological) father in a custody dispute? "The reason, if it is a good reason, has to be traceable to some notion of policy rather than just be the result of arbitrary personal preferences or antipathies, or class bias, or some other thoroughly discredited ground of judicial action" (*id.*) But the major premise "cannot be logic." (*id.*) Logic gets you from the major and minor premise to the conclusion. It does not help you get premises. The major premise ("The legal mother of a child is its birth mother") might be derived from a premise that is more general and basic, but at some point in the process of deriving one premise from another you get to a premise "that cannot be obtained or proved by deduction" (*id.*)

Since the correct choice of premises on grounds of policy is more uncertain than the correct deduction of a conclusion from its premises, the formalists preferred to focus on the process of deduction rather than on the choice of premises. They liked to give the impression that the premises were self-evident—meanwhile packing as much into the major premises as possible, to shorten the chain of deductions. The result is Platonism: the idea that concepts exist "out there," like trees or rocks, rather than are created. (Posner 1986, *id.*)

In the same case (*Baby M*), a lower court had previously awarded the infant to the wife and her husband on the quite different principle that the contract they and the surrogate had made was legally enforceable because there was consideration in the form of a legal benefit given to the surrogate (she received a $10,000 fee for her services). The deduction goes like this: "An enforceable contract is a promise supported by consideration. The surrogate's promise to the married couple to hand over the newborn infant was supported by consideration. Therefore, the promise is a contract." Why enforce only promises supported by consideration? Again, the reason has to be traced to some notion of policy. There may be a deduction of the major premise from a "higher" premise that is said to be "self-evident" (for example, a promise without consideration is a logical impossibility), but this requires an argument, and the argument is inevitably an argument about policy, not about semantics.

A second feature of Legal Realism is its rejection of the formalist idea that most of the rules and principles of private law (tort, contract and property) are an apolitical derivation from the common law employed in the nineteenth and early twentieth century American law. The realists argued that there is no such thing as a neutral or apolitical legal principle to be derived from the very idea of a contract, a tort, or property. The major premise in the arguments of formalist judges could always be exposed as decisions involving their personal, moral or political considerations. In the preceding case, the higher court's decision to grant the right of custody to the birth mother was based on the policy that "to the extent possible, children should be brought up by both of their natural parents." The court goes on to justify this policy by appealing to the best interests of the child.[1] A child, instead of starting off its life with as much peace and security as possible, finds itself immediately in a tug-of-war between contending mother and father" (*In the Matter of Baby M*, 1988). The point made by the Legal Realist is that no matter what decision the court reaches, it is *always a political decision* -- in this case it is based on the desire to honor contracts between consenting parties where there is consideration, and/or to protect what it believes to be the best interests of the child.

13.2 Critical Legal Studies

Although the early realists and their allies "were largely concerned with demonstrating that the existing private-law rules were politically biased in favor of the wealthy... their deeper philosophical point was that any set of private-law rules would be politically biased in some way" (Altman 2001, 115). Private law, including family law, was essentially political, and "the only way to evaluate any system of private-law rules is on the basis of some political position or ideology" (Altman, 115). If the tort, contract, property, and power-conferring rules of family law (trusts, wills, marriage, divorce, adoption) are necessarily political, then the question for a Legal Realist is whether these rules should represent the politics of a largely white, male, Christian, wealthy majority or the politics of a diverse group of many races, ethnicities, genders, sexual preferences, religions, and people from all levels of

[1] [As the result of this surrogacy contract] "a child, instead of starting off its life with as much peace and security as possible, finds itself immediately in a tug-of-war between contending mother and father" (*In the Matter of Baby M*, 1988). For a full discussion of the debate over the validity of surrogate mother contracts see Chap. 11.

wealth and income. Both the early realists and their contemporary counterparts in the Critical Legal Studies movement choose the latter course. Their stated aim is to "promote progressive values through the law… [by using] the legal system to reduce inequalities of wealth and power in society" (Altman, 115).

Critical Legal Studies (CLS) is a "direct descendant of American Legal Realism" (Tushnet 1986, 505). CLS accepted the criticism made by the early realists that the assumptions made by formalists that judges can draw on a relatively small collection of abstract concepts—CLS focused on "liberty of contract" and "property rights" --- as the basis for decisions in particular cases and either deduce results from the necessary meanings of the concepts or intuit them from the social understanding of their meanings" (Tushnet, 506). Legal Realists correctly argued that "the concepts were so abstract that they led to contradictory conclusions, and because of social divisions—between employers and organized labor, for example—there could be no broadly shared social understandings on which intuitions could properly be based" (Altman, 106).

While accepting the main ideas of their predecessors, CLS proponents go much further in the critique of modern philosophical theories of law. They reject the mainstream positions that the rule of law exists and the related notion that there is a unique form of legal reasoning, defined as a "distinctively legal method of deciding a case … that is clearly different from a political or moral approach to the case" (Altman, 286).

13.2.1 Legal Reasoning

The phrase "legal reasoning" implies that there is a form of reasoning employed in the law that is distinct from the type of reasoning that ordinary people use in moral or political arguments. If two friends have a private debate about the moral justification of abortion, one of them might argue that "abortion is murder" and give as her reason that "the fetus is a person just like us." Her friend might counter with the argument that abortion is justifiable on the ground that "a woman has the right to do whatever she chooses to do with her body." According to Legal Formalism, both of these people are using incomplete, unclear, arbitrary rules to arrive at their conclusions. Legal reasoning, they contend,

> … uses a complete, clear and consistent body of rules that dictates a single correct answer to any legal question. The job of the judge is to find the applicable rule for a case and then deduce by means of a syllogism the correct answer from the rule in conjunction with the facts of the case (Altman, 292).

According to the formalist a decision on abortion employing legal reasoning would look like this:

Major Premise.	Statement of the Texas Penal Code, Article 1191, prohibiting abortion.[2]
Minor Premise.	John Doe, M.D. administered to a pregnant woman with her consent a drug or medicine and thereby procured an abortion.
Conclusion.	Therefore, John Doe, M.D. has violated the Texas Penal Code.

In this example, it is clear that the argument is valid. The statute cited in the major premise was passed by the Texas legislature and the text of the statute dictates its application. We shall assume that the facts supplied in the minor premise are also true. If the premises are true, then the conclusion must also be true. And the major premise is correctly applied to the facts presented in the minor premise. If two people living in Texas in 1972 had a dispute about the *legality* of abortion they need only look at Article 1191 of the Texas Penal Code to settle the dispute. But if the same two people have an argument about the *morality* of abortion there are no authoritative rules and no common, neutral "moral judge" to which they can both appeal to settle their differences.

There are two replies to this that can be made by the Legal Realist. First, the claim about the difference between legal and moral reasoning works only because we are dealing with a case of statutory not common law. But this is a pyrrhic victory. What is gained by showing that legal reasoning is a deduction by means of a syllogism is lost when one realizes that the major premise is ultimately the product of a legislative policy debate about abortion law. That debate inevitably contains moral appeals to what individual legislators believe will make "good" or "just law" when deciding whether there should be legal restrictions abortion in the form of a penal code.

Second, if the formalist uses common law cases to make her point about legal reasoning, then the argument collapses, as shown in the syllogism used to decide the *Baby M* case cite above (Sect. 13.1). The first premise of the syllogism is a judge's (not a legislator's) choice made on the basis of policy. The judge decides that the legal mother of a newborn child is its birth mother because she believes for a variety of reasons that this is the best policy to pursue. The judge could just as well have endorsed the lower court judge's decision that it is good public policy to enforce a contract in which a birth mother (prior to insemination) has agreed to hand over her newborn for consideration ($10,000). This difference between policy considerations in a single case makes us wonder about other cases. How much indeterminacy is there in legal reasoning?[3]

---

[2] "If any person shall designedly administer to a pregnant woman or knowingly procure to be administered with her consent any drug or medicine, or shall use towards her any violence or means whatever externally or internally applied, and thereby procure an abortion, he shall be confined in the penitentiary not less than two nor more than five years; if it be done without her consent, the punishment shall be doubled. By `abortion' is meant that the life of the fetus or embryo shall be destroyed in the woman's womb or that a premature birth thereof be caused" (Greenhouse and Siegel, 2012).

[3] See also the example of "reliance-based" rules of recovery as an example of how social policy is used to resolve contract disputes (Sect. 11.4).

The answer is "A great deal of indeterminacy." Consider again the reasoning of a trial court in Florida dismissing a woman's law suit seeking recovery for damages suffered by her and members of her family by her husband when he had attacked them with a machete, inflicting serious injury upon them (Sect. 8.4.2). The trial court's argument for dismissal was deductive. It began with a major premise that simply said that one spouse may not sue the other in tort, even where that tort is the intentional one of assault and battery. The second premise is: This is a suit in tort for assault and battery brought by the wife of the man who committed the tort. From these two premises we get the conclusion: The husband is immune and this suit is thereby dismissed. However, once the courts decided to take a careful look at the common law basis for the interspousal immunity doctrine, it became clear that "the public policy reasons for applying it do not exist" (*Waite v Waite*). The implication is that these policy reasons may have existed at one time, but they do not exist now! It is the kind of answer that is at the root of the CLS accusation that legal reasoning is indeterminate, subject to the constant changes over time of societal and judicial values.

CLS theory contends that "the law is mostly indeterminate, [and] if most such issues and questions have no determinate answer—then the whole idea of legal reasoning begins to look very dubious" (Tushnet 1986). Judges are not engaged in a unique type of reasoning when they decide common law cases. They are reasoning in the same way that two or more people reason when they are debating a moral or political topic. The only difference is that judges are using their deductive argument to make an "authoritative" decision that the litigants before them will be compelled to obey.[4] But because the major premise they use in their argument is a statement ultimately based on a debatable policy or moral position, the reasoning is essentially the same as we find in political or moral debates. This is exactly what happened in the *Baby M* case, and according to those feminists who have been influenced by CLS theory, it is exactly what historically has happened in cases that have negatively impacted the lives of women (such as those early cases giving tort immunity to husbands who intentionally injured their wives). Certain moral and political decisions were made in forming the common law doctrine of coverture. These decisions prevented married women from having a legal identity separate from that of their husbands (Sect. 5.3.2). It was only after a painful and prolonged struggle that women broke these bonds. But this only proves the CLS case for indeterminacy. Although new authoritative decisions have been made to replace the old ones, the new decisions are just as political. CLS now has its foot in the door and can legitimately call for a change to progressive values in the law. If all judicial decisions based on common law are indeterminate, then formalists no longer have an argument for the inevitability of a judicial decision based on common law.

[4] "[T]hey are making from scratch an authoritative political decision that the litigants in the case before them will be compelled to obey, unless the decision is overturned on appeal by a judge in a higher court" (Altman, 293)

13.2.2 Stare Decisis *and the Rule of Law*

The previous remarks have consequences for the oft-repeated idea that our government adheres to the rule of law. This phrase is ambiguous, but we shall take it to mean that where there is the rule of law the government is required to exercise its power in accordance with well-established and clearly written rules, regulations, and legal principles. CLS theorists would contend that the legal reasoning of the judiciary employing the rules, regulations and legal principles are neither "clear" nor "well-established." Common law examples of this have been cited in the preceding section (Sect. 13.2.1). The common law rules that comprised the practice of coverture were once "clear," but have long since been abandoned.

CLS progressives are not the only theorists who point out that the rule of law has been abandoned by the courts -- even when considering constitutional cases. In Chap. 4 we briefly discussed the acknowledged fact that the U.S. Supreme Court does not regard its own decisions in prior cases to be "inexorable commands." There are circumstances in which it will abandon these earlier cases and the rulings which were based on them. For example, although the Court in *Planned Parenthood v Casey* was careful to enunciate a standard (for overruling previous decisions) to which they would adhere (see Sect. 4.3), Justice Scalia in a strong dissent in a later case (*Lawrence v Texas*), pointed out that this standard was simply ignored when it overturned a precedent "rendered a mere 17 years" earlier in *Bowers v Hardwick* (478 U.S. 186, 1986). In *Bowers* the Court had upheld a Georgia statute criminalizing "homosexual sodomy," a decision which also involved private consensual sex between two adults. This opinion would ordinarily set a precedent for future cases, but the decision in *Lawrence* was to strike down on due process grounds a Texas law criminalizing private sexual acts between persons of the same sex. Scalia's dissent to this decision underscores the high degree of discretion that the Court has to ignore its prior rulings. To this extent he would agree with the CLS attack on *stare decisis*.

> I do not myself believe in rigid adherence to *stare decisis* in constitutional cases; but I do believe that *we should be consistent rather than manipulative in invoking the doctrine*. Today's opinions in support of reversal do not bother to distinguish–or indeed, even bother to mention–the paean to *stare decisis* coauthored by three Members of today's majority in *Planned Parenthood* v. *Casey* (*Lawrence v Texas*, 539 U.S., 2003)

Scalia quotes the relevant passage in *Planned Parenthood* in which the Court majority had earlier defended *stare decisis*:

> Where, in the performance of its judicial duties, the Court decides a case in such a way as to resolve the sort of intensely divisive controversy reflected in [*Roe v Wade*], … its decision has a dimension that the resolution of the normal case does not carry … [T]o overrule under fire in the absence of the most compelling reason … would subvert the Court's legitimacy beyond any serious question. (*Planned Parenthood v Casey,* 505 U.S., 1992).

Scalia points out that there was "widespread opposition" to the 1986 ruling in *Bowers*. It was as "intensely divisive" as the decision in *Roe v Wade* (1973). But instead of defending *stare decisis* in *Lawrence v Kansas* by *refusing* to overrule Bowers, the Court majority said that the divisiveness is "a reason *in favor* of overruling it" (*Lawrence*, 15–16) This is exactly the opposite of what the Court had previously declared in its standards for overruling a precedent case. It is also the sort of maneuver that proves the point made by CLS theory. When previous constitutional law cases are so easily cast aside as precedents, then the Court undercuts the promise of predictability embedded in the rule of law.

13.2.3 Family Privacy

Another CLS attack on traditional legal theory in general and formalism in particular is to argue that there is no area of private conduct in which "individuals should be at liberty to act without interference by government or law" (Altman, 205) As previously discussed at length in Chap. 5 (Sect. 5.2), the attack begins with the simple observation that zones of privacy are defined and created by the legal system. If it is claimed that a woman and her spouse have privacy to use artificial means of contraception in their own bedroom, then this is only because there are legal rules that prohibit public invasions of a person's home to prevent such this kind of use. It is then pointed out that the very act of defining a zone of privacy should be seen as a kind of legal intervention. Therefore, this makes it conceptually impossible for there to be a "private" sphere of family life from which government should be barred. The state intervenes by virtue of the fact that it has created by law the very area that it makes private.

The reply to this objection is it makes the assumption that a decision *not* to legally intervene in the conduct of an individual (i.e. to refrain from legally prohibiting a particular action) is to be construed as a kind of intervention (Sect. 5.2). Of course, this assumption *guarantees* the conclusion that a sphere of private life does not exist. But the hypothesis that the state *always* intervenes in our lives is now completely *untestable,* and therefore immune to refutation. For not only does the state intervene when it prohibits or requires a certain kind of conduct, but it also intervenes when it does *not* prohibit or require that conduct. In other words, CLS has so defined the concept of legal intervention that no example of non-intervention that we choose to submit could possibly count as evidence against the hypothesis. It follows that the CLS conclusions that there is no such thing as non-intervention and no such thing as a sphere of privacy are *logically empty.*

13.3 Feminist Legal Theory

Before we discuss feminist legal theory (FLT) and the influences on it of CLS, we should attempt to understand how FLT views the status of women in American society. In one sentence, FLT contends that women are now and have always been unjustifiably and systematically discriminated against and oppressed by men. "Discrimination" is a term used to designate unfair treatment. "Oppression" is a term used to designate discriminatory treatment that is built into the very structure of society, that is, built "into its practices, laws, norms, customs and institutions" (Altman, 204). "Patriarchy" is the term used to designate the unfair treatment and oppression of women by men.

Patriarchy takes several forms. Part of the unfair treatment and oppression of women is seen in the traditional view of the family and the role of women in it. For example, women are expected to bear most of the burden of taking care of and raising children. They are believed to be responsible for most domestic chores. Men are regarded as the ultimate decision makers in the household. Working women are deprived of jobs and opportunities routinely given to men. As a result, they do not hold nearly as many positions of power, wealth and influence in society as their male counterparts.

It is easy to find examples of how patriarchy is built into the laws of non-Western societies. In some Middle East countries, a woman can work and travel only with the written permission of her husband or male guardian, and she cannot obtain a divorce without the husband's cooperation (who can obtain divorce simply by filling out a divorce form). Saudi Arabia is seen as the world's most repressive country when it comes to women's rights. "The Wahhabi form of Islam requires women to submit to male guardianship all their lives, which means that men decide where women go outside their home, which school to attend, whom she marries,[5] whether she works and even what medical treatments she takes. Saudi Arabia remains the only country that forbids women to drive" (icdblogsphereteam 2013).

Is there anything comparable to Middle Eastern patriarchy in western countries, including the United States? One answer is that although there were some patriarchal laws and practices in early American common law, such laws and practices no longer exist. The discriminatory marriage and property laws that were part of coverture have long since been discarded.[6] According to liberal feminists,[7] patriarchy is dead.

The liberal feminist declaration of the death of patriarchy has been greatly exaggerated, according to CLS-inspired radical feminism. There may be little evidence of patriarchy in case law, but "patriarchy is alive and well" (Smith 1993) in the informal norms, rules, and practices of society. These norms dictate that the woman,

---

[5] Readers will recall the example at (Sect. 3.2) of a young Moroccan woman who was required to marry her rapist.

[6] Under the doctrine of coverture, "a married woman or *feme covert* was a dependent, like an underage child or a slave, and could not own property in her own name or control her own earnings, except under very specific circumstances. When a husband died, his wife could not be the guardian to their under-age children. Widows did have the right of "dower," a right to property they brought into the marriage as well as to life usage of one-third of their husbands' estate. Though a married woman was not able to sue or sign contracts on her own, her husband often did have to obtain her consent before he sold any property his wife had inherited." (Harvard Business School 2010). See also the discussion of the Family Privacy Doctrine at section "Intrafamily harm and the family privacy principle".

[7] Altman makes a distinction between liberal and radical feminism. The liberal feminist believes that patriarchy has been largely eliminated from Western societies. Radical feminism believes that it still exists. (202)

not the man, shall be the principal caretaker of their children, her word is not taken as seriously as are the words of a man in powerful social institutions, and "girls are systematically encouraged to have lower expectations for themselves than do boys" (Altman, 203). As a probable result of these social factors, gender inequality remains a serious unsolved problem. The phrase "gender inequality" refers to a disparity of power and status between men and women. And this is exactly what we currently have in much of the United States workforce.

- According to the U.S. Census Bureau, women made up 50.8 % of the population in 2010. Also in 2010, women became half of all workers in the U.S. Yet this mere presence of women in the workforce is anything but a show of equality when men hold the top management positions in a variety of professions in extremely unrepresentative numbers: In 2011, women ran only twelve of the Fortune 500 companies.
- In 2010, women made up 31.5 % of all lawyers but were only 19.5 % of partners in U.S. law firms according to Catalyst. Additionally, 11 % of the largest law firms in the U.S. had no women on their governing committees.
- No state has ever achieved federal or state judgeships gender equality. Women held only 23 % of all federal judgeships and only 27 % of state judgeships in 2010. In its 220-year history, only four women justices have served on the Supreme Court although we currently have the all-time high of three justices out of nine.
- Today in the 112th Congress women hold 17 Senate seats out of 100 and hold 92 out of 435 House seats.
- The United States has never had a woman President.
- Men outnumber women at a rate of 73 % vs. 27 % in all sectors of employment for science and engineering as of 2009.
- Obviously, there are large disparities in the number of women managers and leaders despite the fact that women make up half of the workforce. This is true gender inequality, a gender difference in power and status. Ignoring gender inequality in the U.S. or assuming the glass ceiling is broken when it's not, is dangerous. In the World Economic Forum's Global Gender Gap Report of 2010, the United States ranked number 19 in terms of gender equality (Ferro 2012)

The author of the preceding litany of wrongs against women writes that "a failure to recognize the problem of gender inequality in the U.S. is the perfect way to assure that we'll never solve the problem" (Ferro, id.). But can any of the functions of family law (Sect. 1.2) be used to correct social (non-legal) forms of discrimination against women, such as those mentioned above?

First, as is now the case in some Scandinavian countries, federal legislation could be passed requiring paid parental leave when a child is born or adopted. For example, in Sweden parents are entitled to share 480 days, or around 16 months, of paid parental leave. Not only mothers but 85 % of fathers take parental leave. (Swedish Institute 2013–2016). Second, gender inequality at work could be dealt with by laws requiring that all employers actively pursue specific goals to promote equality between men and women. For example, federal law could prohibit discrimination against any employee who is, has been or is willing to take parental leave. Third, in order to cover the pay gap between men and women,[8] federal legislation could be passed requiring either equal pay for equal work or by requiring pay equity for work of equal value. In the former case, equal pay compares the pay of incumbents in the same or very similar jobs. In the latter, pay equity compares the value and pay of different jobs, such as nurse and electrician.

There is another, more controversial solution specifically targeted at women and the goal of providing them with a level playing field in the competition with men for an equal chance to make it up the chain of command in the workforce. The solution of requiring paid parental leave applies equally to men and to women. Under Swedish law both genders are equally entitled to take leave when a child is born or adopted. But there is a second approach. It involves recognizing that there are certain differences between men and women that make it unfair to women when society requires that the rules be the same for both. This is most obvious in the United States when a woman wants to take a leave of absence during the final stages of her pregnancy but is denied disability benefits from the same company for the period of time she is not at work. If she had been unable to work because of accident or illness she would have received disability benefits. Women get pregnant and are sometimes disabled by their pregnancy. Men do not get pregnant. To deny women a benefit on the basis of this difference between women and men is discriminatory.

The "difference" approach to correct gender inequalities is illustrated by a 1974 Supreme Court case (*Geduldig v Aiello* 1974). Carolyn Aiello experienced disability as result of complications during her pregnancy. She was denied benefits from California's Disability Fund under the state's Unemployment Insurance Code. Aiello and other disabled women who were also denied benefits for the same reason challenged the statute as a violation of the Equal Protection Clause of the Fourteenth Amendment, claiming that by disallowing payments related to pregnancy, California inevitably discriminates against women. The U.S. District Court agreed and declared the statute unconstitutional. The state of California appealed this decision to the Supreme Court, but the court overruled, arguing that the list of conditions covered by the disability insurance system is not exclusive. Other conditions were not covered that affect both men and women. Furthermore, there are conditions not covered by the system that affect both men and women. Moreover, if all disabling conditions were included, this would result in lesser amounts of funding for all other more serious conditions. Altman interprets the majority decision as saying that the distinction is between pregnant persons and non-pregnant persons (that is, the disabling condition), not between women and women (that is, gender). On this basis the Court ruled that there is no unconstitutional discrimination under the Fourteenth Amendment (Altman, 217).

[8] Compiling data from the Census Bureau, the Department of Education and the Bureau of Labor Statistics, AAUW calculated the median salaries for full-time employment in all 50 states and the District of Columbia. In the U.S., the average woman is paid 23 percent less than the average man (The Huffington Post. 2014).

Radical feminists would object to the Supreme Court ruling in *Geduldig* by rejecting the premise that attention to the difference between men and women regarding pregnancy is "special treatment." They see it as a leveling of the playing field, as a way of giving pregnant women equal opportunity. Since women are living in a patriarchal society, they need programs that treat them differently in order to have a fair chance to achieve economic independence. Here is an analogy. Imagine a society in which a large population of persons do not have the same ability to speak, read or write the language of the majority population. This makes it much more difficult for them to read the law texts that are written in the language of the majority. There is no way to correct this disability, and there are no texts available in their language. It would hardly be fair treatment if professors used exactly the same standards to grade both groups of students. Those unable to fully understand because of their disability are unfairly treated if that difference is ignored and exactly the same rules are applied to them as to the students who do not have the same disability. The best solution, of course, is to make sure that all students have an equal chance to succeed on the same examination. This can be accomplished by correcting the language deficit of those who have the disability. And, by analogy, the best way to level the field on which men and women "play" is to create a society in which patriarchy is eliminated and no one suffers on account of gender.

Gender equality could be achieved in the U.S. Congress by requiring that a number of seats in the Senate and the House of Representatives be reserved for women proportionate to the percentage of adult women in the population. Quotas for women have already been instituted in 45 countries.[9] Since women are currently at 50.8 % of the population they would be allocated 51 of the 100 seats available in the Senate and 222 of the 435 seats available in the House. This would certainly correct the current unequal representation of women in Congress, but it would also open the door to those who would want to correct the enormous gap in Congress between white and the non-white populations who have historically suffered from discrimination and oppression. If we reserve seats in Congress for women, then why not also reserve seats for African-Americans?[10]

---

[9] "A number of countries have adopted measures intended to improve the political representation of women. The International Institute for Democracy and Electoral Assistance (IDEA) global database on quotas for women lists 45 countries where quotas for female candidates are presently mandated (either by constitutional provision or by national law) at the national or sub-national level. And there are many more countries where parties have implemented voluntary quotas for female candidates. Whether or not these measures are effective is another issue, but countries and parties are at least interested in appearing to promote greater gender-balance in their representative assemblies" (Bird 2003, 3).

[10] "Only a few states have passed laws to correct the under-representation of ethnic minorities, and in most cases these laws apply to dominant national minorities, and not to polyethnic immigrant minorities. In addition, most of the countries where parliamentary seats are reserved for national minorities are either new or non-democracies, where such measures are required to maintain ethnic peace or to limit the autonomy of national minorities. There are also a handful of established democracies where seats are reserved for designated indigenous communities. There are no established democracies that have adopted quota laws for ethnic minorities (in the fashion that many have for women" (Bird, 3).

Returning to (and ending with) the problem of patriarchy as it occurs in the traditional family, I see no legitimate way to use the tools of family law to correct *internal* gender inequalities in the family. How could a democratic society intervene with mandatory laws prohibiting families from allocating the role of taking care of and raising children exclusively to women, making women responsible for most domestic chores, or denying them the role of equal decision maker in the household? Do we assign social workers to each and every family and charge them with the task of making monthly unannounced visits to see if there is conformity to the state-imposed model of a family that practices gender equality in the assignment of child-rearing duties? Should we allow the state to undertake programs that require constant audio and video monitoring of family activity within the home? What standards should the state adopt to determine when forcible intrusion is necessary to investigate possible violations? How are we to determine whether these standards are morally justifiable? We have seen how the family privacy doctrine has been misused to shield families from state intervention in cases of spousal and child abuse (section "Intrafamily harm and the family privacy principle"), but at the same time there is considerable resistance to removing all of the barriers to state intervention.

Questions for Thought and Discussion

1. Why is the debate between formalism and realism restricted only to cases arising within the common law? Why does it not extend to statutory and constitutional law?
2. What is the main point of contention between formalism and realism? Use a common law case to illustrate.
3. Posner says that the first or major premise used to draw a conclusion in common law cases is crucial. Why is this premise so important? How would the major premise be defended in one or more cases in Chaps 11 and 12?
4. What is Critical Legal Studies, and how did it emerge from Legal Realism? What does it have in common with Legal Realism? What are the differences (if any)?
5. To what extent does radical feminist legal theory use Critical Legal Studies to reach its conclusions about women's legal equality?
6. Despite the arguments and skepticism of CLS and feminist legal theory do you think that a case can still be made that there is a rule of law in our legal system and there is a form of legal reasoning to which we all should subscribe and defend?
7. Where do you stand in the debate between liberal and radical feminists about the equality of women under the law in the United States?

References

Adams, David M. 2013. *Philosophical Problems in the Law*. Fifth ed. Boston: Wadsworth.
Altman, Andrew. 2001. *Arguing About Law. Second Edition*. Belmont CA: Wadsworth. *Baby M, in the Matter of.* 1988.

Bird, Karen. 2003. The Political Representation of Women and Ethnic Minorities in Established Democracies: A Framework for Comparative Research. https://www.hks.harvard.edu/fs/pnorris/Acrobat/stm103%20articles/Karen%20Bird%20amidpaper.pdf. Accessed 29 Sept 2016.

Ferro, Laura. 2012. Gender Inequality in the U.S. Today. *Trust Women and Change the World*. http://www.trustwomenpac.org/2012/03/gender-inequality-in-the-u-s-today/. Accessed 29 Sept 2017.

Geduldig v Aiello. 1974. *417 U.S. 474*.

Greenhouse, Linda and Reva B. Siegel. 2012. Before Roe v Wade: Voices that shaped the abortion debate before the Supreme Court's ruling. http://documents.law.yale.edu/sites/default/files/BeforeRoe2ndEd_1.pdf

Harvard Business School. 2010. Women and the law. *Women, Enterprise and Society*. http://www.library.hbs.edu/hc/wes/collections/women_law/. Accessed 27 Sept 2016.

Holmes, Oliver Wendell. 1897. The Path of the Law. http://www.constitution.org/lrev/owh/path_law.htm. Accessed 29 Sept 2016.

Icdblogsphereteam. 2013. A Comparison of Women's Rights: Middle East and Western Society. *Institute for Cultural Diplomacy*.https://culturaldiplomacyandhumanrights.wordpress.com/2013/05/29/a-comparison-of-womens-rights-middle-east-and-western-society. Accessed 27 Sept 2016.

Posner, Richard A. 1986. Legal Formalism, Legal Realism and the Interpretation of the Constitution. *Case Western Reserve Law Review* 37: 179.

Smith, Patricia, ed. 1993. *Feminist Jurisprudence*. Oxford: Oxford University Press.

Swedish Institute. 2013-2016. Gender Equality in Sweden. https://sweden.se/society/gender-equality-in-sweden/. Accessed 28 Sept 2016.

Tushnet, Mark. 1986. Critical Legal Studies: An Introduction to its Origins and Underpinnings. *Journal of Legal Education* 36: 505.

MIX
Papier aus verantwortungsvollen Quellen
Paper from responsible sources
FSC® C105338

If you have any concerns about our products,
you can contact us on
ProductSafety@springernature.com

In case Publisher is established outside the EU,
the EU authorized representative is:
Springer Nature Customer Service Center GmbH
Europaplatz 3, 69115 Heidelberg, Germany

Printed by Libri Plureos GmbH
in Hamburg, Germany